£10

SUSSEX RECORD SOCIETY

Barbican House, High Street, Lewes, BN7 1YE.

The enclosed Volume 91 *Sussex Clergy Inventories* is distributed to members against the subscription for the year 2007.

Fittleworth

A true and perfect Inventorie of all such
goodes Cattell and Chattells w[hi]ch did belonge
to Ralphe Blinstone of the p[ar]ishe of
fittleworth in the County of Sussex
deceassed taken viewed and p[ri]sed by
william Holmes and william Maxbell
and others the xxx[th] daye of June An[o]
D[omi]ni 1637 as followeth

Imp[rimi]s wearinge App[ar]ell & Money in his purse — 40 s
It[e]m one ffeather bedd one feather bolster
one feather pillowe, one truckell bedstedle
two Coverletts one blankett & one Matt — 50 s
It[e]m one bed ticke of corse Canvas one old
bedstedle two blanketts & a Coverlett and
one old Matt — 20 s
It[e]m three payer and one sheet two
table Clothes, two table Napkens three
towells, one wallett — 22 s
It[e]m one little round table, two old Trunckes
one Chest, one box, three Chayers — 16 s
It[e]m one old sword one staffe & a sertuis
glasse — 5 s
It[e]m about halfe a rood of woll & some hoppes — 12 s
It[e]m 14 bussells of wheat, one bussell and a
helfe of this, & three hennes twoo bagges — 33 4 d
and one pose
It[e]m all his harnes — 20 s
It[e]m one halfe bussell measure one peck
& one halfe peck, small leaden weights — 14 s
It[e]m one table and a frame Bacon joyned
stoles — 13 4 d
It[e]m two kettles one yron pott, two skillets
one little spitt, one fryer pan, one payer of
gridirons, two yron wedges, one payer of
pottharckes, one little payer of tonges
one Cleaver, & one Chopping knyfe — 25 s
It[e]m one flitch of Bacon, one hurdell — 5 s
It[e]m two pewter dishes, two porrengers five
spones, one salte, one brasse Candlesticke two
latten Candlestickes, one latten dripping pan, one
fryenge pan — 6 s

Inventory of Ralphe Blinstone of Fittleworth, 1637. **(57)**

SUSSEX CLERGY INVENTORIES

1600–1750

EDITED BY

ANNABELLE HUGHES

SUSSEX RECORD SOCIETY
VOLUME 91

Issued to members of the Society for the year 2007

Published 2009 by
Sussex Record Society
Barbican House,
High Street,
Lewes,
East Sussex, BN7 1YE.

ISBN 978 0 85445 073 2

Printed by Hobbs the Printers Ltd., Totton, Hampshire.

SUSSEX RECORD SOCIETY

VOLUMES ISSUED BY THE SOCIETY

vi

Volumes marked with an asterisk can be obtained from the Hon. Secretary, Sussex Record Society, Barbican House, Lewes, East Sussex, BN7 lYE.

CONTENTS

ILLUSTRATION

INTRODUCTION

This volume offers an edition of fully transcribed probate inventories for an identifiable social group — parish clergy — between 1600 and 1750, which can be compared and contrasted to illustrate their living conditions and social status. The chosen period provides a manageable volume of 181 documents emanating from the two archdeaconries of the diocese of Chichester, mostly now in the county record offices of East and West Sussex, but augmented from the National Archives. Parish clergy were chosen as a professional group which is easily defined, and for whom supplementary evidence can be found among other ecclesiastical records. From experience of transcribing over 800 probate inventories across the county, it was also clear that they were generally a group representative of the wider community, ranging from the very lowly and poverty-stricken to the level of county gentry.

Additional information, where it exists, is provided in the form of brief biographical and testamentary details for the subject of each entry,[1] and a glossary has been appended of archaic words in the inventories, some of which cannot be found in the *Oxford English Dictionary*, although there are a few that have eluded definition to date. This has been compiled by drawing on a variety of published lists and publications on the history of agriculture, furniture and fittings.[2] In some cases variations have been included, as this was the period before spelling had become fully standardised. In many cases the meanings of words that appear strange can be better deduced when read aloud with a 'rural' accent, or placed in context. Others have been understood after comparison with glossaries in other works, although there can be regional variations in both nomenclature and recording custom, as with words relating to beds and bedding and to farm stock and implements. Some of the buildings in which the clergy lived still survive, even if no longer owned by the church, and in a few cases can be identified in specific inventories.

The motivation for producing this volume arose from the experience of using probate inventories for studies of buildings, in order to illustrate elements of social history and material culture as reflected through possessions and changes over time. With the usual caveats,[3] this was particularly useful when the document was itemised under room headings, as this gave an indication of size of dwelling, use of space and the relationship between different functions. The value of analyses of large groups of

---

[1] Biographical notes have been contributed by John Hawkins, the principal contributor for the Chichester Diocese entries in the Clergy of the Church of England Database 1540–1835.

[2] For some examples see Bibliography.

[3] See, for example, Arkell, T., Evans, N. & Goose, N. (ed.), *When Death Do Us Part*, ch.4.

inventories set against surviving historical structures became apparent when attempting to understand developments in standards of living and social status. This was especially so when inventories could be related to specific buildings. Clergy inventories offered extra dimensions: clergymen were a social group who were likely to possess books (an indicator of levels of literacy); their dwellings were more often identifiable if they survived; and there is often information about the buildings in other sources, such as terriers, visitations and faculty papers.

Until 1858, probate, the legal process for the transmission of property after death, was in the hands of the church, through its courts. Sussex inventories were normally dealt with in the Bishop of Chichester's consistory courts, which covered two separate areas, Chichester Archdeaconry (the western half of the county) and Lewes Archdeaconry (the eastern half). In addition there were further courts for certain parishes which were under the separate (peculiar) jurisdiction of the Archbishop of Canterbury or the Crown.[4] The estates of wealthier people, or those with property in more than one diocese, would be processed in the Prerogative Court of Canterbury, which had jurisdiction over the whole of southern England and much of the Midlands. Three documents were required in order to obtain grant of probate: a will, an inventory of 'goods and chattels' properly valued and taken as soon as possible after the death, and the accounts kept by the executors or administrators appointed for the deceased. If the deceased had died intestate (without making a will) the inventory and accounts had to be provided for the court to grant letters of administration for the estate. Complete sets of all the relevant documents survive for only three of our clergy (**99, 111, 118**), and fall within the period 1677–1682. Two accounts survive with administrations (**58, 155**) and one where there is nether will nor administration (**21**); all have been included in Appendix 2. The official who recorded the proceedings was the Registrar of the court. He ensured that wills were copied into special registers, the inventories and accounts were filed, and the grants were recorded in the Act Books. The process did not always go smoothly, as one case illustrates, where there are two separate inventories for one man (**64, 65**) with a six-year gap, and another (**181**) where the accompanying endorsement indicates a similar breakdown.

Legislation in 1529 had aimed at bringing some order to the process of producing probate documents, but there were still differences between what was prescribed and what actually happened. The process did conform more closely to the stipulations, but the availability of fully literate local appraisers resulted in documents that varied considerably in presentation and quality.

The headings for inventories generally followed a standard format, albeit with minor variations. They included the name and sometimes status of the deceased, the

---

[4] In this volume, the existence of Archbishop's peculiars, particularly in East Sussex, may have slightly skewed the representation.

parish in which he died, the date on which the inventory was taken and the names, parishes of residence and sometimes status of the appraisers.[5] As these men were chosen from relatives, legatees, neighbours or colleagues, they too can provide useful information.[6] No marked difference in their status has been observed, and although in the case of Thomas Holland of Kirdford (**91**) it was recorded that additional men were appointed to value his books; sadly no details survive.

Although 181 inventories were identified, eight of these proved to be so illegible or fragmentary as to be useless for inclusion apart from a heading. Of the 181, 97 have surviving wills, and in a few cases, such as John Buckley of Shipley (**135**) the will provides information where the inventory is useless.

Repository	Inventories	Parishes	Unusable	Wills	Date range
WSRO	136	89	4	65	1613–1741
ESRO	19	19		13	1710–1735
TNA	(W. Sussex) 11	6	2	5	1667–1696
	(E. Sussex) 15	11	2	6	1661–1700
Totals	181	125	8	89	1613–1741

Table 1. Sources of Inventories

Although the production of inventories remained an essential part of the probate process in the ecclesiastical courts, their preservation declined during the eighteenth century. In Chichester diocese the surviving inventories date almost entirely from the period 1600–1750, a pattern that is typical of many other dioceses. Even within the diocese the survivals for the Chichester Archdeaconry (West Sussex Record Office) outnumber the other collections by a wide margin, and representation for the county is skewed towards the west, with 132 usable documents from 89 parishes. Present thinking is that this has to do with differing standards of record-keeping between Chichester, the cathedral town, and Lewes, where only 19 usable documents survive for 19 parishes, and where there is known to have been a policy of 'clearing out' early documents.[7] It may be significant that most of the parishes with more than one surviving document are close to Chichester, and the number of East Sussex inventories in the National Archives may be a reflection of a greater incidence of well-endowed livings. In view of the declared interest in literacy, two further inventories that are outside the time-frame have been included as they contain books listed by title. Henry Caldey held the living of Cuckfield when he died at Oxford in 1451, leaving a library of twenty-five volumes (**182**); when John Wood died at Rusper in 1791, he left over one hundred and ninety volumes (**183**). A recently published directory of parish libraries identifies such institutions in six Sussex parishes —

---

[5] To save space in this volume, the headings have been put in a standard format.

[6] Although women were often executors, none has been found among appraisers.

[7] Personal communication: East Sussex Record Office.

Amberley, Brede, Heathfield, Horsted Keynes, Lewes and Rye — and in the case of Heathfield it seems to have been established by a legacy of 229 books from a relative of a vicar instituted in 1655.[8] The Amberley library was extant in 1865 and consisted of 31 volumes with a date range of 1691 to 1728.[9] Although the origins of such collections coincide with the period covered, none relates to any of the inventories here included, but it is an element that needs bearing in mind.

The survival range of inventories through the period shows a significant drop from 1640 to 1650 (the Civil War) and peaks in the 1680s; this agrees with the general coverage of the period in the numerous West Sussex ones. Tentative and rather crude calculations using estimated life tenure and clergy numbers suggest that there may be an overall survival rate of 20–30%.

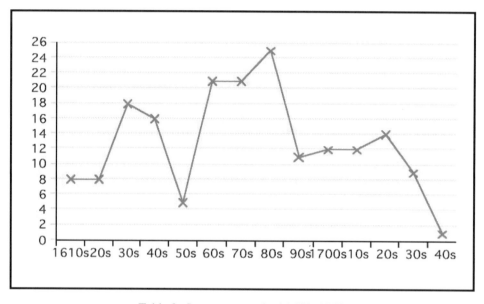

Table 2. Inventory survival 1600–1750

Over the period covered, valuations were recorded in sterling — pounds, shillings and pence[10] — and during the seventeenth century were often in Roman numerals. Some documents even contain a mixture of Arabic and Roman. There is evidence of rounding up or down, and of the use of accountancy units, like the mark (13s 4d) which was two-thirds of a pound, and its fractions (6s 8d, 3s 4d). The format is wildly variable, so has been standardised for this edition.

---

[8] Perkin, M. (ed.), *A Directory of Parochial Libraries of the Church of England and the Church in Wales*, revd edn (London: Bibliographical Society, 2004); WSRO Ep II/42/3.

[9] Clarkson, G.A., 'Notes on Amberley, its Castle, Church, etc.', *SAC*, vol.17 (1865), 236.

[10] 12 pence to the shilling, 20 shillings to the pound.

Inventories were intended to list merely 'moveables', that is personal as opposed to real estate, although the distinction was not always clear.[11] Some introductory headings actually mention credits, rights and/or debts, but these may be included whether specified or not, as may bonds, leases and rents.

There are a number of sources for the period covered to which the student can go for supplementary information. For example, two diocesan surveys have been published previously by the Sussex Record Society.[12] During the earlier survey of 1686–1687, in 175 parishes 29 parsonages or vicarages were in need of repair, and eight were without a clergy residence. The later survey by Bishop Bowers (1724) includes an entry about the condition of the rectory and/or vicarage house and its associated buildings for a majority of the parishes as well as valuations of the living, which can be tested against relevant inventory valuations to discover any relationship between clergy wealth and the livings they held. Entries recorded where repairs were needed or had been carried out, houses that were 'very old' or virtually fallen down, those that had been burned down, and those that had been 'new built'. In Midhurst deanery the commissioners noted how many rooms there were in a number of the houses. Fifty-one parishes in all were without a clergy residence.

'Terriers'[13] or surveys of glebe property survive for many parishes for the years 1615, 1635 and 1665 (usually in relation to a metropolitan or primary visitation), although they vary considerably in the amount of information given about buildings, most being fairly minimal, and some additional relevant information can be found in parish registers and accounts.   Sequences of change to the vicarage at Cuckfield can be traced through terriers and accounts and Edmund Cooper of Woodmancote (1666–82) noted in the registers the repairs, adaptations, and changes he made to both the parsonage house and the church, often including the costs, as well as charting a bitter feud with parishioners over pews.[14] Primary sources, such as the journal of Giles Moore,[15] and secondary literary sources, like Anthony Trollope's Barchester novels, can be used to provide additional social background. Diocesan records of applications for faculties include some relating to eighteenth- and nineteenth-century demolition and replacement of parsonage houses, and occasionally provide surveys of the buildings to be replaced.

The work of Roger Manning, Anthony Fletcher, Peter Jenkins and Andrew Foster — to name but a few — has provided useful detail on the diocese of Chichester in

---

[11] The fruits of an analysis of items in inventories were published in 2004 by Routledge in Overton, M., Whittle, J., Dean, D. & Hann, A., *Production and Consumption in English Households 1600–1750*.

[12] Ford, W.K. (ed.), *Chichester Diocesan Surveys 1686 and 1724* (SRS, vol.78).

[13] WSRO Ep I/25 and II/17.

[14] Sykes-Maclean, H. (ed.), *The Registers of the Parish of Woodmancote ... 1582–1812*.

[15] Bird, R. (ed.), *The Journal of Giles Moore* (SRS, vol.68, 1971).

this period, while the landmark work on the clergy remains that of Rosemary O'Day.[16] From these sources we know of the efforts of Bishop Richard Curteys, appointed in 1570, to raise standards during his twelve-year episcopate, and these can be summarised for the period as follows. Although a zealous reformer, he supported the hierarchical structure of the church and wanted to reform from within. He did everything he could to encourage the preaching of the word in Sussex, and to make livings financially more attractive to better educated and qualified men. There was a strong Puritan movement in the diocese and many laymen had the right to present to Sussex livings, so presentations were often of university-trained preachers from colleges with an equally strong Puritan bias, such as Pembroke, Clare and Emmanuel at Cambridge, and Magdalen, Queen's and Exeter at Oxford. By 1640, a high proportion of graduates had been recruited into the diocesan clergy. Where the bishop held the patronage, graduates were almost exclusively selected, as also in livings that were in the gift of the Crown. This was all part of the concerted efforts to raise the standard of parish clergy and give the newly established national church a better standing and greater credibility in the eyes of the public.

Information gleaned from the inventories should also be set against a background of the struggles between Archbishop Laud and developing Puritan influences (notably in East Sussex), the upheavals of the Civil War, the emergence and rise of sects and nonconformity during the Commonwealth, and the Restoration of the monarchy with the imposition of the Prayer Book of 1662. The evidence of personal possessions in inventories should be tested against the thesis of polarisation between wealthy career clergy and pluralists, and poor incumbents and curates. Fragmentation of income between rector and vicar could lead to the lack of accommodation and funds to house clergy actually working in the parish.[17] That Queen Anne's Bounty was established in 1704 signifies some recognition of this problem. Originally a fund to supplement the income of poorer clergy, it was also used as a source for loans to improve or replace clergy houses.

The eighteenth century saw a rise in the numbers of clergy who were younger sons with no prospect of inheritance, and from gentry families and clerical dynasties, such as the Woodwards of West Grinstead. The inventories of Richard and William Boley (**176, 37**), Robert and Walter Tomlinson (**159, 160**) and William and John Priaux (**126, 127**) suggest that the latter phenomenon had its roots in earlier decades. The fact that names were still subject to variations in spelling may mask even more links, such as between William Corderoy and John Cowdry, and Richard Lewes and Joseph Lewis.

---

[16] For example Manning, R.B., *Religion and Society in Elizabethan Sussex* (1969); Fletcher, A., *A County Community in Peace and War: Sussex 1600–1660* (1975); O'Day, R., *The English Clergy: the emergence and consolidation of a profession 1558–1642* (1979); Jenkins, P.R., 'The Rise of a Graduate Clergy in Sussex, 1570–1640', *SAC*, vol.120 (1982).

[17] In the case of Bury, a combination of impropriation and non-resident clergy resulted in the co-existence of rectory and vicarage, both of which were leased.

The inventories describe the clergy by a variety of titles — though the majority simply used the term 'clerk'. It is worth noting that 46 clergy were described by a more specific term, with the caution that this could reflect several factors: their status in the administration of the Church, their perception of themselves, or how others perceived them. Of these 20 were vicars, 13 rectors, 6 ministers, 4 parsons and 3 curates. Rector, vicar and parson (all incumbents of benefices) and curate usually reflect ecclesiastical status, whereas minister and clerk could be more a question of perception. It is worth exploring whether there is any significant difference between the apparent lifestyles of these categories, as reflected in valuations, belongings, size of houses or book ownership. Did these descriptions also reflect how they were regarded by their parishioners?

Analysis carried out in the course of transcription paid particular attention to information given in relation to dwellings, as the majority are arranged under room headings, and to literacy, as evident in the valuations of books. Of the 173 inventories from which it was possible to extract information only 29 made no mention of rooms. Of the rest, half had 6–10 rooms (inclusive) and eleven had over 15 (16–30) three of the occupants of which were described as rector.

Up to 5 rooms	6–10 rooms	11-15 rooms	Over 15 rooms	Total properties
25	72	36	11	144

Table 3. The range of numbers of itemised rooms

The detailed chronological analysis which follows the introduction can provide a more instantly visual comparison of a number of elements such as the valuation of possessions and books with the size of the house by rooms, and changes in room names and the incidence of stock and crops over time. It illustrates the diminishing importance of the 'hall', the rare appearance of 'cheesehouse' as opposed to the almost ubiquitous 'brewhouse', the increasing incidence of 'parlour' and the first appearance of 'pantry' in 1671. From 1633 'loft' and 'garret' are used almost interchangeably, but the former does not appear after 1706, and there is a marked increase in 'cellar' from the 1690s. These must reflect changes in construction and adaptation of buildings as well as fashions in use of space. The truism that inventories do not always record all the rooms in a house (if they were empty or did not contain items belonging to the deceased) is supported by the number of times the existence of ground-floor rooms is only implied by the phrase 'chamber above'.

The analysis also highlighted the dangers of making categorical assumptions from a small sample. In a recent publication using about 8000 inventories from Cornwall and Kent to illustrate patterns of production and consumption it is stated that 'Unique to Kent among the south-eastern counties was the wash-house, distinguished from other rooms by having a water supply, which began to appear in the 1630s'.[18] It is not clear whether this means that the named 'wash-house' or the distinction of a water supply was unique to Kent, but there are records of sixteen wash-houses from 1638 in this Sussex sample, although I cannot recall coming across any specific mention of a water supply and cannot imagine how that could be deduced.

To return to examples of possible misunderstanding, although George Smyth (**44**) was vicar of East Marden and rector of North Marden his will shows that the 30-room house on which his inventory was taken was Binderton House, drawn by Samuel Grimm in the 1780s. According to the 1615 terrier, Binderton was 'annexed [to West Dean] as in the days of Henry VIII', Smyth's ancestors lived close to the church from at least 1524, and one Thomas, 'designing to build a great house [in 1677] had utterly demolished an old Parish Church or chappell there ... Because it stood in his light.' The replacement chapel was never consecrated and still stands, semi-derelict. Sebastian Pittfield's inventory was taken on his dwelling in East Ashling (**61**),[19] but other information showed that he spent his working life in Hampshire, being rector of Warblington from 1671 until his death. Presumably he found a house there more to his liking than whatever was provided over the border.

Wider studies of local inventories have established that 'chambers' were generally first-floor rooms, often located by relationship to the ground-floor room below. Comparisons between documents can give an idea of the size and arrangement of the house and, taken with the objects listed, also provide some impression of standards of living. This group can then be set against other local inventories to arrive at a clearer understanding of the relative social position of clergy. Some individual inventories contain details which illuminate the understanding of others: for instance, in Walberton in 1650 the bedding of Thomas James (**162**) was valued by the weight of the feathers — something which goes towards explaining the relatively high values always placed on such items and any variations within them.

The existence of a hearth can usually be assumed from collections of fireside implements (andirons, tongs, bellows, etc.) but this is not absolutely foolproof, as these may not have belonged to the deceased. The type of implements recorded can also be used as an indicator of where cooking was taking place, and this can contribute towards an understanding of the slow change in function of the medieval 'hall' from the 'heart' of the house to purely a reception area. Hearth tax returns for 1662 survive for the eastern rapes, but only for Bramber rape in the west. However, it is useful to compare numbers of hearths between a rape from each division, Bramber and Lewes, where clergy can be

---

[18] Overton, M., Whittle, J., Dean, D. & Hann, A., *Production and Consumption in English Households 1600–1750*, 124.
[19] Actually in Funtington parish.

identified. To make the comparison more useful in the block graphs below, the town of Lewes has been removed as there is no comparable urban centre in Bramber.

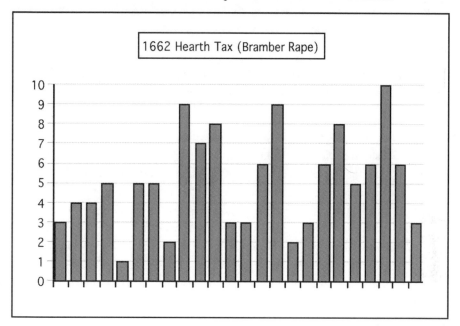

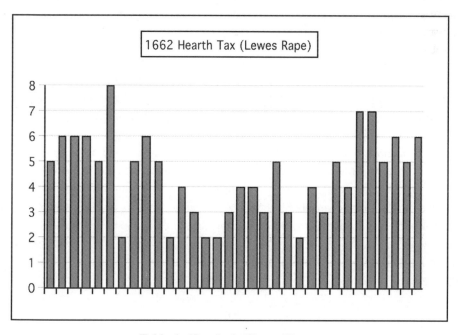

Table 4. Hearths in Clergy Houses

There is a range of between 1 and 10 for Bramber clergy, with a concentration between 3 and 6 and an average of about 5 hearths. The range for Lewes is from 2 to 8, concentrated between 2 and 6, with a slightly lower average of about 4.75, but two clergy appear to be paying tax on more than one property — Magnus Byne and Robert Baker. On the whole, the groups appear to be very similar.

In Bramber six inventories were taken for clergy who paid hearth tax. There are seven inventories taken on houses elsewhere that would probably have been taxed in 1662.

Another item worth noticing is the incidence (in 83 inventories) of stock and/or crops, which must have relevance to farming of the glebe, and so to the clerical income. It should also show that there was a subject of common concern between clergy and their parishioners in rural parishes, but the incidence was not evenly spread. Before 1680, it was 54 out of 91 inventories (over half), while after 1680 it was 29 out of 82 (just over a third). Several factors could be examined to explain this difference, such as the point in the agricultural year when the inventory was taken and the possibility of an increase in leasing out of clerical glebes and changing sources of clergy income. This can also be tested against the records of glebe land still in existence in 1724, which varied from amounts under an acre to quite considerable agricultural areas and woodland. Given that 32 parishes in peculiars across the diocese were not included, in the four western deaneries 95 out of 120 parishes had recorded glebe (79%), and in the eastern deaneries there was glebe in 107 of 136 parishes (78%),[20] so a majority of clergy were still concerned with agricultural matters to some degree.

The vast majority of the inventories (148) record books, valued as a separate item in most cases. The valuations ranged from as little as 2 shillings (**142**) to £100 (**79**). Joan Dils has shown how the valuations of books must be treated with care, as they were often made by laymen who were not always literate, seldom made allowance for differing sizes or quality and often lumped them together with other items. She goes so far as to claim that examples where both the number and value of books are given cannot be taken as guides to the worth of other clerical libraries 'so tenuous is the correlation between the total value and number of books'.[21] Superficially, at least, this is borne out by the evidence of this group of inventories, but the valuation of books as a percentage of the total valuation may distinguish between the true scholars and poorly educated (or poorly paid) clergy. Matthew Woodman (**78**) had 400 volumes valued at £15, but although 'about 800 books' were in Thomas Pelling's study (**122**) the valuation of £100 included at least half a dozen other items.

---

[20] SRS, vol.78.

[21] Dils, J., 'The Books of the Clergy in Elizabethan and Early Stuart Berkshire', *The Local Historian*, vol.36 no.2 (May 2006).

In three cases a little more detail is given about the nature of the books. Samuel Dowlin's 'Bible and ... Cottons sermons' were worth 3 shillings (**69**) and Robert Waters (**133**) had 'Divers books of divinity and physicke and surgery' valued at 14 shillings. Samuel Fowler's collection (**48**) was witness to wide interests: 'a Parsell of books as dixenaries sermon bookes mathematickes Arethmaticke some Lattin some for Prayers some for Gardening some Geographie some manuscripts some Playe bookes some old some young' was valued at just 15 shillings. On this subject wills provided useful supplementary information. John Buckley's inventory (**135**) was too damaged to be worth transcribing, but his will referred to a Bible, law and school books, the books in his study and (Foxe's?) Book of Martyrs; Rowland Prigg (**173**) left his 'library and manuscripts' valued at about £2 to his wife; and John Collins (**77**) left his £80 worth of books between his two nephews, 'the One to divide them and the Other to choose'.

Room names and other contents can also give a guide to the scholarly habits, aspirations or pretensions of the clergy. A study was mentioned or implied (by 'chamber over') in 72 inventories and the four that mention a 'library' (**15**, **44**, **86**, **178**) had between £8 and £100 worth of books. Both Malachy Conant (**12**) and Thomas Pelling (**122**) had 'globes' in their studies, in the former case described as 'celestiall and terrestriall', and pictures and maps are also mentioned in a number of cases. Aside from £40 worth of books, William Priaux (**126**) had 'twelve Cesars' worth £5, which would have been busts, set upon the top of the bookcases. This was a fashion which gave rise to the system by which the Cotton collection was catalogued.

Wills may contain references to items that can be compared to the inventories, including books as legacies, which are sometimes mentioned by title (as in **84**, **128**, **135**); and in one case the value of a nine-volume set is given at £16 (**32**). There can also be noteworthy references that seem to highlight personal interests and beliefs as well as raising questions about motivation, such as money for 'the redemption of Turkish slaves' (**104**), stipulation for a burial to be without 'vain riotous intemperate and gluttenous pompes and ceremonies too often used' coupled with a personal statement of belief several pages long (**112**) and one instance of detailed provision for a maid (**125**).[22]

As noted above, episcopal records can be a fertile hunting ground for additional information about the structures and condition of rectories, vicarages and parsonages. Reports by rural deans in the early nineteenth century on the fabric of churches and parsonages include descriptive references to some of the houses that must have been subjects of seventeenth-century inventories, and these can be usefully compared with item 6 in the articles of enquiry for Bishop Bowers's Survey of 1724, on the 'condition of Rectory or Vicarage house'.[23] In 1724 at Ticehurst and Whatlington the 'mansion houses' were in good repair, whereas by 1817 the parsonages 'are old buildings, the latter

---

[22] Several inventories specify servants' rooms.
[23] SRS, vol.78.

unfortunately stands on low ground, no Incumbent has, it is probable, resided there for many years';[24] and Ticehurst was still described as 'very old' in 1821. Brede's mansion house was in 'pretty good order' in 1724, but 'very old' in 1821. Respectively omitted and in 'good repair' in 1724, houses at Houghton and Laughton were 'very dilapidated' by the 1820s, and at Playden the 'antient house, but in good condition' in 1724 was later a 'mere cottage' while Pevensey vicarage though 'in good repair' in 1724 was 'a miserable Cottage only just covered from wind and weather' by the nineteenth century.[25] Differences between reports must reflect several circumstances apart from damage due to the passage of time, such as absentee incumbents, continuous neglect, lack of funding or the will for repairs and changing expectations for clergy housing. However, although many buildings feature in the 1724 survey, it has proved extremely difficult to make positive identification with those described in this group of inventories.

Faculty and church building papers are not concerned with church buildings alone, but include the clergy dwellings, sometimes with drawings and specifications for work to be done.[26] Although Queen Anne's Bounty was a source for loans for new houses, it also provided sums for what were often 'cut-and-shut' operations, such as at Clapham. Part of the west end of the parsonage there — a 'large old and inconvenient Building its walls consisting cheifly of Timber and Pannells', that is, timber-framed — was blown down in a great storm of 1734, and details are given of the repair work including a rebuilt chimney with bread oven and walling of brick and flints.[27] In 1737 the south part of the vicarage at Nuthurst, measuring 29 ft by 16 ft, was demolished, and cellars made under the hall.[28] The parsonage at Bignor in 1743 was 'part Thatcht part tiled' and also had 'walls of Timber and pannells'.[29] The ruins at Binsted, which had burnt down soon after 1740, were described as having been 44 ft by 17 ft with 'pannell work' 12 ft high. In spite of being ruinous, details are given of how it should be rebuilt, rather than replaced, and even that the new house was to be thatched.[30] In cases where there were two houses, such as at Boxgrove, or two benefices were united, such as Yapton and Walberton, one house was demolished and the materials, or money raised from their sale, used to repair and/or extend the other.[31]

Horsham provides a good example of how a seventeenth-century inventory (John Collins, **77**) illuminates the rather more technical information relating to two

[24] WSRO Ep I/41/65.

[25] WSRO Ep I/41/66; see also Ep II/41/145.

[26] WSRO Ep I/40 and 41 (Chichester Archdeaconry); Ep II/27 and 41 (Lewes Archdeaconry) and also the equivalents for the peculiars of Chichester City, Pagham and Tarring, and South Malling.

[27] WSRO Ep I/40/2.

[28] WSRO Ep I/40/5.

[29] WSRO Ep I/40/8.

[30] WSRO Ep I//40/11.

[31] WSRO Ep I/40/47, 49.

campaigns of improvement and building in the nineteenth century on the vicarage site. Soon after his appointment in 1821, Hugh Rose complained that the vicarage 'is so mean and inconvenient as to be unfit for my occupation ... in parts of the offices ... I am unable to stand upright'. He was, apparently, a tall man.[32] A correspondingly dire survey was produced by William Loat, a builder, who then won the contract to add a wing and extensively repair and renovate. His plans and elevations are the only surviving depiction of the old vicarage with 'a Portall Southward right against the Vesterie joyning to the Chancell' where John Collins had a 'pinne to hang a Cloke upon' in the long gallery. Less than twenty years later, the vicarage was deemed 'incapable of repair or amendment except by pulling down and rebuilding'; it was done forthwith and a further survey, specifications and drawings were produced for the building that stands today.[33]

What began as an apparently straightforward proposal to publish a collection of transcriptions of original documents with a common theme, developed into a much more complicated project, as it seemed appropriate to include information from relevant probate records and biographical details from the Clergy of the Church of England database to augment the information given in the inventories. Analysis carried out in the course of the project focused on house sizes (by room and function) and relative valuations, and this confirmed that there was a range of representation among the clergy from the very poor to the relatively wealthy. It raises interesting questions: about comparative values of livings and how these might be reflected in the living standards of the clergy as shown by their dwellings and possessions, about the value and extent of glebe land and any changes over the given period, about variations in the numbers and values of books owned, and how these might have been reflected in the quality and 'colour' of clerical ministry. It also identified scope for more correlation and comparison between the surviving inventories and the various diocesan surveys and faculty reports, and I hope that readers will find many more ways in which the information here printed can be used to illuminate a range of studies both ecclesiastical and social.

---

[32] Nockles, P.B., 'Hugh James Rose', *Oxford Dictionary of National Biography*.
[33] WSRO Ep I/41/23, 24.

Name	Year	Rooms*	Parish	H	K	B	M	Br	Bh
Smith R	1613	10	W Itchenor	(x)	(x)	(x)	x		x
Wilsha T	1614	6	Westbourne	x		x			
Guy R	1614	3	Midhurst	(x)	x				
Ruffe W	1614	N/A	Bepton						
Leigh J	1614	9	Selham	(x)	x	x			
Waters R	1617	6	Shipley	x		x	x		(x)
Mustian P	1617	N/A	Slinfold						
Warner H	1620	8	Earnley	(x)	x	x	x		
Heare T	1620	3	N Stoke	x	x				
Carus W	1620	9	Arundel	x		(x)	x		
Antrobus R	1622	N/A	Shipley						
Gibbens W	1622	6	Lancing	(x)	x	x			
Chitty J	1623	N/A	Stedham						
Whalley W	1625	8	Sidlesham	x	x	x		x	
Keay J	1625	9	N.Mundham	(x)	2		x		
Forman J	1629	2+	Northchapel		x		x		
Boley R	1630	2	Wiggonholt	x	x				
Harryson T	1630	10	Donnington	(x)	(x)				x
Sephton T	1632	14	Bignor	x	x	2	(x)	x	x
Spencer H	1632	6	Amberley	(x)	x		x		
Browne J	1633	8	Rusper	(x)			(x)		
Beeding W	1633	7	Petworth	(x)	(x)	x	x		
Stepneth W	1634	5	Graffham	x	x				
Thompson A	1634	10	Aldingbourne	(x)	(x)	x		x	
Heape F	1634	5	Binsted	(x)	x				x
Page G	1635	2	Warningcamp	x					
Blinstone R	1637	N/A	Fittleworth						
Hutchinson J	1637	17	W Grinstead	x	(x)	(x)	x	x	x
Bowley W	1638	5	Coldwaltham	x	x	x			
Blaxton G	1638	8	W Thorney	x	(x)	x			x
Taylor J	1639	11	Sidlesham	(x)	(x)	x			x
French H	1639	3	Selsey	x					
Holney T	1639	9	Lancing	x	(x)	x	x		
Andrewes W	1640	9	Nuthurst	(x)	(x)	x	x		
Jeoffrey W	1640	N/A	Coldwaltham						
Prichard J	1641	9	Selham	(x)	x	x	x	x	
Colley H	1641	7+	Harting	x	?x	x	x		x
Collins J	1642	19	Horsham	x	x	2	x	x	x
Stalman L	1643	12	Steyning	x	x			x	
Nye H	1643	11	Clapham	(x)	(x)		x	x	
Dowlin S	1644	N/A	W Grinstead						
Tredcroft E	1644	6+	Warbleton	(x)	x				
Marshall J	1644	N/A	Ford						
Edgly G	1645	N/A	Nuthurst						
Holland T	1647	11	Kirdford	(x)	(x)	(x)		x	x
Knight J	1647	8	Elsted	(x)	x	x	x		
German D	1647	8+4	Woolavington	(x)	x	x	x		
White J	1648	9	Climping	(x)	(x)		x	x	
Hill W	1648	3 (inc)	Arundel						
James T	1650	N/A	Walberton						
Page A	1652	3	Madehurst						

KEY H = Hall K = Kitchen B = Buttery M = Milkhouse Br = Brewhouse Bh = Bakehouse
Ga = Garrett Cl = Closet Cha =Chamber Pa = Pantry Wa = Wash-house/Sink
*Totals may include rooms not covered by the classifications in the succeeding columns

Ch	P	Cel	En	St	L	Ga	Cl	Cha	Pa	Wa	Books	Valuation	S+C	Name
	(x)										£2	£103.11.2	√	Smith R
	x							3				£345.1.0	√	Wilsha T
											£5	£11.4.8		Guy R
											£6.13.4	£153.9.0	√	Ruffe W
	x			x				3			c£20	£501.4.0	√	Leigh J
	x										14s	£65.17.4	√	Waters R
												£4.19.6		Mustian P
	(x)						x				£2	£123.5.2	√	Warner H
x											2s	£4.18.0		Heare T
	(x)			x	x			1			£12	£118.6.4	S	Carus W
												£60.14.10	√	Antrobus R
	x						x					£112.0.0	√	Gibbens W
											£3	£27.0.4		Chitty J
			3								£5	£113.16.6	C	Whalley W
	(x)			x				1			£10	£174.12.7	√	Keay J
											£2	£166.15.0	S	Forman J
											c£8	£98.15.0		Boley R
	x			x				3			£8	£109.18.8	√	Harryson T
	x	2	(x)	x							£5	£205.8.6	√	Sephton T
				x				1			£5	£73.14.4	√	Spencer H
	(x)			x		x					c£10	£172.11.2	√	Browne J
	x										£4	£78.7.0	√	Beeding W
	x			x				1			£5	£27.16.8	S	Stepneth W
	(x)			x				1			£4	£119.19.2	S	Thompson
	x										£1	£40.16.2		Heape F
								1			£10.2.2	£135.11.4		Page G
											£1	£22.16.6		Blinstone R
	2	x	x			x	x	2			c£32	£532.12.2	√	Hutchinson
	(x)										c£5	£102.16.0	S	Bowley W
								1		x	£6	£36.10.2		Blaxton G
	(x)			x		x	x				c£7	£80.1.8	√	Taylor J
				x				1				£4.14.4		French H
	x			x	x			1			Yes	£19.9.0	√	Holney T
	(x)			x							£30	£298.19.4	√	Andrewes
											5s	£5.4.10		Jeoffrey W
	x							2				£18.9.6		Prichard J
								3			£5	£100.18.4		Colley H
	(x)	x	x	x			x	5			£80	£473.18.5		Collins J
	(x)	x		x	x	x	x	2			£10	£116.8.2		Stalman L
	(x)							3			£20	£153.10.0	√	Nye H
											3s	£53.0.6		Dowlin S
	(x)							1+				£194.19.8	√	Tredcroft E
											£5	£39.18.0	√	Marshall J
											£23.5.0	£99.0.0		Edgly G
				x			x	1			£30	£215.8.10		Holland T
	(x)							1			£2	£260.19.0	√	Knight J
	(x)			x				3			£30	£402.18.0	√	German D
	(x)	x									£10	£216.17.0	√	White J
	(x)									(x)	£6	£171.16.6	S	Hill W
											£5	£58.15.0		James T
				x	x			1			£4	£16.18.10		Page A

Ch = Cheesehouse   P = Parlour   Cel = Cellar   En = Entry   St = Study   L = Loft
S+C = Stock and/or crops   (x) = Room with chamber over   ( ) = chamber over

Name	Year	Rooms*	Parish	H	K	B	M	Br	Bh
Welborne G	1652	10	W Stoke	(x)	(x)		x		
Gray A	1655	10	Up.Marden	x	(x)				
Maior M	1657	4	Stoughton	x	x				
Biggs J	1661	15	Little Horsted	(x)	(x)	x	x	x	x
Chaloner J	1661	5	Stopham		x		x		
Knight J	1662	1+	W Itchenor		x				
Cruso A	1663	1	Sutton						
Alexander L	1663	8	Iping	(x)	(x)	x			
Tomlinson R	1663	10	Trotton	(x)	x		(x)		
Attersoll W	1664	12	Burwash	(x)				x	
Maynard J	1665	3+	Arundel	low rooms					
Greenhill S	1666	N/A	Cuckfield						
Lewes R	1666	7	Parham	x	x				
Hallywell H	1667	16	Ifield	(x)	(x)	x	x	x	
Jones L	1667	6	Coombes	x	x			x	
Dennis R	1667	4	Stopham	(x)	(x)				
Corderoy W	1668	8	Thakeham	(x)	x		x		x
Moore G	1668	N/A	N Mundham						
Hinde W	1669	3	Fittleworth	(x)	x				
Fowler S	1669	3	Earnley		x	x			
Wiggs A	1670	N/A	Ashburnham						
Meade T	1670	14	Rudgwick	(x)		(x)	2	x	
Worgar S	1670	12	Ferring	(x)	x	(x)	(x)	x	
Garbrand N	1671	14	Washington	(x)	(x)	x		(x)	
Manning E	1672	18	Coombes	(x)	(x)		(x)	(x)	x
Snelling H	1672	9	Elsted	x	x	x	x		
Burges T	1673	9	Graffham	x	(x)	x			
Middleton R	1674	19	Buxted	x	(x)	(x)	(x)	x	
Lawrence P	1674	12	Tangmere		(x)	(x)			
Tangley S	1675	3+	Bosham		x	x			
Carr R	1675	9	W Chiltington	(x)	x	x	x		
Canner C	1677	12	Climping	(x)	(x)			x	
Garrett T	1677	12	Barlavington	x	x	x	x		
Blaney D	1677	11	Merston	(x)	x	x	x		
Priaux W	1677	19	Rusper	x	(x)		x	x	x
Owen W	1678	2	Westbourne						
Sidgwick G	1678	9	Westbourne		(x)	x		x	
Prynne T	1679	N/A	Westbourne						
Eyles G	1679	7	West Dean		(x)				
Moore G	1679	17	Horsted Keynes	(x)	(x)	x	x	x	
Carr T	1680	10	N Mundham		x		x	x	
Peart S	1680	10	Horsted Keynes	x	(x)	x	(x)	x	
Wilson T	1680	12	Ashurst	(x)	(x)	x	x	x	x
Moore W	1680	6	Ifield		(x)	x		x	
Conant M	1680	12	Beeding	(x)	(x)		x	(x)	
Banckes H	1680	17	Thakeham	(x)	(x)	x		x	x
Lowe T	1681	6	Selham	(x)				x	
Smyth J	1681	N/A	Rudgwick						
Howell W	1681	4	Fittleworth		x	x			
Taylor J	1682	9	Nuthurst	x	x				
Thornton T	1682	10	Sutton	x	x	x			

KEY H = Hall K = Kitchen B = Buttery M = Milkhouse Br = Brewhouse Bh = Bakehouse
Ga = Garrett Cl = Closet Cha =Chamber Pa = Pantry Wa = Wash-house/Sink
*Totals may include rooms not covered by the classifications in the succeeding columns

Ch	P	Cel	En	St	L	Ga	Cl	Cha	Pa	Wa	Books	Valuation	S+C	Name
	(x)			x				1			c£6	£104.17.2	√	Welborne G
	x	x		x				1			c£1.10	£88.10.2		Gray A
				x				1			c£5	£31.14.0	√	Maior M
	(x)			x				2		(x)	£5	£231.2.0	S	Biggs J
	(x)			x							£5	£187.9.8	√	Chaloner J
											£10	£110.5.10		Knight J
				x							£20.16	£35.3.1		Cruso A
	(x)			x								£42.2.0		Alexander L
	x	x						3			£2.6	£73.13.10	√	Tomlinson
	(x)	x	(x)			x		1			Yes	£271.4.2	√	Attersoll W
				x			1+				£10	£620.0.0		Maynard J
												£34.7.0		Greenhill S
	x				2			2				£88.15.0	√	Lewes R
x	(x)		(x)			x	3					£498.10.0	√	Hallywell H
	(x)						x				£5	£33.17.0	√	Jones L
												£68.9.8		Dennis R
		x	x							x	£5	£87.3.2		Corderoy W
											£7.8	£10.0.0		Moore G
				x							£5	£416.14.2	√	Hinde W
								1			15s	£48.14.0		Fowler S
											£3	£13.17.10		Wiggs A
	x			x		x		3			£5	[£117.3.11]	√	Meade T
x	x							1			£10	£117.2.4	√	Worgar S
x	(x)	x		x				1	x		£50	£289.6.0	√	Garbrand N
x	(x)	x		x	x		3				£15	£78.4.0	√	Manning E
	x							3		x	£2	£132.0.0	√	Snelling H
	(x)			x					(x)			£278.0.0	√	Burges T
	2	2		2				3			£3	£110.0.11	√	Middleton R
	(x)		( )	x				1		(x)	£60	£416.3.8	S	Lawrence P
								1			£3	£52.15.0		Tangley S
	(x)			x				1			£35	£208.0.0	√	Carr R
	(x)	x		x		x			( )		£20	£456.10.6	√	Canner C
	(x)			x	x			3		x	c£5	£160.10.10	√	Garrett T
	(x)		(x)	x						x	£5	£296.12.6	√	Blaney D
x	(x)		(x)	x	3			1	x	(x)	£40	£244.0.0		Priaux W
				x				1			£6	£45.2.0		Owen W
	(x)			x				2			£6	£239.10.0		Sidgwick G
											£20	£85.6.0		Prynne T
	x							2			c£3	£55.0.10		Eyles G
x	(x)			x				2			£100	£1678.15.0	√	Moore G
	x			x				4			£20	£568.8.0	√	Carr T
	(x)			x							£10	£172.10.6	√	Peart S
	(x)			x			x				£5.2.3	£233.17.7		Wilson T
				Libr				1			£8	£111.9.11		Moore W
	(x)			x		x	x				c£50	£249.11.6	S	Conant M
	(x)	x	( )	x			x	1		( )	£40	£1337.19.8	√	Banckes H
	(x)			x							c£4	£98.12.6	√	Lowe T
											9s 6d	£76.12.1		Smyth J
								1				£62.12.4		Howell W
	x						x	3			£10	£141.0.3		Taylor J
	(x)		(x)					3				£357.7.4	√	Thornton T

Ch = Cheesehouse   P = Parlour   Cel = Cellar   En = Entry   St = Study   L = Loft
S+C = Stock and/or crops   (x) = Room with chamber over   ( ) = chamber over

Name	Year	Rooms*	Parish	H	K	B	M	Br	Bh
Drake J	1682	12	Oving	(x)	(x)	x			
Putt R	1682	N/A	Thakeham						
Woodman M	1684	N/A	Horsham						
Eldred J	1685	N/A	Whatlington						
Avery W	1685	7	Warnham	(x)		(x)		x	
Lewis J	1685	8	Bersted	( )	(x)	x		x	
Swaffield J	1685	6	Firle			x		x	x
Pittfield S	1686	16	Funtington	(x)	(x)		x	x	
Tomlinson W	1686	7	Treyford	(x)	(x)				
Stepney A	1687	4	Fernhurst	(x)	(x)				
Prigg R	1688	6	Westfield	( )		x			
Wright F	1688	N/A	Lyminster						
Spencer R	1690	6	Goring		x	( )		x	
Lisle J	1690	N/A	N Stoke						
Harrison J	1691	11	Stoughton		x	x		x	
Day H	1691	7	W Itchenor	(x)	(x)	x	x	x	
Coles E	1692	N/A	Storrington						
Griffin T	1694	8	Burpham	(x)	(x)			x	
Jackson J	1694	11	Funtington	(x)	(x)		x		
Dodwell W	1695	5+	W Grinstead						
Brague T	1696	N/A	W Stoke						
Cowdry J	1697	13	Botolphs	(x)	(x)	( )	x	x	x
Seamer R	1699	13	Northiam		(x)	2	(x)	x	x
Adams R	1703	8	Hunston	(x)	x	(x)		x	
Sorocold M	1704	9	Goring		(x)		x	(x)	
The same	1709	9	Goring		(x)			x	
Dennis J	1705	13	Stopham		(x)	(x)	x	(x)	
Spencer C	1705	7	Westbourne						
Boardman I	1706	9	Sompting		(x)	(x)		x	
Oram T	1706	12+	Billingshurst		(x)	(x)		x	x
Lane E	1706	10	N Mundham		(x)	(x)			
Brown W	1708	11	Parham		(x)			x	x
Collins R	1709	N/A	Hunston						
Holder J	1709	9	Aldingbourne	(x)	2			x	
Green W	1710	9	Selmeston		(x)			x	
Hoyle J	1710	12	Newick		x	x		(x)	x
Travers T	1711	6	Plumpton		(x)	x			
Smyth G	1711	30	West Dean	(x)	x	x	x	x	
Newton E	1712	8	Lewes		(x)			(x)	
Forsyth D	1712	N/A	Wartling						
Priaux J	1712	21	Rusper		(x)	(x)	(x)	x	
Rootes W	1713	N/A	Chailey						
Gratwick J	1714	7	Bolney	x	x	(x)	x		
Townsend R	1717	7	Midhurst		(x)			x	
Padie S	1718	8	Wiston	(x)	(x)			x	
Wright H	1718	4	Upwaltham		x				
Bysshe T	1720	10	Eastbourne		(x)	(x)		x	
Jones R	1720	N/A	Bury						
Griffith W	1721	10	W Hoathly		(x)	x	x		
Woodyer J	1721	12	Oving	(x)	(x)	(x)		x	
Litleton E	1721	11	Bignor	(x)	(x)			x	

KEY H = Hall K = Kitchen B = Buttery M = Milkhouse Br = Brewhouse Bh = Bakehouse
Ga = Garrett Cl = Closet Cha = Chamber Pa = Pantry Wa = Wash-house/Sink
*Totals may include rooms not covered by the classifications in the succeeding columns

Ch	P	Cel	En	St	L	Ga	Cl	Cha	Pa	Wa	Books	Valuation	S+C	Name
	(x)	(x)		x				2			£40	£174.15.0	S	Drake J
											£5	£38.5.2	C	Putt R
											£15;	£97.15.0		Woodman
											£12.16	£145.12.5		Eldred J
	x			Libr							£10	£60.4.0		Avery W
	(x)										£2.10	£94.14.4+		Lewis J
	(x)						1				£4	£39.16.2		Swaffield J
		x				2		3	x		c£10	£515.8.0	√	Pittfield S
	(x)								x		£15	£85.16.0		Tomlinson
											5s	£11.19.6		Stepney A
	(x)									x	£2	£170.15.0		Prigg R
												£11.11.0		Wright F
	( )										£10	£650.8.3	√	Spencer R
											£7	£84.4.6	S	Lisle J
	(x)			x		x	x	3			c£50	£106.11.8		Harrison J
											£2	£32.0.0	S	Day H
												£48.16.0		Coles E
	(x)			x							£3	£54.1.0	S	Griffin T
	(x)	x		x				1		x	£20	£82.13.0	C	Jackson J
			(x)		x			2			£4	£59.2.4	S	Dodwell W
											c£50	£376.0.0		Brague T
	(x)	x				x					£30	£631.4.6		Cowdry J
	(x)			x			x	1			£15	£565.15.3	√	Seamer R
	(x)											£96.10.0		Adams R
	(x)	x				x					£5	£101.5.0	√	Sorocold M
	2					2			x			£65.5.0		The same
	(x)	x	(x)	x							£5	£61.8.6	√	Dennis J
	x			x				3			£10	£53.11.6		Spencer C
	(x)			x					x		£5	£388.4.0	√	Boardman I
	(x)		(x)		x	x		1			£3.13.4	£388.8.6		Oram T
	(x)			x			x	1		x	£3.1	£478.3.6	√	Lane E
	(x)	x		x				3			c£8	£38.8.10		Brown W
											£6	£47.5.0		Collins R
	(x)	x		x							£8	£40.19.10		Holder J
	x			x				3	x		£40	£146.14.8	√	Green W
	(x)							5			£50	£1356.1.9	√	Hoyle J
		x									£3	£101.5.9		Travers T
x	2	x		Libr		x	5	4		x	c£100	£616.12.0	√	Smyth G
		x		x		2					c10s	£57.0.2		Newton E
											£2	£19.13.6		Forsyth D
	2	2	(x)	2		2	4				c£30	£236.6.1		Priaux J
											£5	£19.11.0		Rootes W
	(x)										Yes	£11.2.0		Gratwick J
	(x)						x	1			£3	£242.8.6		Townsend R
	(x)			Libr							£10	£157.14.6		Padie S
	x	x						1			£1.15	£38.15.0		Wright H
	(x)	x				2						£173.5.0		Bysshe T
											£10	£932.3.0		Jones R
	(x)	x		x		x				x	£5	£141.16.0		Griffith W
	(x)			x				1			c£20	£1228.9.3		Woodyer J
	(x)	x	x	Libr				1			£40	£122.7.0	√	Litleton E

Ch = Cheesehouse P = Parlour Cel = Cellar En = Entry St = Study L = Loft
S+C = Stock and/or crops (x) = Room with chamber over ( ) = chamber over

Name	Year	Rooms*	Parish	H	K	B	M	Br	Bh
Iver E	1721	11	Ditchling	x	(x)			(x)	
Scrivens T	1722	10	Poling	(x)	(x)				
Parr S	1722	10	Peasmarsh		x				
Prosser J	1723	12	Winchelsea		(x)	x		x	
Knowles W	1723	N/A	Bosham						
Woodeson R	1725	17	Findon	(x)	x			x	x
Smith C	1725	N/A	Broadwater						
Fowle R	1728	10	W Chiltington	(x)	x	(x)		(x)	
Watkins G	1728	9	Chiddingly		(x)	(x)		(x)	
Baker P	1730	20	Mayfield	(x)	(x)			x	x
Stedman J	1732	7	Hamsey	x	x				
Pelling T	1732	17	Rottingdean	x	(x)			x	(x)
Willan R	1732	13	Ashington		x	x	x		x
Dodderidge J	1734	13	Whatlington		(x)	2		x	
Denham T	1735	10	Hollington		(x)	(x)		x	
Smythe T	1735	6	Hartfield		x			(x)	
Bullis J	1738	16	Billingshurst	(x)	(x)		x	(x)	
Baker H	1739	7	Fernhurst		(x)	x		x	
Brownsword J	1741	11	Ashurst		(x)	(x)		(x)	
Wood J	1791	16	Rusper		(x)			x	

KEY H = Hall K = Kitchen B = Buttery M = Milkhouse Br = Brewhouse Bh = Bakehouse
Ga = Garrett Cl = Closet Cha =Chamber Pa = Pantry Wa = Wash-house/Sink
*Totals may include rooms not covered by the classifications in the succeeding columns

Ch	P	Cel	En	St	L	Ga	Cl	Cha	Pa	Wa	Books	Valuation	S+C	Name
	(x)	x						2	x		£5	£128.1.5		Iver E
	x							2		x	£5	£96.0.0	√	Scrivens T
	x	x		x		x		4	x		£25	£395.8.7		Parr S
	(x)	x				x		3			£20	£231.3.4		Prosser J
											£5	£35.14.6		Knowles W
	x	x		x			x	4	3		£5	£974.17.0	√	Woodeson
											£4	£216.18.2		Smith C
	x	x						1			£1	£48.5.0	√	Fowle R
	(x)						x					£39.10.0		Watkins G
	2	3		(x)		x	x	2			£20	£717.13.0		Baker P
	x	x		x				2			£4.4	£38.19.2		Stedman J
	(x)	4		x		x		1	2		c800 v	£1064.13.0	√	Pelling T
	x			x		x		1	x		c£9	£527.14.0	√	Willan R
	(x)	(x)		2							c£2	£55.12.9		Dodderidge
	(x)	x				x		1			c15s	£38.3.6		Denham T
	x	(x)										£186.8.9		Smythe T
	2	2		x		x		3			£30	£141.19.9		Bullis J
	(x)								x			£120.17.6		Baker H
	(x)							2				£72.8.3		Brownsword
	2	2		x		2	1	3	x	x	c193 v	£589.2.8		Wood J

Ch = Cheesehouse   P = Parlour   Cel = Cellar   En = Entry   St = Study   L = Loft
S+C = Stock and/or crops   (x) = Room with chamber over   ( ) = chamber over

ACKNOWLEDGEMENTS

This volume would not have seen the light of day if it had not been for the enthusiasm and assistance of past and present members of the Record Society Council, and especially the dedication of the Literary Directors, Andrew Foster and Roy Hunnisett, with their gentle insistence on content and form; and I am further indebted to Roy Hunnisett for undertaking the index. Janet Pennington and Joyce Sleight generously identified and transcribed probate accounts; Roger Davey and Philip Bye have provided valuable help in extracting probate information. I should like to make particular mention of Peter Wilkinson, the Honorary Secretary, whose cheerful encouragement sustained me through the intricacies of production, and who always seemed able to find willing and skilled technical volunteers, vital for the formatting work. The assiduous work of John Hawkins, the principal contributor for the Chichester Diocese entries in the Clergy of the Church of England Database, has left few ecclesiastical sources untapped in the course of supplying the biographical details of the clergy. Sue Rowland provided her usual high level of expertise in producing the maps from mere numbers and lists of parishes. There have been considerable technical problems in getting the text into its final digital form; and these could not have been surmounted without expert assistance from John Barnes, Nick Clark and David Hawker.

ABBREVIATIONS

ESRO		East Sussex Record Office, Lewes
	W/A	Archdeaconry of Lewes: Registers of wills
	W/B	Archdeaconry of Lewes: Original wills
	W/INV	Archdeaconry of Lewes and peculiar of South Malling: Probate inventories
	W/SM/D	Peculiar of South Malling: Registers of wills and probate and administration acts
PCC		Prerogative Court of Canterbury
SAC		*Sussex Archaeological Collections*
SRS		Sussex Record Society
TNA PRO		The National Archives: Public Record Office
	PROB 4	Prerogative Court of Canterbury: Engrossed inventories exhibited from 1660
	PROB 5	Prerogative Court of Canterbury: Miscellaneous inventories, accounts, and associated documents
	PROB 6	Prerogative Court of Canterbury: Administration act books
	PROB 11	Prerogative Court of Canterbury: Registers of wills
WSRO		West Sussex Record Office, Chichester
	Ep I/25	Diocese and Archdeaconry of Chichester: Church terriers
	Ep I/29	Diocese and Archdeaconry of Chichester: Probate inventories
	Ep I 31	Diocese and Archdeaconry of Chichester: Probate diaries
	Ep I/33	Diocese and Archdeaconry of Chichester: Probate accounts
	Ep I/40	Diocese and Archdeaconry of Chichester: Faculty and consecration papers
	Ep I/41	Diocese and Archdeaconry of Chichester: Church building papers
	Ep II/17	Archdeaconry of Lewes: Church terriers
	Ep II/27	Archdeaconry of Lewes: Faculty papers
	Ep II/41	Archdeaconry of Lewes: Church building papers
	STC I	Archdeaconry of Chichester: Registers of wills
	STC II	Archdeaconry of Chichester: Original wills
	STC III	Archdeaconry of Chichester: Probate acts and administrations
	STD I	Peculiar of City of Chichester: Registers of wills

PRESENTATION AND CONVENTIONS

The inventories are arranged alphabetically by parish, and each has been given an entry number (to which the figures in bold type in the introduction and the Arabic numbers in the index refer). The introductory headings have been standardised to include only the parish, date, name of the deceased and his title (where stated), and names of the appraisers. The signatures and/or marks of the appraisers have been omitted. Dates in headings, probate abstracts and biographies are rendered in New Style.

Within the body of the inventory the original spelling and capitalisation have been retained. Although the text has been formatted in the interests of space and clarity, the columnar appearance of most of the inventories has been maintained as closely as possible. 'Ye' is rendered as 'the'; the recurring 'Item', which can appear in various guises, has been standardised, as has the initial 'In primis'. Interim accounting summaries (such as sums 'carried over') have been omitted. Room headings have been indented throughout and Roman numerals have been changed into Arabic. Where a zero has been represented by a dash or a blank, it has been replaced by '0'. Common abbreviation marks, such as those for 'er' or 'ar', have been expanded, as has the ampersand. Where dots appear in the printed text or values, these indicate indecipherable or absent details. In the currency columns, amounts have been given in accordance with modern conventions (e.g. '25s' and '18d' are rendered as '£1 5s' and '1s 6d'). Titles of books have been left in the form used in the inventory or will.

Most of the original inventories have an accompanying note indicating that they were exhibited in court (usually on the day the will was proved or administration granted). This has normally been omitted unless it provides information not given in the will or administration.

Each inventory is accompanied by an extract from the will or administration (if found). Following this is a brief biographical account of each subject. Catalogue marks are given at the end of the inventories and probate extracts.

BIBLIOGRAPHY: THE INVENTORIES

Arkell, T., Evans, N. & Goose, N. (ed.), *When Death Do Us Part: understanding and interpreting the probate records of early modern England* (Oxford, 2000)

Blencowe, R. W., 'Extracts from the Journal and Account Book of the Rev. Giles Moore, Rector of Horstead Keynes, Sussex, from the year 1655 to 1679', *SAC*, vol.1 (1853)

Chinnery, V., *Oak Furniture, the British Tradition: a history of early furniture in the British Isles and New England* ([Woodbridge], Antique Collectors' Club, 1980)

Dils, J., 'The Books of the Clergy in Elizabethan and Early Stuart Berkshire', *The Local Historian*, vol.36 no.2 (May 2006)

Fletcher, A., *A County Community in Peace and War: Sussex 1600–1660* (London, 1975)

Ford, W.K. (ed.), *Chichester Diocesan Surveys 1686 and 1724*, (SRS, vol.78, 1994)

Foster, A.W., 'Chichester Diocese in the Early 17th Century', *SAC*, vol.123 (1985)

Hughes, A., 'Horsham Probate Inventories', *West Sussex History*, no.53 (April 1994)

Hughes, A., 'Horsham Probate Inventories: an update', *West Sussex History*, no.59 (April 1997)

Jenkins, P. R., 'The Rise of a Graduate Clergy in Sussex, 1570–1640', *SAC*, vol.120 (1982)

Kenyon, G. H., 'Kirdford Inventories 1611 to1776, with particular reference to the Weald Clay Farming', *SAC*, vol.93 (1955)

Kenyon, G.H., 'Petworth Town and Trades 1610–1760', *SAC*, vols 96 (1958), 98 (1960), 99 (1961)

Manning, R.B., *Religion and Society in Elizabethan Sussex: a study of the enforcement of the religious settlement 1558–1603* (Leicester, 1969)

Milward, R., *A Glossary of Household, Farming and Trade Terms from Probate Inventories* (Derbyshire Record Society Occasional Papers, no.1, reprint 1983)

Moore, J.S., *The Goods and Chattels of our Forefathers: Frampton Cotterell and district probate inventories 1539–1804* (London, 1976)

O'Day, R., *The English Clergy: the emergence and consolidation of a profession 1558–1642* (Leicester, 1979)

Overton, M., *A Bibliography of British Probate Inventories* ([Newcastle upon Tyne], Department of Geography, University of Newcastle upon Tyne, c. 1983)

Overton, M., Whittle, J., Dean, D. & Hann, A., *Production and Consumption in English Households 1600–1750* (London, 2004)

Pennington, J. & Sleight, J., 'Steyning Town and its Trades 1559–1787', *SAC,* vol.130 (1992)

Sykes-Maclean, H. (ed.), *The Registers of the parish of Woodmancote in the county of Sussex: baptisms, burials and marriages 1582–1812* (Brighton, 1932)

Williams, I.L., 'A First Look at Midhurst Inventories', *West Sussex History*, no.49 (April 1992)

Williams, I.L., 'Restoration Midhurst: the evidence from probate inventories', *West Sussex History,* no.57 (April 1996)

BIBLIOGRAPHY: THE BIOGRAPHIES

Much of the biographical information on the clergy printed at the end of each entry in the text has been supplied from the Clergy of the Church of England Database 1540–1835 (http://www.theclergydatabase.org.uk). The database was itself compiled mainly from primary sources, most of the Sussex material being drawn from the diocesan records in the West Sussex Record Office: Bishops' Registers, Act Books, Liber Cleri, Subscription Books and Parish Registers. They have been supplemented by a variety of printed and other sources. The most important for the further study of Sussex clergy are listed below.

Armytage, G.J. (ed.), *Musgrave's Obituary prior to 1800*, 6vols (Harleian Society, vols 44–49; 1899–1901)

Burke's Landed Gentry

Dallaway, J. & Cartwright, E., *A History of the Western Division of the County of Sussex*, 2 vols in 3 (London, 1815–1832)

Emden, A.B., *A Biographical Register of the University of Oxford A.D. 1500–1540* (Oxford, 1974)

Ford, W.K. (ed.), *Chichester Diocesan Surveys 1686 and 1724* (SRS, vol.78, 1994)

Foster, J., *Alumni Oxonienses: the members of the University of Oxford 1500–1714*, 4 vols; *1715–1886*, 4 vols; (Oxford, 1891)

Foster, J. (ed.), *London Marriage Licences 1521–1869* (London, 1887)

Harleian Society: Visitations

Hennessy, G., *Chichester Diocese Clergy Lists; or clergy succession from the earliest time to the year 1900* (London, 1900)

Horsfield, T.W., *The History, Antiquities and Topography of the county of Sussex*, 2 vols (Lewes, 1835)

International Genealogical Index (CD ROM & microfiche; Church of Jesus Christ of Latter-day Saints, Salt Lake City)

Le Neve, J, *Fasti Ecclesiae Anglicanae 1541–1857: Chichester Diocese*, comp. J.M.Horn (London, 1971)

Matthews, A.G., *Calamy Revised, being a revision of Edmund Calamy's account of the ministers and others ejected and silenced 1660–1662* (Oxford, 1934)

Miscellanea Genealogica et Heraldica

National Burial Index for England and Wales (CD ROM; Federation of Family History Societies)

Oxford Dictionary of National Biography

Peckham, W.D.(ed.) *The Acts of the Dean and Chapter of the Cathedral Church of Chichester 1545–1642* (SRS, vol.58, 1959)

Sussex Archaeological Collections

Sussex Marriage Index up to1837 (CD ROM; Sussex Family History Group)

Sussex Notes & Queries

Venn, J. & J.A., *Alumni Cantabrigienses: a biographical list of all known students, graduates and holders of office at the University of Cambridge from the earliest times to 1900*; Part 1*, to 1751*; Part 2, *1752–1900*; 10 vols (Cambridge, 1922–1954)

Victoria History of the Counties of England

Wood., A. à, *Athenae Oxonienses*, 4 vols (London, 1813–1820)

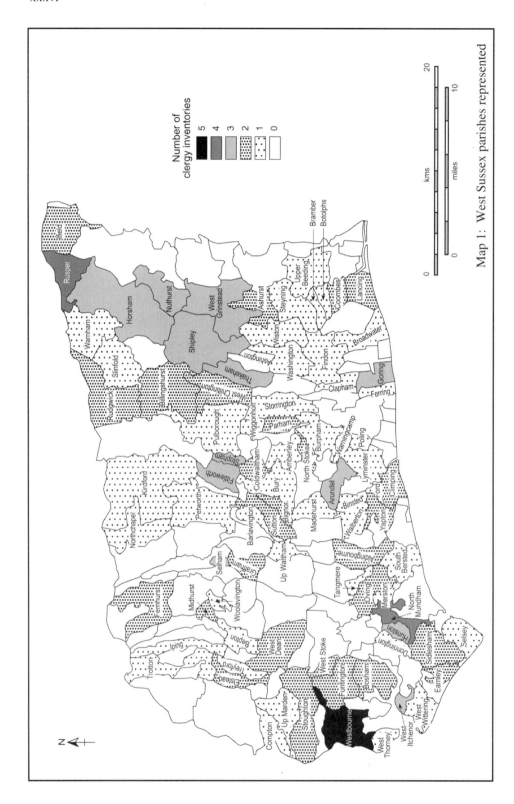

Map 1: West Sussex parishes represented

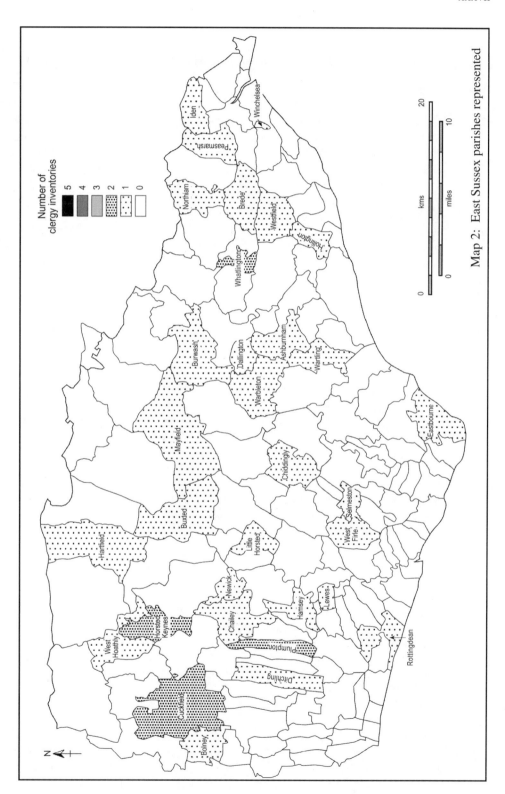

Map 2: East Sussex parishes represented

LIST OF INVENTORIES

No.	Name	Parish	Year	Value	Title	Court
1	Thompson, Allan	Aldingbourne	1634	£119.19.2	vicar	Chichester
2	Holder, John	Aldingbourne	1709	£40.19.10		Chichester
3	Spencer, Henry	Amberley	1632	£73.14.4		Chichester
4	Carus, William	Arundel	1620	£118.6.4		Chichester
5	Hill, William	Arundel	1648	£171.16.6	minister	Chichester
6	Maynard, John	Arundel	1665	£620.0.0		Chichester
7	Wiggs, Alexander	Ashburnham	1670	£13.17.10		PCC
8	Willan, Robert	Ashington	1732	£527.14.0		Chichester
9	Wilson, Thomas	Ashurst	1680	£233.17.7		Chichester
10	Brownsword, John	Ashurst	1741	£72.8.3		Chichester
11	Garrett, Thomas	Barlavington	1677	£160.10.10		Chichester
12	Conant, Malachy	Beeding	1680	£249.11.6	vicar	PCC
13	Ruffe, William	Bepton	1614	£153.9.0		Chichester
14	Lewis, Joseph	Bersted	1685	£94.14.4		PCC
15	Litleton, Edward	Bignor	1721	£122.7.0		Chichester
16	Sephton, Thomas	Bignor	1632	£205.8.6		Chichester
17	Oram, Thomas	Billingshurst	1706	£388.8.6		Chichester
18	Bullis, John	Billingshurst	1738	£141.19.9		Chichester
19	Heape, Francis	Binsted	1634	£40.16.2	vicar	Chichester
20	Gratwick, John	Bolney	1714	£11.2.0	vicar	Lewes
21	Samuel, Tangley	Bosham	1675	£52.15.0	vicar	Chichester
22	Knowles, William	Bosham	1723	£35.14.6		Chichester
23	Cowdry, John	Botolphs with Bramber	1697	£631.4.6	minister	Chichester
24	Horne, Samuel	Brede	1687			PCC
25	Smith, Charles	Broadwater	1725	£216.18.2		Chichester
26	Griffin, Thomas	Burpham	1694	£54.1.0		Chichester
27	Attersoll, William	Burwash	1664	£271.4.2		PCC
28	Jones, Roger	Bury	1720	£932.3.0		Chichester
29	Middleton, Robert	Buxted	1674	£110.0.11		PCC
30	Rootes, William	Chailey	1713	£19.11.0		Lewes
31	Watkins, Giles	Chiddingly	1728	£39.10.0		Lewes
32	Carr, Robert	West Chiltington	1675	£208.0.0		Chichester
33	Fowle, Richard	West Chiltington	1728	£48.5.0		Chichester
34	Nye, Henry	Clapham	1643	£153.10.0		Chichester
35	White, John	Climping	1648	£216.17.0		Chichester
36	Canner, Christopher	Climping	1677	£456.10.6		Chichester
37	Bowley, William	Coldwaltham	1638	£102.16.0		Chichester
38	Jeoffrey, William	Coldwaltham	1640	£5.4.10		Chichester
39	Jones, Lawrence	Coombes	1667	£33.17.0		Chichester
40	Manning, Edward	Coombes	1672	£78.4.0		Chichester
41	Greenhill, Samuel	Cuckfield	1666	£34.7.0		PCC

No.	Name	Parish	Year	Value	Title	Court
42	Russell, Richard	Dallington	1700			PCC
43	Eyles, George	West Dean	1679	£55.0.10		Chichester
44	Smyth, George	West Dean (Binderton)	1711	£616.12.0		Chichester
45	Iver, Elnathan	Ditchling	1721	£128.1.5	vicar	Lewes
46	Harryson, Thomas	Donnington	1630	£109.18.8		Chichester
47	Warner, Henry	Earnley	1620	£123.5.2	parson	Chichester
48	Fowler, Samuel	Earnley	1669	£48.14.0		Chichester
49	Bysshe, Thomas	Eastbourne	1720	£173.5.0	vicar	Lewes
50	Knight, John,	Elsted	1647	£260.19.0	minister	Chichester
51	Snelling, Henry	Elsted	1672	£132.0.0		Chichester
52	Stepney, Abel	Fernhurst	1687	£11.19.6		Chichester
53	Baker, Henry	Fernhurst	1739	£120.17.6		Chichester
54	Worgar, Stephen	Ferring	1670	£117.2.4		Chichester
55	Woodeson, Richard	Findon	1725	£974.17.0	vicar	Chichester
56	Swaffield, John	Firle	1685	£39.16.2		PCC
57	Blinstone, Ralph	Fittleworth	1637	£22.16.6		Chichester
58	Hinde, William	Fittleworth	1669	£416.14.2		Chichester
59	Howell, William	Fittleworth	1681	£62.12.4		Chichester
60	Marshall, John	Ford	1644	£39.18.0		Chichester
61	Pittfield, Sebastian	Funtington	1686	£515.8.0		PCC
62	Jackson, Joseph	Funtington	1694	£82.13.0		Chichester
63	Spencer, Richard	Goring	1690	£650.8.3		Chichester
64	Sorocold, Michael	Goring	1703	£101.5.0		Chichester
65	Sorocold, Michael	Goring	1709	£65.5.0		Chichester
66	Stepneth, William	Graffham	1634	£27.16.8	parson	Chichester
67	Burges, Thomas	Graffham	1673	£278.0.0		Chichester
68	Hutchinson, James	West Grinstead	1637	£532.12.2		Chichester
69	Dowlin, Samuel	West Grinstead	1644	£53.0.6		Chichester
70	Dodwell, William	West Grinstead	1695	£59.2.4		Chichester
71	Stedman, Joseph	Hamsey	1732	£38.19.2	curate	Lewes
72	Smythe, Thomas	Hartfield	1735	£186.8.9		Lewes
73	Colley, Hugh	Harting	1641	£100.18.4	vicar	Chichester
74	Griffith, William	West Hoathly	1721	£141.16.0	vicar	Lewes
75	Denham, Thomas	Hollington	1735	£38.3.6	rector	Lewes
76	Hunt, William	Horsham	1635	£6.5.6		Chichester
77	Collins, John	Horsham	1642	£473.18.5	vicar	Chichester
78	Woodman, Matthew	Horsham	1684	£97.15.0		Chichester
79	Moore, Giles	Horsted Keynes	1679	£1678.15.0	rector	PCC
80	Peart, Stephen	Horsted Keynes	1680	£172.10.6		PCC
81	Biggs, Joseph	Little Horsted	1661	£231.2.0		PCC
82	Dallinder, John,	Hunston	1662	£127.12.0		Chichester
83	Adams, Robert	Hunston	1703	£96.10.0		Chichester
84	Collins, Roger	Hunston	1709	£47.5.0		Chichester
85	Hallywell, Henry	Ifield	1667	£498.10.0		PCC

No.	Name	Parish	Year	Value	Title	Court
86	Moore, Walter	Ifield	1680	£111.9.11		PCC
87	Alexander, Leonard	Iping	1663	£42.2.0		Chichester
88	Smith, Roger	West Itchenor	1613	£103.11.2	parson	Chichester
89	Knight, John	West Itchenor	1662	£110.5.10		Chichester
90	Day, Humphrey	West Itchenor	1691	£32.0.0		Chichester
91	Holland, Thomas	Kirdford	1647	£215.8.10	vicar	Chichester
92	Gibbens, Walter	Lancing	1622	£112.0.0	vicar	Chichester
93	Holney, Timothy	Lancing	1639	£19.9.0	minister	Chichester
94	Newton, Edward	Lewes	1712	£57.0.2		Lewes
95	Wright, Francis	Lyminster	1688	£11.11.0	vicar	Chichester
96	Page, Adam	Madehurst	1652	£16.18.10		Chichester
97	Gray, Anthony	Up Marden with Compton	1655	£88.10.2		Chichester
98	Baker, Peter	Mayfield	1730	£717.13.0	vicar	Archbishop
99	Blaney, David	Merston	1677	£296.12.6		Chichester
100	Guy, Richard	Midhurst	1614	£11.4.8		Chichester
101	Townsend, Richard	Midhurst	1717	£242.8.6		Chichester
102	Keay, John	North Mundham	1625	£174.12.7		Chichester
103	Moore, George	North Mundham	1668	£10.0.0		Chichester
104	Carr, Thomas	North Mundham	1680	£568.8.0		Chichester
105	Lane, Edmund	North Mundham	1706	£478.3.6		Chichester
106	Hoyle, Joseph	Newick	1710	£1356.1.9		Lewes
107	Forman, John	Northchapel	1629	£166.15.0		Chichester
108	Seamer, Richard	Northiam	1699	£565.15.3		PCC
109	Andrewes, William	Nuthurst	1640	£298.19.4	rector	Chichester
110	Edgly, George	Nuthurst	1645	£99.0.0	rector	Chichester
111	Taylor, John	Nuthurst	1682	£141.0.3		Chichester
112	Drake, John	Oving	1682	£174.15.0		Chichester
113	Woodyer, John	Oving	1721	£1228.9.3		Chichester
114	Lewes, Richard	Parham	1666	£88.15.0		Chichester
115	Brown, William	Parham	1708	£38.8.10		Chichester
116	Parr, Stevens	Peasmarsh	1722	£395.8.7		Lewes
117	Beeding, William	Petworth	1633	£78.7.0		Chichester
118	Bennett, James	Plumpton	1682	£657.13.1		PCC
119	Travers, Thomas	Plumpton	1711	£101.5.9		Lewes
120	Scrivens, Thomas	Poling	1722	£96.0.0		Chichester
121	Rawlinson, Richard	Pulborough	1669			PCC
122	Pelling, Thomas	Rottingdean	1732	£1064.13.0		Lewes
123	Meade, Thomas	Rudgwick	1670	£[117.3.11]		Chichester
124	Smyth, John	Rudgwick	1681	£76.12.1		Chichester
125	Browne, Joseph,	Rusper	1633	£172.11.2		Chichester
126	Priaux, William	Rusper	1677	£244.0.0		PCC
127	Priaux, John	Rusper	1712	£236.6.1		Chichester
128	Leigh, John	Selham	1614	£501.4.0		Chichester
129	Prichard, John	Selham	1641	£18.9.6		Chichester

No.	Name	Parish	Year	Value	Title	Court
130	Lowe, Thomas	Selham	1681	£98.12.6		Chichester
131	Green, William	Selmeston	1710	£146.14.8	vicar	Lewes
132	French, Hugh	Selsey	1639	£4.14.4		Chichester
133	Waters, Robert	Shipley	1617	£65.17.4		Chichester
134	Antrobus, Ralph	Shipley	1622	£60.14.10		Chichester
135	Buckley, John	Shipley	1679	£400.3.2		PCC
136	Whalley, William	Sidlesham	1625	£113.16.6		Chichester
137	Taylor, John,	Sidlesham	1639	£80.1.8		Chichester
138	Mustian, Philip	Slinfold	1617	£4.19.6	parson	Chichester
139	Boardman, Isaac	Sompting	1706	£388.4.0	vicar	Chichester
140	Chitty, Joseph	Stedham	1623	£27.0.4		Chichester
141	Stalman, Leonard	Steyning	1643	£116.8.2	vicar	Chichester
142	Heare, Thomas	North Stoke	1620	£4.18.0	curate	Chichester
143	Lisle, Joseph	North Stoke	1690	£84.4.6		Chichester
144	Welborne, George	West Stoke	1652	£104.17.2		Chichester
145	Brague, Thomas	West Stoke	1696	£376.0.0		PCC
146	Chaloner, John	Stopham	1661	£187.9.8	rector	Chichester
147	Dennis, Robert	Stopham	1667	£68.9.8	rector	Chichester
148	Dennis, John,	Stopham	1705	£61.8.6		Chichester
149	Coles, Edmund	Storrington	1692	£48.16.0	rector	Chichester
150	Maior, Matthew	Stoughton	1657	£31.14.0		Chichester
151	Harrison, John	Stoughton	1691	£106.11.8		Chichester
152	Cruso, Aquila	Sutton	1663	£35.3.1	minister	Chichester
153	Thornton, Thomas	Sutton	1682	£357.7.4	rector	Chichester
154	Lawrence, Paul	Tangmere	1674	£416.3.8		PCC
155	Corderoy, William	Thakeham	1668	£87.3.2		Chichester
156	Banckes, Henry	Thakeham	1680	£1337.19.8	rector	PCC
157	Putt, Robert	Thakeham	1682	£38.05.2	vicar	PCC
158	Blaxton, Godfrey	West Thorney	1638	£36.10.2		Chichester
159	Tomlinson, Walter	Treyford	1686	£85.16.0		Chichester
160	Tomlinson, Robert	Trotton	1663	£73.13.10		Chichester
161	Wright, Henry	Up Waltham	1718	£38.15.0	rector	Chichester
162	James, Thomas	Walberton	1650	£58.15.0		Chichester
163	Tredcroft, Edward	Warbleton	1644	£194.19.8	rector	Chichester
164	Avery, William	Warnham	1685	£60.4.0		Chichester
165	Page, George	Warningcamp	1635	£135.11.4		Chichester
166	Forsyth, David	Wartling	1712	£19.13.6	curate	Lewes
167	Garbrand, Nicholas	Washington	1671	£289.6.0	vicar	Chichester
168	Wilsha, Thomas	Westbourne	1614	£345.1.0		Chichester
169	Owen, Warberton	Westbourne	1678	£45.2.0		Chichester
170	Sidgwick, George	Westbourne	1678	£239.10.0		Chichester
171	Prynne, Thomas	Westbourne	1679	£85.6.0	rector	Chichester
172	Spencer, Christopher	Westbourne	1705	£53.11.6		Chichester
173	Prigg, Rowland	Westfield	1688	£170.15.0		PCC
174	Eldred, John	Whatlington	1685	£145.12.5	rector	PCC

No.	Name	Parish	Year	Value	Title	Court
175	Dodderidge, John	Whatlington	1734	£55.12.9		Lewes
176	Boley, Richard	Wiggonholt	1630	£98.15.0	minister	Chichester
177	Prosser, John	Winchelsea	1723	£231.3.4		Lewes
178	Padie, Samuel	Wiston	1718	£157.14.6		Chichester
179	Harrison, John	West Wittering	1663			Chichester
180	German, Daniel	Woolavington	1647	£402.18.0		Chichester
181	Dalgarno, Robert	Yapton	1671	£15.0.0		Chichester
182	Caldey, Henry	Cuckfield	1451	£8.18.6		Oxford: University Chancellor
183	Wood, John	Rusper	1791	£589.2.8		PCC

SUSSEX CLERGY INVENTORIES 1600-1750

PART 1: ALDINGBOURNE TO FUNTINGTON

1. Aldingbourne 17 June 1634 ALLAN THOMPSON, vicar [1]

Appraisers: William Peckham, John Smyth, John Truslowe, Henry Whittington

	£	s	d
In primis Eleven shepe	4	2	8
Item one Sorrell Mare bridell and saddle etc	6	0	0
In his Bedchamber			
In primis one Bedstede a Feather bed 2 bolsters 2 blankets 1 pillow and one Coverlett with curtaines and vallance	5	10	0
Item 2 Tables and Six jointe Stoles		18	0
Item 2 oald chayres a deske and 2 little lowe cushion stoles		7	0
In his Study			
In primis his bookes there	4	0	0
Item a Table a chayre and 2 shelves		3	4
In the hall			
In primis one long Table and 2 Formes		18	0
Item a Cupboard a little side Table and 2 chaires	1	11	0
Item 7 Cushions and two Cupboard cloathes		8	0
Item A Stillatory [*sic*] and one glasse grate		7	0
In the Buttery			
In primis 3 Tubbes 2 barrells 2 firkins and 1 piner [*sic*]		9	0
Item a stande and a planke with some other small things			6
In the Chamber over the Parlor			
In primis A Bedstede a Feather bed 1 feather bolster fower blanketts 1 pillow a covlett and Curtaines of grene Say	5	5	0
Item a dozen and halfe of pewter dishes 3 Candlestickes 3 Salt sellars a Bason and a Chamber pot and 12 spoones	1	9	0
Item A Presse and two chestes		15	0
Item 23 payre of Sheetes	9	12	0
Item 2 diaper table cloathes 2 Cupboard cloathes and a dozen of diaper table napkins	2	0	0
Item 3 other Table cloathes 4 doz and 3 Napkins 6 pillow beares and other small pieces of linnen	4	0	0
In the Chamber over the hall			
In primis A Bedstede a Featherbed a bolster and two blanketts	1	5	0
Item 2 Chests		5	0
Item a Trundell Bedstede		1	0
In the Kitchin			
In primis a fornace 3 brasse potts a kittle 3 skilletts a chaffin dish a Warming pan a morter and Candlesticke	2	5	0
Item 2 Iron potts 2 driping panes 3 Spits and a Clever		14	0
Item A Jacke or Tarnspit 3 Andirons a pair of Tongues a pair of pothookes and an Iron barre		17	0
Item 2 tables and a boal and traies a charne and a chayre		14	0

In the chamber over the kitchin

In primis A Bedstede and flock bed		16	0

In the Brewhouse

In primis A salting trough 4 Tubbes a Coope and a Cheesepresse with other Lumber		8	0
Item A muskett with the furniture	1	0	0
Item in mony	2	12	0
Item A ring		6	0
Item his Wearing apparell	6	13	4
Item in debts	20	0	0
Item in mony to be raised upon a pece of land to him mortgaged	30	0	0
Item A Barne appointed by him to be sould	4	0	0
Item in all other small Lumber		6	0
Sume	119	19	2

Exhibited: Margaret Warner als Thompson, daughter

[WSRO Ep I/29/1/28]

Will: made 5 June 1634; proved 14 July 1634
Son: Daniel; daughter: Margaret (Warner) executrix
Overseer: Physician Anthony Howes of Chichester (left book, 'Zaucheus de operbus dei')
Witnesses: Nicholas Slaughter, Henry Couke   [WSRO STC I/18/328]

[1] Ordained deacon 1576, priest 1577 (bishop of Chichester). Vicar of Aldingbourne 1577–1634, patron William Kitching (advowson granted by dean and chapter of Chichester). Died 1634.

2. Aldingbourne 31 March 1709 JOHN HOLDER [1]

Appraisers: Francis Halsey, Adam Bredham

	£	s	d
In primis his wearing Apparrell and money in purse	30	0	0
In the Parlour			
Item For Thirteen Leather Chaires One of them a Arme Chaire	1	6	0
One Bulrush Chaire		1	6
One Table		7	0
One pair of Andirons		3	6
In the Hall			
Item One long Table and Two Forms Two pair of andirons one Press One Joynt Stool One — A little Table on him	1	8	0
In the Cellar			
Item Four Drink vessells One little Table One Reeming Tub One Water Pot		14	0
In the Back kitchen			
Item Five Drink vessells one — one Powdering Tubb One Salting Trough	1	1	0
In the Kitchen			
Item For 3 hollow back Chaires Two Tables One Oake One Deal One Beacon racke One Cubberd One Dresser of Drawers	1	3	0

One Jack One pair of Dogs Fire pan and Tongs Two spitts One pair of Cottrills One pair of Gridirons One Fender One Trist One Choping

knife Three Smoothing Irons Two Candle Sticks Chaffing Dish One driping pan One pair of Bellows Two kittles One houre glass Pestle and Morter One Bed pan One pair of Pothooks	1	0	0
Item For 68 pound of Pewter seven pence a pound	1	19	8

In the Wash House

One Furnace One Kittle Two Iron potts One Skimmer	1	10	0
One Brewing Vate One Tun tub One Bucking Tub 3 kivers One Item one Pasty pan One Iron pan		3	0

In the Parlour Chamber

Item One Bedsteddle matt and Cord One Coverlid One Blankett		5	0
One Bed One Boulster weighing 88 pound at 5d p pound	1	16	0
For six Chaires Turkey work and One Chest		16	0
Two pair of Sheets Three Tableclothes 3 Pillowbeares Two Towells 12 Napkins 6 Diaper wth a Table cloath And six other	1	2	0

In the Hall Chamber

Item For a Truckle bedsteddle mat and Cord and Blankets		4	0
One Bed Two Bolsters weighing 99 pounds at 8d p pound	3	6	6
For seven Chaires And One Table and Press		18	0
Item the Deced's Study of Books	8	0	0
Item Moneys owing to the decd supposed to be about	10	0	0
Suma Totalis	40	19	10

[WSRO Ep I/29/1/96]

Will: made 10 March 1709; proved 1 April 1709
Nephew: Anthony Wilkes, executor
Witnesses: John Wakeford junior, John Helsey, Adam Bredham   [WSRO STC I/31/139]

[1] Possibly Oxford, New College. Called LLB 1677. Ordained deacon 1674. Rector of All Saints, Chichester, c. 1674, patron archbishop of Canterbury. Vicar of Chidham 1677, patron Henry Buckley; of Aldingbourne 1681–1709, patron dean and chapter of Chichester. Died 1709.

3. Amberley 20 July 1632 HENRY SPENCER [1]

Appraisers: George Rose, Edward Greene, Daniel Braby, Edward Holand

	£	s	d
In primis his purs and Aparile	5	0	0

In the loft over the Chamber

Item 1 olde ione bedstedle 1 feather bed 2 fether boulsters 1 coverlet a blanket a linnen bedticke	2	0	0
Item 1 little bedstedle a featherbed a flocke boulster one oulde rudg and a blanket	1	10	0
Item a trunke 2 litle boxes a cradle		3	6

In the loft over the hale

Item in corne readie wimed wheate maulte and barlie	5	1	0
Item 4 sackes 1 poake		5	0
Item 3 naile of hempe		6	0
Item 2 naile of buter 12 litle Cheeses		10	0
Item in other old Lumberment		2	0

In the chamber

	£	s	d
Item a bedstedle with curtaines a featherbed and linen bedticke a feather boulster 2 pillowes a blanket a coverlet	5	0	0
Item one other bedstedle a featherbed 2 feather boulsters a pillow a blanket a coverlet	2	10	0
Item an other litle bedstedle a flocke bed with other thinges therto belonging		10	0
Item 1 press 1 chest 1 deske a litle rounde table	1	10	0
Item 16 payre of sheetes	4	0	0
Item 7 pillowcoates 3 table cloathes 1 dozen of napkins 3 towells and other linen	2	10	0
Item in bookes	5	0	0
in the hale			
Item 1 table 1 forme 1 bench 3 Chayers a cuboard		12	0
Item 6 Cushions		9	0
Item in peuter	2	7	8
in the kitchin			
Item in bras	1	10	0
Item in Ireon kettles 4 spitts 1 payre of tongs 2 fire Shovel 2 payer of pothangers 1 payre of pothookes		18	0
Item 2 tubes 2 ferkins a cheesepres 2 bucketes with other lumberment	1	0	0
Item 1 pestle 1 morter		1	6
in the milkhouse			
Item 6 truges 2 ferkins a litle tun with other lumber	1	0	0
Item 1 flitch of bacon		10	0
in trenckes house			
Item 1 Chaire a bedstedle 2 forme a table a trunke		5	0
in prates house			
Item a litle table and a bench		1	0
in the barne			
Item in haye and boardes with other lumber	1	6	0
Item 3 kine 2 bul 3 yong beast	10	0	0
Item a mare and a fole and two coultes	5	0	0
Item a Sowe 7 pigs 2 yong hoges	2	6	8
Item 3 acres of wheate	4	10	0
Item 2 acres of barlie	2	10	0
Item 1 acre of pease 1 acre of tares	1	10	0
Item 5 acres of grass	2	10	0
[Total]	73	14	4

[WSRO Ep I/29/3/20]

Will: made 27 Jan 1631; proved 7 Aug 1632
Wife: Joan, executrix; sons: James, eldest (bed, moveables at Chiltington house); Henry (great press, bed on south side of chamber, boards now on floor of chamber, furniture in hall); daughter: Anne (bed, pewter, moveables in Amberley copyhold)
Witness: Robert Pannett   [WSRO STC I/18/203]

[1] Called BA 1603. Ordained deacon and priest 1603 (bishop of Colchester). Licensed curate of North Stoke and Houghton 1604–?1632. Died 1632.

4. Arundel 16 June 1620 WILLIAM CARUS [1]

Appraisers: Thomas Freeman, Richard Wooldridge senior, Richard Page, Francis Homfrey

	£	s	d
In the halle			
In primis two tables one Bench and a fourme		5	0
Item two Chaires two dressers and two shelves		2	0
Item five prongs two Spadestaves one drawyng wyndowe 1 chopping block 4 bucketts with yron bayles and without a bayle			8
Item fower yron spitts two pothengers a pair of pothookes 3 payer of Andyrons one fyre shovell a payer of tongues one yron hayhooke three Iron dripping panes a Cheesell a graffing sawe and knyfe three Chopping knyves 1 Cleaver 2 pair of gredyrons and a tosting yron	2	12	0
Item two yron potts		5	0
[Tear on fold] Item 4 brasse . . . and a pair of . . .		3	0
Item five posnets 1 bell posnet a Chafingdish and a ladle of brasse		10	0
Item 1 morter and pestle 1 ladle and skyme brasse		5	0
Item fower brasse Candlesticks		4	0
Item one Furness of brasse	1	3	4
Item two Candlesticks 2 quarts and 2 pynte potts 4 Salts 2 Chamber potts ten porrengers and fyve litle Cupps all pewter	1	3	4
Item 2 Cupps a litle bottle and ten Spoones of pewter		2	0
Item one doze occumy spoones		2	6
Item two flytches of bacon		12	0
Item potts and Cruses of earth Tankerds a Cullender eathern panches pannes and dishes bottles Cupps and such like		6	0
Item wooden dishes trenchers litle basketts a shovell spitter pickax two yron wedges One Ax and a hatchett		4	8
Item two brushes Candlesticks of wood and other smale Thinges		2	0
Item two frying pannes		1	6
Item two Skrynes		4	0
In the parlor			
Item one table and frame fyve Joyned stooles 1 bench 1 Setle 2 Joyned Cubberd 1 Syde Cubberd a rownd table with litle shelves three Chaires and one great Mappe	3	0	0
Item one feild Bedstede Matt and Coard with Canapye and Curtens 1 featherbed one feather boulster and pillowe 2 blankets and a Coverlett	6	3	4
Item six turky Cishions 1 Carpett fower Curtens and Seaven ould Cushions	2	13	0
Item two black quishions one Cubberd Cloth 1 Cubberd for glasses one other Joyned Cubberd wth boxes glasses 1 litle desk lock and key certayne Lynen therein glasse bottles a payre of tables three dossen of trenchers and other smale thinges		17	0
Item a wyndowe Cushion Coveringe		2	6
Item all his Bookes	12	0	0
Item one payer of Castyron Andyrons and a payer of tongues		4	0
Item one ould Callyver furnished and a Javelin		3	0
In the Buttery			
Item fower Tubbs keever three kylderkins 4 virkines two pynnes 1 ould			

Cubberd 2 shelves 1 shutting wyndowe with crocks and smale Lumber	16	0
Item one Tubb wth seaven naile of butter	17	4

In the Milke howse

Item one ould table five shelves a reming tubb 1 powderinge tubb 2 keevers 4 bowles 6 Trugs 6 Milkpannes Crocks and pipkines		13	2
Item a Bowltinghutch and 1 tubb wth Meale		5	0
Item 1 Charne 1 Cheespres Cheesmots hoopes vallows and other smale thinges		6	4
Item seaventeene Cheeses and 8 lb of butter		12	0
Item Leaden waights 4 lbs			6

In the Wheatlofte

Item three Tronkes 1 chest 2 boxes a hamp a flockbed 2 feather pillowes one half bushell 1 peck and 1 bag with 1quarter wheat	1	5	0
Item a frame for a stale and a looking glasse		2	8
Item six quarters of Malte	3	12	0

In the Chamber over the Parlor

Item two Standing bedstedles trundle bedsteed matts and Coardes	1	0	0
Item fyve Chestes and two ould Chaires		15	0
Item three featherbeds and a flockbed 2 feather boulsters 2 flock boulsters 2 Feather pyllowes	5	10	0
Item three payr of Blanketts 2 Coverletts 1 Rugg and a half dossen of Bedstaves	2	14	0

[Tear on fold]   The Studye and . . . chamber

Item a deskboard shelves two Curteins and Curten Rodds		3	4
Item a halbeard		2	0
Item Thirty seaven payer of Sheetes	13	18	0
Item fower payer of pillow Coats		14	6
Item 13 table clothes and fower dossen of napkines	2	11	4
Item two Cubberd Cloathes		3	4
Item 13 hand towells		3	4
Item three handtowells and 3 yards course lynnen		8	6

In the Loft over the Buttery

Item two Wheeles Three Saddles for men one woman's Sadle Cloth and Brydle	1	6	0
Item a table 2 shelves a leather sacke a Brydle tytt yarne wynders Cushion and 2 stawbucketts		7	8
Item hemp and Flexen Towe		10	0
Item a Lanthorne a Ridder and other Lumberment		2	6
Item 12 lb of Lynnen yarne		12	0

In the Gates and backsyde

Item Seaven Cordes of wood	2	6	8
Item the well Curbe frame wynch roap and Chayne		13	4
Item a Coope a Wheelbarowe Tubbs and other Lumber		5	0
Item two ladders two Racks and 2 hogtrowes		6	0
Item two ladders two Racks and 2 hogtrowes	3	18	0
Item six kyne and two wanyer Calves		16	0
Item the Poultry		2	0
Item his wearinge Apparrell	5	0	0
Item mony in his purse	1	10	2

Item of good debts			15	0	0

Summa Totall   118   6   4

[WSRO Ep I/29/8/11]

Probate act for lost will: 27 June 1620
Wife: Catherine, executrix   [WSRO STC III/F/161]

[1] Of Westmorland. Oxford, Merton, matriculated 1582 aged 20; Queen's, BA 1586, MA 1589. Ordained deacon and priest 1590 (bishop of Chichester). Vicar of Arundel 1595–1620, patron Crown. Died 1620.

5. Arundel ... 1648 WILLIAM HILL, minister [1]

Appraisers: James Morris, John Alberry, Nathaniel Older

	£	s	d
Item 2 feather beds 2 feather bolsters 4 pillowes 2 Coveringes 2 blanketts 1 payre of Curtaines and vallence 1 bested 1 baskett Chayre 1 Side Cubord 1 Chest 2 Cubbord-cloathes 1 payre brandirons 1 little table 1 wooden Chayre 6 glass bottles	9	14	4
In the Chamber ov[er] the wash[?]place			
Item 1 cradle 2 bedsteds		8	0
In the Chamber ov[er] the parlor			
Item 1 bedsted 1 payre Curtaines and vallence and rods 1 Rugg 1 feather bed 2 bolsters 1 Chest 3 boxes 1 Coveringe 1 truckle bedsted	4	2	6
Item there 12 payre of sheets 12 Course towells 12 napkins 5 table cloathes 3 Payre of pillow coats all	5	0	0
In the Studdey			
Item for Bookes	6	0	0
Item 1 table 1 deske 1 stoole and shelves		10	0
Item in Readie moneys there	45	1	8
Item 1 watch	2	10	0
Item 1 horse	12	0	0
Item 4 Calves	7	0	0
Item 5 Kine 2 Ewes and 2 lambs	21	0	0
Item 1 Colte	6	0	0
Item moneys in London	30	0	0
Item his wareing Aparrell	5	0	0
Maior Joseph Yonge oweth	5	0	0
debts due more	[*sic*] 80	0	
[Total]	171	16	6

[WSRO Ep I/29/8/85]

Administration 30 May 1648
To wife, Mary   [WSRO STC III/K/84]

[1] Called BA 1624. Ordained deacon 1624 (bishop of Rochester), priest 1625 (bishop of Chichester). Vicar of Felpham 1624–1648, patron the rector; of Arundel ?1645. Curate of New Fishbourne 1626. Licensed preacher Chichester archdeaconry 1631. Died 1648.

6. Arundel 12 Oct 1665 JOHN MAYNARD [1]
Appraisers: Nathaniel Cuffley, William Pellett

	£	s	d
In the lowe roomes			
In primis 7 tables 13 leather Chaires 4 wrought Chaires 4 Lerg[?]			
Chaires 3 other Chaires 9 Cushiones I pair of virginalls 13 joined			
stooles 5 pair of Andirons 5 p of dogs 6 pr of tongs 5 fire pan 2			
Cubberds 1 Safe 1 Jack 4 p of pothangers 9 spits 4 driping pans a brass			
morter 4 Iron pots white earthen ware a musket and sword two firnises			
tubs and brewing vessells 1 press and other small things	39	15	0
In the chambers			
Item 5 feather beds 15 boulsters 6 pillows 20 blanckets 3 Coverlets 2			
ruggs two flockbeds 7 bedsteds 4 p of Curtaines and vallents 5 Chests 3			
truncks 1 press 1 p of drawers 2 side bords	37	0	0
Item in plate a Clock a watch and silver box	27	0	0
Item in linen	26	0	0
Item pewter and brass	13	0	0
Item books in his study	10	0	0
Item 8 cord of wood in the gate and other lumber	6	0	0
Item his Wearing apparell and mony in his purse	10	0	0
Item a lease of the house he lived in	50	0	0
Item in ready money	400	0	0
Item for lumber about the house	1	5	0
Suma totalis	620	0	0

[WSRO Ep I/29/8/110]

Administration 13 Oct 1665
To wife, Elizabeth   [WSRO STC III/H/361; STC III/I/8]

[1] Vicar of Arundel 1663; of Lyminster 1664. Died 1665.

7. Ashburnham 17 Jan 1670 ALEXANDER WIGGS [1]
Appraisers: Matthew Wing, John Bowyer

	£	s	d
In primis his purse and wearing apparrell	4	16	8
Item mony in his boxes and Truncks	4	11	2
Item his books	3	0	0
Item two truncks and severall small boxes		10	0
Item A lookinglass and other small things		10	0
Item a silver box		10	0
Debts (as yet) none appears		0	0
Sum totalis	13	17	10

[TNA PRO PROB 5/2815]

Will: made 27 Dec 1669; proved 5 Jan 1670
Executor: Anthony Nethercott, vicar, Ashburnham   [TNA PRO PROB 11/332]

[1] Born Hildersham, Cambs.   Cambridge, Jesus, matriculated sizar 1617, BA 1622, MA 1625. Ordained deacon 1628 (bishop of London) aged 25.   Licensed curate and schoolmaster of Withyham 1634.   Died 1669.

8. Ashington 1 Nov 1732 ROBERT WILLAN [1]

Appraisers: John Farley, Thomas Sturt

	£	s	d
In primis Waring Apparell and money in purse	10	0	0
4 Heifers and Two Steers	16	10	0
Two Steers and One Heifer	5	5	0
16 Sheep and One Lamb	7	13	0
One Shod Waggon	7	10	0
One Horse Rooller		15	0
3 Horse Harrows	1	0	0
One Ox Harrow		10	0
One Horse Dung Cart	1	10	0
One plow		10	0
Winnowing Tackle and Bushell a Shall and 5 Prongs	1	13	0
Two Ladders		4	0
5 Horses and their Harness	24	10	0
3 Colts and One Mare	12	15	0
Two Sadles	1	5	0
6 Cowes One Calfe and One Bull	23	19	0
4 Hoggs	6	0	0
5 Shutts	4	0	0
Deal Boards		15	0
Geese		12	0
Another Colt	3	7	0
Oates in the Barne and in the Ricks	53	0	0
All the Wheat	47	0	0
Hay	40	0	0
Barley French Wheat and Pease	5	18	0
In the Buttery Chamber			
Three Beds and all belonging to them. A pillion and Cloth and other small things	10	2	6
In the Kitchen Chamber			
One Bed and all that do belong to him Two Guns a Desk Trunk Box and other odd Things	5	17	6
In the Parlour Chamber			
One Bed and all that do belong to him A Chest of Draws A Large Seeing Glass 6 Cane Chaires a Square Table Doggs Fire Shovell tongs Fender and other odd Things	21	4	0
In the Mens Chamber			
One Bed and all belonging to him	1	5	0
In the Garrets			
The Wooll a Side Saddle some Wheat and other odd Things	12	0	0
In the Study			
One square Table One round the Library of Books A Silver Watch a			

Silver box and other odd things	11	3	0

In the Parlour

One round Table Nine Cane Chaires A Great Chair a Table Fire pann Tongs and other odd things	1	19	0

In the Corner Cupboard in the parlour

Silver Salts Silver Spoones China with Silver Spoones and other odd things	2	2	6

In the Mill Room

A Still Mill 4 drink Vessells A warming pan a brass Chaffing dish and other odd things	2	1	6

In the Buttery

Ten drink Vessells One Stand One Stand Tubb 4 powdering Tubbs Silver and other odd things	2	15	0

In the milkhouse

A brass Kittle Two Lids Two Churns One milk buckett A butt Tubb Cheeses butter a Bowle Wooden platter with Shelves and other things	5	0	0

In the Pantry

A Copper porridge pott Frying pan Three Kittle a brass Kittle and Little Iron pott a brass Same pan Shilfes and other things	2	9	6

In the Brewhouse

A large Furnace Two Vates Tun Tubb Two Kivers Two drinks Vessells Two bucketts Glass Bottles A Cheese press and other things	3	15	0

In the Kitchen

Pewter dishes pewter plates A Dresser a Clock a Case a Jack Two Spitts Pothooks Gridirons Two doggs Iron back Tea kittle a Box Iron Stillions Cleaver Table Corton Bellows fire pann Tongs and other Things	8	13	0
Linen	30	0	0
4 Hives of Bees	1	4	0
Due from his Tennant	10	0	0
Bond debts	50	0	0
Debts good and bad	56	15	6
Dung	1	10	0
Wood and Faggotts	9	6	0
Sacks and Wimsheet	1	10	0
Other things forgott and unseen		10	0
Sum tot of this side	169	8	6
Sum tot of the first side	292	1	0
Sum tot of the second side	66	4	6
Sum tot is	527	14	0

[WSRO Ep I/29/9/43]

Administration 24 Sep 1733
To wife, Lucy   [WSRO STC III/O/67]

[1] Son of Robert, rector of Edburton. Oxford, Magdalen Hall, matriculated 1703 aged 17, BA 1707. Ordained deacon 1706 (bishop of Chichester), priest 1710 (bishop of Ely). Licensed curate of Beeding 1706. Rector of Ashington 1710–1732, patron Mary Willan, widow. Married Lucy Bennett at Buncton 1728. Died 1732.

9. Ashurst 7 Oct 1680 THOMAS WILSON [1]

Appraisers: Richard Greenfeild, yeoman, William Longmer, Steyning, butcher

	£	s	d
In primis his wearinge Apparell and ready money in his house	45	5	0
Item due to him for halfe A yeares Tithe att Michaellmas last	20	0	0
Item due to him upon bond	105	10	0

In the Kitchen

Item fourteene pewter dishes foure Porringers foure little pewter Potts
one pewter Cullender and Bason three brasse Kettles twoe bell Brasse
Potts twoe Skilletts of the same twoe Chaffine dishes one Iron Pott one
brasse Morter one Iron and Stone Morter three spitts twoe paire of
potthookes twoe paire of potthangers twoe paire of Tongs one Fire
Shovell one Iron Slice and Pronge one little Table three Joyned Stooles
foure Chaires one warmingpann twoe Iron drippinge panns one Jacke
three brasse Skimmers one brasse Ladle one Cleaver twoe Chopping
knives one paire of Gridgirons one Iron Kettle one brasse Pann and one
paire of Brandirons   5   0   0

In the Hall

Item twoe Formes one Table one Cupboard three pewter dishes one
pewter Flaggon Foure Candlestickes twoe Chayres one pewter still and
one Clocke in the Entry   2   0   0

In the Parlour

Item One Table three Joyned Stooles foure leather Chayres one other
Chayre one paire of Brandirons and Fire Shovell one Sideboard and one
silver Bowle   4   0   0

In the Milkehouse and Buttery

Item twelve Truggs one Keeler one powdringe Tubb six Barrells twoe
Cheesepresses one Kenninge Tubb one three legged Tubb one Charne
and other Lumber   2   15   0

In the Brewhouse

Item one Furnace Foure Tubbs one Keeler and one Iron Pott   2   10   0

In the Bakehouse

Item one Cupboard one Keeler and one old Tubb   15   0

In the Kitchen Chamber

Item one Bedsteddle one Featherbedd one Feather Boulster one Flock
Boulster twoe Blancketts one Coverlett and all thinges belonginge to
the Beds   2   0   0

In the Hall Chamber

Item one Featherbedd twoe Feather Boulsters twoe Feather Pillowes
Curtains and Vallence one Coverlett twoe Blancketts one Presse three
pewter dishes one old Trunke twoe Chayres and one Table Chaire   5   12   0

In the Parlour Chamber

Item one Feather Bedd twoe Feather Boulsters twoe Feather Pillowes
twoe Blancketts one Rugge Curtaines and Vallence one little
Bedsteddle under the other wth a Featherbedd one Feather Boulster one
Flock Boulster twoe Blancketts one Coverlett one sideboard twoe
sideboard Chushions one lookinge Glasse twoe Chests one Truncke
foure greene covered Chayres one Chest in the halfe space Five paire of
Tire Sheetes twoe paire of Tow Sheets Five dozen of Napkins Five

paire of Pillow Coates six Towells twoe Tableclothes twoe		
sidebordclothes twoe Cupboard Clothes six naile of Tire and Towe	17 0 0	
In the little Closett		
Item old Bottles and other Lumber	10 0	
In the Study		
Item Bookes and other Lumber	5 2 3	
without Doores		
Item three Cowes twoe Hoggs and the Hay	16 0 0	
Item thinges unseene and forgott	13 4	

                                            Suma totalis   233 17   7
                                            [WSRO Ep I/29/11/41]

Will: made 23 June 1680; proved 12 Oct 1680
Wife: Joan, executrix; sons: Thomas, John, Samuel (trunk + lock, sister Mary's cabinet);
daughters (both under 21): Mary (3 silver spoons, 2 pairs sheets); Anne (2 silver spoons,
2 pairs sheets)
Overseers: John Gratwick of Eatons, William Whitebread
Witnesses: William Harris, Elizabeth Child   [WSRO STC I/27/127]

[1] Rector of Ashurst 1660–1680, patron John, earl of Thanet. Possibly married Joan Moris at
Keymer 1666. Died 1680.

10. Ashurst 3 May 1741 JOHN BROWNSWORD [1]

Appraisers: John Muzzal, Charles Cutress

	£	s	d
First Whareing Apparel and Money in Purse	2	0	0
In Goods Debts	16	10	0
In the Kitchen			
One Clock and Case	8	0	0
One Dresser with Drawers	1	5	0
One fowlding Table		4	0
One Meal Trist		8	0
One Roasting Jack		10	0
Two Spitts		9	0
Four Pewter Dishes and Six Plates		9	6
One Salt Box			6
One Tea Kettle		5	0
One pair of Potthangers One pair of Gridirons One Fender a Trist fire			
Pan and Tongs a Chaffing Dish		9	6
One Wharming Pan		5	6
Fifteen Small cloths five Napkins Three Cloths		13	8
Four brass Candlesticks One Iron One flat Iron One Box Iron and			
Heaters brass Snuffers Two Coffy Potts One Candle Till One Flower			
Box		16	6
A Good Huzzy and Bellows		1	2
Five Stone Muggs		1	9
One Arm Chaire and 5 other Chaires		7	0
One old Lanthorne One Bason			8

In the Dresser a Case of Eight Drawers	2	0
Six Knifes and Forks and a Baskett	8	4
In the Pantery		
One Powdering Tub One flower Tubb One Tin Dripping Pan Three		
Small Crocks One Chocolate Pott and Crewett	8	4
In the Great Parlour		
One Corner Cupboard	7	6
One Round Table	14	0
One Mahogany Table	10	6
One Tea Table and Tea Pott and Four Dishes and Saucers Four Coffy		
Cans and Saucers and Slop Bason	15	0
One looking Glass	12	0
Eight Cane Chairs	1 0	0
One pair of Dogs [?]Offere Pan and Tongs One Brush	4	0
In the Little Parlour		
One Corner Cupboard	10	0
One Decanter Three Glasses four Cups	2	0
One Gun	10	6
Six Rush Bottom'd Chaires	7	0
In the Buttery		
Five Barrells One Earthen Pan One Tin Funnell	13	2
In the Brewhouse		
One brass Furnace	15	0
One Bucking Tub One Vate	15	0
One Slice	1	6
One Plate Rack	2	6
Two Pailes One Tin Kettle One Earthen pan a Sope box and Chaires	4	2
In the lower Pantery		
Two Pottage Pott One Frying Pan	9	6
Four Earthen Pans Two Puding Pans One Sauce Pan and [?]Grable	3	10
One Boiler	1	0
Thirteen Dozen of Glass Bottles	19	6
One Stone Bottle	1	0
In the Kitchen Chamber		
One Chest of Drawers	10	0
One Bed and Steddle and Curtains and Rodds and Three blanketts One		
Quilt One Boulster Two Pillows	5 5	0
One dressing Table and Glass	10	0
Five Cane Chaires with Rush Bottoms	5	0
Four Pair of Sheets and one odd one 8 pillowbers	1 7	6
In the Parlour Chamber		
One Bed and Stedle One Boulster Two Pillows One Quilt Three		
Blanketts and Curtains and Rods and all belonging thereunto and		
Window Curtains	6 6	0
One Chest of Drawers	10	0
One Dressing Table	8	6
One Closestool and Earthen Pan	8	0
Five Cane Chaires	10	0

In the Brewhouse Chamber

	£	s	d
One Bed and stedle One Boulster One Quilt Three Blanketts and Curtains	9	10	0
One Small Table		9	6

In the buttery Chamber

	£	s	d
One bedstedle and Matt and Cords and top and Curtains and Rodds	1	1	0
One Coffy Pott and Stand	1	5	0
One Salver		12	0
Two Candlesticks and Snuffers		9	0
The seat in the Field		6	0
One Garden rake and Spiter and hand Bill		4	0
One Mare	6	0	0
One Horse	8	10	0
One Bridle Sadle and housing		8	0
Things Unseen and forgoten	1	10	0
	72	8	3

[WSRO Ep I/29/011/71]

Administration 4 May 1741
To John Elphick, John Brownings and William Jeffery, principal creditors, wife,
Elizabeth Brownsword having renounced   [WSRO STC III/P/244]

[1] Son of William, vicar of Sompting and rector of Coombes. Oxford, Queen's, matriculated 1732 aged 17, BA 1735. Ordained deacon 1736, priest 1738 (bishop of Chichester). Died 1741.

11. Barlavington 12 July 1677 THOMAS GARRETT [1]

Appraisers: Joseph Tester of [S]utton, gent, William Langley of Sutton, yeoman

	£	s	d
In primis For the wearing Apparrell of the Deceased and money in his purse	20	0	0
In the Parlour			
Item A Drawing Table 6 Chaires 6 Leather Stooles 2 Chushions One paire of Andirons 1 paire of Tongs White Ware and Glasses	4	5	0
In the Hall			
Item A Table a Forme 2 Chaires 2 Stooles a Still	8	0	0
In the Kitchin			
Item A Table and Forme 4 Chaires		7	0
Item In Brasse 3 Kettles 1 Pot 3 Skilletts 2 Chaffing dishes 2 Skimers 1 Warming Pan a Mortar	1	13	0
Item In Pewter 23 Dishes and Sawcers 1 Flagon 1 pint Pot 6 Porringers 1 Cawdle Cup 6 Candlestickes 2 Salts 2 Chamber Pots	1	19	0
Item In Iron 1 Kettle 4 paire of Pothangers 5 spits 1 Jacke 3 Dripping Pans 1 paire of Gridirons 1 paire of Andirons 1 paire Dogs 1 Slice 1 Fire pan 2 paire of Tongs 2 Tosting Irons 1 Iron Plate 1 Fender 1 Flesh hooke 1 Clever 1 Chopping knife 5 Smoothing irons 3 iron pots 3 paire of Pot hookes 4 Skilletts a Mustard Ball	2	11	0
Item For Bacon	3	0	0

	£	s	d
In the Sinke			
Item 1 Cheese presse 1 Brewing Fatt 4 Tubs 4 Buckets 4 Kivers		15	6
In the Milkehouse			
Item 3 Tubs 1 Churn 1 Traye Earthen Pots Butter and Salt		5	0
In the New Roome			
Item 3 dozen of Bottles 1 Frying Pan ..		0	0
In the Buttery			
Item 13 Vessells 3 Tunnells	1	10	0
In the Round Chamber			
Item 1 Chest of Drawers 1 Chest 1 Deske 1 Side Cubboard 1 Fether bed 1 Bolster 1 Pillow 3 Blanketts 1 Cov[erlet] Curtaines and Vallance 1 Cupboard cloth 1 Cushion 1 Glasse 1 paire of Andirons 2 Chaires 2 Stooles 1 Trunke	7	12	6
In the Parlour Chamber			
Item 1 Bedsteddle 1 Fetherbed 2 bolsters 2 Pillows 1 Rug 1 Coverlet 1 Blanket Cu[rta]ines and Vallence 2 Chests 1 Presse 1 ..op ...esse 1 paire of Andirons	5	6	0
In the Study			
Item 1 Table 1 Deske Bookes	5	10	0
In the Roome next the Parlour Chamber			
Item 1 truckle bedstedle 2 fether beds 3 Bolsters 3 Blankets 2 Coverlets	4	0	0
Item 20 paire of Sheets 8 Table cloths 3 dozen and a halfe of Napkins 8 Pillow Coats	13	0	0
In the Mault loft			
Item Wheat 30 Bushels 5£ 5s 0d Barley 6s Hopps 1£	6	11	0
Item Mault Mault Shovel and Haire cloth	3	0	0
Item 11 Sacks and 1 winnow Sheet	1	0	0
Item A Quern Scales and Weights		6	0
Item Cheese 1£ 5s 0d Wooll 1£	2	5	0
Item 1 Sow and Piggs 30s 3 hoggs and 4 Piggs 3£ 4s	4	14	0
Item 1 Bull 1 Cow 1 Heifer and calfe 2 yearlings 1 weanyere	12	5	0
Item 3 Horses	9	0	0
Item 1 Waggon 1 Dung pot 1 Plow 3 Harrows 1 Chaine 1 yoke Harnesse	5	5	0
Item Wheat 6 acres Barley 8 acres Pease and Fitches 4 acres Oats 3 acres	32	0	0
Item Wood and Faggots	1	0	0
Item Sadle and Bridle		10	0
Item Lumber things unsee[n] forgotten and unprized	1	0	0
Item Desperate Debts	2	0	0
Tot	160	10	10

[WSRO Ep I/29/12/13]

Will: made 3 May 1676; proved 18 July 1677
Wife: Ellenor, executrix; sons: Edward, Richard
Overseers: Joseph Tester of Sutton, gent (brother-in-law), William Langley of Sutton
Witnesses: Thomas Thornton, John Hayler   [WSRO STC I/26/139]

[1] Probably curate of Barlavington 1657. Ordained deacon and priest 1660 (bishop of Ardfert, Ireland). Curate of Duncton 1660–1675 (or 1677). Rector of Egdean 1671–1677, patron Sir Henry (*?recte* Sir William) Goring, bt. Died 1677.

12. Beeding 4 June 1680 MALACHY CONANT, vicar [1]

Appraisers: Mr John [Cowdry] of St Buttolphs, — Backshell, Michael Piper both of Beeding

	£	s	d
In primis his weareing Apparrell and money in his pocket	8	3	..
Item money due upon Bond	100	0	0
In the Parlour			
One dozen of Russia leather Chaires one Couch of Russia Leather and six Velvet Cushions	..	..	..
Item two Tables and theire Carpetts fower window Curtaines	1	0	0
Item one paire of brass Brandirons one paire of Coale irons one paire of Tongs one fire shovel and a paire of Bellows		16	0
Item three Pictures in Frames		6	0
Item tenn peeces of Arras	3	0	0
In the Hall			
One Table fower joynd Stools one armd Chaire and six Cushions one Sconce and two halberts		8	0
In the Milk house			
One chirne two keelers six Milk troughes one powdring Tubb nine Beer vessells one safe one trencher rack one frying pan two stands two dozen of bottles	2	0	0
In the Kitchen			
One Table two dressers one forme fower chaire one cupboard a still a Cradle a case of knives a Jack two gunns a paire of Brandirons a paire of tongs one fire shovell three dozen of plates eighteene Pewter dishes four pewter candlesticks	5	15	0
Item thre spitts one dripping pan one pair of toasting irons a gridiron two cleavers one chopping knife four Candlesticks one pasty pan		11	0
Item a fire slice and fork two leaden waites one iron waite a marble mortar and a brass mortar a bellbrass pott two kettles four skilletts one table one spoon one skimmer one warming pan	1	2	0
Item foure Flitches of Bacon	2	10	0
In the Brewhouse			
Two Furnaces one brew Fatt a tun tub and other brew vessells two iron potts an iron barr two bucketts and other things in that roome	2	14	0
In the Kitchen Chamber			
One feather bedd and all things belonging to it	5	0	0
One trundle bedd and boulster with all things together as it stands	2	12	0
One chaire a looking glass a paire of brandirons a fire box and a trunk		5	0
In the Closett			
A Chest of Drawers two stands a hanging shelfe two sellars of glasses one dozen of silver spoons silver Tankard three porringers one sugar box a silver tumbler and other things in the said roome	11	10	0

In the Brewhouse Chamber

One bedd and steddle and all belonging to it	4	0	0

In the Hall Chamber

One bedd and steddle and all belonging to it   4   10   0

one Chaire one desk a Looking glass one Trunk one Chest two tables two suites of diaper two suits of holland and twelve paire of sheets two suites of flaxen table linnen and other course linen   10   16   0

In the staire Case

A Clock one press one side board   2   0   0

In the Parlour Chamber

One bedd and steddle wth all belonging to it   10   13   4

One trunk one table two Chaires four stools a Looking glass a paire of brandirons a paire of tongs and fire shovel and fower pictures with the Curtains and hangings   2   10   0

In the Garretts

Two Tables two wooden bottles a spinning wheele two Chests one bedd and all belonging to it   1   11   0

In the Study

His study of books two Globes (vizt) Celestiall and Terrestriall a book of Mapps and others loose maps and all other things in the study   50   0   0

Without doores

Two Cows one horse one yeareling heifer and two Hoggs   12   10   0

Item one dung Cart and wheeles one wheele barrow a spitter and shovell an ax and a saw a hamar and Chisell and other small tools   17   0

Old hay   14   0

For things unseen and forgotten   1   0   0

Sum tot   249   11   6

[TNA PRO PROB 4/11081]

Administration 9 June 1680

To widow Jane   [TNA PRO PROB 6/55]

[1] Son of John, of Salisbury, Wilts, cleric. Oxford, Exeter, matriculated 1651; Magdalen, demy 1653–1655, BA 1654, fellow 1655–1657, MA 1657, BD 1665, librarian 1665. Cambridge, incorporated 1668. Ordained deacon and priest 1660 (bishop of Oxford). Curate of Horspath, Oxon, c. 1664–1666. Vicar of Beeding 1667, patron Magdalen College. Prebendary of Middleton 1669–c. 1678. Chaplain to Denzil, Lord Holles, overseas. Died 1680; buried Beeding.

13. Bepton 9 Dec 1614 WILLIAM RUFFE [1]

Appraisers: Thomas Hitchcocke, John Andrews, John Chandler

	£	s	d
In primis one standing bedstedell one Truckell Stedell one fether bede two fether bolsters one kiverlett and two blanketts prized at	3	0	0
Item one Cupbord two Chaires and Six Joyne Stooles and eight cushones	2	12	0
Item one bed pane		6	8
Item one Table and one forme		5	0

Item one Standing bedstedell one fether bed two kiverletes and one blankett	3	10	0
Item one truckell stedell one flocke bed one blanket one kiverlett and one bolster	1	0	0
Item fower Chestes and one box	1	6	8
Item his bookes in his studdy	6	13	4
Item one bedstedell one flocke bed two cushons one flocke bolster and 4 pillowes	1	0	0
Item certayne wooll	3	0	0
Item the hempe	1	0	0
Item one presse		8	0
Item about tenn paire of Sheetes	3	0	0
Item two dozen of table Napkines		16	0
Item fower table clothes and five toweles		13	4
Item seven pillowebers		7	0
Item one other bedstedell and certayne hoppes	1	0	0
[Following five lines torn]			
Item one Caldron three kittelles th. . . and three skillettes			
Item one Stylle one limbecke and the p. . .thereunto			
Item one Skime. . . fower candlestickes			
Item one Iron bar and one Treset two broches. . . paire of pothangers three paire of pothookes three. . . andirons and five Iron wedges	1	0	0
Item Barrells firkins tubes one half bushell one fate two tables and other wooden stuffe	2	0	0
Item one morter and two frying panes		6	8
Item seven platters six pewter dishes two chamber pottes three salts three dozen of spones wth other smalle pewter	1	10	0
Item three score and ten chesses	3	0	0
Item ten nayle of butter	1	6	8
Item seventeen bushelles of mault	1	10	0
Item eight bushelles of beanes	1	6	8
Item one bushell of [?]hastes		5	0
Item two hogges of bacon	1	10	0
Item eleven trugges and bowelles wth other lumberment of wooden stuffe		10	0
Item all the aples at		10	0
Item his wearinge aparell and money in his purse	10	0	0
Item the wheate in the barne	24	0	0
Item the barley in the barne	6	0	0
Item the oates in the barne	3	0	0
Item one Ryke of hay	5	0	0
Item two fatt hogges	2	0	0
Item nine leane hogges	2	0	0
Item two horses	7	0	0
Item five kyne and two bullockes		15	0
Item fiveteene ewes	4	16	0
Item all the poultry		10	0
Item one carte two paire of wheles one dungpott one sadell one Sedelap two harrowes and two paire of harness	1	0	0

Item one Culliver and one dagge one sword one Rapier and one hanger	1	0	0
Item the wood and Timber	13	6	8
Item the wheate upon the ground	10	0	0
Total	153	9	0

[WSRO Ep I/29/17/3]

Will (Nuncupative; administration with will annexed): made: 28 Nov 1614; proved 14 Jan 1615
Wife: Elizabeth
Witnesses: Thomas Hitchcock, John Andrew, John Ch[…][WSRO STC II/M Dean 1614]

[1] Called BA and MA 1607. Possibly curate of Woolbeding c. 1606. Rector of Bepton 1607–1614, patron Thomas Hitchcocke, yeoman. Married Elizabeth (possibly Elizabeth Searle at Sompting 1597). Died 1614.

14. Bersted 17 Oct 1685 JOSEPH LEWIS [1]
Appraisers: Robert Chapman, …

	£	s	d
In primis His wearing apparrell and ………..			
In the Parlour			
Item One [?]Ovall table ….. Chaires…pair…..One fire pan ….Iron grate……	7	..	..
In the Parlour Chamber			
Item One Olive table two Olive stands One dressing box One Looking glass One Chest with drawers One close stooll and pan Six searge chaires One featherbed and bolsters Two pillows a Sett of Curtaines with double valence One quilt with bedsteadle and Curtaine rods Two Window Curtaines One pair of Andirons Firepan and tongs a Childs Cabinet and Two Blankets	22	1	6
In the Hall Chamber			
Item One Trundle bed Two blankets a Flock bed and bolster One feather pillow One old Greene Rug One desk One little trunck Two boxes Two hampers One flasket Two shelves	1	7	6
Item His Books	2	10	0
In the Kitchen Chamber			
Item One feather bed and bolster Two pillows Two blankets One Counterpane and Curtains Four Chaires One Trundle Bedsteadle one Featherbed to it and bolster and pillow One Blanket One Coverled One pair of Andirons One pair of bellows One small Looking glass One Large bedsteadle Mat and Cord One Large trunck Two old boxes	7	12	6
Item Two pair of Canvas Sheetes	14	0	0
Item Four pair of large Canvas Sheetes	1	16	0
Item One pair of fine Canvas Sheetes	14	0	0
Item Two pair of old Sheets	1	0	0
Item One dozen of Napkins marked with J.P.	3	6	0
Item Six Napkins of severall sorts	1	6	0
Item Six Tableclothes	11	0	0
Item Sixteen Towells and Two Dresser clothes	3	0	0

In the Brewhouse

Item One vate One bucking tub Two Keevers One Washing Keever
One water tub One large iron pot and Iron grates to it Three wood
platters One old Stand One tray One [?]Jutt One plate dryer Two
buckets One wood Morter and pestle One tin'd meate broyler One fish
plate One woort dish One ladle One Skimmer Four other wood dishes
One brass Furnace with Iron grates One old Vate Stirrer and earthen
ware   4   11   10

In the Yard

Item in Faggots and Wood and Two boards and about Three
Chaulderon of Sea Coale and a Well Rope   4   5   0

Linnen More in the Drawer

Item Three Dozen of Flaxen napkins	1	4	0
Item Nine Diaper Napkins	4	6	0
Item Eighteen Damask Napkins	15	0	0
Item Four Holland Pillow coates	8	0	0
Item Three Damask Table clothes	1	4	0
Item Four Diaper Tableclothes	1	0	0
Item Three Holland Sheetes	3	0	0
Item Three homemade Tableclothes	12	0	0
Item One pair of small pillowcoates	1	0	0
Item Four Diaper towells	4	0	0
Item One pair of cradle Pillow coates	2	0	0

In Plate

Item One large silver Cup with a cover to it One small cup Three Silver
pottingers Six salts   6   0   0

In the Buttery and Under the Stairs

Item Four drink Vessells One Stand One powdring tub One frying pan a
tilter and shelves Three searches One Meale bag one wood bole and a
wooden plate One pair of Ninepins One Saddle One Sidesaddle and
bridles to them and One Tunnell and an old table   1   18   0

In the Kitchen

Item One Deale table Nine Rush bottom Chaires One Seacole grate and
range Two pair of pothangers One pair of Andirons One pair of Doggs
One fender One pair of gridirons One cleaver One chopping Knife Six
iron Skivers One pair of large Tobacco tongs One tin'd candlebox Four
smoothing Irons One box Iron and frame Two heaters Two tin'd
dripping pans One tin'd pudding pan One Coffee pot One tin'd pastrie
pan One drudger Two pepper boxes One pair of Snuffers and pan Two
Extinguishers One toasting iron Two chafeing dishes One iron slice
One tin'd tunnell Two Jacks and weights One basting ladle Two brass
skillets One brasse Kettle One Iron Skillet Two brass potts One pewter
Chamber pot Two Copper drink pots Two brass Candlesticks One tin'd
one One iron one and One wooden one One tin'd Sugar pot One
warming pan One apple roster Three brass skrews Six Sawcers Six
pottingers Four pewter Candlesticks One tin'd Sugar dust box One py
plate One cheese plate Five large pewter dishes Seven smaller One
Dozen of Mazareene plates Seven old plates Three Dozen of Cake pans
Six tinn tart pans One Cupboard One Dresser and shelves One Cradle

	£	s	d
with Bed and bolster and blanket Two glass Crewets One spit	9	13	0
Item five Dozen of glass bottles	12	6	0
Item In hay	18	0	0
Item A Nag and a Mare	4	10	0
Sum	94	14	4
Item Debts Sperate owing to the Deced the sume of One Hundred and Six pounds	106	0	0
Item In Desperate Debts owing to the said Deced the sume Of Two Hundred Twenty Nine pounds	229	0	0

[TNA PRO PROB 4/19992]

Administration 5 Oct 1685
To wife, Mary
Marginal note: re-grant June 1691, the original letters having expired, to William Whitear, clerk, guardian of the widow Dorothy Lewis, minor, until she attains the age of 2l. [TNA PRO PROB 6/61]

[1] Born Salisbury, Wilts, son of Griffith, gent. School at Salisbury. Cambridge, St John's, admitted sizar 1679 aged 17, matriculated 1680; Jesus, 1680, BA 1683. Ordained deacon 1683, priest 1684 (bishop of Chichester). Died 1685.

15. Bignor 24 June 1721 EDWARD LITLETON [1]

Appraisers: Samuel Ayling, William Hunt

	£	s	d
In primis In the Kitchen			
one old Jack two Spits 2 shriding knives 1 old Cleaver 2 iron skivers 1 tin Candlebox 4 iron Candlesticks		9	6
Two Pothangers Two small Iron Dogs 2 old barrs Tongs Gridirons Fender pot plate Iron Slice		10	6
2 dozen and Five pewter plates		18	1½
Eleven pewter dishes Twelve Old plates Three Cheesplaits with an Old Standard one old Strainer the weight 3 pound	2	10	3
Two Old warming pans one stewpan 2 brass Skimers one small brass morter and pestle Five brass Candlesticks snuffers and Stand one Egg spone and frying pan	18	11	0
2 small boiling pots 3 Skelets 2 old small brass Kettles 1 old saucepan		16	0
One old Tin dripping pan one old Cover one old puding pan one small Coffee pott Ten old patty pans 1 old pepper box		2	0
One woden Trey 1 Dish one Wooden Scales one small Dresser bord one old ovall Table Seven old Chairs and six old Knives and forks and Drinking pots and some small Draws and beacon Rack		14	6
Item in the Brewhouse Mash Tub bucking Tub			
5 Kivers 2 Old Tubs Two pales	1	0	6
one furnass		17	6
Item in the Hall			
one old Table and Firme 1 old box Iron and Heaters and a spinning wheel		4	0

Item in the Parlour
2 Oval Tables 1 Clock and Irons fire pan and Tongs 4 slop basons of Chainey and 5 dishes 2 pair of Curtains and rods to the same	3	8	0

Item in the Seller
12 small beer vessells 2 powdering Tubs 3 old stands	1	10	11
6 dozens of bottles Quarts and pints		9	0
One pillion and pillion cloth		3	6

Item in the Parlour Chamber
1 table 2 Stands Dressing Box 1 looking Glass 2 Cabinets a Press to hang Cloaths in an old Chest of Drawers a Japan [space] 5 old Cane Chairs 2 brass Andirons firepan and tongs 2 iron Dogs 1 small Stone Ring one old Close Stool and Pann 5 Curtains and 2 Rods	3	5	1
Fine Linnen 3 pair of Sheets 5 table Cloths 2 Sideboard Cloths 4 dozen of Napkins One towell and Four Pillow Coats	4	3	0
Childbed Linnen and a Courel		15	3
Coarser Linnen 8 pair and one Sheet 14 old Napkins 6 old table Cloths 13 old Towells 5 old Pillow Coats and a Wallet	2	11	0

Item In the Chamber over the Passage
One old bed and bedsted 3 blankets one quilt one bolster Curtains and Vallance Mat and cord	3	0	0
One truckle bed and bolster 2 blankets	1	5	0
One old Chest one old trunk and Flax in them 4 yards of Rowls		15	0
Four todd of Wooll	3	7	6
One bag of hopps wt 94lbs one pocket of hopps 9lbs	1	18	0

Item in the Hall Chamber
One bed and bedsted 1 bolster 2 pillows 3 blankets One Counterpain Curtains and Vallans	4	0	0
Another bed bedsted 1 bolster 3 pillows 5 old healing Curtains and Vallans	2	0	0
One small table and Cabinet 1 old trunk 1 deal box 1 other box 1 small Looking Glass 1 firepan and tongs		12	0
4 old Silver Spoons 1 Fork 1 tobacco Stopper	1	0	0

Item in the Lobby
14 old sacks 1 bill hook old ax and 1 Saw		12	0

Item in the Barn
1 old Bushell and Gallon 2 old Fann 1 Shovell 2 prongs		14	0

Item in the Stable
Cart harness and 2 old Sadles Bridle Shovell and Prong		12	0

Item in the carthouse
one old Waggon 2 harrows 1 old Plow	3	12	6
2 Load of hay	1	8	0
4 Acres of Wheat	6	4	0
2 Acres of Barley	3	4	0
2 Acres of Tares and 15s in hay sold	3	0	0
3 young hogs	3	3	0
2 old horses and other Lumber	1	10	0
Wearing Apparell	2	13	0
Money in Pockett		18	6

Item in the Library

	£	s	d
Books valued by Dr Longwith and Mr Bettesworth	40	0	0
Moneys received from Hardham	3	0	0
Moneys received from Mr Mills	1	12	0
Moneys received for Hay		6	0
Due from the Prebend	4	0	0
Preaching at Houghton an uncertain debt	1	10	0
[total]	122	7	0½

[WSRO Ep I/29/20/27]

Administration 6 Oct 1721
To wife, Mary   [WSRO STC III/N/30]

[1] Son of Edward, of Shropshire. Oxford, All Souls, matriculated 1681 aged 17, BA 1685. Cambridge, Christ's, MA 1690. Eton College, fellow 1726. Rector of Merston 1689–1701, patron Crown; of Bignor 1701–1721, patron Crown. Vicar of Amberley 1701–1721, patron bishop of Chichester. Prebendary of Bishopshurst 1706–1721. Died 1721.

16. Bignor 3 March 1632 THOMAS SEPHTON [1]

Appraisers: Thomas Stanley, William Pellatt, John Cook gents, John Shaw

	£	s	d
In primis his apparell and money in his purse prized at	10	0	0
Item his books and other things in his studye	5	0	0
Item in the hall			
one press cupbord at	1	10	0
Item there one table longe and one round table twelve ioynt stooles and two chaires at	1	7	6
Item there 6 turkie workt cushions		16	0
Item there a corslett furnished and bowes and arrowes at	1	10	0
Item there one Jack at		10	0
Item there one litle fowling peece at		10	0
Item there one Andiron one iron slice one pair of tongs one pothanger one fender two tosting irons and one paire of bellowes		6	8
In the litle buttrie			
Item there one binne one safe one bread grate one glasse bottle baskett skales and glasses and shelves and 4 pann dishes at		13	4
In the butrie			
Item one garner one table cupbord one wheele a halfe bushell a peck and a gallon at		1	0
In the parloar			
Item there one table one cupbord two Setles one old chest and one old chaire at		19	4
Item there one paire of andirons fire pann and a paire of tongs at		8	0
Item there one fetherbed two blankets one fetherbolster 4 fether pillowes one Rugge and five curtaines at	6	13	4
In the outer sellar			
Item there one hogshead 3 barrels one firkin on great barrell one safe one salting trough and one table with other lumberment there at		13	0

In the inner sellar

		£	s	d
Item there two hogsheads two barrells and a verkin at			12	0
Item there one pott of butter at			8	0
Item there certaine salt fish at			3	0
Item there one furnace		3	0	0
Item one vate and all other brewing vessells there		2	0	0
Item there 5 bushells ground mault			12	6

In the kitchen

		£	s	d
brasse one ketle and 2 smale skelletts two ladles and a slice a paire of pothookes at			12	0
Item there 4 kettles 2 brasse potts 2 bell possnetts 3 brasse candlesticks and one chaffing dish at		2	19	4
Item one pestle and morter 2 iron kettles one iron pott and a paire of pothookes at		1	6	0
Item two latin covars at				8
Item two latin dripping panns two iron dripping panns at			18	0
Item there 4 spitts two andirons one paire of pothookes one paire of tonges one iron ovenpeele one fender one rolerake at		1	0	0
Item there three chamber potts			4	0
Item an apple roster at				8
Item there two tables one skellet a breader a forke and a ladle wth all other lumberment there at			6	8

Item in the litle buttrie

		£	s	d
2 shelves crockes wth other lumberment at			6	8
Item beam and blades and waights at			10	0
Item a banpott latin at			1	0

In the bakehowse

		£	s	d
Item a boulting hutch one tubb one keever 1 bushell and ½ of ground wheat a little Sacke wth other lumberment there at			12	0

In the roome over the milkhowse

		£	s	d
Item one wheele 1 lb lathes and other lumberments			4	0
Item on bedstedle two flockbeds two boulsters a fether pillow two coverletts two blancketts at		1	10	0
Item there one sadle bridle wth other lumberments			13	0
Item 7 nayle of hemp			2	0
Item there hoppes at		1	10	0
Item there mault 4 quarters and a half quarter mault		4	10	0
Item there oat meale and the tubb with other lumberments			4	0
Item one whimsheet 8 sacke 2 poaks and a hame		1	0	0
Item oates at			3	4
Item 8 ewes and 8 lambes at		2	10	0

In the Chamber over the parlour

		£	s	d
Item there one presse at		1	0	0
Item one bedstedle one warming pan three chests at			15	0

In the chamber over the entry

		£	s	d
Item there one bedstedle three boulstars one pillow one coverlett and 2 blanketts at			10	0
Item the yellow curtaynes and a … yellowe at			13	4

Item there two flockbedds one flockboulster and one coverlet one blanckett at	2	0	0
Item there one trunck three chests one box at	1	10	4
Item there 24 paire of sheets at	16	0	0
Item one bedteeke at	1	6	8
Item there 4 dozen and 5 napkins at	2	1	0
Item there 13 table clothes at	2	2	4
Item 15 hand towells and ten pillowberes at	1	8	0

In the closet

Item one still		15	0
Item a voyder and a plate	1	1	0
Item aples and other lumberments at		6	0
Item there plate two boules one tankerd 4s spoones one double salt at		12	0

In the Chamber over the parlour

Item there one bedstedle 3 boulsters fether one pillow one downe bed and one fetherbed one coverlett two blancketts att	14	0	0
Item one truckle bed one chest one blanckett one m'n coverlett a livery cupbord one clostool one chaire with other lumberments at	2	13	4
Item there one Andiron one paire of tongs and one slice at		2	0
Item woole five todd at	6	0	0
Item pewter 76 lb at	3	6	0
Item two flagons a bason and Ewer 2 basons 2 pewter candlesticks 4 porrengers 6 Sawcers 1 plate one cup and one salt seller	1	10	0
Item in the chimney and elsewhere bacon three hoggs at	4	0	0
Item the wood timber faggotts and loggs at	6	0	0
Item the well buckett and chaine		6	8
Item two horse and 2 kene	12	0	0
Item fowre acres wheat on the ground	5	0	0
Item Fowre acres vetces and beanes at	2	13	4
Item one cart with all other his implements of husbandry at	2	0	0

in the barne

Item there sixe quarters of barley at	5	10	0
Item five quarters of wheat at	7	0	0
Item vetches and hay at	1	10	0
Item sixe hogges at	3	0	0
Item the querne wth racks bord and all other lumberments thear at	2	0	0
Item a cocke and henns		1	0
Item in ready money and debts	10	0	0
Item two carpetts and curtains at		13	4
Item tyre and larde at		10	0
Item one litle gould ring		6	8
Sum totalis is	205	8	6

Probate: Joseph Sephton, son

[WSRO Ep I/29/20/27]

Will: made 23 Feb 1631; proved 11 July 1632
Wife: Ellinor (beds, pewter); sons: George, eldest (silver tankard and spoon, gold seal ring, Downehams 2 vols); John, second (clothes, silver salt and bowl, dagger, bed; all

books, giving mother and brother 'such English books as he can best share'; brother-in-law: Richard Lewes (?Parham)
Witnesses: Nicholas Y[…]ing, William Collinson [WSRO STC/I/18/185]

---

[1] Of Lancaster. Oxford, Brasenose, matriculated 1593 aged 17, BA 1597, MA 1600. Ordained deacon and priest 1603 (bishop of Chichester). Rector of Bignor 1603–1632, patron Crown; of Selham 1614–1622, patron Jennet Leigh, widow. Master of hospital of St James and St Mary Magdalen, Chichester, 1624. Married Joan Lewes of Sutton at Sutton by licence of 1607; second wife Ellinor. Died 1632; buried Bignor.

17. Billingshurst 15 March 1706 THOMAS ORAM [1]
Appraisers: Thomas Butcher, John Sturt

	£	s	d
In prs his wearing apparrell and money in his Purse	6	0	0
Item bookes in his Study	3	13	4
In the Parlour			
Item one Oval table Twelve Turkeywork Chairs one little Table brandirons fire pann tongs bellowes Pictures wexwork things and windo Curtaines	4	11	0
In the Parlour Chamber			
Item one Feather bed bed Stead quilt curtaines and all things to the same bed and bedStead belonging	12	0	0
Item one Chest of drawers Six Caine Chaires one little Oval Table two Stooles one paire of Andirons one Seeing glass one joyned press and winder Curtaines	4	19	6
Item in Plate	16	15	6
Item in fine Linnen one dozen of diapper Napkins one diapper table cloth one dozen of hugerbag Napkins one tablecloth of the Same one dozen of fine Tyer Napkins one tablecloth of the Same three paire of Fine Sheetes and five paire of Pillocoats	9	16	0
Item more fine linnen Three paire of Sheetes one paire of Pillowcoats	2	8	6
Item more fine linnen one Table Cloth Three Napkins one Sideboard cloth two hand towells and one little table cloth		19	6
In the Entry Chamber			
Item one Feather bed bedstead and all to the same belonging	2	10	0
Item one Chaire		1	10
In the Study			
One Table one Chaire		2	5
In the Space on the Stairs			
Ten Cushens and one Stoole		11	0
In the Garrett			
Item fower Kilderkins Fower firkins and one Bird Cage	1	1	8
In Backhouse Fower Chaires one winder curtaine one water pott Fower Scutchens two haire broomes		7	10
Item in the Kitchen Chamber			
one Fether bed and all thereunto belonging	4	0	0
Item two Chaires one Trunk one Box one seeing glass and winder Curtaines		8	4

In the Chamber over the buttery

Item one Feather bed and all belonging to itt one Mill puff bed and all belonging to itt	3	6	8
Item two Chaires one Saddle and one Baskett		7	9
Item in Butter and Lard two decanters in glasses small glass bottles and ten [?]cole salts	1	1	0

In the Roome on the Staires

Two Chests one Side board one Pillober one close Stoole two Searchers and Sume old boxes	1	0	0

In the old Chamber

Item two Kivers Eight Sackes one Bag one Meale Tub and one old spinning wheele	1	2	0
Item Seaven paire of Towen Sheetes Five paire of pillow coates Eight hand towells Three table Cloaths Three napkins	3	2	4
Item in more Linnen Six Napkins two table cloaths Fower hand towells		10	5

In the brewhouse

One brass Furnace one Iron Furnace one Vate one cooler one Bucking Tubb one Three leg tubb two halfe Tubbs Three bucketts two brass Skilletts one pair of bellows and some other small things	3	19	2

In the Butterys

Sixteen dozen of glass bottles	2	5	0
Item one case of Knives		4	0
Item Eight Ferkins one barrell one butter tubb two powdering tubbs one Kiver one Table one Safe one Stone Morter one frying pan one pair of blades one bole Six Spoones and other small things	2	7	6
Item two Flitches of bacon	2	0	0

In the Kitchen

Item two tables one Jack one paire of Andirons fire pann tongs one Iron plate two Spits 41 pewter plates 13 pewter dishes Eight chaires Five candlesticks Five porengers one Still and Severall other small things	13	1	2
Item one Sider press and all belonging to itt	2	10	0
Item in wood and Faggotts		13	4
Item for things not seen and forgotten		11	11
Item in good debts and upon Bond	270	0	0
Item in Despate Debts	20	0	0
Tot Sume is	388	8	6

[WSRO Ep I/29/21/189]

Will: made 10 June 1704; proved 22 March 1706
Wife: Ann, executrix; son: John; daughters: Ann (Laker), Sarah, Mary (Butcher)
Witnesses: William Booth, William Greenfield, John Burrell   [WSRO STC I/30/828]

---

[1] Born Shrewsbury, Salop, son of Thomas, of Shrewsbury. Cambridge, St John's, admitted sizar aged 17 and matriculated 1660, BA 1664, MA 1667. Ordained deacon and priest 1663. Vicar of Billingshurst 1663–1706. Licensed preacher 1675. Married Ann Meade at Rudgwick 1667. Died 1706; buried Billingshurst.

18. Billingshurst 5 Jan 1738 JOHN BULLIS [1]
Appraisers: John Farley, John Garton

	£	s	d
Wearing Apparell and Money in Purse	12	0	0
In the best Chamber			
One Bedstedle and Curtains Quilt and Three Blanketts one Feather Bed One Bolster Two Pillowes One Sack Bottom Seven Chairs One Table and [?]Twilight One Standing Glass Two pair of Window Curtains and Two Iron Rods One Fender One pair of Dogs a Fire Shovel and Tongs	12	14	6
In the Hall Chamber and Stair Case			
One Hanging Press One Cloak and shutter	7	10	0
In the Study			
A Library of Books	30	0	0
A Table Desk and Stand One Bag of Hops and One Ladder	1	1	6
In the Chamber over the Kitchen			
One Bedstedle and Curtains one Feather Bed Two Bolsters Three pillows Three Blancketts One old Rug One Scrutore One pair of Chest of Drawers One Table One Dressing Box One Bugle Box One Cabinett pictures and Trifles Three pistols one Blunderbuss One Sword and Two Bells	8	10	0
In the Closett			
Bottles and a few odd Things		5	0
In the Nursery			
One Bedstedle on Featherbed One Bolster and Curtains One Chest Two Boxe Two Trunks One Closestool One Pillion and an Old Tub	3	0	0
In Maid's Chamber			
Two Bedstedles Two feather Beds Two Bolsters Four pillowes Three Blancketts Four old Trunks Ten Cushions unmade	4	10	0
In the Great Parlour			
Thirteen Cane Chair one Easy Chair and Case One Oval Table One Punch Bowl Two pair of Holland window Curtains Two Iron Rods Two Shutters pictures One pair of Brass Andirons Tongs and Fire Shovell and an Iron Fender	4	2	0
In the Hall and litle Parlour			
Two round Tables One Dozen of Black Chairs a pair of Bellows One pair of Dogs Fire Shovell and Tongs a Fender One Trevett Curtains and pictures a Hair Broom and Cloath horse	1	10	0
In the Bottle Room			
Four Dozen of Pints and Quart Botles One Firkin One Dozen and Ten patty pans One Tobacco pot a Stool and Shelves		11	6
In the Kitchen			

One Jack Chain and Weights Five Brass Candlesticks Two Brass
Snuffers and One Stand One Extinguisher Two Save alls One Brass
Mortar and Pestle One Iron Mortar and Pestle Three Coffee Pots One
Chocolate Pott and Two Mills One Pepper Box One Flower Box One
Pasty Pan a large Knife and fork Four Iron Candlesticks Three Box
Irons Six Heaters One Housewife One Coffee Mill a large Iron Skewer
Tobacco Tongs a Cupboard and Six Cannisters One pair of Stilliards
and Weight Two Spits Two pair of Dogs Tongs and Fire Shovell Two

Pair of Pothooks One Chaffing dish One chopping knife Salt Box One
Mallet and Hammer a Brush one Candle Box One Tea Kettle One
Lanthorn One Table One Bunting hutch a Dresser and Shelves Nine
Pewter Dishes Two Dozen and Eight pewter plates Two Salvers Three
Rings Eight Glasses Five tea potts Four White Mugs Three Brown
Muggs One large pott Earthenware and China Hedge Sheers a Hoe a
Hand Bill [?]pirsile potts a Warming pan Bellows a Bacon Rack Two
Rush Candlesticks Seven Chairs a Fender a Tea Board Three Curtain
Rods a Portmanteau and Mare pillion Six Knives and forks One old
Knife and Four Forks and Two Silver Spoones   10   11   3
     In the Milk House
Three Dozen of Pint and Quart Bottles Seventeen Pewter Plates Six
Dishes One Cistern One Still One Brass Kettle Two Brass Potts One
Iron pott one Dripping Pan One Frying Pan Two powdring Tubs Scales
and Weights 13lb One Watring pot One Mouse trap Two Wooden
platters One Tray Three Brass Skilletts One Saucepan a Spinning
Wheel One Scain Winder an Iron ware frying pan A Salting Trough and
Form One Gallon and Sieve Earthen Ware and shelves and a few odd
Things   5   15   0
     In the Two Cellars
Thirteen Drinking Tubs Four Stands One Tunnell Three Brass Cocks
One Pair of Gridirons Four Bucketts One Dozen of Bottles One Beer
Stooper Old Lead a prong Two hoes one Rake one Bill a pair of Slings   3   5   6
Linnen in the Chest
Four pair of Sheets One pair of Sheets not whitend One Damask one
huckaback and Two Diaper Table Cloths One Dozen of Diaper One
Dozen and Four Damask Napkins and One Dozen of Huckaback
Napkins Four pillowcoats Five Hand Towels and a Childbed Baskett
Linnen in the Deal Box Seven pair of Sheets and an odd one Five
pillowcoats Three hucaback Two Diaper and One homemade Table
Cloth Six Huccaback and One Diaper Napkins and Eight Hand Toweles 12   16   6
     In the Brewhouse
Two Furnaces One Vate One Bucking Tub Three Tun Tubs Five Kivers
Three Stands One Cyder Press a Horse a Handsaw a long Saw One
Wire Sieve a Strainer Four Dozen of Bottles One half Bushell One
Brewdish a Hair Cloth a Spitter an Iron pyepeel an Iron Fork a Shool a
lett three Rakes a Garden Line a Still Bottom a Hammer a Cloath horse
Two Ladders Feather and Lumber and Eight Cord of Wood   12   5   0
     In the Stable
Hay Dung a Sadle and Bridle A WheelBarrow Hog hutch New Boards
and a Mare   11   12   0
                   [total]   141   19   9

Memorandum Mr Perkins has one pair of New Boots and Two Pair of
New Shoes in his Hand to sell

           [WSRO Ep I/29/21/233]

Administration 9 March 1738

To Thomas Gratwick, principal creditor, Catherine Bullis, wife, having renounced

[WSRO STC III/O/126]

[1] Born Ely, Cambs, son of Thomas. King's School, Ely. Cambridge, Christ's, admitted sizar 1696 aged 17, matriculated 1697, BA 1701, LLB 1725. Ordained deacon 1702 (bishop of Ely), priest 1704 (bishop of Chichester). Curate of Coveney, Cambs, c. 1702; of Cuckfield 1704. Vicar of Billingshurst 1706–1738, patron Sir Henry Goring, bt. Rector of Sullington 1725–1738, patrons John Hawes and Richard Russell, clerks. Married Catherine Green at Selmeston 1711. Died 1738.

19. Binsted 6 July 1634   FRANCIS HEAPE, vicar [1]

Appraisers: John White, Robert Presett, John Page

	£	s	d
in the parlour			
One Featherbedd boulster two pillowes two blanketts on rugg a beddsteedle and Curtains	5	0	0
a Table and Chayre		16	8
4 Cushions and a Carpett		11	4
two yron potts and a dripping pan		11	0
two brass kittles 2 brass skelletts		8	0
two pewter dishes a caste and yron and a spitt		7	0
a keellor a bowle a sive and a baskett		3	6
a payer of sheets		6	0
a doosen napkins and a payer of sheetts		8	0
a pin'd pewter pott		1	0
a Candlestick and salt		1	6
a payer of Tables		2	6
an ould Chamber pott		1	0
two small pins		2	0
Theise good[s] Beedinge ware given Mr Heape by will			
In the halle			
his wearing apparell and mony in his purse	2	10	0
a sylver bowle and three spoones	2	0	0
a Cuppboard		15	0
a green Chaire		3	0
Wainscott		14	0
a forme		1	6
In the kittchen			
an yron mill		10	0
a Jacke Lyne and Chayne		10	0
a brass kittle 2 brass skilletts a chaffing dish		11	6
two yron potts a brass kettle and a spitt		8	0
two Yron Racks a Cast andyron a slyce a fyer pan a payer of tonges a greddyron two pair of potthangers a payer of potthoockes		14	0
a pickaxe a spitter and some old yron		1	6
three bucketts		1	0
In the Back house			
Two Tubbs two barrells a greate bowle and a skrene		12	0

two ioyned stooles	1	8
In the Halle Chamber		
a halfe headed beddsteedle a bedd bowlster blankett and a payre of sheetts	2 10	0
a standing bedd curtains valence covalet two bowlsters two pillowes two blancketts and a payre of sheets	5 0	0
on Chest a Carpett a payer of Cushions and an old Cupp board cloth	10	0
three emptie chests	6	0
a truncke full of Lynnen	2 0	0
an old Chayre and some old Cushions	2	0
eight pewter dishes	16	0
a truckle beddstedd a bunting hutch an old tubb and an old coverlet	5	0
his books	1 0	0
Withoute doors		
A horse bridle and saddle a yong mare and her colt	7 0	0
An old payer of wheeles an ould cartt a dung ... and chills	10	0
a Pile of wood	2 2	0
Things unseen and forgotten	2	6
The wholl sum is	40 16	2
	[WSRO Ep I/29/22/1]	

Will: made 8 June 1634; proved 7 July 1634
Wife: Elinor (bed); son: John (dec); daughter: Frances Racton, widow

[WSRO STC I/18/323]

[1] Cambridge, Trinity, matriculated sizar 1585, BA 1589. Ordained deacon and priest 1593 (bishop of Worcester). Rector of Whatlington 1598, patron Sir George Browne. Vicar of Binsted 1605–1634, patrons John Pritchard and Jane Shelley, widow. Licensed preacher 1605. Married Joan Browninge of Udimore, widow, by licence 1600; Eleanor Sephton (possibly widow of Thomas, rector of Bignor, **16**) at Binsted 1633. Died 1634.

20. Bolney 12 Feb [1714] JOHN GRATWICK, vicar [1]
Appraisers: John Bridger, Samuel Standen, James Lintott

	£	s	d
In the Brewhouse			
One Furnace a porridge pott and some old Tubbs	1	0	0
In the Kitchen			
One Small Table and Seven Small pewter Dishes Some old Chairs one old brass Kettle a parcell of old Books a pair of Andirons and Some other Lumber	1	9	0
In the Buttery			
A keeler a possidge pott and two old Sives a Bunting Hutch valued at		7	0
In the Drink Room			
A few Empty Casks two joynt Stools a Small Table		7	6
In the Hall			
One old Spinning Wheell one woollen wheele one Chest		6	0
In the Parlor Chamber			
Two Bedds and Bedstedles three Chests one Trunk one Box one Chaire			

	£	s	d
and some old Books and Six pair of Sheets three Table Cloths	4	0	0
In the Buttery Chamber			
One Flock Bedd two old Chestes a Small Table		17	6
For wearing Apparrell and Money in Pockett	2	15	0
[Total]	11	2	0

[ESRO W/INV 500]

Will: made 19 Jan 1714; proved 9 March 1714
Wife: Anne, executrix; sons John, Samuel; daughter: Susanna (Flood)
Witnesses: Thomas Cannon, John Butler, Thomas Fest, John Parson, Edward Burtenshaw

[ESRO W/A 48.363]

[1] Ordained deacon and priest 1661 (bishop of Chichester). Vicar of Bolney 1662–1714, patron prebendary of Hova Villa. Married Catherine (died 1670); Margaret Butler of Cuckfield at Bolney 1670 (died 1678); Anne Savage at Bolney by licence 1679 (died 1716). Died 1714; buried Bolney.

21. Bosham 18 Feb 1675 SAMUEL TANGLEY, vicar [1]

Appraisers: Warburton Owen, clerk, John Godfrey, tailor, Robert Whitaker, tanner in Westbourne

	£	s	d
In primis his wearing Apparrell and money in his purse	4	0	0
Item 1 silver Tankard 1 silver bole 6 Silver spoones 1 old brass watch 2 Rings one 11s piece of Gold	7	10	0
Item 20 dishes of Pewter 3 porringers 1 Salt cellar 1 Flaggon 1 Bason one Chamberpott 1 Stewpanne 1 Lattin panne 2 Candlestickes 3 Sawcers	2	10	0
Item In his Lodging Chamber			
1 featherbed 1 feather bolster one feather pillow 1 Rugg 1 Coverledd one blanckett 2 Bedstedles and Valens and Curtaines	5	0	0
Item more in his lodgeing Chamber			
1 Diaper Tablecloth 2 paire sheetes 20 Napkins 3 other Table Clothes 2 Pillowbeeres 4 Towells 1 Shirt and Bands and Cuffes	1	10	0
Item in the same Chamber			
1 Trunke 1 Chest 1 Deske 1 Chaire 1 p Andirons 1 p Cotterells wt some other Lumber	1	0	0
Item Books in the same roome	1	10	0
Item in the Buttrye			
2 Skilletts 1 brasse kettle 2 brasse potts 1 Brasse Chaffing dish 1 Warmeing panne 1 Brasse skimer		12	0
Item in the same Buttrye			
2 Barrells 6 Bottles and other Lumber		10	0
Item in the Kitchin			
11 chaires 2 stooles		16	0
Item in the same Roome			
1 Brasse pestle and Mortar 1 p of Andirons 1 spitt 2 smoothing irons 1 spitt 1 p of Tongs 1 fire shovell 1 slice 1 p of Cotterells 1 p Gridirons 1 Lookeing glasse 1 p of Bellows		14	0

Item in Wm Redwells Roome where he inhabited in Bosham		
1 flitch of Bacon and some other pounds of Bacon	19	0
Item in the Church Litten and about the Vicaridge		
some few small Stickes of Timber wood and faggotts	1 0	0
Item in Will Hales house in Westbourne		
1 Still 1 Posnett 1 dripping panne one Pistoll 1 spitt 1 salt cellar	1 0	0
Item Wheete sowed in the feilds and for the Tillage of the same	1 5	0
Item In Mr Tangleys house in Westbourne		
In the Hall		
1 Table 1 Side cupboord 2 Chaires and 1 other litle Table	1 6	0
Item In the Chamber over the Hall		
4 p of sheetes 5 pillow beares 3 Table clothes 2 Towells	2 0	0
Item in the same Roome		
1 Bedsteddle 1 side cupbord 1 Trunke 1 Chaire 1 stoole 1 Boxe 1 carpett and one Cupbord cloth	1 10	0
Item in the Chamber over the Kitchin		
1 Chest 1 Trunke and one Bedstedle	6	0
Item in the litle Chamber below		
1 Bedd 1 Bolster 1 Bedstedle 2 old Blancketts wth Curtains and Valens	1 10	0
Item in the same Roome		
1 Chest of Drawers 2 old side Tables one Chaire wth a Hose stoole in the same	1 0	0
Item in the Chamber over the litle low chamber		
1 Bedstedle 1 Bedd 1 Matt 1 Chest with other Lumber	1 0	0
Item In the 2 inner Buttryes		
4 Kivers 1 salting trough 2 stand 2 Formes 1 Smoothing boorde and 1 meale bagg of leather	16	0
Item In the litle passage to the Buttryes		
1 old Table 1 old Chest 1 Barrell of a Gunne	4	0
Item In the Kitchin		
4 Chaires 1 Table 3 Stooles 1 Barrell 1 brewing Tubb 1 Bucking Tubb 1 firkin 2 Pillowes 1 Cushion 1 Cupbord cloth	5	0
Item in the same Roome		
1 Jack to turne meate	5	0
Item in the same 1 Furnace 4 brasse potts 2 Brasse Ketles 3 brasse skilletts	2 10	0
Item in the same Kitchin		
7 spitts 1 iron Kettle 1 p of iron doggs 1 p gridirons 1 p Pincers 1 fryeing panne 1 ironbacke 1 Fender 1 p of Potthookes 1 brasse Ladle	1 0	0
Item in the same roome		
2 Pewter dishes 1 halfe bushell 1 Gallon and 1 halfe Galln and 1 p of Tongs	4	6
Item in the Barne		
Barley in the Mow	4 0	0
Item in the old house		
16 severall Boords	1 0	0
1 Sider presse and 1 trough	2	0
1 single Wheele belonging to a Wheele barrow	2	0

Item in the Gate		
1 Sticke of Timber	16	0
Item in Wm Hales house		
1 skimer		6
1 flaggon	1	0
Item due from Rich Crockeford of Idsworth	1	0	0
Item 2 Vessells and 1 pickaxe 1 Bill 1 wheele barrow	7	0
Item Bookes in his house in Westbourne	1	10	0
Item other pcells of Goods discovered lately 1 Ladder 1 Syth 1… and one Trey	3	6
Item 1 pewter quarterne		6
Summa totalis	52	15	0

[WSRO Ep I/29/25/89]

No will or administration found
For probate account see **184**.

[1] Curate of Chidham c. 1662; of Bosham from 1663. Vicar of Bosham 1672–1674, patron dean and chapter of Chichester. Died 1674.

22. Bosham 14 Oct 1723 WILLIAM KNOWLES [1]
Appraiser: Richard Withers, clerk

	£	s	d
In primis money found in his pockett		6	0
Item Due from the Revd Mr Whithead	15	0	0
Item Due from the Revd Mr Luff	11	8	0
Item the Deceaseds Wearing Apparell	3	0	0
Item his Books	5	0	0
Item a blind horse and sadle and Bridle worth about	1	0	0
tot	35	14	6

[WSRO Ep I/29/25/157]

Administration 9 June 1724
To brother, Abraham Knowles; Robert Knowles, Thomas Knowles, John Plumpton and wife, Alice, John Southworth and wife, Catherine, brothers and sisters, all having renounced　　　　　　　　　　　　　　[WSRO STC III/N/41]

[1] Of Lancashire. Dublin, Trinity, BA 1713. Cambridge, King's, MA 1722. Possibly curate of Merston 1721.

23. Botolphs cum Bramber 11 Jan 1697 JOHN COWDRY, minister [1]
Appraisers: Mr John Wheeler, Robert Devonish

	£	s	d
In primis his wearing apparel and his purse	10	0	0
3 Cowes 2 horses 2 fat hogs	17	0	0
One lean hog five shuts	4	0	0

One Rick of hay one dung cart two harrows One Wimer One bushel half a bushel One Shall and Ridder Ten Sacks	8	0	0
The Kitchin			
Two dozen of plates Sixteen pewter dishes two flaggons two pewter Candle-Sticks two basons two pye plates	2	5	0
Two brass Ketles One bras pot foure brass Skellets two brass Candle-Sticks One brass Mortar One Chaffing dish and Sawcepan One Jack three spitts two pair of tonges two fire shovels three skivels Cleever One dripping pan One pair of Andirons three iron potts	2	15	0
One Table foure joyned Stools two dressers two Shelves One beacon Rack Three chaires One Cubboard Lanthorne One iron backe	1	5	0
The Hall			
Two tables One Settle One side board One press Napkin One Still Glass cage forme two Chaires	1	15	0
The Parlour			
One long tabl One round table One litle table tenn Chaires One stool One clock two pair of Andirons One fire shovell and tonges One pair of bellowes	2	5	0
The brew-house			
One furnace One vate Six tubbs One Tunne	2	10	0
The Milk house			
Two buckets ten Milk trayes One churne One pair of butter blades One dozen of Wood-trenchers twenty small Cheeses	1	0	0
The bake house			
One bakeing Keeler One fine Sieve		5	0
The Seller			
Eight Vessels One powdring tub One dozen and half of bottles		15	0
The Parlour Chamber			
One bed three boulsters three blankets Curtains and Valens bed-sted Matt and Cord	3	10	0
Two great chaires Seven litle chaires two stooles Six Cushions four chaires One chest of drawers One Glass-cage one looking glass One White Quilt two pair of Andirons One pair of tonges fire shovel and bellows One litle table	3	13	6
The Chamber over the Hall			
One bedsted Matt and Cord two beds two boulsters three pillowes two blankets and One Rugg	5	0	0
More in the Hall Chamber			
One bedsted matt and Cord One bed two boulsters two pillows Curtains and Valens	3	10	0
One press One table three chaires One Coffer two diaper tabl Cloaths one dozen and half of diapper Napkins	1	17	6
Eight pair of Fine Sheets Twelve paire of Course Sheets two dozen of Napkins two fine table Cloaths	9	2	0
Chamber over the buttery			
One bedsted Matt and Cord One bed One boulster three blankets Curtains and Valens	2	0	0
One litle flock bed One boulster blanket and Coverlet bedsted matt and Cord		10	0

One Cubboard two Chestes One dozen of hand Towels Six pair of pillow Coates and other linnen used about the house	2	1	6
Chamber over the Kitchin			
One bed sted matt and cord One flock bed One boulster two blanketts and a Rugg	1	0	0
In the Garret			
One Chair and old furnace		15	0
The Colledg lease of Brambur cum Buttolphs for one year Charges and taxes deducted	80	0	0
The two and thirtieth part of a Vessel At Sea the William and Sarah Ketch	12	10	0
In plate of Silver	10	0	0
Lent upon a Mortgage	400	0	0
The Study of bookes	30	0	0
Desperate debts	10	0	0
Things out of sight and forgot and other old Lumber	2	0	0
[total]	631	4	6

[WSRO Ep I/29/26/9]

Administration 23 July 1697
To wife, Mary   [WSRO STC III/M/3]

[1] Oxford, Magdalen, chorister 1648, matriculated 1649, demy 1650–1654, BA 1653, fellow 1654–1660, MA 1655. Rector of Bramber with Botolphs 1658–1697, patron Magdalen College. Died 1697; buried Botolphs.

24. Brede ...1687 SAMUEL HORNE [1]

[Original damaged/illegible]   [TNA PRO PROB 4/4451]

Will: made 28 Nov 1683; proved 22 Jan 1687
Sons: Samuel, executor, Thomas, Joseph; daughters: Elizabeth, Sarah
Overseers: Brother-in-law Thomas Bromfield of Lewes, Samuel Symmonds of Kent
Witnesses: George Tilden, John Dyne, Thomas Fuller   [TNA PRO PROB 4/386]

[1] Oxford, Oriel, matriculated 1650, BA 1653. Rector of Brede 1656–1686. Married Elizabeth Bromfield at Udimore 1658; Elizabeth Sampson of Maidstone, Kent, widow, at Cranbrook, Kent, by licence 1665. Died 1687.

25. Broadwater (Offington) 14 Jan 1725 CHARLES SMITH [1]

Appraisers: Nathaniell Hobbs, William Andrew

	£	s	d
In primis Ready Money in the House	66	11	12
Item Wearing Apparell	3	0	0
Linnen		15	0
Books and Pamphletts	3	0	0
A Watch	2	0	0
A Clock		15	0

A Looking Glass		3	0
Two Pistolls		5	0
One Close stool frame		2	6
Two Sadles and Two Bridles		6	0
A horse	5	0	0
A Note of	10	0	0
A Bond of	90	0	0
A Ring		15	0
Arrears of rent due from Mr Marsh	14	0	0
Arrears of Rent from Mr Sheppard due at Michaelmas last	9	0	0
A quarter due from Each at Christmas last besides the above mentioned sums	7	0	0
A Debt of	3	1	0
For old Lumber and other Odd things		5	0
A parcell of Books in London worth	1	0	0
Total	216	18	2

Forgott to be inserted in the Inventory 9 Odd pieces of gold value uncertaine
Two silver Buttons for the Wastband of A pair of Breeches
A small parcell of Wood
Exhibited by Charles Smith, son   [WSRO Ep I/29/29/126]

Will: made 20 July 1721; proved 7 Oct 1725
Son: John (clothes between sons); 3 younger children
Executors: John Young of Goring, Richard Bridger of Coombes, John Mathews, vicar of Steyning
Witnesses: Nathaniel Hobbs, Elizabeth Hobbs, John Swaysland   [WSRO STC I/33/356]

[1] Of Sussex. Westminster School. Cambridge, Peterhouse, admitted 1665 aged 16, Warren scholar 1665, BA 1669. Signed for deacon's orders 1670 (bishop of London). Vicar of Sompting 1671–1690. Rector of Coombes 1677–1690, patron Richard Caryll, esq. Deprived of Sompting and Coombes as a nonjuror. Buried Broadwater 2 Jan. 1725.

26. Burpham 26 Jan 1694 THOMAS GRIFFIN [1]

Appraisers: John Knowles yeoman, John Walder carpenter

	£	s	d
In primis his wearing apparell and money in his Purse and his watch	6	5	0
Item the Books in his Study as praised by Mr Woodeson	3	0	0
Item in the Kitchen			
6 Pewter dishes 6 plates		18	0
Item more 1 still 2 porringer 1 Brasse morter		12	0
Item 7 Candlesticks 3 drink potts 1 furnace	1	0	0
Item 1 Jack 2 Spitts 2 Dripping pans 2 Chaffing dishes		16	0
Item fire pan and Tongs gridiron and Pothangers 3 potts fender and racks slice and forke iron skivels Candle box basting Ladles 2 ketles 1 Case of knives	1	11	6
Item in the Hall			
13 Chaires 2 tables 1 presse 1 Cradle	1	11	0

Item 1 Clock 1 Skreen 7 maps 1 glasse cage	2	13	0
Item Andirons Tongs fire pan and bellows 1 Cubbord	1	4	0
Item in Parlor			
6 lether chaires 2 Tables 2 arm Chaires	1	4	0
Item the base Viol and hangings	1	15	0
Item in the Hall Chamber			
1 Bed quilt 3 blankets and bedsted Curtains and valens	6	0	0
Item 1 dosen Chaires 2 Andirons 1 Chest of Drawers	1	12	0
Item in Parlor Chamber			
1 Bed wth all therunto belonging 1 glasse 2 stooles 1 Table and andirons	4	0	0
Item in the wash house			
3 Tubs 4 Keevers 1 wel buckett and rope 3 water bucketts	1	8	0
Item in the drink house			
5 Vessells 1 poudring tub		15	0
Item 3 dosen of Botles 1 warming pan		9	6
Item 2 mares sadles and Bridles 1 pillion	5	5	0
Item 4 Ewes	1	12	0
Item 1 Shutt		12	0
Item hay	1	10	0
Item 16 watles 1 gate 1 Bare		18	0
Item 4 pair of Sheets and 2 dosen of Napkins 3 Tableclothes	3	3	0
Item Lumber goods seen unseen and forgotten		5	0
	54	1	0

Exhibited by Margaret Griffin widow   [WSRO Ep I/29/31/51]

No will or administration found

[1] Ordained priest 1676 (bishop of Chichester). Possibly curate of St Martin's, Chichester, c. 1677. Vicar of Burpham 1679–1694, patron dean and chapter of Chichester. Curate of South Stoke 1691. Died 1694.

27. Burwash ... 1664 WILLIAM ATTERSOLL [1]
Appraisers: William Woodhouse, John ...
[Original damaged]

	£	s	d
[In primis]wearing apparrell [and rea]dy m[oney in] his purse	..	..	..
In the hall Chamber			
Item [?] feather bedd and Bolster 1 greene rugg with darnix Curtaines with other thinges thereunto belonging	..	..	..
Item I halfe headed bedstead 1 old f... with the furniture thereunto belonging 1 ... bedstead with a flocke bedd and bolster with ... thereunto belonging	..	..	..
Item 4 [?]joine chestes and 2 trunkes and ... and one deske			
Item 1 double guilt salt 1 silver beere ... 23 silver spoones And one small tast...	..	..	..
Item 1 paire of andirons one fire shovel tongs and bellowes	..	..	..
Item 8 paire of flaxen sheetes 18 ti[re] and table clothes and 30 ...	..	..	..

Item 12 paire of course sheetes ... napkins ... table cloathes and towell
and 16 towells ... of course tow .. .. ..
     In the study Chamber
Item one featherbed and bolster 1 yellow rugge with linsey woolsey
curtaines ... bedds ... matt with ... .
Item 2 joyned chestes and one trunke .. .. ..
     In the [?]oimes Chamber
Item 1 old flocke bedd and bolster and boarde bedstead and all
thereunto belonging .. .. ..
Item 18 pound of tyre and flax .. .. ..
     In the hall
Item 32 pewter plattes and 16 small peeces 2 candlestickes 3 chamber
[potts] one salt and one ... bason .. .. ..
Item 3 brasse kettles and three skilletts 1 chaffing dish 2 skimmers and
one ... .
Item 1 jacke 3 spittes 2 paire of andirons ... panne ... oven tonges and ...
chopping knives 1 gridiron ... and one fowling peece .. .. ..
Item 1 table and forme 4 stooles 1 dresser and foure cushions .. .. ..
Item foure flitches of bacon .. .. ..
     In the parlour
Item 1 table 7 joyned benches … leather chaires 3 stooles Court
Cupboard ... paire of andirons and fire shovel and tonges twoe carpets
and … .. .. ..
     In the study
Item 1 presse 2 joyned stooles in the study and five shelves .. .. ..
Item the bookes there .. .. ..
     In the Celler
Item three little beere vessells 2 … tubbs 16 truggs 1 crocke of ... 2
keelers … .. .. ..
     In the next roome to the Celler
Item 2 frying panns 3 iron pottes and some other small thinges .. .. ..
     In the Brewhouse
Item ... little firkins 6 keelers 1 brewing tubb 1 bucking tubb ... 1 cheese
presse and weightes 1 brasse furnace 2 iron kettles and some other
small thinges .. .. ..
     In the parler Chamber
Item 1 feather bedd and bolster ... rugge joyned bedsteadle cord and
matt with all thereunto belonging 4 stooles 1 old sideboard 1 cushion 1
old curtain and one greene say side board clothe .. .. ..
     In the Inner Roome
Item about 20 bushells of oates and three cheeses .. .. ..
     In the Garrett
Item about 20 bushells of wheate and about 6 bushells of oates .. .. ..
     Without dores
Item 4 Cowes .. .. ..
Item 2 oxen and 3 yeareling heiffers .. .. ..
Item 2 three yeareling steeres .. .. ..
Item 2 two yeareling heifers .. .. ..
Item 3 twelve monthlinges .. .. ..

	£	s	d
Item 2 horses	..	..	..
Item 2 hogges	..	..	..
Item 4 small piggs	..	..	..
Item 2 hay rickes	..	..	..
Item hay in the barne	..	..	..
Item I horse harrow	2	0	0
Item 20 boards		15	0
Item things unseene and forgotten		10	0
Suma totalis	172	14	2
Debts			
Item due from William Cuplocke of Framefeild upn mortgage	30	0	0
Item from Richard Thunder upon bond	6	10	0
Item from Mr Ambrose Frewen upon bond	25	0	0
Item due from him more by note under his name	8	0	0
Item from John Norris by bill	9	0	0
Item from Mr Richard Delves by bond	20	0	0
Suma Debitorum	98	10	0

[TNA PRO PROB 4/25491]

Will: made 27 Jan 1664; proved 5 May 1664
Wife: Elizabeth, executrix; son: William (minor); nephew: William, son of brother John of Bramber
Overseers: Edward Polhill, Mr William Durrant of Street
Witnesses: John Cruttenden, William Woodhouse   [TNA PRO PROB 11/314/49]

[1] Born Mayfield 1591, son of William, rector of Isfield, author. Tonbridge School. Cambridge, Peterhouse, matriculated 1608, BA 1612, MA 1615. Ordained deacon 1615 (bishop of London), priest 1616 (bishop of Chichester). Vicar of Laughton 1633–?1662, patron Sir Thomas Pelham, bt. Licensed preacher Chichester diocese 1635. Rector of East Hoathly by 1653; ejected 1662. Married Elizabeth Delve at St Swithin's, London, 1648. Died Burwash 1664.

28. Bury 1 March 1720 ROGER JONES [1]
Appraisers: Clement Hull, John Bedwell

	£	s	d
In primis Money in his pockett and wearing apparell	15	0	0
Money upon mortgage of land	490	0	0
Money due to him as pr book	400	0	0
Money due pr bills	15	0	0
Arrears of Rent	33	0	0
Feather bed Beadstead and 3 blanketts	4	0	0
Table Couch chest of drawers and 2 chairs	1	0	0
Two Tables	1	0	0
Clock	2	0	0
Three Barrels		3	0
Books	10	0	0
Things unseen or forgott	1	0	0
	932	3	0

[WSRO Ep I/29/33/77]

Will made 10 Dec 1719; proved 5 March 1720
Nephew: Hugh Lloyd, executor
Mary Dance 'constant attendance…in all of several sicknesses' (bedchamber furniture, clothes, household goods)
Witnesses: Edward Powell, Clement Hull, Clement Upperton   [WSRO STC I/32/280]

[1] Called BA 1701. Possibly ordained deacon and priest 1681 (bishop of Chichester). Curate of Lurgashall c. 1695; of Bury from 1701. Died 1720.

29. Buxted 15 May 1674 ROBERT MIDDLETON [1]
Appraisers: John Mullet, John Earle

	£	s	d
In primis his wearinge Apparell and money in his purse	5	0	0
In the great Parler			
Item One long table one little eight square table twelve wood chayres and a childes chayre	2	4	6
In the Hall			
Item One still and bottom one napkin presse one paire of yarne winders and a cloath beater		3	4
In the Buttery next the great Parler			
Item Two hoggsheads three stanns and three douzen of bottells	1	1	1
In the chamber over the great Parler			
Item Foure bushells of barley foure bushells of Oaten Malt and two parcells of hopps	1	5	0
In the chamber over the great Buttery			
Item One old bedsteddle one old matt and cord		3	0
In the Studdy			
Item Soape and larde one chest a hanging shelfe and a treble viall		13	6
In the little Parler			
Item One table one red leather carpett one greate woodden chayre tenn high red leather chayres two lowe red leather chayres one side board and a paire of tongues	2	10	2
In the Kitchinge			
Item Six pewter dishes one pewter bason two pewter porrengers eighteene spoones and other small peeces of pewter foure douzen of trenchers two iron candlesticks two tinn candlestickes and two white candlesticks one tinn driping pan one tinn cover one tinn water pott one tinn sacer two sauce panns one drudger one grater and one white earthen salt	1	13	1
Item One great iron pottage pott foure other small iron potts one iron kettle one brasse kettle one iron skillett one brasse posnett one old iron chafendish one paire of brandirons one iron cape potthangers and hookes a smoake Jack one paire of tongues one fire shovell one gridiron one iron peele two spitts one basting ladle one clever one iron driping pan one iron morter and pestell two smothing irons and two heaters one old frying pan one warming pan and a paire of bellows	3	18	9
Item one Bacon rack one bunting hutch foure pailes one hand Jett one chest of drawers one salt box one ioyned stoole and a table board to it			

foure old chayres one spinning wheele two sives and a chopping knife	2	12	8

In the Buttery next the Kitching

Item One Safe		2	6

In the Brewhouse

Item One Furnace one Mashinge fatt two bucking tubbs three Wort tubbs one washinge keeler one shoote one hogge tubb one other old tubb one hand dish and a halfe bushel	2	7	8

In the little Strong beere Sellar

Item Foure Barrells		16	6

In the Small beere Sellar

Item Two old barrells one firkin one kilderkin one old spinninge wheele and a tunnel		9	6

In the milke house

Item Two milke leads one double cheese presse one bacon trough one cherne two olde powderinge tubbs and lidds one keeler one table and two tressells two hanging shelves a crock cherne one forme three cheese bailes and followes one woodden platter and seaven crocks and pans	1	18	9

In the chamber over the milkhouse

Item One old bedsteddle and coard two boulsters one Flockbedd and a blanckett		11	4

In the Parler Chamber

Item One bedsteddle one feather bed two boulsters two pillowes three blancketts one rugg curtanes and curtaine rodds vallents and cover matt and coard and a little carpet	5	12	8
Item One chest of drawers one hangin shelfe one little table one large lookeing glasse one small lookeing glasse one picture one stand three little stooles one paire of brandirons one paire of tongues and an old firepan	2	15	6
Item One little silver porrenger six paire of sheetes eight pillowe beeres six table cloathes foure douzen of napkins and foure towells	5	15	0

In the chamber over the Studdy

Item one halfe headded bedsteddle curtaines curtaine rodds vallens cover matt and coard	1	12	0

In the maides chamber

Item One Flock bed one feather boulster one blanckett one rugg old curtaines and vallents one truckle bedsteddle one old feather bedd and a boulster	1	16	0

In the Kitching chamber

Item One bedsted one feather bedd two boulsters two pillowes one blanckett one rugg a matt coard and curtaine rodds one table two chests one stoole and one old armed chayre	3	16	11

In the Studdy next the Kitching chamber

Item one deske		3	0
Item all manner of Bookes	3	0	0
Item debts sperate and desperate	5	0	0

Without doores

Item The hay	3	0	0
Item Eight thousand of old hoppolles	8	0	0

	£	s	d
Item Three Cowes	9	10	0
Item One old oasthaire and one other oasthaire	1	4	0
Item Two old broaken harrowes		4	0
Item Oates and Barley in the strawe	2	0	0
Item One hay cutter and two sives		2	2
Item One Sowe and seaven sheetes	3	5	0
Item Two hough troughes		5	0
Item Wood and fagotts		15	0
Item one old horse one old mare bridles and saddles	5	5	0
Item the Dung	2	0	0
Item The Wheat upon the ground	17	0	0
Item Things out of sight and forgott		3	4
The summe totall of this Inventory	110	0	11

[TNA PRO PROB 5/4616]

Administration 6 Aug 1674
To wife, Mary   [TNA PRO PROB 6/49]

[1] Called BA, possibly MA. Rector of Buxted c. 1661–1673. Died 1674.

30. Chailey 2 Oct 1713 WILLIAM ROOTES [1]
Appraisers: John Langford, Walter Vinall

	£	s	d
In primis his Weareing apparell and Money in Purse	10	0	0
Item A Chest of Drawers	1	1	6
Item An old Watch	1	0	0
Item Three Beere vessells		6	0
Item Bookes	5	0	0
Item An old Mare	1	10	0
Item Old Lumber		13	6
tot	19	11	0

[ESRO W/INV 459]

Administration 14 Aug 1713
To sister, Anne Fowle   [ESRO W/B 15.110r]
[1] Son of William, rector of Fletching and Chailey. Oxford, Christ Church, matriculated 1674 aged 16, BA 1678, MA 1681. Ordained priest 1682 (bishop of Chichester). Rector of Chailey 1686–1713, patron Richard Towle of Newick, gent. Possibly vicar of Compton. Died 1713.

31. Chiddingly 1728 GILES WATKINS [1]
Appraisers: William Ward, Joseph Wacklin
[Original damaged]

	£	s	d
Apparrell and Pockett Money	7	0	0
Furniture and Linnen in the Kitchen Chamber	16	0	0
Goods in the Brewhouse Chamber	3	0	0

Furniture in the Closett	1	0	0
Buttery Chamber	1	0	0
Furniture in the Kitchen	6	0	0
Furniture of the Parlour		10	0
Furniture of the Buttery	1	0	0
Furniture of the Brewhouse	3	0	0
Furniture of the Parlour Chamber	1	0	0
	39	10	0

[ESRO W/INV 2049]

Will: made 22 Feb 1728; proved 4 May 1728
Wife: Ann, executrix
Witnesses: Elizabeth Jeffrey, James Pilbeam　　　　　　[ESRO W/A 52.473]

[1]　Son of William, of Stroud, Glos. Oxford, Wadham, matriculated 1712 aged 18, BA 1716. Ordained priest 1723 (bishop of Chichester). Curate of Chiddingly 1723; vicar 1725–1728, patron Crown. Married Ann Jeffrey at East Hoathly by licence 1721. Died 1728.

32. West Chiltington 14 Dec 1675 ROBERT CARR [1]
Appraisers: Henry Harwood, John Norman
[Original damaged]

	£	s	d
In primis his wearing Aparrel money in Purse	..	..	..
In the Room over the Parlour			
Item Bed and Bedstead and other necessaries thereto belonging	6	..	..
In the Same Roome			
Item half a dozen Chaires	..	15	..
Item one Press a Table Truckle Bed and Bedstead	1	15	0
In the Parlour			
Item one Bed and Bedstead wth other necessaries thereto belonging	4	0	0
Item one Chest of Drawers wth a Carpett	1	0	..
Item Nine Chaires and two stooles and window Curtaines	1	4	..
Item for Brandirons Tongs and fireshovell		10	..
Att the Staires head			
Item one Clock	1	0	0
In the Hall Chamber			
Item two Featherbeds and one … Bed wth other things thereto belonging … Item a pair of Brandirons Fireshovell Tongs Table and Chair		8	..
In the old chamber			
Item two Bedsteads and a flock bed thereto belonging	1	0	0
In the Study			
Item for his Library	35	0	0
Item the Table and Desk		3	..
Diaper Linnen Item two dozen of Napkins two Table Cloths and two cupboard Cloths	3	0	..
Item for Tenn pair of tire linnen sheetes napkins and Three Table Cloths	8	0	..

	£	s	d
Item for four pair of Tow sheetes and Five Table Cloths wth other Linnen	15	..	..
Item for Plate		..	..
Item two Truncks and Childebed Linnen wth a Red Mantle and white Silke Mantle	2	..	..
In the Hall			
Item two Tables and Carpetts	..	..	..
Item halfe a dozen Chaire Cushions	..	..	..
Item the still and Brand[irons]	..	..	..
Item for Growing Corne....... the Ground	..	..	..
Item for Wheate in the Barne	..	..	..
Item Pease in the Barne	..	..	..
Item for hame and strawe ready threshed	..	..	..
In the Little Barnes			
Item for Hay and Tares hame	..	..	..
Item for two Fatting Hoggs	..	..	..
Item for two Leane Hoggs	2	5	..
Item for a long Fur Ladder		4	..
Item one Dray and Ladder		4	..
Item for the grey Mare	2	5	..
Item for the Little Mare	1	13	..
Item for sheepe	3	0	..
Item a Wellbuckett Rope and Chaine		3	..
Item for Wood Fagotts and Refuge Timber	3	0	..
Item the Furnases and other brewing vessell	7	0	..
Item money upon Booke for Tythe and Timber	68	8	..
In the Beere Buttery			
Item Three Kelers and foure Bucketts		10	..
Item 4 Barrells and two Firkins		17	..
Item 2 Hogsheads		10	..
In the Milkhouse			
Item a Meale Trough and two Searches		5	..
Item two Leatherne sacks		6	..
Item foure Linnen Sackes a Wim Sheete and an halfe Bushell		17	..
Item for Three Sadles a Pannell and a Pillion		19	..
In the Kitchen			
Item two Brass Kettles one brass Pot foure brass Skilletts and Candlesticke	2	5	..
Item two pair of Brandirons 2 pair of Pothangers Fire pan Tongs and Fire Prong		..	..
Item a Jack and Foure Spitts two Iron Dripping Pans and two box Irons box Irons	1	1	..
Item two Iron Potts and an Iron Kettle	..	..	..
Item for Pewter	..	..	..
Item for hemp and Fl[ax]	..	..	..
Item foure Chaires............. Cradle little Table Bu[tter] and Cheese and all o[ther] things forgotten	..	..	..
Suma Totlis	[208	0	0]

Exhibited 4 Jan 1676   [WSRO Ep I/29/48/76]

Will: made 6 Feb 1674; no probate

Wife: Hannah, executrix (choose up to 12 practical books); daughter (by 1st wife): Grace (2 childbed suits of linen, red blanket with silver lace, 2 pairs sheets, table cloth, dozen napkins, cupboard cloth, his bed and fittings)

Trustees for second family: Samuel Bedford, (brother-in-law) Edmund Coles (rector, Storrington), Richard Ridder, London clerk, John Marryon senior of Bramber, eldest son: Alan (Critical annotations in 9 vols folio cost £16); son: Robert (Hebrew Bible in 4 vols of Plattens prining, Junius, Exemmellins [*sic*] upon the whole Bible and 12 of best books in study at his choice; remainder of library, printed and mss between the two daughters (by Hannah): Hannah and Mercy (half each household goods and linen)

Witnesses: Thomas Mellersh, Richard M ... , John Edaw   [WSRO STC I/26/174]

---

[1]   Son of Alan, rector of West Chiltington. Cambridge, Trinity, matriculated 1643, scholar 1646, BA and fellow 1647, MA 1650. Chaplain to earl of Warwick. Rector of Braintree, Essex, 1662–1675; of West Chiltington (succeeding his father) 1668–1675. Subscribed for institution at Willingdon 1664 but not instituted. Died 1675; buried West Chiltington.

33. West Chiltington 15 June 1728 RICHARD FOWLE [1]

Appraisers: Thomas Nye, Edward Downer

	£	s	d
In primis Wearing apparrell and Money in his purse	4	0	0
In the Parlour			
Twelve Cane Chairs a Clock Two Tables Two arm'd Chairs and other small Things	3	0	0
In the Hall			
Six Chairs Two Tables Firepan Tongs and Andirons	1	0	0
In the Kitchen			
Nine pewter dishes Two dozen and half of plates one Iron Rack one pair of Andirons Three Spitts one Jack one Skreen Firepan and Tongs Two dripping Pans Two Tables one Bacon Rack and other small things	4	10	0
In the Brewhouse			
One Furnace one Bucking Pott Five Tubbs One Kettle Three Bucketts and other small things	3	10	0
In the Buttery			
One Bunting Hutch Two Porridge Potts Two Frying Pans and other small things	1	0	0
In the Hall Chamber			
One Bed and all belonging to it one Close stool one couch	4	10	0
In the Brewhouse Chamber			
Six pair of Sheets Five Table Cloths one dozen of Napkins and other small things	2	10	0
In the Little Chamber			
One Bed and all belonging to it	2	10	0
In the Buttery Chamber			
One Flock Bed and Steddle		15	0
In the Cellar			
Eight Kilderkins Six dozen of Bottles one Tundish	1	10	0
Four acres of Wheat	12	0	0

	£	s	d
One acre of Hay	1	0	0
Two Cords and half of Wood	1	5	0
one Saddle and Bridle		15	0
Books	1	0	0
	48	5	0

[WSRO Ep I/29/48/126]

Administration 10 July 1728
To John Newman and Ann White, principal creditors; Ann mother, having renounced

[WSRO STC III/N/78]

[1] Son of Richard, of Fletching. Oxford, Magdalen Hall, matriculated 1698 aged 18, BA 1702. Ordained deacon 1704 (bishop of Chichester). Curate of Ditchling 1704. Rector of West Chiltington 1705–1728, patron Ann Moreton. Died 1728.

34. Clapham 18 Sept 1643 HENRY NYE [1]

Appraisers: Thomas Oliver, Edward Sowton, John Cooper

	£	s	d
In the hawle Chamber			
In primis Item his wearing aparell and money in his purse	10	0	0
Item one bedd wth that belonging to it	4	0	0
Item ten payre of sheets and 2 dussen of Napkins and other Lynnen	3	0	0
Item two chests and one boxe		10	0
In the parlor Chamber			
Item a high bedd and a truckle bedd furnished	5	0	0
Item Five payer of sheets Fower tableclothes and a dussen of Napkins wth other linnen	50	0	0
Item two chests a trunk and a square table	1	0	0
Item certayne wooll	3	0	0
In the outward Chamber			
Item a presse a bed and a bedstedle	1	10	0
In the kitchen Chamber			
Item a bedd and bedstedle	3	0	0
In the Inner Chamber			
Item two bedds and two bedstedles	2	0	0
In the Manns Chamber			
Item a bed and two bedstedles	1	0	0
In the Parlor			
Item his lirarye[sic] of bookes	20	0	0
Item a livrye cupborde a square table and a Cowtch	1	10	0
In the hawle			
Item a table and forme eight joyned stoles two chayers two brandirons	1	10	0
In the kitchin			
Item the brasse kettles and pots and other brass	1	10	0
Item the pewter	1	10	0
Item a table cupbord a Jack an Iron pott brandirons and other things belonging to the kitchen	2	10	0

In the Milkhouse			
Item butter and Cheese and other Things there	1	0	0
In the brewhouse			
Item a Furnes and brewing vessels	2	0	0
Item wheete and Mault and Sackes	1	10	0
Without Dores			
Item three horse beasts	10	0	0
Item Five Kine three younge beasts	13	0	0
Item Fower swine	2	0	0
Item Three acres and halfe of wheate	6	0	0
Item six acres of barley	6	0	0
Item Five acres of Tares	1	10	0
In the barne			
Item haye	10	0	0
Item a Cart and wheels a plow and dungcort	1	10	0
Item tymber and wodd and other lumber about the howse	2	0	0
Item Money Due by bonds and other wise	40	0	0
Suma totalis	153	10	0

[WSRO Ep I/29/50/16]

Will: made 16 Aug 1643; proved 29 July 1645
Wife: Lettice, executrix; son: John (all study books, clothes); 'youngest children'
Witnesses: Edward Sowtten, John Whegacombe, Edward Lucas, Richard Grantham

[WSRO STC I/21/61b]

[1] Of Sussex. Oxford, Brasenose, matriculated 1609 aged 20, BA 1611; called MA 1614. Ordained deacon and priest 1614 (bishop of Oxford). Vicar of Cobham, Surr, 1615. Rector of Clapham 1620–1643, patron Sir Thomas Holland.

35. Climping 31 May 1648 JOHN WHITE [1]

Appraisers: Christopher Elliott, John Duke, William Gawen

	£	s	d
In primis his wearing aparell and mony in his purse	10	0	0
9 pair of tire cheetes at	4	10	0
11 paire of tire pillowcoates at	1	10	0
1 Shirte of Damaske at	2	0	0
1 Table Cloath one Towell 1 Cubberd cloath of diaper at		15	0
5 Tire table cloaths at	1	5	0
2 doz and halfe of tire napkins at		15	0
3 Tire towels at		6	0
14 paire and 1 course sheete at	5	0	0
11 course table Cloaths at		10	0
14 Course Towels at		7	0
1 Doz and halfe of course napkins at		9	0
Sum is	27	7	0
Cattell			
In primis 2 steers at 4 years old	8	0	0
5 bullocks at 1 yeare old	16	0	0

3 bullocks at two yeare old	15	0	0
3 kine and 3 Calves at	7	0	0
1 Mare and colt 1 Lame Horse at	5	0	0
21 Sheepe and 14 Lambs at	13	10	0
Sum is	64	10	0

In the Halle Chamber

In primis 1 livry bedsted and bed and all things to it at	3	0	0
1 fether bed and joined bedsted wth all things to it	5	0	0
1 Truckle Bedsted 2 Blankets 1 rug 1 bolster at		10	0
3 Joyned Chests 2 trunks 9 boxes 1 old Chest joyned chest Chaire 4 Cushins Stooles one Square table 1 paire of Andirons and tongs at	3	0	0
Item Orrice Covlid at	1	0	0
4 doz pewter at	6	0	0
halfe a dozn of butter dishes 14 small plates 11 porringers 9 saucers 10 spoones 3 Candlesticks 3 salts 2 pye plates five Chamber pots 3 pewter potts at	3	0	0
1 paire of tables 5 els of sackinge wth other old Lumberments at	5	0	0
Sum is	26	10	0

In the Paller Chamber

In primis 1 livry bedsted and Fether bed 2 bolsters 4 pilloes 2 blankets 1 ruge at	2	13	4
1 bedsted 2 blankets at	1	10	0
1 joyned Chest 1 trunk 1 press for cloaths at	1	0	0
Sum is	5	3	4

In the Paller

Item 1 Table and frame and side cubberd eight Chaires 4 stooles 1 deske 2 Andirons at	1	10	0
Sum is	1	10	0

In the milkehouse

Item 3 doz of milke treyes 3 bowles one meale tubb 1 Kiver 1 old chest wth 2 nayle of flaxen towe 2 butter tubs 1 Charne wth other Lumber at	2	0	0
Sum is	2	0	0

In the Hall

Item 1 table and Frame 9 joyned stooles 3 cubberds 1 Chaire 1 paire of cast andirons 1 Still a paire of Racks 1 Musket 1 birdinge peece 2 swords 1 iron barr wth other Lumber at	5	0	0
Sum is	5	0	0

In the Kitchen Chamber

Item 2 paire of shutt harness 2 linen and two woollen turns 3 old tubs 6 prongs one wymsheete and 17 sacks at	2	0	0
2 bedstead 1 Fether bed 2 Flocke bed 1 old blankett 2 covlids 2 bolsters 1 round table at	1	10	0
2 Roade sadles 1 side sadle 2 pillions 2 Sadle Cloaths 2 bridles 1 panell and other lumber at	4	0	0
Sum is	7	10	0

In the Brewhouse

Item 1 furnice 2 Tuns 2 mash vates and other Brewing vessells at	3	0	0
Sum is	3	0	0

In the Seller

Item 9 barrells 3 pins 1 silting trowe at	1	10	0
Sum is	1	10	0

In the Kitchen

Item 4 Iron potts 3 brass potts 4 brass ketles 3 brass Chaffeinge dishes 3 brass posnetts 2 Skymers of brass 1 brass slice 1 brass ladle 2 bastinge ladles 2 brass Candelsticks one brass Morter 1 warminge pan 1 bell morter	5	0	0
Item 4 dripping pans 6 spitts 1 paire of beefe prongs 1 Cleaver 2 Shriddinge knives and 3 smoothinge irons 3 Andirons 1 Fender 1 paire of gridirons 2 paire of pothangers 1 Iron barr 1 paire of tongs 1 fier shovell and Slice at	2	0	0
1 Steele Mill 1 Iron Jacke at	1	0	0
Bacon at	1	0	0
1 Table and Furme 1 Cuberd and grate 4 Chaires 2 lynnen wheeles one spence and other lumber at	1	6	8
Sum is	10	6	8
Item 1 Fether bed and bolster at Houghton	1	10	0
Sum is	1	10	0

In the gate and Barne

Item 1 paire of shod wheeles and the tire of A nother paire 2 Dunge potts 1 Cartt 1 plowe 4 Harrowes 1 rowler 2 ladders and harness at	6	0	0
1 Garnard 1 Cheese press 1 bm 2 racks and two Mayngers wth other things belongeinge to husbandry at	2	0	0
Sum is	8	0	0

Corne groweinge

Item 8 Acres of wheate 9 Acres of barley 9 Acres of pease 4 acres of pease and tares 3 acres of Oates at	43	0	0
Sum is	43	0	0
Item bookes in the studye at	10	0	0
The whole sum is	216	17	0

Exhibited 13 June 1648 by wife, Jane White   [WSRO Ep I/29/51/31]

No will or administration found

[1] Possibly son of John, cleric and author. Called MA 1615. Ordained deacon and priest 1615 (bishop of Norwich). Vicar of Climping 1620, patron Eton College. Coadjutor of West Tarring 1620. Vicar of West Tarring, Heene and Durrington 1621, patron archbishop of Canterbury. Married Jane Michell at Houghton 1639. Died 1648.

36. Climping 15 Oct 1677 CHRISTOPHER CANNER [1]

Appraisers: Thomas Peache, John Standen

In primis	£	s	d
In the Parlour			
Item his wearinge apparell and money in his Purse	107	0	0
Item one Bed and Bedstedle and all that belong unto him	5	0	0
Item sixe Turkeyworke Chaires and Two Stooles		14	0
Item hangings one Carpett and Table	2	0	0

Item Two paire of Brandirons one looking glas Tonges and Bellowes with a fire shovell	1	0	0
In the Sellar			
Item six hogsheads one Barrell and Two Kilderkins		12	0
Item six duszen of Bottells and one Pudringe Tubb		6	0
In the Hall Chamber			
Item one Bed and Bedstedle and all things thereunto belonginge	3	10	0
Item one Presse one little Table and Carpitt Two Chaires one Stoole Two old Trunckes		10	0
Item one Paire of Brandirons fire Shovell and Bellowes and Tonges		2	6
In the Parlour Chamber			
Item one Bed and Bedstedle and all belongeinge to him	4	0	0
Item one Chayer Two old Stooles Two litle Tables Brandirons fire Shovell and Pis one paire of Pistolls		10	0
Item the hangings		10	0
In the Pantrye Chamber			
Item one Bedstedle and Bead and Bolsters and Ruge and Blankett	2	0	0
Item in the Stayercase one Clocke		5	0
In the Hall			
Item one Large Table and Carpett one Rowne Table six Chayres and Two Stooles		16	0
Brandirons and a grate		6	0
Item Curtaine and Curtaine Rods		2	0
In the Kitchin			
Item Two Brasse potts one Iron Pott Two Brasse Kittles Three Skilletts Two Brasse A Chafing dish Three Brasse Candle Stickes		12	0
Item one Duszen of Pewter dishes and Three duszen of Plaitts Two Flagons Two Candle Stickes one Bason six Porringers	1	10	0
Item one paire of doges one fender Tonges and Slice and fire Pronge Two Pothangers spitts and a Jacke		8	0
Item one Table Two Chaires one dresser and Bacon Racke		6	0
In the Kitchin Chamber			
Item one Bed and Bedstedle and all things therunto belonginge and other Lumber	1	10	0
Item in the Studdy the Bookes	20	0	0
In the Garrett			
Item Twelve Bushells of Appells		10	0
Linen Item Ten paire of Sheetes fower paire of Pillowbers six Table Cloathes and Three diaper Table Cloathes Two duzen of diaper napkins one long Table Cloath halfe a duszen of Towells	2	10	0
In the Brewhouse			
Item one furnis one vate and Tun Two Ceellers Two Kevers	1	5	0
Item Twentie quarters of wheate	30	0	0
Item Twentie quarters of Barley	18	0	0
Item Three quarters of Peason	2	10	0
Item Three quarters of oates	1	0	0
Item six Bushells of Teares		12	0
Item in the Stable Two horses one maire	10	0	0
Item Two Cowes	5	0	0

	£	s	d
Item one Carte one dunge Carte one Plough and two harrowes	3	2	0
Item one Loade of Hay	1	0	0
Item Two Hoggs seaven shutts one Sowe	1	10	0
Item due for halfe a Loade of Wheate	5	0	0
Item one mortgage	60	0	0
Item one Bond	30	0	0
Item one Bond	30	0	0
Item one Bond	20	0	0
Item one Bond	10	0	0
Item one Bond	10	0	0
Item one Bond	50	0	0
Item one Bond	10	0	0
Item wood and other Lumber Carte harnes and plough harnes	2	0	0
Suma Totalis huius Inventory	456	10	6

[WSRO Ep I/29/51/62]

Will: made 10 June 1677; proved 17 Oct 1677
Wife: Deborah, executrix
Overseer: John Millington of Newick
Witnesses: Christopher Seleam, Anne Richbee, Thomas Peckham

[WSRO STC I/26/156b]

[1] Son of Christopher, of Tewkesbury, Glos. Oxford, Pembroke, matriculated 1639 aged 16; Christ Church, BA 1642, MA 1646. Vicar of Climping 1670–1677, patron Eton College. Rector of Ford 1670–1677, patron bishop of Chichester. Prebendary of Gates 1661–1677. Died 1677.

37. Coldwaltham 1 March 1638 WILLIAM BOWLEY [1]

Appraisers: John Wallwin, John Knowles, Richard Hed

	£	s	d
In primis his weareing apparrell money in his purse and his bokes wth his deske	5	0	0
In the halle			
Item one table wth a forme and benches one Joyne Stoole three Chayres one side table one Joyned Cheast	1	0	0
Item one Cubbard one glasse cage one payer of pott hangers one payer of brand Irons one payer of Tonges and a fier shovell and a payer of bellowes	1	10	0
Item beefe and bacon wth other Implements there	1	0	0
In the Parlor			
Item one Fetherbed wth a Joyned bedstedl one rugg two bolsters fowre fether pillowes and one blancket	2	0	0
Item 1 trundell bedstedle a flockbed two boulsters and two blanckets		16	0
Item one cheast three boxes and a warming pann		8	0
In the Chamber over the parlor			
Item one flockbed two Fetherbolsters one flock boulster one Coverlet thre blanckets and one round table	1	6	8

In the kitchin

	£	s	d
Item six peeces of brass wth a brasse candellsticke	1	6	8
Item tenn peeces of pewter one dussen of Spones and one pewter candellsticke		13	4
Item one greate Iron pott		6	8
Item one spitt one Iron Candellsticke and a chopping knife		1	6
Item three buckets fower tubes one dresser wth shelves and other lumber		10	0

In the buttery

	£	s	d
Item two barrells 3 firkins one powdring tubb Six Crockes one Cheeseprese one ould cubbard one tunn two Serches two Sives wth other lumber		16	0
Item linnen in the howse wth some hempe	2	0	0

In the gates

	£	s	d
Item one mare wth a bridell and saddle one hogg wth some haye and woode	3	13	4
Item halfe an acker of hy on the ground		6	8
Item things forgotten unseene and so unprised		2	0
debtes oweing to the deceased at the time of his death			
Item due unto him one specialtie from divers persones	80	0	0
Some total	102	16	0

[WSRO Ep I/29/54/18]

Will: made 6 Feb 1637; proved 7 March 1638
Wife: Elizabeth, executrix; son: Richard; daughters: Mary (iron pot, pewter, bed), Elizabeth; brother: Edward
Witnesses: John Wallwin, Edward Boley   [WSRO STC I/19/92]

[1] Biographical details not found.

38. Coldwaltham 10 Nov 1640 WILLIAM JEOFFREY [1]

Appraisers: John Lawrence clerk, John Wallwyn, Thomas Barber

	£	s	d
In primis His waring apparell and Mony in his purse	2	0	0
Item His Books		5	0
Item In debts from John Wallwyn	2	19	10
Sum totalis	5	4	10

[WSRO Ep I/29/54/23]

Administration 11 May 1641
To William Chandler, clerk, one of creditors   [WSRO STC III/H/170]

[1] Possibly ordained deacon and priest 1631 (bishop of St David's); and curate of Stopham in 1630s.

39. Coombes 5 Sept 1667 LAWRANCE JONES [1]
Appraisers: William Langford, Henerie Comer

	£	s	d
In primis his wearing parrell and money in his purse	2	0	0
Item his bookes	5	0	0
in the bruhous			
Item two Cilderkins and ould tubes		10	0
Item one furnis an oyron pot and a kitle		16	0
in the kitchen			
Item two Chaires one table and furme one Warming pan brand oyrons and spit		14	0
Item one jacke two paire of pot hangers		5	0
Item one kettel one frying pan		3	0
Item two spining wheales		2	6
in the parler			
Item one table six Chaires one paire of brand oyrons on payre of tongs one fier pan and a payre of bellows	2	0	0
. In the Closet			
Item two bask one Case of knives and trenchers		1	6
In the halle			
Item one table two Chaires		4	0
In the parlor Chamber			
Item one bead and beadstedle wth other thinges thereto blonging	3	0	0
Item two beads and two beadstedles	2	0	0
Item pewter and boles		16	0
Item linan in the hous	3	0	0
Item two Cowes	4	0	0
Item two horses one Cart and dong Cart	3	10	0
Item Sheepe and lambs	3	4	0
Item three hoges and seane piges	2	10	0
Item the hay		16	0
Item things unsin and forgoten		5	0
Sum totalis	33	17	0

[WSRO Ep I/29/57/6]

Administration 6 Sep 1667
To Mary, wife   [WSRO STC III/I/36]

[1] Oxford, Magdalen Hall, BA 1648; Jesus, fellow and MA 1651, vice-principal 1656. Rector of Welby, Lincs, 1662; of Coombes 1662–1667. Married Mary Snelling of Ferring at Tangmere 1664. Died 1667.

40. Coombes Feb 27 1672 EDWARD MANNING [1]
Appraisers: John Cowdrey, Edward Manning

	£	s	d
In primis his wearing apparell and money in his purse	1	10	0
Item in the Parlour chamber			
One bed and bed steadle Curtaines Valences Two bolsters One blanket			

a rugg matt	3	0	0
Item six chaires and stooles with covers		8	0
Item a paire of Andirons tongs and fire shovell		2	0
Item a Table carpet two window curtaines		4	0
Item in a closet joyning to the chamber			
severall bottles and A dozen of trenchers and		3	0
Item Hempen tow upon the parlour chamber staires		2	6
Item in the Hall chamber			
a bed two bedsteedles Two bolsters One blanket a rugg Curtaines and Valences and matt	2	0	0
Item two chests two Trunkes Ten paire of sheetes foure dozen of Napkins Halfe a dozen of table cloaths and other new linnen	5	0	0
Item in a closet joyning to it			
an old Trunk and an old pair of Andirons		1	0
Item in the chamber over the milk house			
a presse for cloaths a chaire two old boxes a close stoole		10	0
Item a Silver Tanket	2	10	0
Item a bed and Bedsteed blanket Coverlet old Curtaines A Matt and	2	0	0
Item in the chamber over the Chitchen			
a flock bed and bedsteedle One blanket and Coverlet One bolster		10	0
Item in a chamber over the Brew house			
Two leathern bags a Garden rake a Keeler old Tub and bowles a spinning wheele and some other lumber		5	0
Item in the corn loafe			
Wheat Oates and Tares	5	0	0
Item his Library or study			
of bookes	15	0	0
A little desk and small table in his study		2	6
Item in the parlour			
One Table and Carpet six leathern Chaires Two paire of Brand irons and a paire of Tonges	1	0	0
Item in the closet joyning to the parlour			
Two white candlesticks small dish		1	0
Item in the milk house			
a Table a churn milk keeler five trugs dripping pan a few crocks a fryng pan six cheeses		15	0
Item in the cellar			
a stand and three barrels		5	0
In the Bake house			
Two potts old frying pan Two flitches of Bacon a cupboard a little Tub	1	5	0
Item in the Kitchen			
On Table Three chaires a box of drawers salt tubb a Jack Three spits 3 paire of Pothooks Item Two pair of brandirons bellowes fire shovell and Tonges and	1	0	0
Item Twelve pewter dishes small and great Two plates Three small skellets Three brasse Candlesticks and a flaggon and some other small things	1	10	0
Item in the Brewhouse			
a furnace and some brewing vessels	2	0	0

Item in the cheese house			
Six small vessels two sheares a pair of slings		10	0
Item in the Barne			
Barly unthresht and a few pease	2	0	0
In the close			
Two Cowes foure pigs	8	0	0
Item in the stable			
an Hors with Harnesse	3	0	0
Item A part of a Rick of Hay	1	10	0
Item sheep fifteene	5	0	0
Item things unseene and forgotten		5	0
Summa totalis	78	4	0

Exhibited by Richard Manning 21 March 1672   [WSRO Ep I/29/57/7]

Administration 24 Feb 1672 and 21 March 1672
To Mary, wife   [WSRO STC III/L/89, 91]

[1] Oxford, Wadham, scholar 1648; St John's, matriculated 1649, BA 1652. Curate of Climping and Ford c. 1662. Vicar of Rustington 1664–1672, patron bishop of Chichester. Married Mary Stent at Midhurst or Stedham 1658; marriage entered in both parish registers; both parties described as of Midhurst in Stedham register. Died 1672; buried Coombes.

41. Cuckfield 12 May 1666 SAMUEL GREENHILL [1]
Appraisers: Edmund King, John King

	£	s	d
In primis brasse and pewter	3	0	0
Item a table and 4 stooles		5	0
Item 3 Iron potts and kettle		12	6
Item a table a forme and Cupbord		16	0
Item a table chayres and stooles	2	0	0
Item a Furnase att	1	0	0
Item Leades trayes and churne	1	0	0
Item brewing Tubbs and Barrells	1	0	0
Item Cheese presse		2	6
Item a feather bedd Blanketts Rugge and Curtaines	8	0	0
Item chayres and stooles	2	0	0
Item 3 feather beds and curtaines and all things belonging to them	8	0	0
Item two old flocke bedds and Blanketts	5	16	0
Item 2 Little tables and Cupbord		7	0
Item two Carpetts		8	0
Item Lynnen sheetes and table Clothes att	5	0	0
Sum total	34	7	0

[TNA PRO PROB 4/13059]

Will: undated; proved 29 June 1667
Wife: Margaret, executrix; (residue and Shropshire annuity); deceased wife, Mary; son Samuel (house etc in Clavering, Essex) ;sons: John, Thomas, Nathaniel; daughter: Anne (house called Bultrowe)

Poor of parish. 40s
Overseers: brother-in-law John Bolton, cousin John Eborne
Witnesses: Randall Page, Sara Bolton   [TNA PRO PROB 11/321/98]

[1] Son of Thomas, of Harrow on the Hill, Midd. Oxford, All Souls, matriculated 1634, BA 1637, MA 1640. Licensed curate of Wivelsfield and curate in Lewes archdeaconry 1637. Curate of Cuckfield from 1638; vicar 1643 on ejection of Dr James Marsh. Married Mary daughter of Thomas Vicars, a previous vicar, aged 16, at Cuckfield by licence 1641; Margaret Bolton of Northaw, Herts, at New Shoreham 1654. Died 1666 aged 50.

42. Dallington ... 1700 RICHARD RUSSELL [1]
[Original damaged/illegible]   [TNA PRO PROB 4/928]

Will: made 7 Nov 1697; 20 Feb 1700
Wife: Susannah, executrix (with brother-in-law John Hawes, clerk, and Lawrence Avery); sons: John (silver seal and watch), Richard (books 'to be a scholar'), Thomas, Nathaniel, Edward (son of wife)
Overseer: George Barnsley, clerk, Sedlescombe
Witnesses: John Wenham, Mary Montague, Elizabeth Hendley
                                                         [TNA PRO PROB 11/454]

[1] Son of a cleric. Oxford, University College, matriculated 1660; Magdalen, demy 1660–1668, BA 1663, MA 1666. Ordained priest 1667 (bishop of Chichester). Vicar of Hollington 1667–1679; of Hellingly 1679–1682; of Dallington 1682–1700. Married Susannah Hawes, ?widow, (possibly his second wife) at Warbleton 1683. Died 1700.

43. West Dean 3 Sept 1679 GEORGE EYLES [1]
Appraisers: Robert Smyth, John Michaell
[Original damaged and fragmentary]

	£	s	d
In primis his Weareing Apparrell [and] money in Purse and Bookes	3	18	0

Item in the Kitchen
one Jack twoe spitts one paire of Andirons twoe fire panns ... paire of Tonges one paire of doggs one Fender one paire of Gridgions twoe old Ireon potts Twoe brasse Skilletts one Iron driping pann one Warmeing pann one Stone morter and pisle one old Table and five Joyned stooles three Lether [c]h[a]ires two ... ldre Chaires   ..   ..   ..
[There follow 13 original lines with only a few words legible]
... pewter ... [ch]amber potts and one other pewter Chamber pott one Jack waite one old Aple Roster one old Cheast three Spoones one little Laten Case pann and tunell sixteene wooden platts thirteene square Trenards ... one ...ten Cu[le]nder and one ... ore Quishions   4   0   0
... the Parlour
three Turkeyworke [ch]aires one other blew armed [c]haire twoe Lether Chaires twoe Round Tables twoe Carpetts one paire of Andirons one paire of Tongs ... Fire pann one brasse Firepann one brasse paire of

Tongs one and Twenty Pictors and Scuttings [*sic*] and one Quishion	1	10	0
Item in the roome within the Palor			
one old Cheast and one old bedstidle		3	6
... Boxes in the said ... d twoe Bottles		1	6
... [r]oome betweene the Palor			
... Kitchen one old Cheast ... Botles ...		10	6

[There follow 13 original lines with only a few words legible]

... of Hempe and Flex sheetes ... other sheete and twoe halfe ... [sh]eete ... two course Table [clo]this more three Twoells more ... one dannishe sheete ... dannishe Table Cloath ... two Dussen and a halfe of Flex and Hempe Napkins five Towells Twoe sidboard Cloaths one Table Cloath more twoe Flex table Cloaths more three Hall and Table Cloathes fower Course Napkins six pillow Coates one smale pillowe Coate Twoe Course Pillowe Coates	6	10	0
Item Fower Wrought Curtain for a bedd and Wrought Valliance one Counterpaine one Cheast Clothe ... [o]f the same a Cover for a Chaire ... [o]f the same 1 Cloath of the same for a Table one of the sa[me] for a sideboard Three peeces of the same for stooles fower peeces of the s[ame] ... bed posts with white Inside hangings for the bedd	4	0	0
Fower old napkins one Towell and Pillowcoate more		2	4
In the drawer			
one Silver Tanckard ... Spoones fowre Silver ... Cupps twoe ... Silver Porringer ... Cadle Cupp and ... Watch ... one gold ... [c]ornelian Ringe			

[2 fragmentary lines]

... [cha]mber ... Fether boulster ... one redd ... peece of greene Rugg ... [b]lanck[e] with old Curtain ... same Bedstidle Matt and ...	2	0	..
... Cheast one Trunck three Boxes one Hamper with some Glasses and one old Chaire twoe fruite dishes and one solibob Pott and Bottle Covered with Lether		5	0
One Pewter Bason one Plash ... p Twoe Screw [ca]ndlesticks and one other do Candlestick twoe galley potts and one basson		5	0
In the Chamber over the Kitchen			
Item One Fether Bedd one Fether boulster and one old Fether boulster Eight blancketts one Red rugg one Counterpaine with Curtens valiance Matt Bedstidle Matt and Courd	3	0	0
... old Truncke twoe old ... chaires one Wicker Chaire one old Box one old sid Cubbard One Chuishion one Close stoole and Pann one old birding peece and twoe old Musketts and Pockett Pistole	1	0	0
In the Chamber over the Stares			
One Fether Bedd one fether boulstar one Canv ... [b]oulstar ... and Courd	1	0	0
...		0	4
...	3	0	0
...		15	0
...	2	0	0
...		5	0
totalis	55	0	10

Exhibited 18 September 1679

Robert Smith and Thos Woodward [WSRO Ep I/29/65/52]

Will: made 3 Sep 1679; proved 12 Sep 1679
Three underage children
Executor in trust: Thomas Woodward, West Clandon, Surrey, clerk
Overseer: Thomas Smith of Binderton
Witnesses: Christopher Spencer, Richard Crockford, Robert Smith

[WSRO STC I/27/64b]

[1] Son of George, of London. St Paul's School, scholar. Oxford, Christ Church, exhibitioner 1660–1664, matriculated 1661 aged 17, BA 1664. Ordained deacon 1666, priest 1668 (bishop of Chichester). Vicar of West Dean 1668–1679. Rector of Westbourne 1679. Died 1679.

44. West Dean (Binderton) … Oct 1711 GEORGE SMYTH [1]

Appraisers: John Sadler, Thomas Peachey

	£	s	d
In primis his Wearing Apparel and money in Sussex	10	0	0
In the Library			
Item Books Thirteen Chaires One Table One Picture Two Andirons Firepan and Furnace	103	0	0
In the Stone Parlour the Library Closet			
Item 1 Table 10 Chaires Carpett 8 Pictores Firegrate	1	0	0
Four Chaires One Carpett Eight Pictures the Firegrate and Andirons 3 Pecttres	19	0	0
[Four lines in original confused and over written]			
In the smoaking Roome			
Item Four Chairs One Couch … 3 Pictures	8	0	0
In the Long Roome			
Item Sixteen Chairs Two Tables Ten Pictures one Couch One Pewter cistern	43	0	0
In the Storehouse			
Item two Chests One table Five Chairs 1 Sppining [*sic*] Wheell Ten glass jars [?]250 dozen of bottles One Still Two Andirons	6	0	0
In the Storehouse Passage			
Item Three Pictures	5	0	0
In the Withdrawing Roome			
Item the Hangings Five Pictures Irons Andirons Tongs Firepan Window Curtaines Flowerpott Given away Three Tables Twelve Chaires Two Stools Two glass Sconces Twenty Seaven Tea cupps	23	0	0
In the Lobby			
Item Five Chairs one Table Three Pictures one Napkin press and Cistern	5	0	0
In the [great] Parlour			
Item the Clock Seaven Sconces the Firehearth Irons Andirons tongs and … Flowerpott and Window Curtaines Gl … way … One Looking glass One Table … stands Fourteen Chaires and Cushions … Table and dishes	25	0	0
In the great [Parlour] Closet			

Item Six Chaires O ... One Table one Chest of draws Three Cushions Given away Two Cushions Twenty Pictures One Tea table and dishes	2	0	0
In the 2 Lobby Closetts			
Item Books Four Chairs Three Tables 4 Cushions	30	0	0
In the Hall			
Item One and Twenty Chairs Three tables Five Pictures Four Andirons Firepan Tongs Cop...	22	0	0
In the little Parlour			
Item Twelve Chairs Four Cushions ... Pictures Four Andirons Firepan and Tongs One Locking press Window Curtaines Two Andirons Given away Two Tables	10	0	0
In the Buttery			
Item Two Foarms One Table One Cupboard one p of Scales	1	0	0
In the Kitchen Closet			
Item Fourty Four Earthen dishes Two drinking Potts One Silly bub pott one Table one Coffee Mill	[no value given]		
In the Kitchen			
Item One Jack 4 Andirons One Fender one Ovenlid Three Tables One Warming pann Five Spitts Four Coppers Three Chaffing dishes One rack Two pairs of Scales One [?]powdry Pan Three pastry Pans ... Two Copper Scewers Two Frying Panns Three Cullenders Three Tin plates One Fish Kettle Three other Kettles Firepan and Tongs Five Potts Fifteen Candlesticks Four Tin[*sic*] hoops Two morters Six Copper dishes one Skimmer 2 brass rings Two Pewter rings Clever Chopping knife Two brass Skilletts Two ... Pint and ½ pint Potts Two Candle boxes 1 Meat Cover Three Gunns Six Lead Weights sixteen pewter dishes two pewter Cheese dishes Two petwer plates Twenty [?]Tafens pewter plates ... dripping Pans Two Sauce panns 2 doz pye plates	20	0	0
In the Kitchen Given away One iron chaffing dish			
Two Churns One Warming Pan One Breadgrater One Morter One Pr of Stillions Three Me … rings Two Coffee Potts one Tunnell Ten Candlesticks Five Dozen and halfe of Pewter plates Fifteen pewter dishes Four Pewter Covers One iron Slice	[no value given]		
In the Sellar			
Item thirteen Hogsheads Three powdering Tubbs one Wooden Tunell Given away 5 and ½ hogsheads 2 hogsheads Twelve dozen of Bottles	2	10	0
In C[?heese] house			
Item 1 Table 1 Tin the ... glies	3	0	0
In the Brushroome			
Item 1 table 1 Picture ... Two Chests One Chest of draws Cloathpress ... and all thereunto belonging 2 trunks	8	0	0
In the Blew ...			
Item Hangings 3 Pictures ... Bed Curtaines and all Things Thereunto belonging … Cushions Two Andirons Firepan Tongs a Sett of dressing Boxes one Looking Glass	10	0	0
In the Stairs Case			
Item Six Pictures 3 Chairs 2 Sconces Given away 1 Clock	15	15	0
The Great Parlour Chamber			
Item Hangings 2 Pictures Given away 1 bed Curtaine and all things			

th[erunto] belonging One Cabinnett and Cover upon it two ... Thing
upon 'em One dressing table boxes and Looking glass next looking
glass 1 table Two Sconces 6 Chairs 4 Stools China on the Mantelpeice
window Curtaines Firehearth Pan and Tongs Close Stool case | 10 | 0 | 0

    Great Parlour Chamber Closett

Item 1 Looking glass Given away 6 Chairs one Cuchions Table
hangings Matting | | 10 | 0

    In Dineing Roome

Item Eight Andirons 2 firepanns 2 tongs 2 fenders Two Pictures | 12 | 0 | 0

    Parlour Chamber

Item Hangings Two pictures Given away Red Curtains and all Things
thereunto belonging Chest of Draws 7 Chaires 5 Cuchions 1 Stoole a
great Looking glass 3 tables dressing boxes and looking glass 1 head
block four Andirons Firepan Tongs Ten table Covers Silver Coffee pott
sugar dish milk pott window Curtains | 2 | 10 | 0

    In the Hall Chamber

Item Bed Curtains and all Things thereunto belonging Looking glass
Hangings 1 Table 4 Andirons Tongs Firepan Chaires 2 Pictures window
Curtaines dressing Box and Looking Glass | 21 | 10 | 0

    In the Nursery

Item 4 Chests of Draws 1 [?]hair trunk 3 beds Curtains and all things
thereunto belonging 3 Chaires 1 picture 4 Andirons Firepan and tongs | 13 | 10 | 0

    In the Garrett

Item Two meal searches 1 meal kiver 1 Chest 2 desks 4 tables 4 Beds
Bedsteds and all thereunto belonging 1 more Bedsted 7 iron Casements
not put up | 8 | 19 | 0

    Smoaking roome Chamber

Item One bed and bedsted | 2 | 0 | 0

    In the Brewhouse

Item the maltmill Furnace and all things belonging to the Brewhouse | 20 | 0 | 0

    In Daryhouse

Item One Butter Charn ... Ten wooden Trays 1 Kiver 1 Wat[er] Tubb 1
renning Tubb 2 Washing [Tubbs] 1 Furnace 4 Cheese[?]moots 2 ...
hoops 2 Buckets Cheese | 4 | 10 | 0

    Abr[oad]

Item One Waggon Dun[g Cart] 2 barrows 1 plow 24 Wooden Chaires 4
Corn roolers 4 garden Roolers One Wheel barrow garden tools 2
Ladders 1 water tubb 1 Bushell 1 hay Rack | 18 | 10 | 0

    In the Wash house

Item Cheesepress Furnace Limbeck 1 table Bucking Tubb | 2 | 10 | 0

    Stable and Coach house

Item Fours horses Two Sadles Three Cartharness 3 plowharness 1
Charriott and Halters 2 bridles Given away 3 Horses One Coach and
Harness | 42 | 0 | 0

Item two hoggs Seven Cows Fourteen Sheep | 38 | 10 | 0

Item Tun of Hay Fifteen Qtrs of Oates 3 Qrs of Horsebeans 3 Qrs and
½ of Wheat Six Qtrs of Barley | 32 | 17 | 0

Item One Salver 11 Spoons 3 Casters 2 Salts silver | 10 | 0 | 0

Item Three Table Cloths Eleven Napkins		5 0 0	

Sum tot   616 12 0

That which is given away not valued   [WSRO Ep I/29/65/78]

Will: made 8 July 1703, codicil after birth of daughter Mary 12 Jan 1705; proved 12 Oct 1711
Wife: Barbara; son: Thomas; daughters: Barbara, Hannah (both under 21)
Kinsman: John Woodward, clerk, executor
Witnesses: Ursula Yates, William Bridges, John and Hannah Wakeford   [STC I/31/411]

[1] Son of Ellis, of Binderton, gent. Cambridge, Emmanuel, MA. Vicar of East Marden 1661–1711. Rector of North Marden 1664–1711. Married Elizabeth daughter of Richard Peckham at Up Marden 1687 (died c. 1691); Barbara daughter of Thomas Woodward, prebendary of Hova Villa, in the bishop's chapel, Chichester, 1693. Died 1711 aged 83; buried West Dean. Lived at the mansion house at Binderton, which is the subject of Grimm's drawing, 1787 (British Library, Add MS 5675 f 34).

45. Ditchling 8 Aug 1721 ELNATHAN IVER, vicar [1]

Appraisers: Henry Wood, John Chatfield

	£	s	d
In primis Wareing Apparel and Money in purse	5	0	0
Item in the Citchen			
One Stock plate three paire of Andirons one Dripping pan and other Impliments about the Chimney	1	15	0
Twenty eight pewter plates Seven Pewter Dishes one pye plate	2	0	0
Three tables Eight Chaires one Stoole		16	0
A Small Jack one Warmingpan one Screen and other Small Impliments	1	12	6
Item in the Haull			
One Clock and case Eight Chaire and one Table	3	12	0
Item in the Parler			
Two Tables 6 Chaires and one paire of Andirons	1	12	0
Item in the Pantery			
One Table and dresser two Pottage Potts Three Skilletts one poudering Tubb one Frying Pan one paire of Scales and Weights thereto one Flower Tubb one Desk box three Dishes and other Small Implements in the sd Room	1	16	0
Item in the Brewhouse			
One Furness One Brew-Vate one Tunn Tubb one Bucking Tubb Six Keelers two Small Tubbs and Koollers one Malt Mill two small Kittles one small Furness one halfe Bushell one Lanthorn and other Small Implements	7	10	6
Item in the Seller			
Eight Drink Tubbs four Stollages Eight Doz of Bottles and other Small Implements	3	5	0
Item in the Citchen Chamber			
One Fether Bed and Boulster two Pillows Three Blankets one Quilt and Bedsted Hangings and Sacking Bottom	3	15	0

Three paire of Course Sheets and one od [*sic*] one Five pair of Flaxen
Sheets Eight Pillow coates Seven Course table Cloaths Eigh [*sic*] old
Flaxen Table cloaths Six Flaxen Towels Six Course Towels one Dyaper

Tablecloth Eight Diaper Napkins and other Old Linen	4	14	8
One Tubb and Wheate and other things		7	6
Item in the Little Chamber			
One Bed and Steadle together with healling and all other thereto belonging	1	10	0
Item in the Maids Chamber			
One Feather bed and Steadle Curtaines and Quilt together with all other things thereunto belonging	4	0	0
Item in the Parler Chamber			
One Feather Bed and Stedle Quilt Bolster Blanketts Hangings and all other things thereto belonging	6	10	0
One Table one Glass one paire of Andirons and other Small things in the Sd Chamber	1	0	0
Item Lumber in the Brewhouse Chamber		7	0
Item Hoppoles	1	10	0
Item Wood and Faggets	1	0	0
Item Well buckett and chaine and Rope		6	0
Item Ready Money	20	0	0
Item the Libery of Books	5	0	0
Item Tyths due at Michaelmas 1721	48	11	3
Item things forgott and unseen		10	0
Total	128	1	5

[ESRO W/INV 1393]

Will: made 19 July 1721; proved 25 Oct 1721
Executor: Nathaniel Osborn
Witnesses: Henry Dungate, Henry Vaus   [ESRO W/A 51.66]

[1] Born Brentford, Midd, son of George. Cambridge, Christ's, admitted sizar aged 18 and
matriculated 1674, BA 1678. Ordained deacon 1678 (bishop of Winchester), priest 1708 (bishop of
Chichester). Curate of Uckfield from c. 1695. Vicar of Ditchling with chapel of Wivelsfield 1715–
1721, patron chancellor of Chichester cathedral. Died 1721; buried Ditchling.

46. Donnington ... Oct 1630 THOMAS HARRYSON [1]
[Poor original]

	£	s	d
In primis in the Hall			
two Tables forme halfe a dozen joyned stooles three joyned Chares and the Bench with the Wenscotte	2	0	0
Item one Cubbard one side Borde	1	0	0
Item one payre of Andirons a payre of tongs a fire pan and a payre of Bellowes		7	0
Item two Bench Quossions		1	8
Item in the Parlour			
one joyned Bedsteddle and Curtaines	1	0	0

Item a Trunck and a side Boarde …	..	..	..
Item in the Bakehouse			
a Silting troughe a tubb a Bolting Hutch wth other Lumber …	..	..	..
Item the manservants Bedd and Bedstedel to lay in two bolsters one Blankett and one Coverlett …	..	..	..
Item in an other lodginge Chamber			
one livery Bedsteddel Fether bedd two fether Bolsters two Blanketts and one Coverlett	2	0	0
Item in the same roome one Truckle Bedsteddel a Fetherbed one fether bolster one blankett one Coverlett wth some other Lumber …	..	..	..
Item in the Appleloft			
Apples Hopps Hempe wth other Lumber …	..	..	..
Item in the Chamber over the Hall			
one waney Bedsteddle a Fetherbed two fether bolsters two pillowes three blanketts and a Coverlett …	..	..	..
Item in the same Roome one waney Bedsteddle a Fether bed one fether bolster two blanketts and the curtaines …	..	..	..
Item three Chests …	..	..	..
Item a Dozen paire of Sheets … table Clothes two diaper napkins and dozen of other napkins …			
Item four pillowbers …	..	..	..
Item one Quilt a Mantell two pillowbers and an yron back in the Chimney …	..	..	..
Item in another Chamber			
one fetherbed two fether Bolsters two pillowes two blanketts one Coverlett and a Chest …	..	..	..
Item in the loft over the kitchen			
a pairr of Scalles wth an yron Beame and a Weaskett with other Lumber …	..	..	..
Item in an other roome			
Breweing vessells Drinkeing vessells foure truggs a round Table and a safe …	..	..	..
Item thre brasse potts three Brasse kettles two skilletts one Bedpan one Chafeing dish one skimer and a brasse furnace …	..	..	..
Item a … with other Lumber …	..	..	..
Item five Spitts two dripping pans one pr of Racks two payre of Wellhangers and a pair of Andyrons …	..	..	..
Item a Jacke to turne with the wei[ghts] …	..	..	..
Item foure laten Candlesticks three brasse candlesticks two duzen of putter two Chamber potts and one … with some other small putter …	..	..	..
[21 difficult and indistinct lines omitted , apparently stock and crops]	..	..	..
the Bookes	8	0	0
Wearinge aparell and Money [in] his purse	8	0	0
Sum tot	109	18	8

Exhibited 13 Oct [1630]: Elizabeth Harrison, daughter   [WSRO Ep I/29/68/10]

Will: made 25 Sep 1630; proved 30 Oct 1630
Wife: Elizabeth; five sons (all books to be sold to use of Thomas); three daughters
Property

Witnesses: Peter German, Nicholas Mos, Robert West   [WSRO STC I/18/31]

[1] Cambridge, Christ's, matriculated sizar 1594, BA 1598; called MA 1607. Ordained deacon and priest 1594 (bishop of Colchester). Licensed preacher Chichester, Lincoln, London and Winchester dioceses 1598. Vicar of Donnington 1598–1630, patron bishop of Chichester. Curate and sequestrator of St Andrew's, Chichester, 1607. Married Elizabeth Hillarie at Donnington 1629. Died 1630.

47. Earnley 1 March 1620 HENRY WARNER, parson[1]

Appraisers: Henry Smyth, Nicholas Colden, William Mansbridge, John Wilson, Humphrey Warner

	£	s	d
In the hall			
In primis one table foure shelves one chare and other old lumberment Theire		6	8
In the parlour			
Item one ioyned table a ioyned frame and six ioyned stooles	1	0	0
Item 3 chaires two little stooles and one little square table		10	0
Item one Cubhard and a cubhard cloth		13	4
Item two old benches two same boards five Cussions		6	0
Item a drie pike-head peece and soorde		8	0
In the loft over the hall			
Item pewter		16	0
Item three bedsteddles one flockbedd an hullbedd two bedd coverings two boalsters		16	0
Item one chest a corne sachar with other implements there	1	0	0
In the loft over the parlour			
Item two fetherbeds one bedsted one Covering a rugg with other appurtenances therunto	10	0	0
Item one other bedsted an old fetherbed with that belongs unto yt		3	6
Item one trundlebedsted an hulbed and an old Coveringe		10	0
Item fyve chests with other lumbermet there	1	0	0
Item in an outlett ioyning to the same loft hempe larde wooll and other implements there	1	0	0
In the kytchin			
Item one pair of andirons one paire of doggs one spitt 2 paire of tongues 2 pair of pothangers a dripping pan 2 pair of potthookes 2 trevets an iron to sett before dripping pans with other iron stuffe		16	0
Item nyne peeces of brasse one iron pott with other brasse	3	0	0
Item six hogges of bacon	4	0	0
Item 2 cheese presses six tubbes a bolting hutch with other lumberment ther	1	11	8
In the milkehouse			
Item 10 trugges wth other milking vessels and all other lumberment there	1	0	0
In the butterie			
Item six barrells five ferkins one churne and other implements there	1	0	0
Item 16 cheeses		16	0

	£	s	d
Item Lynnen Item six table cloaths 2 towells napkins 2 dosen tenn paire of sheets with all other Lynnen	4	10	0
Item his apparell and money in his purse	6	0	0
Item one silver salt one boule 2 spoones	5	0	0
Item his bookes	2	0	0
Item wheate threshed and wimbeld 11 quarters	10	0	0
Item 5 bushell of pease and one bushell of beanes			12
Item wheat in the barn unthreshed	8	0	0
Item barley unthreshed	5	0	0
Item sacks an old wimsheet a willie a bushell and a corne shovell		10	0
Item otes fetches and hey	2	0	0
Item hennes and geese	1	3	0
Item 8 hogges	1	13	4
Item two kyne with calves by ther sides four without calves and two yearling bullocks	17	0	0
Item two rackes 3 ladders		3	4
Item 13 sheepe	3	5	0
Item thre horsbeasts and harness to them	13	6	8
Item two plowes and tymber in the hall house with other implements there		10	0
Item one dungg pott thills and wheeles they stand upon with two harrowes	1	13	4
Item one long cart a paire of wheeles one dung pott a paire of thilles Other implements of husbandrie	1	12	4
Item woodd and tymber		10	0
Item 5 acres of wheate upon the glebe		5	0
Item 3 acres upon the lease land	3	0	0
Item more nyne bushell of pease and two bushell of beanes	1	4	6
Item old iron		5	0
Item one old fowling peece		6	0
Sum totall	123	5	2

[WSRO Ep I/29/72/5]

Will: made 14 Feb 1620; proved 8 April 1620
Wife: Mary, executrix; sons: George, William, Samuel (all under 21); daughters: Elizabeth, Gartred, Catherine (all under 17); sister's daughter: Jean Webster
Overseer: brother-in-law, George Rogers
Witnesses: John Tomson[?], Humfrie Warner   [WSRO STC II/Original W26]

[1] Called MA 1602, 1604. Ordained deacon and priest 1602 (bishop of Ely). Rector of Earnley with Almodington 1604–1620, patron bishop of Chichester. Died 1620.

48. Earnley 22 April 1669 SAMUEL FOWLER [1]
Appraisers: Robert Parker, Thomas Colestock
At the instance and request of William Lelam a creditor to the estate

	£	s	d
Without Doores			
Item one little white Maire valewed att	5	0	0

Item 2 piggs in the Gaite att	1	4	0
Item one Cocke one henn 3 duckes att		2	0
Item 2 quarters of wheate Pt unthreshed	3	0	0
Item 1 quarter of Oates de … Will Lelam		12	0

In the Kitchin and Butterie

Item one litle table and 2 three leged stooles		1	6
Item 4 smale dishes 2 porengers 1 pint pott 1 Chamberpott one Candlesticke		8	0
Item 4 kettles whereof 2 very smale 1 brass candlestick 1 warming pann one Laidle	1	5	0
Item Trenchers Earthen porengers drinking Nogins and 2 wier candlestickes att		1	0
Item 2 P tongues 2 old Fier Shovells a clever A Frieing pann one cotterell 1 P pott hookes		3	6
Item a brass pott that leake att		7	6
Item a lookeing Glass att			6
Item 4 drink vessells att		13	0
Item one saife one Lanthorn 3 wooden dyshes		1	6
Item 2 serches one sive 1 baskett one adle		1	6
Item one wooden Boule one half Boushll One Gallon 2 kervers one Buckett	8	1	8
Item a spitter a shovell and Racke att		1	4
Item the lopp of a tree att			6

In the Chamber

Item the bedinge and bolster sorie stuff Pt Flocke and old att	1	5	0
Item darnix curtaies and vallians 3 Blanketts and 1 Rugg wth the old Carpett att	1	5	0
Item 2 pictures att		2	0
Item 4 P sheetes and ½ old and decayed	1	4	0
Item 2 Table clothes very old and tender wth dozen ½ of napkins and towells	1	4	0
Item 3 shirtes 2 wascoates		10	6
Item bandes and cuffes wth a hawkeing bagg		3	0
Item peeces of Broken Groates bittes of silver wth a Silver dram cupp		8	0
Item 2 smale trunckes and 4 deskes		14	0
Item in that Chamber 1 Boush ½ of Beans		3	0
Item Linen redie to make handkercher att		5	0
Item Ratt eaten Candals att		2	0
Painteing stuffe in a boxe att		1	0
Item a Parsell of Books as dixenaries Sermon Bookes mathematickes Arethmaticke some Lattin some for Prayer some for Gardening some Geografie some manuscripts some Playe bookes some old some young att		15	0
Item a parcell of old Iron wth tooles in a boxe		5	0
Item his weareing apparell decayed att	2	5	0
Item two old sackes and the Rotten Haye att		5	0
Item the mayd velld Mr Lelam in Gold and Silv[er]	1	11	0
Item a Ring and a Spoone valued att Wch the Mayde had in her possession		12	0

	£	s	d
Item more dellrd sayd Lelam at his death in Gold	20	16	0
Item more two Ringes valewed by the Goldsmith		11	6
Sum totalis	48	3	6
Since dell by the mayde to me in the presence of Mr Mills		10	6
	48	14	0

Exhibited by Richard Manning, notary public, for the administrators, 5 May 1671

[WSRO Ep I/29/72/12]

Administration 19 April 1669
To William Leland of Earnley, principal creditor   [WSRO STC III/I/77]

[1]   Oxford, Christ Church, matriculated 1654, BA 1657, MA 1660.   Rector of Earnley with Almodington 1667–1669. Died 1669.

49. Eastbourne ... 1720 THOMAS BYSSHE, vicar [1]
Appraisers: Thomas Sinnack, John Mortimer

	£	s	d
In the Kitchen			
For one Dozen of Leather Chairs	1	10	0
For two Tables and four Chairs	1	0	0
For one pair of Brandirons two pair of Tongs and one Fire Shovell		6	6
For two pair of Window Curtains		4	0
In the Parlour			
For 10 Cane Chairs and Cushions	5	0	0
For three Tables and a Corner Cubbard	1	1	0
For one pair of Andirons one pair of Tongs and a Fire Shovell		5	0
For one large Glass	1	0	0
For two pair of large Window Curtains and two Window Squabbs	1	1	0
For the Hangings of the Room	1	10	0
In the Buttery			
For two brass Kittles one Warming Pan a Chaffing Dish a Sauce Pan three pair of Cande Sticks a peper Box two Save Alls and one pair of Snuffers	1	15	0
For one bell Brass Pott and three Skilletts		13	0
For one Copper Tea Kittle one Coffee Pot and one Sauce Pan		16	0
For one large Iron Kittle 3 Potts one Mortar and Pestle a pair of Gridirons one double Ring and one Driping Pan	1	18	0
For Six Iron Candle Sticks one Cleaver two Smoothing Irons two Cane irons and some other small things		10	0
For two Tinn Coffee Pots a Driping Pan a Lanthern a Candle Box and Some other Tinn Things		6	6
For Nineteen Pewter Plates 10 Dishes one Bason two Candlesticks	1	11	0
For one Table one Dresser and some wooden things		14	0
For one Stone Mortar and some Earthen Ware		10	0
In the Brewhouse			
For one Copper Furnace	5	0	0
For Six Tubbs and five Keelers	2	6	0
For two Mawkins four Barrells and some small Casks	1	8	0

For one pair of Andirons Fire Shovell and Tongs one pair of Creepers one pair of Creepers one Iron Prong two pair of Pott Hooks 1 Kittle one Slice and 6 Iron Skewers	17	0
For one Jack two Spitts one frying Pan one fender	15	0
For two Water pails Four Wooden Platters one pair of Bellows one Prong 2 Chairs and some other Wooden things	7	6
For two Leathern Bags and two Sacks	9	0
For one Well Buckett and Roap	6	0

In the Seller

For Five barrells 3 Stollages two Powdering Tubs two Keelers one Trunnell and some other small things	1	17	0
For twenty Dozen of Bottles	2	0	0

In the Kitchen Chamber

For one Bed as it Stands	7	0	0
For one Chest of Draws	2	0	0
For one table a Dressing Glass and Box		18	0
For four Chairs		14	0
For one Press	1	1	0
For two pair of Window Curtains		12	0
For Creapers Fire Shovell and Tongs		4	0
For hangings of the Room	1	0	0

In the Buttery Chamber

For one Bed and Some other things	2	5	0

In the Parlour Chamber

For one Bed as he Stands	10	0	0
For one Chest of Draws	3	0	0
For one Table Dressing Glass and Carpet	1	0	0
For Five Cane Chairs and Cushions	2	0	0
For one Pair of Andirons		2	0
For Hangings of the Room	1	0	0

In the Kitchen Garret

For one Feather Bed as it Stands	3	0	0
For one Table two Chairs		4	0

In the Parlour Garret

For one Bed as it Stands	1	10	0
For one Chest and one Trunk		7	6
For one Side Saddle one Pilleon a Portmanteau and a Limbeck	1	8	0
For three Dozen of Plates	1	12	0
For 18 Dishes and a Pie Plate	1	6	0
Linnen For two Dozen of Damask Napkins and 3 Table Cloaths	2	14	0
For one Dozen and a half of Flaxen Napkins		15	0
For two Dozen of fine Diaper and 2 Table Cloaths	2	2	0
For one Dozen of fine Flaxen and 2 Table Cloaths	1	0	0
For one Dozen and a half of Diaper		18	0
For Seven pair of fine Flaxen Sheets	8	15	0
For ten pair of Coarse Sheets	5	0	0
For Six Huccaback Towells		9	0
For Seven pair of fine pillow Coats	2	0	0
For one Dozen and a half of Coarse Towells		9	0

	£	s	d
For 2 Dozen of Coarse Napkins		12	0
For four small Diaper Table Cloaths	1	0	0
For three Fine Diaper Towells		5	0
For Knives and Forks		10	0
For Silver Plate	25	0	0
For a Watch	3	0	0
For China	1	10	0
For two Horses Saddles and Bridles	11	0	0
For Wearing Apparell and Money	25	0	0
For things not observd	1	0	0
	136	18	6
	36	6	6
Totl	173	5	0

[ESRO W/INV 1244]

Will: made 3 Oct 1716; proved 24 June 1720
Wife: Elizabeth, executrix; brothers-in-law: Thomas and John Woodyer
Witnesses: Gerald Reeves, Thomas Holland, William Marten   [ESRO W/A 50.239]

[1] Son of Christopher, of Cuckfield. Oxford, St John's, matriculated 1677 aged 17; Oriel, BA 1681. Cambridge, incorporated 1704; Christ's, MA 1704. Ordained deacon 1681, priest 1682 (bishop of Chichester). Master of Cuckfield Grammar School 1682–1704. Curate of Lindfield from c. 1687. Rector of Tarring Neville with South Heighton 1698–1720. Vicar of Eastbourne 1704–1720, patron treasurer of Chichester cathedral. Married Elizabeth Woodyer at Wivelsfield 1691. Died 1720.

50. Elsted 30 April 1647 JOHN KNIGHT, minister [1]
Appraisers: Walter Tomlinson, Richard Randall senior, John Stott

	£	s	d
In primis The wearinge Aparell and the money which the said John Knight had in present possession	5	0	0
Goods in the Hawle			
One Table and frame one chaire one form one joyned stoole one saw with some other small things	1	0	0
Goods in the Parlour			
A Clock	3	0	0
Item one Table and Frame one livery Cupbord Fowre ioyned stooles and one chaire	2	0	0
Item one Cubord	1	0	0
Item Fowre Cushion stooles two cushion Chayres		12	0
Goods in the litle chamber			
One Querne one Gunn one Musket and one small Flockbed	2	0	0
Goods in the milkhowse			
One Safe two Chernes with small things	1	0	0
In the Buttry			
Six Barells one kneading trough with other small things	1	0	0
In the kitchin			
Three spitts two Iron drippinge pans an Iron Jack one table three			

chayres two ioyned stooles two iron potts two paire of pothangers one
Iron oven pill two paire of brandirons one paire of tongs etc | 4 | 0 | 0
      In the hawle chamber
Three bedstedles two Feather bedds three chests two boxes one presse
two Coverletts two boulsters one side table and one chayre | 10 | 0 | 0
      In the parlor chamber

	£	s	d
One high bedsteddle one halfe bedstedle with thappurtenances	6	0	0
Item two chests sixe stooles one livery cupbord	1	10	0
Item in Linnen sheets table cloathes napkins with some other linnen	10	0	0
Item in Pewter three dozen one Flaggon Fower Candlesticks	2	5	0
Item in Brass two kettells one brasspot three skilletts one Furnisse and two warming pans	2	10	0
Item one Featherbed boulsters Curtaines Bedstedle with thappurtenances	5	0	0
Item one Trunke		10	0
Item one table and Frame and one Forme	1	0	0
Item one Table and frame		6	0
Item Eight Quarters of Malt	8	0	0
Item Fowre hoggs of Bacon	3	0	0
Item two Quarters of Wheate	4	0	0
Item one Waggon two dungpotts ploughs yoakes chaines etc	10	0	0
Item one brewinge Fatt and one hoggetrough		6	0
Item Fifteene acres of wheate	15	0	0
Item Five acres of Oates	3	0	0
Item Six acres and a halfe of Pease	4	0	0
Item Six acres of barley	4	10	0
Item Six Kine	18	0	0
Item Two oxen	8	0	0
Item Three 2 yearlinge beasts	6	0	0
Item Five 1 yearlings	7	0	0
Item Three Weand Calves	1	10	0
Item Eighteene small sheepe	5	0	0
Item Two Mares	7	0	0
Item Nine hogs and piggs	5	0	0
Sum total	178	19	0
Item there is a lease of Lidseys Parsonage	80	0	0
Item Books	2	0	0
Sum totalis	260	19	0

[WSRO Ep I/29/80/7]

Administration to Anne, wife 25 May 1647   [WSRO STC III/K/55]

[1] Rector of Elsted 1625–1647. Married Ann Burton of Elsted at Elsted 1626. Died 1647.

51. Elsted 29 Oct 1672 HENRY SNELLING [1]

Appraisers: William Downer, John Knight

	£	s	d
In primis his wearing apparrell and money in his purse	5	0	0
In the kitchen			
Item two cupbords one table one furnasse three spitts three chaires one forme two old dripping pannes and other old Lumber	2	0	0
In the hall			
Item one table and forme		10	0
In the parlour			
Item the bookes of the Deceased	2	0	0
Item one bed with furniture one table six stools one side cupbord and other things	4	0	0
In the low Chamber			
Item one bed with furniture to him belonging	1	0	0
In the Inner chamber			
Three chests one trunck one side cupbord one presse twelve paire of sheets foure dosen of napkins two table clothes two paire of pillowbers and other old linnen	8	0	0
In the outer chamber			
Item foure beds with furniture with some other lumber	5	0	0
Item twelve dishes of pewter foure flaggons two chamber potts with other small pewter	1	5	0
In the Washhouse			
Item three potts three kettels foure skilletts One warming pann and one frying pann	1	10	0
In the Buttery and Milkhouse			
Item six barrells foure verkins two butte charnes foure kivvers one bucking tubb two dozen of treyes foure bucketts and other small wooden materialls	2	10	0
Item for butter and cheese and other provision	1	5	0
Without dores ~~in the~~			
Item for wheate and barly unthreshed	20	0	0
Item for oates and hay unthreshed	10	0	0
Item for pease and teares unthreshed	3	0	0
Item for one paire of oxen one Cow and calfe	10	0	0
Item for three small horsebeasts	6	0	0
Item one waggon one dungpott two plowes two harrowes and other materialls belonging to husbandry	6	0	0
Item Six hoggs and seavem small shutts	6	0	0
Item things seene and unseene in and about the house		10	0
Item in desperate debts	37	0	0
Item ten saxes		10	0
Suma totalis	132	0	0

[WSRO Ep I/29/80/12]

No will or administration found

[1] Oxford, Balliol, BA 1629. Ordained deacon 1629, priest 1630 (bishop of Oxford). Rector of Elsted 1647–1672; of North Marden 1662–1664. Vicar of Lyminster 1669–1672. Died 1672.

52. Fernhurst 9 March 1687 ABELL STEPNEY [1]
Appraisers: William Clarke, John Challen

	£	s	d
In primis his wareing cloathes and money in his purse	2	0	0
in the hall			
three tables five chaires three joyned stooles two paire of brand Irons three formes one paire of tongs and other utensills	1	0	0
in the Citching			
one furnace one [?]candlestick two brass Skilletts three Iron pots one Iron Kettle three spits one driping pan 2 gridirons one warming pan with other stuff	1	5	0
one fate 4 Keelers one tubb other stuff five firkins one stand and other utensils	1	2	0
in hall Chamber			
two beds a feather bed and a flock bed two bed sheets and all belonging to the beds two chests one chaire	1	10	0
in the Citching Chamber			
three shelves		2	6
for bookes		5	0
five pewter dishes		5	0
Six paire of Sheetes with other linnen	1	10	0
One horse one pigge	1	10	0
Two fliches of bacon	1	10	0
	11	19	6

Exhibited 30 March 1687 by William Stepney, son   [WSRO Ep I/29/82/64]

No will or Administration found

[1] Called MA 1681. Curate of Fernhurst from c. 1675; of Linchmere from 1681. Died 1687.

53. Fernhurst 31 Jan 1739 HENRY BAKER[1]
Appraisers: Richard Luffe, William Lucas

	£	s	d
First Wearing Apparell and Money in purse	11	0	0
In the Parlour			
Two Tables Six Silver Spoons Seven Chairs one pair of small Andirons and some China Ware	1	17	0
In the Kitchen			
Two tables Six Chairs one Jack and Cupbord with drawers therein two pothooks One pair of Andirons a Fire pan and Tongs Six pewter dishes Twenty pewter plates two Spitts four Candlesticks two pair of Billows and two Box Irons	2	11	0
In the Pantry and Drink House			
Eight Beer Barrells four Dozen of bottles One frying pan and One old			

	£	s	d
desk	1	10	0
In the Brewhouse			
One brass Furnace one Vate one Tubb two Kivers one brass Skillett two tea Kettles one Buckett and two poridge potts	1	15	0
In the Parlour Chamber			
Three feather beds two Steadles two Quilts two Coverlids Curtains Vallence and all thereunto belonging Six Chairs One Chest of Drawers one other Chest one Box one looking glass and one Clock	11	6	0
In the Chamber over the Kitchen			
One feather Bed and Steadle Curtains Coverlid Vallence and all thereto belonging One pressbeed frame One chest one cloathes Press and all the Linnen	6	17	6
Seven Chairs a looking Glass a Bedstead and Table a [blot] Pan some old bookes old well buckett and rope and a hog Cestern	1	18	0
Wood and Old Lumber		2	6
Four Gold Rings	1	0	0
Half a Dozen of Knives and forks		2	0
Due to the deced on Note of hand from Wm Wackeford	28	0	0
Due to Ditto on Note from Mr Geo Osborne for principal and Interest	37	18	6
Due to the deced from the Right Honble Anthony Viscount Montague	13	10	0
Due from Mr Henry Boxall for a Years Rent for a Meadow	2	0	0
Total	120	17	6

[WSRO Ep I/29/82/102]

Administration 19 March 1739
To Anne Baker and Mary Baker, daughters   [WSRO STC III/P/5]

[1] Son of Henry, of Midhurst. Oxford, Exeter, matriculated 1682 aged 17, BA 1686. Ordained deacon 1687 (bishop of Chichester). Licensed curate and preacher of Fernhurst 1687. Curate of Lodsworth 1691. Rector of Linch 1699. Died 1738.

54. Ferring 15 July 1670 STEPHEN WORGAR [1]

Appraisers: John Snellinge, gent, John Pannett, Henry Manning

	£	s	d
In primis his Wearinge apparell and mony in his purse	10	0	0
In his Beddchamber			
Item two Feather Bedds two Feather bolsters one blankett one Coverlett one bedd stedle curtaines and valence curtaine rodds the beddstedle matt and coards	8	0	0
Item the hangeings in that chamber		12	0
Item six Flower Chayrs and two stooles		18	0
Item one Lookeing glass	2	0	0
Item one payre of dogg Andirons and a Little table		2	0
In the Chamber over the Hall			
Item one Featherbedd two Feather bolsters one Rugg curtaines vallence and beddstedle	4	10	0
Item one press in that Chamber		5	0

In the Buttery Chamber

Item one Flockbedd one Flockbolster one Feather bolster one blanckett one coverlett and a little beddstedle		6	8
Item one truncke and a close stoole		6	8

In the Chamber over the milkhowse

Item one Feather bedd two Feather bolsters two blancketts one Coverlett one beddstedle curtaines valence matt corde two pillowes two stooles and One Chayre	3	..	..
Item one Truckell beddstedle one flockbedd one flockbolster two blanketts matt and corde	1	5	0
Item one Joyned Cheast		6	8

In the Parlor

Item one draweinge table one Carpett one side boarde Cloath and Cushen	2	0	0
Item one douzen of Rushe Chayres	1	16	0
Item one Clock	1	10	0
Item one payre of Andirons fyre shovell and tongs		5	0

In the Hall

Item one Little table one Chayre one cubbertt and one carpett		4	0

In the Butterie

Item two duble barrells one kilderkin one firkin three tubbs two keelers two searches one tunnell a little powdering tubb one Frying pan and a Charne	1	6	8

In the Inner butterie

Item two kilderkins one dubble barrell two stallages and old Cubbert and shelves		10	0

In the milkhowse

Item nine milketrayes and the shelves		15	0

In the Brewhowse

Item one Brass Furnace and the brew Fate	2	0	0

In the Cheesehowse

Item the Cheese press hoops and vallowes		6	8

In the Kitchen

Item the pewter in the whole	3	2	0
Item one still		9	0
Item three brass keetles three brass possnetts and warming pann		7	0
Item two Ironpotts two potthangers two payre of potthookes two payre of tongs two Fyer shovells two Fyer Forkes one payre of brandirons one payre of smale racks and three spitts	1	2	8
Item the bacon in the Chimney	1	0	0
Item one Jack		10	0
Item one bacon rack one table and Frame one morter and pestle one lanthorne one …cketts two latten dripping pans the dishes and trenchers and spoones	1	0	0

The Lynnen

Item sixteene payre of sheetes	5	6	8
Item Five douzen of napkins	1	5	0
Item Fifteene table cloths	2	5	0
Item three course table Cloths		3	0

	£	s	d
Item seaven Cubbert Cloths		17	6
Item ten payre of pillowcoats	1	5	0
Item Fourteen towells		7	0
In plate	3	10	0
Item one Lookeing glass		1	6
Item the studdy of bookes			
Without doores			
Item in wood and Fursse	1	0	0
Item two hoggs	1	6	8
Item one Cowe	2	10	0
Item one horse	6	0	0
Item the wheate on the ground	13	0	0
Item the Barley on the ground	7	10	0
Item the pease and teares on the ground	2	0	0
Item the hey and horseharnes And Implements of husbandry		10	0
Item eight hives of bees	1	4	0
Item a dung court and wheeles		5	0
Item things that were not seens And forgotten	1	10	0
Some totall	117	2	4

[WSRO Ep I/29/83/24]

Administration 19 July 1670
To wife, Sara   [WSRO STC III/I/115]

[1] Possibly curate of Heathfield. Vicar of Ferring with Goring and Kingston by Sea by letters patent of Lord Protector 1657; vicar of Ferring by institution 1661–1670. Died 1670.

55. Findon 8 May 1725 RICHARD WOODESON, vicar [1]

Appraisers: Richard Batcock, John Butters

	£	s	d
In primis The Deceasd his wearing apparell and Money in his house and purse	78	3	6
Item in the Parlour			
one large glass a clock a corner cupboard a large oval Table a little square table a Great chair a couch bed 9 Cane chairs whereof one great one a limnd Piece and some printed ones of no great value window curtains Andirons fender fireshovel etc	7	19	0
Item in the Hall			
a long great table a small oval one a Skreen 4 leather chairs a press cupboard an old printed piece two old sconces ore the Chimney Andirons etc	1	6	0
Item in the best chamber			
Tapistry Hangings a workd bed with Quilt blanketts etc a little Square table and drissing glass a chest of Draw 3 stools two Cane Chairs a Close Stool with the pan a Picture ore the Chimney window curtains Andirons etc an old dutch ovel table etc	13	12	0
Item in the hall Chamber			
an old Chest of Draws a Cloaths press a Feather bed two bolsters and			

curtains the Hangings of the Room a little table a Great leather Chair a
leather Stool two Cane Chairs and a Glass ore the Chimney a pair of
Andirons window curtains and a Red Trunk etc | 4 | 7 | 8

Item in the little Chamber adjoyning

a featherbed Bolster Curtains and papr Hanging a little square table two
old Chairs and a stool Window Curtains an old Trunk etc | 3 | 2 | 6

Item in the Study

Books and paper etc | 5 | 0 | 0

Item in the Hall Chamber Closet

my mothers Books a large Silver Tankard and Salver a two handled
Cupp a porringer 3 salts 10 spoons whereof two guilded 9 Silver
teaspoons etc | 16 | 15 | 0

Item in the maids Chamber

1 bed 2 stedles and pillows etc 2 old Chests and a still etc | 1 | 9 | 0

Item in the man's chamber

2 feather Beds 2 bedsteads etc a Bagg of Hopps etc | 2 | 16 | 0

Item all the Linnen in General | 9 | 16 | 6

Item In the Kitchen

11 Dishes 3 dozen and 8 Plates Toaster Cullendar 1 Salts dripping pan 2
tables 2 forms 3 spitts smoothing Irons stilliers Jack Grate Shovel poker
Tonges slice and Fork Spitrack pothooks fender Warming pan 4 Bra 3
Iron Candlesticks cleaver Bellows Pestle and Morter Copper pot 2
saucepanns Frying pan Skillet 3 … Kettle Panns Dishes and platters etc | 9 | 0 | 6

Item in the Bakshouse

[?]Grice Bagg and sifters meal Tubbs Dow Tubb and Scales etc | | 9 | 0

Item in the Brewhouse

well bucket Rope Chain Brew Tubb Tun Tubb Cooler 4 other Tubbs
Keeler 4 Pales a Limbeck copper Furnace wooden Horse etc | 4 | 17 | 0

Item in the Inner Pantri

4 Powdring Tubbs Butter Tubb Crocks Panns and old Table etc | 1 | 6 | 0

Item in the outward Pantry

Brass Kettle and Stew Pan 3 beer vessells etc | 1 | 6 | 0

Item in the Cellar

5 Drink vessells 5 doz of Bottles etc | 1 | 12 | 6

Item in the Garden Room

Linnen Cupboard and Press Glass Cage and Glasses etc | | 8 | 0

Item in the little Pantry adjoyning

A Candlechest other little things there etc | | 9 | 6

Item in the Granary

10 bushell of oats 14 Bush of Wheat 3 bush of Tail Barly 12 old and 12
new sacks a woolspoke a Bushell peas…. and 2 shovells 2 shoals
prongs and rakes spade Handbill and ax etc | 8 | 12 | 0

Item out of Doors

2 Hoggs 1 Horse 1 Mare 400 Faggots a Chaldron of Coals Hay bullock
Racks etc | 21 | 13 | 6

Item for Things forgot or unseen | 1 | 0 | 0

		£	s	d
Item Money at Interest		300	0	0
	Tot	494	17	0
Desperate Debts				
In primis to Delahay lent upon Interest		200	0	0
Item for ten years Interest of the Same at 6 per Cent		120	0	0
Item lent Mrs Denham on Bond threescore pounds		60	0	0
The Interest thereof for		480	0	0
	Totall	974	17	0

Exhibited 21 July … [WSRO Ep I/29/84/73]

Will: made 12 Oct 1724; proved 1 March 1726
Eldest son: Richard, executor (with sister-in-law Elizabeth Heming, spinster); five children
Witnesses: John Mathers, Elizabeth Richardson [WSRO STC I/33/293]

[1] Son of John, of Windsor, Berks. Oxford, Magdalen, chorister 1662–1672, matriculated 1670 aged 17, demy 1672–1677, BA 1673, MA 1676. Vicar of Findon 1676–1725, patron Magdalen College. Married Dorothy Hemming at St Martin's in the Fields, Westminster, Midd, 1702. Died 1725.

56. Firle 12 June 1685 JOHN SWAFFIELD [1]
Appraisers: Sackvile Graves, James R …

	£	s	d
In primis his apparrell and money in his purse	10	0	0
Item Stilliards		5	0
Item Pewter in the Kitchin	1	0	0
Item Brasse in the Kitchin		6	7
Item Tins		1	0
Item Iron potts Spitts andirons etc	1	10	0
Item a Clock	1	0	0
Item Bacon [*sic*] Item Chaires Tables Settles etc		10	0
In the Buttery			
Item 9 Barrelles	1	0	0
Item 5 Dozen of Bottles and Glasses and potts		15	0
Item knives			6
Item powdering tubbs Sive etc		2	6
In the Brewhouse			
Item 2 small furnaces	2	0	0
Item tubbs		10	0
Item Coales		10	0
Item a Still and Sack etc		6	0
Item a Saddle		4	0
Item in the Parlour			
table and Chaires etc		6	0
In the Best Chamber			
Item 2 bedds hanging bedstead and a bed cloth	5	0	0
Item a Chest of Drawers and Lookeing Glass	1	10	0
Item Chaires a table		12	0

Item Andirons bellowes etc		5	0
Parlour Chamber			
Item Sheetes and Napkins and other Linen	5	0	0
Item a bedd bedstead bedcloths and hangings	2	0	0
Item Bookes	4	0	0
Item Lumber and other things		2	6
Sum	39	16	2
Item desperate debts about the sume of	6	0	0

[TNA PRO PROB 4/9083]

Will: made 4 May 1685; proved 13 June 1685
Son (under age); daughters
Executors: Mr John Shore and Mr Henry Snooke
Witnesses: John Earsby, John Hinckley, Mary Waycort   [TNA PRO PROB 11/380/77]

[1] Possibly Cambridge, St Catharine's, admitted sizar 1673. Ordained deacon 1677, priest 1678 (bishop of Salisbury). Vicar of Glynde 1680; of West Firle 1681–1685, patron dean and chapter of Chichester. Licensed preacher Beddingham 1680; Chichester diocese 1681. Curate of Beddingham 1682. Wife Martha (died 1681). Died 1685.

57. Fittleworth 23 June 1637 RALPHE BLINSTONE [1]
Appraisers: William Polinge, William Marckes

	£	s	d
In primis his wearinge Apparell and Money in his purse	2	0	0
Item one Feather bedd one feather bolster one feather pillowe one truckell bedstedle two Coverletts one blankett and one Matt	2	10	0
Item one bed ticke of corse Canvas one old bedsteddle two blanketts and a Coverlett and one old Matt	1	0	0
Item three payer and one Sheet two table Clothes and 6 table Napkens three towells one wallett	1	2	0
Item one little round table two old Truncks one Chest one box three Chayers		16	0
Item one old sword one scaffe wth [?]a speatuie glasse		5	0
Item about halfe a Tod of wooll and some hopps		12	0
Item 14 bushells of wheat one bushell and a halfe of Rie and Fower sacks two bagges and one poke	1	13	4
Item all his Boockes	1	0	0
Item one halfe bushell measure one pecke and one halfe pecke smale leaden weights	1	2	0
Item one Table and a frame seaven Joyned Stooles		13	4
Item two ketles one Iron pott two skillets one little spitt one fyer pan one payer of potthoockes one little payer of tonges one Clever and one Choppinge knyfe	1	5	0
Item one ~~sheshe~~ fletch of Bacon one buckett		5	0
Item two pewter dishes two porrengers Six spoones one Salte one brasse Candlesticke two latten Candlesticks one latten drippinge pan one fryeinge pan		6	0
Item one liverie Cubberd one kever		4	4

Item Fower Firkens Fower tubbs one boule	8	0
Item ~~tornes~~ two tornes one pronge one Iron rake one Corne shovell one spitter one becke one hatchett	5	0
Item one old Sadle a pannell	2	0
Item two young hogges	15	0
Item one Table wth tressels two Ladders boardes wood and faggotts and all other Lombrie	1 0	0
Item one Mare and a Colt two hens and a Cocke	1 13	4
Item one Barne which is moveable if he be removed Within ten dayes next after his decease	5 0	0
Som totalis	22 16	6

[WSRO Ep I/29/86/26]

Will: made 28 March 1637; proved 28 June 1637
Wife: Jane; son: Ralph; cousin: William Blinstone of London (bequeathed sword)
Property and land
Burial at Egdean
Witnesses: Edward Fogden, Mary Hampton, widow   [WSRO STC I/19/66]

[1] Ordained deacon 1592 (bishop of Chester), priest 1601 (bishop of Colchester). Rector of Egdean 1621–1637, patron Crown. Licensed preacher Chichester diocese 1635. Died 1637.

58. Fittleworth 19 Feb 1669 WILLIAM HINDE [1]

Appraisers: Edward Fogden, … Winson

	£	s	d
for the hale			
In primis 1 Jacke 1 payer of Andirones 1 payer of tonges 1 fender 2 musketts wth bandallers and sourds 1 morter one payer of fetters 1 tostingiron 1 fire pann 1 ~~Chaffing dishe~~ Chirne 1 treste1 Cutting knife wth other [?]forme	1	7	4
Item 1 brass skillett 1 warming pan one Candlesticke 1 lanthorne and other brasse		8	0
for the kitchin			
Item 16 peeces of pewter 2 Chamber potts 2 Candlestickes 3 porringers 2 saucers 3 saltselers and other small pewter	1	17	2
Item 3 table 1 frame 2 joyned stooles 9 Chayres 3 Cubbords 4 drinke vesles 1 tube 1 keever 1 powthering tube one stand 1 …… 1 hutch 1 payer of billowes 1 salte box 2 buckets 22 trenchers and other wooden thinges	3	2	8
for the lofte over the hale			
Item 1 joyned bedstedle 6 old trunkes 1 Chest and one box and 6 bed [?]stames	1	11	4
t 1 fether bed 1 boulster 1 pillow 6 blankets wth the Cushens	3	5	8
Item all his wearinge Apparrell and money in his A Purss and some desparat debtes	12	10	4
Item in Redy money and sillver plate	355	1	6
~~Item 18 payer of sheets 3 dozen of napkins 11 table clothes towells and other linnen for the Study Item all his Bookes~~	~~5~~	~~0~~	~~0~~

For the Barnes

Item 10 qters of wheat 3 qters of Rye 12 Qters of barley 4 qters of oats 2 bushels Of pease 4 bushels of tares and some hay	35	10	0
Item all one bridle 1 sadle 1 speeter one Shovell 1 pronge 1 beill hooke 3 lokes		10	6
Item 3 ladders and wood bordes 1 rake Some hopes and hempe 5 sives and Reeders and other lumbrey	1	2	4
Item one shutt		8	0
Suma totalis	416	14	2

[WSRO Ep I/29/86/46]

Administration 22 Feb 1669
To William Hinde, gent, son   [WSRO STC III/I/72, 103]
For probate account see **185**

[1] Cambridge, Christ's, matriculated sizar 1612, BA 1616, MA 1620. Oxford, incorporated 1627. Ordained deacon and priest 1619 (bishop of Peterborough). Vicar of Fittleworth 1625–1655, patron bishop of Chichester; sequestrated 1655; restored by 1662 until c. 1669. Licensed preacher Chichester diocese 1635. Died 1669.

59. Fittleworth ... 1681 WILLIAM HOWELL [1]
Appraisers: Richard ... , John Fowler, Nicholas Coates
[Original damaged and incomplete]

	£	s	d
In primis his wearing apparel and money in his purse	5	0	0
...chamber			
... chaires ... bench a table a rac pott ... andirons a paire of ... shovell and tongs ... a mapp ... the hangings ... roome	3	10	0
...			
... tables one forme six chaires a muskett a sowrd and a paire of bandyleeres a paire of iron racks a paire of andirons fyre pann and tongs a paire of gridirons a fender a jack five smoothing irons an iron dripping pann a salt boxe a paire of bellows ....cradle a paire of bras scales fower pewter dishes five pewter pye plates two spitts a cupboard for spice earthen weare and Lumber	3	7	0

    Kitchen

Item a furnis a brewing vate a mesh tubb six kivers two tunns a bucking tubb two paire of pott hangers two paire o[f] pott hooks two iron potts one iron kettle one bras kettle three bras skilletts a bras Skimmer a bras Ladle a bras warming pann a bras candle stick two tinning candlesticks two ..e candlesticke three tinning dripping pans a fish plate a pye plate a tinning cover for meate a ... Sawce pann ... pewter porringers fower pewter sawcers a tinning aple corer a tinning pott a pewter bason fower pewter platters One pewter Chamber pott fower white ... chamber potts one iron ... an iron morter and pestle ... cleaver a shredding knife a dozen wooden trencher plates three ... trenchers three ... halfe bushell one peck ... measures a paire of snuffers a tinning plate for them a lantorne two woodden peeles a hanging safe two woodden trayes a

[?]ntt a spitter a Couell a bill and Lumber		3	15	0
... buttery				
....powdring tubb a salting ... sacks stands ...			..	..
...	[Total]	15	0	0

[WSRO Ep I/29/86/46]

Administration ... 1681
To Robert Scutt of Petworth, creditor, during minority of children: William, Margaret, Humfrey and Thomas. [WSRO Ep I/31/5/16]

[1] Oxford, St John's, MA. Ordained deacon 1660, priest (bishop of Chichester). Curate of Petworth c. 1666. Vicar of Lyminster 1666–1669; of Fittleworth 1669–1681, patron bishop of Chichester. Prebendary of Fittleworth 1673–1676; of Somerley 1676–1681. Rector of Egdean 1677–1681, patron Sir William Goring, bt. Died 1681.

60. Ford 5 June 1644 JOHN MARSHALL [1]
Appraisers: John ?Patte, Thomas Martin

	£	s	d
In primis five qtrs of wheat	17	0	0
Item burnt old mear		10	0
Item three kyne	7	10	0
Item tenn sheepe	2	10	0
Item one hogg		10	0
Item one Fetherbed one Fether boulster 2 pillows a payer of Blancketts one coverlett and a paire of Curtaines	3	10	0
Item one flockbedd three payer of sheetes one table cloth and a side Cubboarde cloath	1	0	0
Item six peeces of pewter a flagon a Double salt	1	0	0
Item one Brass pott on brass skellitt One Chamber pott		16	0
Item a brass kettle a burnt furnace A burnt jack and a spitt		10	0
Item two old Tables and a piece of a Side Cupboard		10	0
Item two old chaires		2	0
Item his bookes	5	0	0
Item his wearing apparrel monie in his purse and debts upon bond	10	0	0
Item things unseen forgotten and of small matter		10	0
	39	18	0

Exhibited by Frances Martin, widow [WSRO Ep I/29/87/10]

Will: made 23 May 1644; proved 22 Oct 1644
Niece: Frances [Martin]
Overseer: Mr John White
Witnesses: John White, Thomas Cosen, Thomas Haseler [WSRO STC I/21/17b]

[1] Of Cumberland. Oxford, Queen's, matriculated 1608 aged 16, BA 1612, MA 1616. Ordained deacon 1613 (bishop of Oxford), priest 1622 (bishop of Chichester). Rector of Ford 1626–1644, patron bishop of Chichester. Died 1644.

61. Funtington (East Ashling) 4 Nov 1686 SEBASTIAN PITTFIELD [1]
Appraisers: Mr Johnn Scardevill, Mr John Clerk

	£	s	d
In the Parlor			
In primis … of green …	1	..	..
…		18	0
Four tables and formes …		10	0
… leather chaires one … Chair and two leather stools	1	2	0
Three Maps		15	0
Three curtain rodds and two valence curtaines	..	4	0
Fire pan and tongs two pair of Andirons and a pair of bellows		10	0
Four bullrush chairs		8	4
One picture of Ezekiell and others	..	0	0
In the Hall			
Item A Clock and the appurtenances	..	0	0
A still		16	0
A Couch frame		2	0
Two Tables and one carpett		4	0
Napkin press with a drawer		8	0
A Forme and three rush chairs		3	0
A cheilds table chair		3	0
Two pair of Andirons		4	0
Curtain curtain rod and pictures		2	2
Two dozen of trenchers		1	6
A Joynd stoole			6
A baskett		1	0
Six cushions		3	8
In the Kitchen			
Item A side table great table and dreshinge board with …..		12	0
Twelve pewter dishes	1	3	0
Two duzen of pewter plates and six pewter sawcers	1	6	0
Eleven pewter porringers	..	10	0
Six candlesticks and a sackbotle		5	0
A pewter bed pan		4	0
One lattin Cr…..			..
One lattin chaffing dish			..
Two lattin patty pans		1	8
One lattin pudding pan			9
One lattin Angle … asle		1	0
A lattin fish plate			7
A lattin dripping pan			..
A lattin candlestick			..
A lattin candlebox			9
A flower box and pepper box			9
Three lattin …		2	2
Three kettles		11	0
A chease pan		7	0
Two warming pans		6	0
Four brass skilletts		4	0

One bell skillett		5	0
Two bell mettall potts		14	0
A bell meatle chafeing dish		..	10
A brass Ladle			4
Two brass skimers		1	0
Two brass frying pans		5	0
A Jack and chain and weight		6	0
Four spitts		5	0
Two iron drippinge pans		5	0
Six iron sinders			..
A tosteinge iron and Cup iron		1	2
Three pair of gridirons		2	6
Three pair of smoothing irons		2	8
Two iron chafeing dishes		4	0
An iron Oven stoper		4	0
A cleaver			6
A fryinge pan		1	6
A skimer and flesh forks			4
Two pair of Andirons and dogs		10	0
Fire pan and tongs		1	6
Two iron potts		..	0
Four pair of pott hangers		5	4
Three pair of pott hooks		2	0
An iron bender			8
Two settles two forms four chairs and a pair bellows		5	0
…. dozen of trenchers			5
Pictures			5
A bread grater			10
A copper pott pestle and mortar		2	6
A litle bell		1	0
…. a glass			4
In the little Parler			
Item a Table three Joynt stooles baskett chair carpet & Pictures		8	0
In the Pantry			
Item A safe three … a fine search and a form		4	0
In the Brewhouse			
Item The wooden ware (viz) Tubbs stands barrells table and Basketts	1	10	0
Two furnaces	3	0	0
In the Dary			
Item The leaden pans		12	0
… th milkpans		4	0
White eartheware		1	0
A butter charne and two tubbs		..	..
A cheese press and hoops		2	0
In the seler			
Item … grose of bottles	1	16	0
Beere	4	0	..
In the parler Chamber			
Item … Quilt featherbed bolster two pillows two blanketts bedstead …	10	0	..

Two …		2	0
… painted hangings with gold leather	3	0	0
A chest of drawers and dressingbox	2	10	0
Table and carpett		6	0
Two druggett chairs		3	6
Three … of painted stuffe		8	0
Eight bullrush chairs		8	0
One lookinge glass		6	0
One Map		3	0
Two window curtains		3	0
Andirons fire pan tongs and bellows		6	0
A Bender and Clocke	3	0	0
In the Hall Chamber			
Item Linnen never used	6	0	0
Nineteen pair of sheets	..	0	0
Pillow coats		14	0
Seven table cloths	1	1..	0
Course napkins		10	0
A druggett furniture	2	4	0
Stripe stuff hangings		14	0
A Cyprus Chest		12	0
A spruce Chest		4	0
Fine Napkins two dozen	2	0	0
Five fine table cloths	3	0	0
Three fine Towells		3	..
Course towels a duzen		7	0
A feather bed bolsters blanketts …. pillow and rugs	7	10	0
One painted callicoe counterpain		7	0
Four rush chairs a trug and a box		5	..
A cradle		4	0
Two pair of fine sheets	2	0	0
A diaper counterpaine		12	0
In the bigger Closett			
Item Boles glasses and other things	1	0	0
In the Kitchen Chamber			
Item A green printed furniture with a bedstead and sackcloth bottom	2	10	0
Feather bed bolster blanketts and pillows and rug	4	0	0
A purple furniture	1	10	0
Bedstead sackcloath bottom bolster pillows blanketts and rug	4	10	0
One table and carpett		6	0
Side board and lookinge glass		2	6
A hanging shelfe		1	2
A Chest of drawers		10	0
Four trunks		9	0
A painted box		1	6
Three pictures and a mapp		10	0
One Spruce box		8	0
Three chairs and a stoole		3	0

In the Maids' Chamber			
Item For a bed and other things	2	10	0
In the little parlor chamber			
Item Bed and furniture	3	15	0
In the cheilds Closett			
Item Plate	30	0	0
In the mans Chamber			
Item bed and furniture	1	15	0
Wool and Lumber	1	5	0
In the Barne			
Item Nine Acres of barly	10	0	0
Fifteen acres of Wheat	18	0	0
Peas	7	0	0
A load of old wheat	6	0	0
Sacks van and winnowinge sheets	1	5	0
A reeke of Hay	2	0	0
Item necessaryes for husbandry	6	0	0
Wood and other Lumber	6	0	0
A great bell	1	10	0
In live goods			
One horse	1	4	6
five sows	12	10	0
… younge beasts	8	0	0
Twelve sheep	5	0	0
Item in books and wearing apparell	10	0	0
Item Money at use	270	0	0
Sum	515	8	0

[TNA PRO PROB 4/6656]

Will nuncupative: made 12 Sep 1686; proved 3 Nov 1686
Wife: Mary, executrix; daughter: Grace (guardian Gabriel Hastings)
Witnesses: John Ridge, Richard Cole, Mary Bembowe   [TNA PRO PROB 11/385]

[1] Probably of a Dorset/Middlesex gentry family. Oxford, Magdalen, matriculated 1649; Wadham, BA 'by favour of Thomas, Lord Fairfax, and Oliver Cromwell' 1649. Ordained deacon or priest or both 1662 (bishop of Bristol). Curate of Wymering, Hants, c. 1668–1670. Rector of Warblington, Hants, 1671–1686, patron Richard Cotton, esq. Died 1686.

62. Funtington (Ashling) 6 Dec 1694 JOSEPH JACKSON [1]
Appraisers: John Forder, Thomas Bonny

	£	s	d
In the Kitchin			
Racks Andirons tongs fireshovels Spitts Jack Bellows tables choppingknife Potthangers Cleaver Chaffingdish Saltbox Smoothing irons Pestle and mortar Candlebox Candlesticks and snuffers Chaires and stool Skewers Fork Flowerbox Pewter Case of six knives Earthen potts and dishes A fowling piece glasses sheep print setting stick Still basting ladle gridiron vall[ue] all as in the margin	3	18	0

In the Washouse			
A furnace a Fatt tuns Chivers tubbs Kettles skilletts scales bucketts			
Brass pott dripping Pan frying pan some wooden dishes flasket basketts vall[ue] all	4	5	0
In the Milkhouse			
Trays Powdring tubb shelfs and dresser		5	0
In the Parlor			
A Couch Chaires table hangings Chimny broom Shovel tongs and doggs vall[ue] all att	4	0	0
In the Hall			
A table Chaires sconce Escucheons Map pictures Andirons vall[ue] att	6	12	0
In the room under the staires			
A side saddle Pillion roadsaddle and hors Bridles Fetters and Cock curry comb horse cloth	3	0	0
In the Kitchin chamber			
A bed and furniture Chest of drawers table Glass stands Chaires and cushions Andirons shovel tongs A ... nest of boxes and escritoir vall[ue]	7	0	0
In the Parlor chamber			
A bed and furniture Chair table fender	3	5	0
In the study			
A great chair Chest and books vall[ue]	20	0	0
In the chamber over the hall			
Two beds bedsted and stool	1	0	0
An old chest trunk and linen	3	2	0
In the Cellar			
Eight vessells sixty gall cyder Bottles	3	0	0
Wearing apparrell	5	0	0
Without door goods			
A well buckett rope and chain Cheespress hogtroughs hutch Plough and chain harrows shovel spitter wood and fagotts ladders Cyder press baggs Cheespress barrell churn apples and hopps Sacks hogwash tubb	5	0	0
In the barn			
barly wheat oates pease	19	6	0
	82	13	0

[WSRO Ep I/29/90/94]

Will: made at Chichester 23 Nov 1694; proved 12 Jan 1695
Wife: Lois, executrix ; sons: Thomas, Joseph, Robert; sister: Elizabeth (deceased) wife of
William Trusler; brother-in-law: Francis Doyly
Books to be sold
Property in Bosham, East and West Ashling
Witnesses: John Ellerger, Richard Shudd, Mary Denton   [WSRO STC I/30/200]

[1] Son of Thomas, rector of West Stoke with Funtington, deprived for nonconformity 1662, owned house at Funtington, died 1669. Oxford, Trinity, matriculated 1682 aged 16, BA 1686. Ordained deacon 1688 (bishop of Chichester). Curate of Sidlesham 1689. Married Lois Tayer of Charlton in Singleton at Singleton by licence 1690. Died 1694.

63. Goring 1 April 1690 RICHARD SPENCER [1]

Appraisers : Hugh Penfold, Edward Weston

	£	s	d
In primis his Apparrell and ready money	20	0	0
Item In the Kitchen at Field Place			
four pewter dishes seven plates one flaggon one poringer and Candlstick all pewter two small brass skilletts		18	0
Item two small iron potts A pair of pott hooks a pair of Pothangers Iron Andirons a pair of Gridirons one spitt fire pan and tongs fire forke and belows		18	0
Item four truggs wooden dishes and about a dozen of Trenchers and four very old stooles and other small things		6	0
Item in the brewhouse			
one keeler five tubbs and old Cask	1	0	0
Item four flitches of bacon	2	11	0
Item one powdring tubb two Cerces old frying pan a parsell of bottles two kilderkins one Hogs head and ferkin and other lumber	1	6	8
In the Chamber over the Buttery			
Item one fetherbed and bolster steddle old Curtains and two blanketts and app[urtenances]	2	0	0
Item two paire of sheets eleven napkins six towells a pair of pillocoats two table cloths and an old Chest	1	5	0
His books of all sorts	10	0	0
Parlor Chamber			
Item one fether bed bolster Rugg and blankett Curtains stedle and App[ur]t[e]n[ances]	3	0	0
Item seven working oxen and hale an ox	31	0	0
Item five two yearling and four twelvemonth bullocks	13	15	0
Four fatt Oxen and fifteen fat sheep	38	0	0
Thirty Ewes and thirteen Lambs	9	0	0
Four young hoggs One sow and fifteen young shoots	6	15	0
One lame Colt	1	0	0
Item wheat at Field Place barnes Thashed and untrashed	8	0	0
Barley there	10	0	0
Oates there	3	0	0
Tares and hay	1	0	0
Item half the waggons Carts plows Harrows fan to winnow with and other tackle	7	10	0
Item two load of Barley sold Mr Page	7	6	8
Item sown on Field Place land nine Quarters of Wheat and five bushells	13	9	6
Tillage sowing and fallowing the wheat land etc	5	12	9
Fallowing barley ground there	3	9	8
Item Tares sow at Field Place farme	3	10	10
Item peas sown there	2	0	0

Tillage and sowing the said tares and pease	4	1	6
At Court Farm In the Kitchen			
Item one table and form five Chaires and old Cupbord		7	0
Item two brass kettles three brass skilletts warming pan skimer and ladle	1	2	0
Item seven pewter dishes five plates two poringers one Candlestick bed pan and Chamber pott	1	8	0
Item one Iron Kettle two spitts two p of pothangers one fire prong fire pan and tongs slice and Andirons pothoks and flesh prong Gridirons and bellows	1	2	0
Item four flitches of bakon	3	0	0
Item Trenchers wooden dishes and other things		2	6
Butterey			
Item baking keeler little table frying pan two sarces and buskett and other small things there		17	6
Milkhouse			
Item a powdring tub salting trough Churn hoops and fallows and eighteen truggs and other wooden things and other small things	1	16	0
In the Hall at Court Farm			
Item one table and five Joyned stooles		12	0
Parler there			
Item one table five Joyned stooles Three leather Chaires and p of Andirons	1	5	0
Little buttery			
Item five beere vessells bottles and stand	1	5	0
Best Chamber			
Item one fether bedd two bolsters one pillow Rugg and three blanketts Curtains valents bedsteddle and appurtences	5	0	0
Item four Chaires two stooles Chest of drawers one Chest and p of Andirons	1	2	0
Item four pair of sheets to pair of pillow coats two doz and halfe of Napkins six tablecloths six towells	3	4	6
Item one lookinglasse		15	0
Parlor Chamber			
Item one fether bedd two bolsters pillow three blanketts and rugg Curtains and valents bedsteddle and apps.	4	0	0
Item one old flock bed wth the Apptences	1	0	0
Item a little table and old trunk		4	0
Servants Chamber			
Item three old beds and three bolsters Ruggs and the steddles wth Appurtences one old steddle and a parcell of wooll	5	6	0
On Court Farm lands			
Item one hundred and twenty sheep and Thirty six lambs	37	0	0
Item eleven sheepe more	5	10	0
Item seven Oxen one bull stagg one Bull and one heifer	12	0	0
Item one sow one bore and twenty shoots	8	16	0
Item three porkers	2	2	0
Item Five horses one Mare and harness	24	0	0
Item wheat	24	0	0

Barly		15	0
Pease	5	6	8
Hay and Tares	3	0	0
Item a wagon two plows two dungcarts and four harrows and other husbandry tackling	12	0	0
Item twenty three whattels		11	6
Item twenty three quarters of barly In the Granary	11	10	0
At Campions barn and Gates andc			
Item five Cows wth Calves and five yearling	21	5	6
Item a Sow and four shoots	2	2	6
Waggon there	2	0	0
Barly there	7	0	0
On Mr Fletchers Farms			
Item four Cowes four Calves and a steer	15	10	0
A parcell of peas	8	0	0
Oates	3	10	0
Item manglers and oats	1	3	4
Sown on Court Farm lands Fletchers and Campions			
Twenty four quarters six bushells and an halfe of wheate	34	14	9
Item tillage plowing and sowing these wheat lands	15	15	6
Item sown ten quarters four bushells and an halfe of Oats on the said Farms	5	5	0
Tillage and sowing the oat grounds	2	5	10
Item Tears sown on the said Farm six quarters and three bushells	4	5	10
Sown pease there seventeen bushells and an halfe	1	15	0
Tillag of the said tare and peas ground	5	18	2
Item fallowing twenty seven acr barly	4	19	0
Item thirty three sacks	2	0	6
Item Lumber small things forgot	1	0	0
Item due to the deceased on bond	10	5	0
Item a ….	1	0	0
Item due to the deceased for tythes	40	0	0
The full sume is	614	9	3
Due from Sr William Goring for Re[nt] of a Farm Called Court Farme	30	0	0
Due from Barnes the Carrior For pigons	2	10	0
Due to the deceased for rent of the seven acres	2	0	0
due for part of a Hogg fold	1	9	0
Tot	650	8	3

[WSRO Ep I/29/092/06]

Will: made 11 May 1689, codicil 9 March 1690; proved 10 April 1690
Wife: Sarah, executrix (with son John); sons: Daniel, Thomas (under 21) Richard (under 21); daughters: Sarah, Hester, Susannah (all under 21); child to be born
Overseers: George Gittins, John Fletcher
Witnesses: William Barnard, William Davis, Elizabeth Snelling   [WSRO STC I/29/58]

---

[1] Oxford, Balliol, BA. Ordained deacon 1661 (bishop of Oxford), priest 1663 (bishop of Llandaff). Vicar of Goring 1663–1690, patron Nathan Weston, gent. Licensed preacher 1663. Married Sarah Gittence at East Preston 1675. Died 1690.

64. Goring 10 Feb [1704] MICHAEL SOROCOLD [1]
Appraisers: … tington, … as Petow…
[Damaged and incomplete]

	£	s	d
In primis his wearing Apparrell and Money	2	..	..
… Kitchin			
Item one clocke one Jack …Tables Iron and other things	4	..	..
in the Parlour			
Item Chaires Glass [t]abes and other things	..	..	..
In the Brewhouse and Seller			
Item one furnass one Cool[er] one Bar[rel] Tubbs Kilderkins verkins and other things		..	..
in the Milkehouse			
Item one brass kettle one powdring tubb and other things		..	..
in the Parlour Chamber			
Item one bed and all thereto be[lon]geing Table Glasse and other things			
in the Passage			
Item one press	..	..	
in the Kitchin Chamber			
Item one bed and all thereto belonging chaires Drawers Glass and other things			
in the Closett			
Item Plate and other things			
in the Brewhouse Ch[amber]			
Item one bed and a[ll ther]eto b[elon]geing	2	..	..
in the Maids chamber			
Item one bed and all theereto [belong]eing seven Pair of Sheets and other …	..	..	..
Item Bookes	5	..	..
Things unseen and forgott	..	..	
Without Doors			
Item One horse one Mare two Cowes two Runts horse harness Hoggs and Piggs	..	..	..
Item two hogg tubbs Boards and Husbandry Ta[ckling] … Item Hay cordwood and Faggots	..	..	..
Item wheat on the Ground	9	..	..
Item Barley unthrashet in the Home barne	5	..	..
… Two and Twenty Bushells of Tares [eig]ht old sacks and other Tares and Wheate …ed in Snows Barne	15	16	0
totall	101	5	0

[WSRO Ep I/29/92/76]

Will nuncupative: made 12 Jan 1703; proved 5 April 1704
Wife: Mary; daughter (unnamed)
Trustees: Mr Mellish, John Young, John Spencer
Witnesses: Joseph Morris, John Spencer, John Foreman   [WSRO STC I/30/669 and 752]
See also **65**

[1] Son of James, of Leigh, Lancs. Oxford, Brasenose, matriculated 1685 aged 17, BA 1688. Cambridge, Jesus, MA 1695. Vicar of Goring 1690–1704, patrons George Fettiplace, esq., and John Tucker, gent. Curate of Lancing 1691; licensed curate there 1702. Married Mary Keyse of Goring at St Mary Magdalene's, Old Fish Street, London, 1699. Died 1704; buried Goring.

65. Goring 11 May 1709 MICHAEL SOROCOLD [1]

Appraisers: Francis Halsey, John Peachey
Goods etc left unadministered by widow Mary Sorocold

	£	s	d
In primis in the Kitchen			
One jacke One paire of Andirons one pair of Doggs Fire Shovel Tonges			
One Fender One pair of Bellows Two pair of Cotterells One Cleaver			
One Choping knife One pair of Gridirons Two Smoothing Irons One			
Iron Driping pan Two spitts One Iron Heater Six Iron Skivels One			
Tosting Iron Two Iron Candlesticks	1	2	0
Two pair Brass Candlesticks One Pair		4	0
Tin goods Brass Morter and pestle		5	0
81 pewter plates		12	0
One Dresser Three Tables One Cubbord		18	0
One Chafing Dish of Iron		1	0
Five old Rush chaires Six knives Six Forks		2	6
One Iron Back		8	0
In the little Parlour			
Nine Cane Chaires One Iron Back One pair of Andirons Firepan and			
Tongs One pair of Bellows One haire Brush		10	0
One Clock and Case	1	5	0
In the Chamber over the little Parlour			
One Bedsted wth a Sacking bottom wth A raised Tester Curtains and			
valliants One bed boulster Two pillows Three Blanketts One Large			
Quilt	10	0	0
Window Curtains and Rodds		8	0
One Glass One Table and Six Chaires	2	0	0
For the Chainey on the Chimney mantle	1	0	0
In the Kitchen Chamber			
One Table Two Chaires One pair of Andirons firepan and Tongs One			
pair of Bellows One Glass		13	0
Two Blanketts Window Curtains and Rodds		15	0
In the Great Parlour Chamber			
One Bedsted matt Corde and Curtains One other Bed One Bolster Two			
Pillows Three Blanketts One Quilt	5	0	0
One Glass One old Chest of Drawers		19	0
One pair of Andirons Firepan and Tongs One Close Stoole Four old			
Sarge Chaires One old Childs Chair		12	0
One pair of fine Holland Sheets	2	0	0
Eleven pair of Sheets	4	0	0
Two pair of Holland pillowcoats		10	0
Twelve homemade fine Napkins		10	0
One table Cloth and Eleven Napkins of Damask	1	10	0

One Table Cloath and Napkins of Huckerback	1	0	0
Twelve Course homemade Napkins		3	0
Nineteen fine thin homemade Napkins		8	0
Five Fine table Cloaths		8	0
Six Course Table Cloaths		5	0
Nine Course Towells Three finer 4 older		5	0
Four a Muzling Twilight		2	6

In the Garrett over the Little Parlour

One Bedsted with a Sacking bottom One Pair of Curtains One
Featherbed Two Bolsters Two Pillows Blankett One Quilt One Table

Two old Sarge Chaires one small Glass	4	0	0

In the Maids garrett

One press Old Blew hanging		4	0
A Sidesadle Thread and Flax		2	6
One palet Bedsted Matt and Cord		4	0
Three Baggs of Feathers		5	0

One Silver small Salver three Casters Two Silver Salts One Silver
Porringer One Small Taster six Spoons flat handle One round handle

Spoone One Mustard Spoone a Small haire Bodkin	12	0	0
Three Wooden Casters Three Glases Nine Coffe dishes		3	0
For a parsell of small vialls		1	0
For Bees wax		1	0

In the Pantrey

Six Dozen of Bottles		10	0
For Shelves and Eight Trays		4	6
Scales and Weights Two Sarches		5	0

In the Brewhouse

One Brewing Furnace one small Furnace One vate and Stand	3	0	0
Five Kivers Four Tubs One large Tunnel		14	0
Two Iron Potts One Iron Kettle		7	0
One Brass Tinned Pott		12	0
One Brass Kettle		6	0
Two Brass Skilletts Two Bucketts		3	6
A Kitchen Coop		3	0
Eighteen Vessells Three Bear Pins		16	0
Three Powdering Tubbs		6	0
One Cord of Wood		16	0
Tot	65	5	0

Exhibited 11 May 1709, by Martha Keyse mother and executrix of Maria Sorocold
widow, deceased   [WSRO Ep I/29/92/77]

Will of Mary Sorocold, of Chichester, made 1 Aug 1708: proved 11 May 1709
                                                       [WSRO STD I/6/53]

---

[1] For biographical details see **64**.

66. Graffham 7 May 1634 WILLIAM STEPNETH, parson [1]
Appraisers: Robert Clark, Benjamin Sandam, George Hill

	£	s	d
In primis in the Hall 2 shorte tables with forms stooles and one Cubboard	1	0	0
Likewise in the Chimney a cast Backe two brandirons cast a fier shovell a paire of tongues two paire of pothangers and two spittes		13	4
Item in the parlour one Bedsted and Trundle bed with two feather bedes furnished	5	0	0
Item in the same roome one Table a ioyned chaire 3 ioyned stooles a ioyned chest 3 trunckes one cofer and one boxe	1	10	0
Item linnen in one Truncke	1	0	0
Item one Carpet and Coverlet	1	0	0
Item in a Chamber 2 beds furnished	2	0	0
Item in his Study in Bookes	5	0	0
Item in his Study one Table one ioyned stoole one Bedsted and one Chest	1	0	0
Item in the Kitchin in wooden vessells	1	10	0
Item in pewter and Brasse there	2	0	0
Item in other wooden lumbrey		3	4
Item one Heyfer and calfe and 3 swine	4	0	0
Item his wearing aparell	2	0	0
Summa totalis	27	16	8

[WSRO Ep I/29/93/21]

Administration 9 May 1634
To Agnes, wife   [WSRO STC III/G/253]

[1] Possibly Cambridge, Peterhouse, admitted 1604, scholar 1604–1608, fellow 1608. Rector of Graffham 1608–1634, patron Crown in minority of Thomas Garton. Died 1634.

67. Graffham 14 May 1673 THOMAS BURGES [1]
Appraisers: Henry Napper, Thomas Mounfeild the elder

	£	s	d
In primis in his weareing Apparrell and moneys in his purse	10	0	0
In the Chamber over the Parlour			
Item one Feather Bed wth the Testor and all other furniture belonging unto him	5	0	0
Item seven Ells of Course Cloth		..	0
Item one Trundle Bed wth that belonging unto him	1	0	0
Item A presse		15	0
Item one paire of sheets six Napkins and five Towells		11	0
Item Twelve paire of Sheets Two Duzen of Napkins two table Cloths wth fower pair of pillow Coats	4	10	0
Item Three Chests one Chaire wth a Box and other necessarys		10	0
Item a Still		5	0
In the Studdie			
Item the Bookes	10	0	0

In the Chamber over the Pantrie

	£	s	d
Item a side Cupboard a little table a Chaire with other Lumber		6	0
Item a flocke Bed		10	0

In the Citchin Chamber

Item Fower quarters of Mault	3	0	0

In the Parlour

Item a Table and three ioyned stooles		10	0
Item Six Chaires and a Livery Cupboard		15	0
Item two paire of Brandirons		6	0

In the Haule

Item a Table five ioyned stooles wth a Cupboard	1	5	0
Item Five Chaires		5	0
Item a Jack two paire of Brandirons two spitts a fire Pan a paire of Tongs and a little table		10	0
Item one duzen of Pewter wth other smaller peices of pewter		10	0

In the Citchin

Item a furnace two Brasse Kettles one Brasse pott three Brasse skelletts	1	10	0

In the Buttery

Item the Barrells stands Tubbs Civers and other Lumber	1	0	0

In the Pantry

Item a fatting Trough and a old Table		5	0
Item the Wheat Thresht and Unthresht	10	0	0
Item the Rye	1	0	0
Item fower Hogs	2	0	0
Item an old Mare		10	0

[WSRO Ep I/29/93/46]

Will: made 5 April 1673; proved 19 May 1673
Wife: Mary, executrix; sons: Thomas, William; daughter Elizabeth, wife of Thomas Lowe rector of Selham; son-in-law Henry Clare of Hurstland and three children
Overseer William Yalden of Blackdown
Witnesses: William Todman, William Ede
Books (named) to son-in-law and overseer
10s to poor   [WSRO I/25/117b]

[1] Son of Thomas, of Heckfield, Hants. Oxford, New College, matriculated 1624 aged 19, BA 1627, BCL 1631; Balliol, MA 1630. Ordained priest 1627 (bishop of Llandaff). Rector of Graffham 1654–1673. Died 1673.

68. West Grinstead 22 Sept 1637 JAMES HUTCHINSON [1]

Appraisers: Thomas Hudson, Edmond Attree, Thomas Whittington

	£	s	d
In primis his wearing apparell and Mony in his purse	50	0	0

In the great Parler

Item one long folding table one aubry Cupbord one greene carpet 6
Cushion chayres 2 ioyned chayres 12 Cushion stooles 2 low chayres 6
turky worke cushions and one long cushion a p[air] of brand irons a

p[air] of creepers fire shovell tongs and bellowes and 5 pictures	7	8	0
In the hall			
Item one long table 2 ioynd formes 2 Chayres 3 stills one earthen bason and frame	2	1	0
In the litle Parler			
Item the table and side table forme 2 chayres 16 ioynd stooles and one low stoole brandirons fire shovell and tongs one carpet and 8 cushions	1	14	0
In the Kitchin			
Item one table and forme 2 short benches one old Cupbord 3 low chayres one dresser a blocke a ioyned stoole 4 shelves and 2 muskets furnished	1	3	0
Item one jacke 5 spits 2 iron ketles 3 iron pots one posnet one great mortar and pestle a stone mortar 2 iron dripping pans a frying pan a grediron 2 chafing dishes a flesh hooke an iron peele brandirons fireshovell and tongs 2 p[air] of pothangers a p[air] of pothookes an iron to lay before the fire a Clever a shredding knife a fire prong a trivet 4 Candlesticks and ... b.t 2 smoothing irons	3	4	6
Item one brasse fornace 3 ketles 2 brasse pots 3 brass mortars and 3 pestles 1 chafingdishe 5 posnets one ladle 2 scummers 2 brasse candle sticks 2 latin candlesticks and one latin dripping pan	4	10	0
Item 2 great iron pots 2 Cans 3 bottles five earthen dishes a lanthorne and a bandpot and houre glass		5	6
In the Brewhouse			
Item one brewing fatt 4 keelers 2 brew tubs 4 halfe tubs 2 renning tubs a butter tubb a 3 leggd keeler a powdering tubbe 2 Churnes a Cheese press 3 milke keelers one stallage a Coupe one bucking tubbe 8 barrells and a firkin 6 payles a tundish 3 wooden platters and 2 wooden bottles and other lumber	3	8	0
In the Bake house			
Item 3 olde tubs a bunting hutch and a great bowle 3 little tubs 2 peeles 2 searces one bushell one halfe bushell one pecke 2 hampers ... of feathers one wicker basket 4 shelves		13	0
In the milkehouse			
Item Trugs 17 two tables 13 shelves one forme 2 p[air] of blades wth the weights one olde tub 2 small keelers 7 cheese hoops 3 mootes 4 Crocks of butter 35 cheese and other earthen ware	3	11	0
In the buttery			
Item one bin a glasse cage 10 dozen of trenchers 4 stallages 2 hogsheads a double barrell and 3 single barrells 4 shelves 12 bottles 4 glasses and other lumber	1	3	0
In the little closet			
Item one old Cupbord a boxe 3 baskets 6 shelves 3 crocks a rundlet and some other small things		7	6
In the malthouse			
Item a maulting fatt a querne a cheesepresse an oasthayre a chest 3 boords a working bench 2 ridders a loade of Charcoale hemp and flaxe and one brake 2 mault shovells and 400 of laths 4 bushells of oaten mault and a grindstone	2	14	6
Item bills prongs pitchforks 2 iron barres sythes shovells spades a			

punche and other implements of husbandry	13	6
In his Study		
Item one litle table and stoole a frame for bookes with 16 shelves a		
p[air] of scales a searce 13 small boxes and his library of bookes	34 10	0
Item glasses galleypots and Apothecaryes drugs	2 0	0
In the Parlor Chamber		
Item one featherbed and bolster 2 pillowes one red rugge 3 blankets a		
Carpet a bedsted curtaines matt and cord Two turkyworke cushians6		
cushion stooles 6 low cushion stooles a looking glass a side Cupbord		
and a Close stoole and the hangings of pepetuana	15 5	0
In the great garret		
Item a quarter of wheate 20 poundes of hops3 wheeles and a sive	1 18	0
In the kitchen chamber		
Item one bedsted wth curtaines matt and cord a feather bed 2 bolsters 2		
pillowes 2 blankets one olde rugge [bor]ded cheste a trundle bedsted a		
flockbed one Coverlet one blanket one bolster 7 trunks and close stoole		
2 boxes 2 chayres and 3 … a mat and cord and a wicker chayre	8 13	0
Silver plate		
Cups salts spoones etc	50 10	0
Linnen		
Sheets ell broad 6 payre fine flaxen sheets ten payre 16 p of course		
sheets 10 payre of pillowbeeres 5 Cupbord cloathes 12 table cloathes 8		
dozen of napkins 3 long towells 6 other towells	32 12	0
In the entry at the top of the stayres		
Item 3 chests a flockbed and bolster a coverlet 2 blankets a flasket 2		
shelves and other lumber a new sadle and bridle	1 12	0
In the maydes chamber		
Item a bedstedle and a mat	3	0
In the buttry chamber		
Item one low ioynd presse one chest one shelfe an olde bedsted a		
featherbed and bolster 2 pillowes matt and cord 2 blankets a covering		
and a chayre	4 0	0
Item one trunke certaine hempe leather feathers and other lumber	10	0
In the garden		
Item 2 beehouses and 4 stalls of bees	10	0
In the Close		
Item wood and timber	2 15	0
Item of healing stone 6 loades	2 0	0
Item one wayne wth a payre of shoed wheeles 2 dung courts and 4		
racks and a payre of unshod wheeles	3 10	0
In the barne		
Of wheate 30 quarters	37 10	0
Of barlye 20 quarters	25 0	0
Of oates ten quarters	5 0	0
Of haye 5 loades	2 10	0
Haye abroad in a stacke 8t loades	5 0	0
A stacke of haye menged wth strawe	1 10	0
Seaven great hogs and 5 piggs at barn doore	8 0	0
Stocke abroad		

Item 4 oxen	20	0	0
Item ten kyne and 2 bulls	35	0	0
Item 2 horses	10	0	0
Item 18 sheepe	6	0	0
Item 2 steeres and 4 weanyers	10	0	0
Item 2 harrowes 5 yoakes 4 chaines and a timber chaine 2 ploughs 3 Chapes	2	3	0
Item one windsheet and 8t sackes	1	0	0
Item poultry and ducks		10	0
Item 4 ladders a packsadle a pannell a payre of waine ropes 2 olde sadles and 300 of bricks and other lumber	1	4	0
Item things unseene unapprized and forgotten	2	0	0
Item wheate upon the ground	5	0	0
Item 5 quarters of wheate	6	5	0
Item due to him for tythe at time of his death	70	13	8
The totall	532	12	2

Exhibited 31 Oct 1637 by James Tichenor and Maria Hutchinson widow

[WSRO Ep I/29/95/29]

Will: made 3 June 1637; proved 31 Oct 1637
Wife: Mary, executrix; son: George (all books, plate)
Witnesses: Robert Monk, George Chapman, Thomas Bacon   [WSRO STC I/19/80b]

[1] Cambridge, Clare, BA 1597, MA 1600, BD 1609. Ordained deacon and priest 1602 (bishop of Rochester). Rector of Parham 1605. Licensed preacher Canterbury, Chichester and Winchester dioceses 1609. Vicar of Amberley 1609–1621, patron bishop of Chichester. Prebendary of Seaford 1616–1637. Rector of West Grinstead 1621–1637, patron Thomas, earl of Arundel and Surrey. Married Mary (possibly Mary Atree at Lyminster 1613). Died 1637.

69. West Grinstead April 1644 SAMUEL DOWLIN [1]

Appraisers: Edward Michell, Thomas Freeman

	£	s	d
In primis his Wearinge Apparrell and Linnen and Woollen left in the hands of William Newman at his death	1	10	0
Item An Old Saddle		1	6
Item An Old bible and a booke of Cottons sermons		3	0
An Old Mare	1	0	0
Item A litle sucking Colt		15	0
Item Two Silver Spoones wch were in the Keepinge of Thomas Whittington which were after claimed by Mr Whetstone as pawned and redeemed by him for		15	0
Item In Moneys	41	19	0
Alsoe In the time of his sicknes hee left in the hands of Wm Newman towards the discharge of the phisicions attendance in his sicknes and other necessaries all which the said Wm Newman said he disbursed	6	17	0
The total sume is	53	0	6

Exhibited by: Edward Johnson 11 April 1644   [WSRO Ep I/29/95/41]

Will nuncupative; made 24 April 1644; proved 10 April 1662 [*sic*]
Executor John Tredcroft, STB (no executor having been named in will)
Bequest of £41 19s for charitable purposes
Witnesses: John Tredcroft, Thomas Whittington, William Newman   [WSRO STC/I/23/5]

[1] Of Wiltshire. Oxford, St Alban Hall, matriculated 1602 aged 17. Ordained deacon 1606, priest 1608 (bishop of Llandaff). Curate of Alderton, Wilts, c. 1608. Vicar of Sherston Magna, Wilts, 1612–1638 when deprived.

70. West Grinstead 1695 WILLIAM DODWELL [1]
Appraisers: Edward Gearing, William Peirce
[Incomplete]

	£	s	d
… Item one Table three Chayres one stoole two Stands one looking Glass two old Deale Boxrs one Glass Cage one paire of Andirons one paire of Tongs and one fire Shovell and Bellowes		10	0
Item Hangings Window Curtaines and rods	1	10	0
Item Books	4	0	0
Item two diaper Table clothes and three and twenty Diaper Napkins		18	0
Item three paire of fine Tire Sheetes and two pillowcoats	1	12	0
In the Studdy Chamber			
Item one Feather Bed and Bedsteddle Matt Cord Curtaines valens one Bolster two Pillowe three Blanketts and one Rugg	5	0	0
Item one table Fower Chayres one Trunke one Close Stoole and Pann one looking Glass one paire of Snuffers and Chaffing Dish		11	0
Item two paire of Andirons One paire of Tongs and Fire Pann and one Pistoll		5	0
Item Window Curtaines …		2	0
In the Corn Loft			
Item Wheate and Oates	2	11	6
In the Long Chamber			
Item two Feather Bedds one Bedstedd and Curtaines Two Bolsters one Rugg and two Blanketts one nest of drawers	2	10	0
Item one Chest five paire of Sheetes and six Towells	1	10	0
In the storehouse Chamber			
Item one Feather Bed Bedstedd Matt Cords Curtaines Valens one Bolster and all things thereto belonging	4	0	0
Item Silver Spoon		7	0
Item two Chaires two Boxes and one Chest of drawers		13	6
Goods without doores			
Item one old Horse	2	5	0
Item two Piggs	1	4	0
Item Geese		6	0
Item Wood and Faggotts		13	0
Item Lumber and things unseen and forgotten		5	0
Sume totall	59	2	4

Exhibited 18 June 1695 by Robert Randall, gent, creditor, Susan Dodwell widow

[WSRO Ep I/29/95/117]

Will: made 8 May 1695; proved 18 June 1695
Wife: Susanna, executrix
Witnesses: John Linfield, John Greatwick, Thomas Pyke   [WSRO STC I/30/232]

[1] Oxford, Lincoln, matriculated 1658; called BA 1664 and MA 1677. Ordained priest 1664 (bishop of Chichester). Rector of Coombes c. 1667–1677; of West Grinstead 1677–1695, patron Walter Coles; of Harting 1682–1695. Died 1695.

71. Hamsey 10 June 1732 JOSEPH STEDMAN, curate [1]

Appraisers: Richard Simmons, John Hooke

	£	s	d
In primis In Cash	1	8	0
Item In the Chamber			
Two Necks Two pair of Sleeves five Bands three old Bands One old shirt One old pair of stockings One old pair of Shoes two Pillow cases three table cloths two Napkins two Perukes two Hats one Walking cane One coat and waistcoat two pair of breeches one old coat one Gown one brush one pillow two blankets one quilt one feather bed one bolster one bedstead with green Curtains lined wth linnen one pair of Sheets worth in all	7	8	0
Item In another Chamber			
Five hand glasses and two old framed glasses for gardens one deal box and one old chest		16	0
Item In the Cellar			
One cask of twelve Gallons one Kilderkin one half hogshead one Powdering tub one butter crock one Fire screen one Gallon measure two brass skelletts one pair of wooden scales and weights one pestle and mortar two wooden platters and one wooden trey	1	13	0
Item In the Kitchen			
One small spit three old turkey chairs one box iron and two heaters one bacon rack with the iron work		11	0
Item In the hall			
two large prints and twenty old small prints		6	0
Item In the Parlour			
One old Watch Clock One silver old Watch one silver spoon one pair of andirons with brass heads and one pair of tobacco tongs	3	5	6
Item In the hands of Mary Ford			
not yet delivered two small gold rings and one small silver spoon	1	1	0
Item In the parish of Southover			
One old gown and cassock	1	5	0
Item In debts sperate and desperate			
Due to the said Mr Stedman from several persons within the parish of Southover and parts adjacent for their composition for tythe for their lands stock or houses within the parish of Southover in all	16	0	0
Item Due for a funeral sermon preached in the parish church of Hamsey at the burying of John Norris and for breaking the ground for him the said John Norris		16	8

Item In the Study at Hamsey			
A parcel of old books	4	4	0
Item On account of things unseen and forgot		5	0
	38	19	2

[ESRO W/INV 2422]

Administration 16 June 1732
To James Miles, clerk, principal creditor [ESRO W/B 17.15v]

[1] Glasgow, MA. Ordained deacon 1721, priest 1723 (bishop of Chichester). Curate of Hamsey c. 1723–1725; of St John sub Castro, Lewes, c. 1725. Sequestrator of Southover c. 1723–1725. Possibly married Elizabeth Umphery at Balcombe 1728. Died 1732.

72. Hartfield 29 April 1735 THOMAS SMYTHE [1]
Appraisers: William Luck, John Medhurst

	£	s	d
In the Kitchen			
In primis His wearing Apparell Purse Purse [*sic*] Keys and ready Money	55	0	0
One Rack with hooks and staples		4	6
The Jack two Spits a pair of Andirons and creepers	1	10	0
One Iron back firepan Tongs pothangers And bellows	1	3	0
Four brass Candlesticks two flower boxes Snuffers two brass dish warmers twelve Scuers two Iron forks one Egg skimmer one Basting ladle		12	0
One dresser two tables seven Chairs and two window shelters two box Irons one Morter And pestle one Chafindish one small Cubbard and Candlebox one tunnel and grater	2	5	0
One warming pan one pair of Stillyards one Crane		10	0
Nine small pewter dishes two dozen and a half of plates	1	15	0
In the Parlour			
One Clock and case	4	0	0
One corner cubbard one weather glass One tea table and coffey mill one set of Chiney one coffey pot one tea kettle	1	18	0
Four tables six Cane Chairs six rush bottom Chairs	2	5	0
One looking glass One pair of Andirons two pair of Tongs one pair of bellows and fire pan 1 backgammon table one silver Tankard Three silver spoons 5 silver tea spoons and a pair of silver tea tongs	6	12	0
In the Brewhouse			
Two coppers one brew fate two tun tubs three Keelers one bucking tubb	7	10	0
One pair of Andirons one slice one iron fork one iron one iron fender one pair of pothangers one Gridiron two porridge pots one Kettle	1	1	0
Four wooden bowls seven Trenchers two Pails three stalledges one cloth horse		9	0
One fry pan one washing pot one fish kettle One collender one dripping pan one tin Cover one small sive		8	0

Three brass skillets one brass pot two brass saspans one meale bagg and three sives	15	6
In the Cellar		
Four hogsheads three Kilderkins one poudring tub and seven small tubs	3　0	0
One safe two Crocks and three mugs	8	0
In the Kitchen Chamber		
One bedsted and hanging one feather bed One bolster two pillows three blankets and one Quilt	6　0	0
One Chest of Draws one scrutore six Chairs	3　15	0
One Iron Back one pair of Andirons one pair of Tongs one firepan Bellows punch Bowl and one small Table	12	0
Thirty three pictures	10	0
In the parlour Chamber		
One Bedsted and Hanging one feather Bed one bolster two pillows three blankets and one coverlid	3　5	0
Three boxes one Chest four Chairs one table Three Candlesticks one pair of Andirons One firepan one pair of Tongs	11	0
In the Cellar Chamber		
One bedsted one feather bed one bolster One pillow three blankets one Coverlid Four Chairs one Table three Candlet	2　10	0
One prest and one Chest	1　10	0
In the brewhouse Chamber		
One Bedsted and bed hangings and things belonging	1　10	0
One close stool bed pan and a straw tub	10	6
Linnen Eight pair of Sheets	3　9	0
Five table Cloths thirteen Towels	8	0
Twenty Eight Napkins	1　3	0
Three pair of sheets more three table Cloths Nine pillow coats	3　0	0
Hop poles	5　0	0
In the stable		
Two sadles one garden Role one wheel barrow a hop pitcher two prongs one old Chest and horsehair hoppokes two sikles and a dog	1　13	6
The Hay	1　0	0
One sledge three Wedges two Axes three hoes three garden rakes one mathook one spade one shovel a pair of hedgeing Coses two hop knives one hanbill	15	11
Two hundred and fifty glass bottles	2　0	0
A pillion and Cloth and girt	15	0
A Sun Dial	1	0
Debts due to Mr Smythe for Arrears of Tythes	35　0	0
Desperate debts	5　0	0
Three baggs and two pockets of Hops in hand	15　0	0
Things unseen and forgot	3	4
Total	186　8	9

[ESRO W/INV 2606A]

Administration 10 May 1735
To widow Margaret　　　　　　　　　　　[ESRO W/B 17.38r]

[1] Son of Nathan, of Appleby, Westm. Oxford, Queen's, matriculated 1703 aged 17, BA 1708, MA 1711. Vicar of Hartfield 1716–1735, patron Thomas, earl of Thanet; rector 1730–1735. Died 1735.

73. Harting 5 Oct 1641 HUGH COLLEY, vicar [1]
Appraisers: Danell Pritchard, Christopher Hallett, Thomas Stamford
[Original damaged]

	£	s	d
... hall			
[three illegible lines]	1	10	0
... Cupbord		18	0
... {s]tooles ...		12	0
[squ]are Table		5	0
... Chaire and two other ...		8	0
... [dr]esser borde ... to set Glasses in		10	0
... [square s]tooles and two [rou]nd stooles		5	0
Twentie peeces of ... of Candlesticks ... plates [?7] Chamber ... potts one pewter ... 3 Basins ... Cupps 8 pewter ...	3	5	0
... Boll and Twelve ...	6	2	0
... Mort[ar] ... Pestle		7	0
... fowre ... two kettles one Brass ... [s]kelletts one Bell Chafer		16	0
... Fornace	3	10	0
... paire of Andirons ... 3 paire of ... plate one Iron ... one Stone ... Cleaver a Fleshooke ... one fire shovell and Chaufinge dishe	1	0	0
... [cu]sshions ... one pair ...		2	0
... Milkhowse			
... one Table and tressles		18	0
... kyver and one other ... Tubbe		15	0
... les and fyre Tonggs		12	0
... Balls		4	0
... Cheese ... other		7	0
... whale ...Serches and other ... vesseles		13	4
... Butterie			
...[?brewi]nge Fat		14	0
... [?drin]ke vessells		16	0
... presse two Tubbs		5	0
... Chamber			
... [weari]nge Apparraile ... [hi]s Pursse ... Gold	10	0	0
... one high Bedsteddle ... [be]dsteddle one sett of ... and one Fether ... Bolsters ... and Bolster foure ... Ruggs 4 Blankets	13	10	0
... Cupbord one little ... Baskett Chaire ... [st]ooles and Chaires 6 ... Trunkes ... Box	1	18	0

… And … one … one pare of … Bellowes one Fire … paire of Tongs		12	0
… of Sheetes	4	10	0
… thes and a Cupborde … Towells 13 pillow … dozen and two …	5	4	0
… [mi]ddle Chamber			
… Bedsteddle one … steddle 3 Fetherbedds … one Flockbolster … Coverletts 4 Blanketts … [curta]ines and valents wth …	10	0	0
… and one Trunke		10	0
… Cha …			
… [t]runks A Closetoole … spun and unspunn … halfe hedded Bedd … Press	2	6	0
… ing howse			
… of Malt		8	0
… of Apples		6	0
… ate			
… and Colt … Bridle and …	6	0	0
… d 2 Shouts	3	15	0
… aboute the howse		10	0
…			
… of wheat … Peaze 11 busshells … Busshells of oats	5	5	4
… Strawe	1	10	0
… in the Gate		10	0
… and harneis		15	0
Bookes	5	0	0
… in the B … Flore	1	10	0
Soma tot	100	18	4

[WSRO Ep I/29/98/48]

Will: made [8?] Feb 1641; proved 29 Oct 1641
Wife Mary, executrix   [WSRO STC II/M Dean 1641 (2)]

[1] Cambridge, Pembroke, admitted sizar 1603, BA 1607, MA 1610. Vicar of Witton, Norf, 1611, patron bishop of Ely; of Harting 1614–1641, patron the rector. Died 1641.

74. West Hoathly 10 March 1721 WILLIAM GRIFFITH, vicar [1]
Appraisers: John Smith junior, John Farmer

	£	s	d
for his weareing Apparrell and Mony in his Purs	10	0	0
Goods in the Kitching Chamber			
A bed and all the furniture belonging A Chest of Draws and a Glass 6 Chares and 6 Cuchings 1 pr Andians and fiar Shovell Tongs 2 Diaper Table Clothes 4 Doz: Napkins 1 Silvar Tanckard and 7 Silvar Spoons 6 Silvar Tea Spoon and a Silvar Cupp	12	0	0

In the Parlar Chamber

1 bed and all the furniture belonging 12 pr of Sheets Corse 7 fine a press and Arm Chare 2 Chestes and 8 Corse Table Clothes 6 Corse Towels and a Glass	3	8	6

In the Garrit

An Old Still and Lumber		7	6

In the Chamber Over the Little Parlar

A bed and All Furniture belonging 1 table	2	10	6

In the Parlar

1 Easy Chare 6 Cayne Chares 1 Ovell Table a Glass Coffee Mill 1 pr Doggs and Chainey 1 Tea Table	2	7	6

In the Kitching

1 Clock 12 Putar Dishes 3 Doz: Plates 1 Dressar 1 Jack 2 pr Andians 2 Spits 1 warming pan 2 Little Tables 1 Small Cubbard 1 furme 4 Coffee Potts 4 Candle Sticks 2 potts 2 pothooks 1 Iron Kittle 1 Iron Plate 1 box Iron and heaters 1 Iron fender 1 brilar 6 Chares 1 Rack	5	2	6

In the Sinck

1 furnace 3 brass Skyllets 1 tea Kittle 2 trays 3 Buckets 1 Driping Pan 1 brass spoone	1	18	0

In the Buttery

7 barrells 1 vate 1 Tun Tubb 1 bucking Tubb 1 3 Legd Keelar 2 powdering Tubbs 1 peele 2 Sives 2 Stands	1	1	6

In the Sellar and Milckhouse

1 backen Keelar 2 Stands 2 Milck Ledds 1 frying pan stand		10	0
Books in the Studdy	5	0	0
Wood and faggats	1	0	0
Hay in the Barne	1	0	0
things unseen and forgott		10	0
Upon Acct	80	0	0
Upon book	15	0	0
Totall	141	16	0

[ESRO W/INV 1332]

Will: Made 23 Feb [year missing]; 12 June 1721
Wife Ann, executrix; sons: Henry, Thomas; daughters: Anne, Gainor, ?Aprines
Witnesses: Joseph Browne, William Brooks, William Burley   [ESRO W/A 51/2612]

[1] Called BA 1684. Ordained deacon 1684 (bishop of Chichester). Possibly curate of Balcombe c. 1678–1686. Curate of West Hoathly 1687; vicar 1690–1721, patron Crown. Died 1721; buried West Hoathly.

75. Hollington 20 Feb 1735 THOMAS DENHAM, rector [1]

Appraisers: William Cramp, Richard Sharpe

	£	s	d
In primis			
his purs and wearing Aparrill of All sorts	5	0	0
goods In the Chichen one Clock one Jack one Tabell one Cubard six Chayers and other things	4	10	0
goods In the parlor one Tabell one glass siex Chayers and other things	1	10	0

In the Buttrey			
three potts one Fry pan and other things		10	0
In the Celler			
seven barrills thre poudering Tubs and other things	3	0	0
In the bruhous			
one Furness four Tubs Four killers one kettell three paiels and other things	2	0	0
In the kichen Chamber			
one bed Two tables Three Chayers one glass and other things	2	10	0
In the parler Chamber			
two beds one Chayer and other things	2	10	0
In the buttry Chamber			
two beds two Chests two Chayers A parsell of books and other things	2	15	0
In the Spare Chamber			
one Chest of Drawers one press two Chests and other things	1	10	0
In the darck Closet			
one Charn three Milck trugs and other things		5	0
Linnon of all sorts	3	0	0
with out doors two Cows	4	10	0
two horses	1	15	0
For wood and fagguts	1	0	0
In good debts	1	0	0
In bad debts		15	0
For things unseen and Forgott		3	6
	38	3	6

[ESRO W/INV 2601]

Administration 13 March 1735
To widow Elizabeth   [ESRO W/B 17.36r]

[1] Born Withyham, son of David, gent. Lewes Grammar School. Cambridge, St John's, admitted aged 17 and matriculated 1700, BA 1704, MA 1717. Ordained deacon 1703, priest 1707 (bishop of Chichester). Curate of Pett 1704. Vicar of Hollington 1707–1710, 1712–1734, patron Charles Eversfield, esq. Died 1734 aged 51; buried Hollington.

76. Horsham 1635 WILLIAM HUNT [1]
[Original damaged and illegible]
Inventory value: £6 5s 6d.   [WSRO Ep I/29/106/47]

Administration 13 Feb 1635
To Thomas Lamb of Horsham, creditor   [WSRO STC III/G/271]

[1] Possibly Cambridge, Trinity, MA; and licensed curate Peasmarsh and Lewes archdeaconry 1624.

77. Horsham 15 July 1642 JOHN COLLINS, vicar [1]

Appraisers: George Edgly clerk, James Ford, Edward Parkhurst mercer

	£	s	d
In primis his wearing apparrell and money in his purse	20	0	0
Item Bookes in his Study	80	0	0
Goods in the Parlor			
One draweing Table six joyned stooles and one side cupboard	1	19	8
Item one old armd chayre of cloth of silver and 2 lowe stooles of the same		8	0
Two lowe chayres of gilt leather		6	0
A carpet and cupboard cloth striped		12	0
A paire of brasse handirons a pair of tongs and fireshovell with brasses	1	4	0
Item 8 cushions		13	0
Fower Curtaines of green (Linsey Woolsey) with curtaine rods to go same		13	4
A Cupbord for glasses and greene hangings		6	0
Two backe chaires and 2 low chaires of green cloth	1	0	0
Goods in the Hall			
A table and 6 joynd stooles		14	0
An Armed chaire and a side cupboard		6	8
A carpet and cupbord cloth		10	0
Seaven Cushions 2 lowe matched chaires and 2 little stooles with needlework		15	8
A pair of handirons with brasses		4	0
A pewter still brasse sconce with raised lid		8	2
Goods in the kitchin			
One joyned cupbord one little table and eight dressers bords and shelves		18	6
One Wainscott window a well bucket with an iron chain and frame		7	6
A furnace to breu in	1	13	4
An arm'd chaire and 2 little chayres		3	6
An Iron Jacke with weights		16	0
Six old cusions a paire of cast hand irons a paire of iron racks a paire of tongs and a slice and a paire of bellows		11	6
A muskett a rest Bandelerrs a sword with a headpiece	1	10	0
Fire spitts two iron dripping pans two tin dripping pans a frying pan gridiron tosting iron and 1 trevett		19	8
Item two pairs of pothangers two pairs of pothooks two iron potts two iron kettles and a birding peice	1	8	0
Item 1 iron clever and a chopping knife		1	0
Nine wooden candlesticks		1	6
Item a brasse morter and iron pestle		6	0
Item a chopping blocke three wooden Tankards and 12 dishes Six bucketts with iron bayses A dresser forme and a blocke two pairs of wooden scales with leaden weights		16	0
In the Saddle House			

Item an old pillion a pannell bridle Sixteene old boards an iron barre 1 Shovell a Chissell an axe and spitte pitchforke an hedging bill two iron wedges a paire of pinchers a paire of traces and fetters and other Lumber	1	16	4
In the Bake house			
Two cheese presses two cheesemotes - hoopes and vallowes a great cheese mote a backing Tubb and a washing Bowl a keeler to wash in two tinne water potts and a pewter Still	1	8	4
In the Hen house			
Two coupes for poultry five spinning wheeles a fire forke and a Slice a paring iron and other Lumber	1	1	0
In the Little Buttery			
Five pinnes and 2 Stands 3 rundlettes and a payre of Slings		12	0
In the Great Buttery			
Two Stands two shelves 5 kilderkins fower leather Bottles other Lumber	1	0	0
In the Entry			
a cover to the Salthouse		1	0
Brewing Vessills One Tunne 1 Mash fatt 10 coolers One cheese Tubb a Meale Tubb 1 Boulting hutch and a Mustard querne	1	18	4
Stands lumber shelves and other things in the Brewhouse		3	4
Sope and candles Sugar and spice	1	0	0
In the Milkhouse			
Butter and cheese		13	4
A safe or Cupbord for meate three planks 8 shelves a Cheese Tubb a poudring tubb two Chyrnes two dozen and 3 treys or truggs a salting trough with a Cover and stand Potts pans and other Crockry ware yarne winders and other Lumber	3	8	4
Goods in the great Chamber			
One high Bedstead carved with a Tester matt and cord	1	6	8
Curtains and Valons of striped Darmicke and Curtaine rodds	1	6	8
One featherbed and Bolster and Matre and 4 Pillowes 2 downe and 2 feather	5	0	0
fower Blanketts 1 Greene rugg	2	4	8
A Trundle Bedsted Matt and Cord		4	0
An Arras Coverlett	2	0	0
Eighteene yards of black and white Cloth	3	0	0
One faire waynescott Cupbord with 3 lockes and keyes and 1 Side Cupbord	1	8	0
A side Table with a Cupbord in it an arm'd Chayre with greene cloth and a wicker Chaire a lowe backe chaire of needle worke 2 low Stooles of the same and 2 lowe Stooles of Irish stitch	1	19	8
A Carpett and 2 Cupbord Clothes of greene Cloth with silk fringe		15	0
Two window Curtaines of striped linsey woolsey with Curtaine rods and two window Curtaines of Needle worke 3 other Cushions of Irish stitch and 4 Cases for Cushions irish stitchs	1	5	4
A paire of Handirons with brasses fireshovell tongs and bellowes		10	0
Two looking glasses		3	6

fowerscore pound of towe threescore pound of tyre and Sixteene pound of linnen yarne	3	0	8
Twenty pounds of wooll		13	4
An old trunke bound with Iron and a Close stoole with a pewter pan a bed stoole and panne with 2 old basketts		15	0
Goods in the Long Gallery			
A long shelfe and a pinne to hang a Cloke upon a Trunke locke and key and a needle worke Cushion wrought with silke	1	4	0
Another Cushion of Crimson Damaske		4	0
In the Little Chamber			
An high Bedsted with Matt and cord Curtaines of Say and Vallons with fringe and curtaine rodds	1	0	0
One featherbed 2 bolsters two pillowes a paire of blanketts one Coverlett of yellow Cloth	5	6	8
A wicker Chayre a little square table a lowe wooden Chaire a little carpett of greene cloth 1 window curtaine and curtaine rod one writing deske and 14 pound of tyer and 2 little shelves	1	2	0
In the Closett			
2 Trunke Boxes and an old Chest one Cabinet locke and key water glasses Gally potts and stone bottles with other Implements in that roome	2	4	0
In the Parlour Chamber			
One joyned bedsted with Tester matt and Cord Curtaines and Valons with Curtaine rodds	1	6	8
One strawe bed one featherbed two bolsters three blanketts 1 Coverlett One halfe headed bedsted matt and cord with a buckram cover	4	13	4
Curtaines and Valons of say one featherbed and bolster one feather bed fower blanketts and an old greene rugg and a white rugg	3	3	4
A waynescott press to hang clothes in 1 little square table and a turnd chaire 3 joyned Chests and one large trunke	1	9	8
Item 1 old wicker Chayre an old little stoole and three old Cushions 3 Curtaines and 2 Curtaine rodds		7	6
Item a paire of Handirons with brasse tops an odde handiron with a paire of little tongs 1 fireshovell and a joynd stoole		5	0
In the Mayds Chamber			
One halfe headed bedsted matt and cord		6	0
Item one Canopie of greene Darnix with 2 old curtaines to the same		3	0
Item 1 featherbed and bolster 1 flocke bolster two old blanketts and an old Coverlett One Trundle bedsted and cord Two old Chests an old forme a boxe and 2 old window Cushions	2	6	2
In the MenServants Chamber			
An halfe headed Bedsted matt and cord		6	0
One Strawe bed a featherbed 1 fether bolster 1 blankett and 2 old Coverletts one falling Table and two shelves with one livery Cloke	1	16	6
In the Study			
A Table an arm'd Chayre shelves A boxe of weights for gold curtaines and Curtaine rodds and a writing Deske		13	10
Linnen			
Twelve pairs of flaxen sheets	8	0	0

Item 4 payre of hempen tyre sheetts	2	8	0
Item 10 payre of Towe sheetts	2	10	0
Item 16 paire of pillowbeers	2	10	0
Eleaven flaxen table clothes	4	0	0
Item 10 dozen and halfe of napkins	4	0	0
Item 3 Diaper Table clothes and a Dozen of Diaper Napkins	2	2	0
Item two Towells and side bord Cloth of Diaper		6	8
Item 3 hand towells and 4 Cupbord cloths	2	4	0
Item 2 dozen of course handtowells		16	0
Item 11 Course Table clothes		11	0
Item silver plate	11	18	6

Pewter

One fayre Bason and Ewer		8	0
One flagon 1 payre of Candlesticks and 1 odd owed beere bowle two aqua vita bottles 4 Candlecups		19	10
Item 20 Nayls of pewter also Basons	8	0	0
Item two little flagons two Ale quart potts Ale pint and half pint pott		9	6
Item One Bason 3 Chamber potts A wine qt pott a pint an halfe pint a qter pott		8	2
Item two pudding pannes an apple korer a Breader of tinne and a bread Grater	3	3	0

Brasse

Fower brasse Candlesticks fower brass potts five brasse kettles two Chaffing dishes five brasse posnetts two warming pans 4 brasse skimmers a brass ladle and two brass spooones	4	0	8
Item one flaskett two table basketts and divers other basketts		6	6
Item 4 Dozen of Trenchers glasses and Crockery ware and bottles and other Lumber		9	0

In the Stable

Two saddles and 2 bridles		6	8
five yokes for oxen three oxes chaynes and an iron Chappe a shovell Male pillion and an iron sledge with other lumber		16	3
Item Nine wattle Gates and 2 racks		5	0

In the Gates

One wayne and wheeles shod with iron two Marling Coates and one paire of wheeles 2 paire of Thills 2 harrows 1 plowe and barley rowler	3	10	0
Item One Corne wayne and paire of wheeles		13	4
Fower hoggs tenne Ducks and a Drake one black mare 4 kine and 4 oxen	44	12	2
Stone at the Delfe	10	0	0
Wheate about 40 Bushells and hay about 6 Loads	10	0	0
Oates 9 Acres Pease 7 Acres and barley 2 Acres and an halfe	24	13	6

Goods in the Corne Lofte

Five flitches of Bacon	2	10	0
Two old Chests fower shelves and other Lumber 32 pound of towe		14	8
Forty Bushells of wheate twenty Bushells of Malt 1 malting skreene	8	8	0
Item 1 shovell and Sieve one halfe bushell 1 halfe pecke bords and other lumber		6	6

Barley 4 bushells a Wyr sheete A seede lip hoopes 7 Sackes one shaull			
Tubbe and other lumber	1	3	0
In the Gardens and Orchard			
Beanes pease and other fruites	1	0	0
Item 1 Grindstone with an iron winch 1 Stone table and frame healing			
stone about 7 yard wood and fagotts	17	11	0
Fower racks for beasts		2	0
Hay in the Barne about 5 loads	3	6	8
Fower prongs 1 Cutting knife an hay spade and a racke		3	0
In Ready money about	100	0	0
Lumber about the house and things forgotten	1	0	0
The sume totall is	473	18	5
In Desperate Debts and due upon the Tithe booke	10	0	0

[WSRO Ep I/29/106/70]

Will: made 2 April 1642; proved 2 Aug 1642
Wife Elizabeth, executrix; nephews John and Stephen Anstey equally to share books
Overseers: James Ford of Petworth, Edward Parkhurst
Witnesses: William Strudwicke, Thomas Forman
Value £473.18.5   [WSRO STC II/S Dean 1642 (1)]

[1] Of London. Eton College. Cambridge, King's, admitted Eton scholar 1603 aged 17, fellow 1606–1612, BA 1608, MA 1611, BD 1618. Ordained deacon and priest 1608 (bishop of Ely). Licensed preacher Chichester diocese 1609. Vicar of Horsham 1608–1642, patron archbishop of Canterbury. Died 1642; inquisition post mortem 1644.

78. Horsham 12 May 1684 MATHEW WOODMAN [1]

Appraisers: Anthony Hilton, James Waller

	£	s	d
In primis his wearinge apparrell the mony and watch in his pockett	10	0	0
Item his study of bookes 400 in number greate and small	15	0	0
Item three fether beds curtains and vallens matts and cords	6	0	0
Item a silver tankard one silver bowle two silver porringers twelve			
silver spoones one silver salt and one shugger dish	9	0	0
Item 2 brasse kettles 2 brasse morters one brasse pott three brasse			
skilletts and other small things	1	5	0
Item 20 peeces of pewter neere 50lb weight	1	5	0
Item 5 payre of sheets 4 dosen of napkins with other old peeces of			
linnen	1	5	0
Item 2 lookinge glasses one chest of drawers one table chaires stooles			
and other lumber	2	0	0
Item due for rent	12	0	0
due upon bond to the deceased	40	0	0
	97	15	0

[EpI/29/106/196]

Will: made 21 May 1683; no probate
Son: Mathew, executor (books); daughters: Elizabeth Waller, Mary Goble
Overseers: 'brothers' Nathaniel Tredcroft, clerk, Anthony Hilton, gent
Witnesses: Anthony Hilton, John Kent, Nathaniel Pellatt   [WSRO STC I/27/387]

[1] Son of George, rector of Thakeham; grandson of Richard, martyred Lewes 1557. Oxford, Magdalen Hall, matriculated 1638 aged 16, BA 1641. Vicar of Slinfold, admitted 1647, collated 1660, ejected for nonconformity 1662. Preached gratis at Horsham. Imprisoned. Married Ann (possibly Ann Henshaw, died 1663); Elizabeth Waller of Horsham, widow, at Horsham 1664, when called gent., late minister of Slinfold. Died 1684.

79. Horsted Keynes 14 Oct 1679 GILES MOORE, rector [1]
Appraisers: Walter Hille, William Young, John Lumb, John Langridge

	£	s	d
In primis money in purse and wearing Cloathes	17	0	0
Item the Study of bookes	100	0	0
Item in plate	12	0	0
Item moneys upon bond	1160	0	0
Item one table deske a trunke and box vallued at	1	0	0
Item things in the great parlour chamber bed and all things	8	0	0
Item one chest One press and livery table and cloaths	2	0	0
Item 8 chaires and cloath Brandirons Tongs and panne	1	10	0
Things over the Milkhouse Chamber			
Item two beds bedsteads Curtains and hangings	6	0	0
Item One Chest drawers 3 chairs and a trunke 1 looking glass			
And other small things	3	0	0
Things over the kitchin Chamber			
Item the bed and all things thereto belonging	5	0	0
Item One Chest One Trunke 3 Chaires and a box		15	0
Chamber over the little Parlour			
Item One bed and all thereto belonging	3	10	0
In a little Chamber joyning			
Item 1 bed bedstead and 3 pillows	2	0	0
In the mans chamber over the hall			
Item the mans bed and things thereto belonging and presse	1	10	0
Item 13 prs of tyre sheets and 1 sheet	8	0	0
Item 7 prs of towen sheets	2	0	0
Item 5 dozen and 5 tire Napkins	2	0	0
Item 1 dozen and 3 Napkins towen		6	0
Item 27 pieces of new cloath	5	8	0
Item 5 tyre table cloaths	1	10	0
Item 13 pillow Coats	1	6	0
Item 6 towells fine and course		6	0
Item 11 Course table cloathes		12	0
Things belonging to the great Parler			
Item 1 great table 1 little table 1 side board	1	10	0
Item 13 Chairs	1	10	0
Item two stills	1	5	0

Item 2 sewers and 2 plates	1	5	0
Item 25 pieces of pewter dishes	2	10	0
Item 4 candlesticks a flaggon a Cullender and other small pewter	1	15	0
Things in the Kitchin			
Item 2 brass kettles a Warming panne 2 brass Skillets 1 Chafendish			
and other brasse	2	4	0
Item 4 iron pots 1 kettle 1 posnet 2 pot Lids	1	4	0
Item 1 dripping pan and other pieces of iron		13	0
Item 2 pr of andirons 2 spets 2 pot hookes fire pan and tongs		17	0
Item 1 Jack gun and Jack weight	2	5	0
Item 1 table 3 Chaires and 4 buckets		10	0
Item 1 brasse mortar a Cage sling Curtaine and rod		8	6
Item 1 frying panne		5	0
Things in the little Parlour			
Item wainscot	2	0	0
Item 1 table side board and 2 Carpets		10	0
Item a green Chaire 6 stooles and Andirons		13	0
Things standing in the hall			
Item 1 table forme chaire and Wheele		18	0
Things in the milkhouse			
Item two Leds 9 Trugs table and a powdering tub	1	10	0
Item all other small things		15	0
Things in the Cheese roome			
Item 1 cheese presse 3 keelers and other things		15	0
The Roome going in the milkhouse			
Item a beam Scale weights Cupboard and other things	1	8	0
In the Beere Roome			
Item 3 barrells 2 Pins and other small things	1	1	0
Things in the Brewhouse			
Item 1 furnace 1 Vatt a tun and a tubbe	8	10	0
Item 5 Barrells Coup two keelers 3 Pins 5 Tubbs 1 Ringer			
Stallage and other things	3	7	0
In the Chamber over the Brewhouse			
Item 2 Oast haires Chaine Curb Well bucket	1	0	0
Item Wood and Faggots	2	5	0
Item 3 Cowes and 2 horses	18	0	0
Item a waggon and horse … carte	7	10	0
Item hay and Corne	[?]10	0	0
Item Hoppes	4	0	0
Item a halfe peck bushell Peck gallon shaul five Chamber pots bedpan			
and two ladders	1	0	0
Item two hoggs	2	10	0
Item 3 Iron plates	1	0	0
Item butter and cheese	1	10	0
Item hop poles		3	0
Item four pounds layd out over Coppice bought of Mr Cotton of			
Slapham	4	0	0
Item a [?]Coule musket sword and Bandileers	1	4	0
Item Tythes due to the deced in the parish	40	0	0

Item things unseen and forgot		5	0
	Sum	1678 15	0

[TNA PRO PROB 4/18013]

Will: made 13 Oct 1673; proved 16 Oct 1679
Wife Susan £10; brother Robert Moore's family and servant; nephew Eustace or niece Elizabeth (silver plate); brother Francis Moore's family; kinsman John Citizen of Streat, clerk (whole library except St Ambrose Works); niece Mistress Citizen
Executors: John Citizen, Francis Moore (all goods and chattels)
Anne Wilkins's family; Susan Mayhew's family; widow Anne Michelborne of Stanmer, Ann Brett of Lindfield, James Butler, John Wood, tanner of Horsted Keynes, Mary Dumbrill of Cuckfield, servant
Poor of Horsted Keynes £5
Witnesses: John Shoulder, Edward Wickerson, Henry Payne

[TNA PRO PROB 11/361/133]

[1] Baptized Hawstead, Suff, 1617, son of Giles, gent. Bury St Edmunds Grammar School, Suff. Cambridge, Gonville and Caius, admitted sizar aged 16 and matriculated 1633, BA 1637, MA 1640. Ordained deacon 1638 (bishop of Peterborough), priest 1641 (bishop of Rochester). In Royalist army, probably as chaplain. Rector of Horsted Keynes, admitted 1656; instituted 1660, patron William Michelborne, esq. Died 1679; buried Horsted Keynes.

80. Horsted Keynes 14 Oct 1680 STEPHEN PEART [1]
Appraisers: John Day, John Lucas

	£	s	d
In primis his wearinge Cloths and mony in his purse	..	6	6
Item 2 cowes and 2 heifers and a calf and a mare	20	0	0
Item The hoggs poultry geese and ducks		4	10
Item The Hay and Corne		7	0
Item the Wood and husbandry tackling	3	0	0
Item in the Stable a [?]sadole and other f ... there		13	4
In the Brewhouse			
Item a furnis and bruing vessells and 2 hogsheads and a well bucket and iron chaine and other things	6	17	0
Item a bee house a hogg trough and other small things	1	2	6
In the Kitchen			
Item 10 pieces of pewter 3 iron potts 2 iron kettles 4 brasse skilletts 1 brasse kettle 3 morters 4 spitts 1 ironplate 1 paire of stilyards 1 fowling piece 4 chaires 1 table 1 paire of andirons 1 paire of tongs 1 clyse and fireshovell 1 Jacke 1 gridiron 2 paire of potthooks together with other small things	10	1	5
In the Parlour			
Item 3 chaires 2 stooles a couch and cupboard 2 carpetts and 2 picheres and a paire of Andirons	1	15	0
In the Hall			
Item a Muskett and bandileers and a Sword and Souldiers Coat and 2 tables 3 chaires 1 still and a paire of Andirons with other small things	3	6	0

In the Dary House

Item a paire of Leads and other small things	1	10	0

In the Buttery

Item 10 drinking Vessells 1 bunting hutch 1 barrell of Vinegar	2	1	0

In the Dairy House Chamber

Item a downe bed and boulster a bedstead and a paire of blankets and
coverled and Curtains and Vallens and a Chest and a Table and 3

stooles and a paire of andirons	3	5	6
Item in a little Closett some odd things		5	6

In his Study

Item his Library there	10	0	0

In the Parlour Chamber

Item a feather bed and a boulster and searge Curtains and Vallens and
other things belonging to it and two trunks and 6 stooles in one of the

trunks 10 paire of sheets and some table linnen with other things	10	5	0

In the Kitchen Chamber

Item 2 featherbeds 1 flock bed and boulster and bedsteads and all

belonging to them	3	5	0
Item a Clocke and Case belonging to it	2	10	0
Item in Debts due at Uckfield	5	0	0
Item for a Lease of Hoppgarden and Hoppoles at Uckfield	35	10	0
Item Due at Uckfield for hopps	6	0	0
Item Due from Edward Page of Uckfield	15	0	0
Item Due for Tithes at Horsted Caynes	20	0	0
Item Things unseene and forgott		6	6
Suma	172	10	6

[TNA PROB 4/10926]

Administration 3 Nov 1680
To Richard Smith uncle and guardian of Thomas, Mary and Richard Peart, minors,
children of the deceased, the widow Elizabeth Peart having renounced.

[TNA PRO PROB 6/55]

[1] Born Giggleswick, Yorks, son of Thomas. Cambridge, Christ's, matriculated 1652; called BA
1679. Curate of Uckfield c. 1662; vicar c. 1678. Rector of Horsted Keynes 1679–1680. South
Malling Peculiar licence to marry Elizabeth Smyth of Uckfield at Uckfield 1662. Died 1680.

81. Little Horsted 7 March 1661 JOSEPH BIGGS [1]

Appraisers: Edmund Packham, Robert Pancris

	£	s	d
In primis wareing apparrell and money in his purse	10	0	0

Item in the Kitchen

one little table one forme one sideboard three Cupboards six Chaires

one dresser board three benches and four shelves	1	0	0

Item one Jack and waights five spits one fender two iron pans on paire
of brandirons one fier shovell one paire of tongs one Iron peele two
paire of pothangers four iron potts one Iron kettle one paire of bellowes

one Clever two pot hookes one gridiron one tosting Iron	1	10	0

Item Pewter and brasse	6	0	0

Item in the Hall

one Table and forme two joyned stooles one bench two Chaires one block one pair of brandirons		13	0
Item one clocke and waights	1	10	0

Item in the Parler

two Tables one livery Cupboard one bench seaven joyned stooles eight Leather Chaires tenn Cushions four Carpetts two sideboards three Curtaines	4	0	0
Item two paire of brandirons one paire of tongs and fier pann	1	0	0

Item in the Parlour Chamber

one joyned bedsted and truckell bedsted two feather beds one rugg one Coverlett two feather boulsters two Pillowes four blanketts and Curtaines	6	0	0
Item one round Table one joyned Chest two Chaires and two stooles one paire of Crepers one fierpan one paire of tongs one seing glasse	1	10	0
Item two paire of blanketts		12	0

Item in the Hall Chamber

One joyned bedsted curtaines and vallens one feather bed Counterpain three boulsters and two Pillowes	5	0	0
Item One presse one joyned Chest one sideboard one Little table three Chaires and four stooles one lookeing glasse	3	5	0
Item one paire of Brandirons one fier pan and a paire of tongs		5	0

Item in the next Chamber

one halfe head bedsted one feather bed one rugg two blanketts one boulster and two Pillowes	2	10	0
Item One presse one table one trunke one Chest seaven boxes one Chayer three brishes one paire of brandirons	1	10	0

Item in the Kitchen Chamber

one halfe head bedsted and curtaines one flocke bed one rugg two blanketts two boulsters and two Chests	1	10	0

Item in the little Chamber

two bedsteds two flock beds two Coverletts two blankets three boulsters one pillow one box	1	4	0

Item in the Studie

two deskes and shelves one Chaire		5	0
Item the Bookes	5	0	0

Item in the wash house Chamber

one bedsted one flocke bed one Coverlett one blankett	1	0	0

Item in the buttery

for playte	12	0	0
Item one cage two basketts one dresser board two shelves and earthen dishes potts and other earthen things	1	0	0

Item in the milkhouse

For milk vessells two Chornes and shelves	7	8	0

Item in the Brewhouse

one furnesse one brewing tub and other tubs and kelers five kilderkins and barrells one Cheise presse one renning tub and keler	3	18	0

Item in the Wash house		
one well buckett Chaine wheeles one keler and washing block	19	0
Item in the Bakehouse		
one meale trofe one boulting hutch one moulding board one kedge one frying pan two sives	10	0
Item two lynnen wheeles and one woolen wheele	5	0
Item one Muskett sword and bandelers one pistoll	2 0	0
Item the still and glasses	1 0	0
Item for lynnen of all sorts	20 0	0
Item for husbandry tooles	5	0
Item for four fletches of bakon and other provision	3 0	0
Item for wheate malt oates and pease	5 13	0
Item without doore		
one horse saddle and bridle	5 0	0
Item six Cowes	30 0	0
Item for hay in the barne	2 0	0
Item for three hoggs	2 5	0
Item for wood and faggotts	2 0	0
Item in money	20 0	0
Item for lumber thing not seen or forgot	15	0
Suma totalis	231 2	0

[TNA PRO PROB 4/10182]

Will: made 29 Nov 1660; proved 20 May 1661
Wife Mary, executrix; daughter: wife of Thomas Butcher   [TNA PRO PROB 11/304]

[1]   Son of George, of Hampshire. Oxford, Merton, matriculated 1621 aged 18; St Alban Hall, BA 1624, MA 1627. Curate of Lindfield. Rector of Little Horsted 1643–1661. Died 1661.

82. Hunston [Feb?] 1662 JOHN [DALLINDER] [1]
[Original damaged and illegible]   [WSRO Ep I/29/108/25]

Administration 7 March 1662
Margaret, wife, having renounced; granted to Master Nicholas Dallinder, father, during minority of JD's children, Ann, Elizabeth and Nicholas   [WSRO STC III/H/242, 257]

[1]   Son of Nicholas, of Chichester, gent. Oxford, Trinity, matriculated 1647 aged 18; Wadham, scholar 1648. Rector of Hunston c. 1659. Died 1662.

83. Hunston 18 March 1703 ROBERT ADAMS [1]
Appraisers: John Sheetin, Timothy Smith

	£	s	d
In primis his wareing Apparell and money in his purse	5	0	0

In the Kitchen
Item one Table one Cubbard one Chaire twoe joyned Stooles one Jacke one paire of Andirons one paire of Doggs foure spitts Twoe paire of Cotterells twoe dripping panns five smoothing Irons one warming

panne and one paire of Gridirons	1	0	0
In the Brewhouse			
Item one Furnace one Brewing Tubb one Bucking Tubb one old Table Eight tubbs and kivers one still old pewter twoe potts one Iron and one Brasse and three ketles	3	0	0
In the Hall			
Item three Tables one Cubbard three Chaires five Joynt Stooles one Forme and one Chest	1	10	0
In the Parlour			
Item one Table foure Joynt Stooles one Chaire six Cloth stooles Brasse Andirons Fire and pann and tongs	2	0	0
In the Seller or Buttery			
Item five drinck vessells three dozen of glasse bottles and Stands	1	0	0
In the Chamber over the Buttery			
Item One Feather Bedd twoe Blancketts and a rugg one Presse twoe Joynt Stooles one pair of Andirons one pair Of tongs and a paire of Bellowes	4	0	0
In the Chamber over the Hall			
Item one Bedd and Bedstedle and all Thereunto Belonging one Chest foure stooles one presse and some old Boxes and one old Table	2	10	0
In the Chamber over the Parlour			
Item one Bedd and Bedstedle and all belonging Thereunto Twoe Chests with Linnen therein one Chest of drawers One side Cubbard one Morter and pestle one Table and three Chaires	5	0	0
Item twoe piggs		15	0
Item pewter	1	0	0
Item …	10	0	0
Item Wood and Faggetts	1	0	0
Item Wheat Barley and Oats	15	0	0
Item one load of sacks one screene and one Fann	1	10	0
Item debts owing to the deceased on bond	40	0	0
Item seven silver spoones	2	0	0
Item in Lumber	1	0	0
	96	10	0

[WSRO Ep I 29/108/39]

Administration 20 March 1703
To John Adams, son   [WSRO STC III/M/39]

---

[1] Son of John, of Chichester, gent. Oxford, Magdalen Hall, matriculated 1637 aged 17, BA 1640, MA 1643. Ordained deacon 1660, priest 1661 (bishop of Chichester). Rector of Singleton 1661, patron Richard, Viscount Lumley; vacated by cession 1666. Vicar of Hunston 1665, patrons Sir James Bowyer, bt, and Thomas Peckham, gent. Wife Mary (died 1700). Died 1703; buried Hunston.

84. Hunston 14 Jan 1709 ROGER COLLINS 'one of the vicars of cathedral church of Chichester'[1]

Appraisers: William Webb, Theodore Aylward

	£	s	d
In primis the Deceaseds Books	6	0	0
Item one Watch	2	10	0
Item Two Canes Eight paire of Spectacles And other odd things		6	0
Item one surplice And his Weareing Apparrell	6	0	0
Item Money in Pocket	7	9	0
Item halfe a years Rent of Hunston Vicaridge	25	0	0
	47	5	0

Exhibited by Judith Scott als Collins, daughter and executor   [WSRO Ep I/29/108/40]

Will: made 1 May 1707; proved 3 Feb 1709
Sons: Charles, (books, except others named, silver watch), William (Plutarch's lives, Mr Ainsworth on Pentateuch, The English Gentleman and Gentlewoman, Mr Clarke's 2nd vol, Mr Elborroughs 2 little books explaining the divine service); daughter: Judeth, executrix (Mr Bleams History upon the Bible, Mr Clarke's lives upon the Antient and Modern Divines, Dr Sparks Festivalls, book called the house of Mourning)
Witnesses: Robert Freeman, Thomas Scott, Jane Freeman   [WSRO STC I/31/126]

[1] Ordained deacon 1662, priest 1663 (bishop of Chichester). Preacher Rumboldswyke 1672. Rector of Rumboldswyke and St Olave's, Chichester, c. 1677; of East Wittering 1688–1707. Vicar of Hunston, instituted 1706 and again 1707, patron Nicholas Covert.

85. Ifield 25 Feb 1667 HENRY HALLYWELL [1]

Appraisers: James Chapman, Arthur Waller

	£	s	d
In primis the goods in the Parlour (Chamber) att		10	0
Item the Goods in the Closett within the Parlour Chamber	1	0	0
Item the goods in the long Chamber	10	0	0
Item the goods in the Hall Chamber	8	0	0
Item the goods in the Closett in the Hall Chamber	5	0	0
Item the goods in the Studdy Chamber att	5	0	0
Item the goods in the old Chamber	12	0	0
Item the goods in the garretts	3	0	0
Item the goods in the Kitchin Chamber	5	0	0
Item the goods in the Parlour	5	0	0
Item the goods in the Hall att	5	0	0
Item goods in the Closett within the hall	1	0	0
Item goods in the Buttery att	1	0	0
Item goods in the Cheesehouse	6	0	0
Item goods in the Milkhouse	10	0	0
Item goods in the Kitchin	12	0	0
Item goods in the brewhouse	10	0	0
Item silver plate	3	0	0
Item 8 fatten beasts	55	0	0
Item 12 beasts	45	0	0

Item 8 beasts	20	0	0
Item 8 horses	20	0	0
Item hoggs att	5	0	0
Item flax att	2	0	0
Item wheate and oates	65	0	0
Item Chalk att	2	0	0
Item Wood and faggotts	5	0	0
Item husbandry tackling	15	0	0
Item 4 oxen att	20	0	0
Item poultry		10	0
Item hog troughs	2	0	0
Item Wearing Cloaths and money	20	0	0
Sum Total	498	10	0

[TNA PRO PROB 4/12491]

Will: made 6 Feb 1667; proved 27 Feb 1667
Sons: Arthur, executor, eldest Henry (all books, bed and bolster in parlour chamber, pair pillows, pair blankets, 2 pairs sheets, 2 pairs pillowcases, tablecloth, dozen flaxen napkins, say curtains and vallance in long chamber, silver bowl); daughters: Mary (Grundy), Ann (bed etc in old chamber next study, various linen, pewter dishes), Margaret (joyned bed in old chamber next stair, own bed and linen, pewter dishes)
Overseers: James Chapman of Rusper, 'sons' Edward Michell and Thomas Grundy
Witnesses: William Borer, Anne Cheesman   [TNA PRO PROB 11/323]

[1] Cambridge, Trinity, matriculated 1616, BA 1621, MA 1624. Ordained deacon and priest 1625 (bishop of Llandaff). Rector of Crawley 1626–1632; of Twineham 1632–1642; patron of both Sir Walter Covert. Licensed preacher Chichester diocese 1635. Vicar of Ifield c. 1651–1667. Possibly married Mary Hatley at Wadhurst 1630. Died 1667; buried Ifield.

86. Ifield 4 Dec 1680 WALTER MOORE [1]
Appraisers: Henry Waller, John Colcock, John Jupp, (William Cole)

	£	s	d
In primis His the said deceaseds wearing apparell and money in his pocketts valued and apprized at	5	0	0
Item In the Chamber on the Kitchin			
two beds and bolsters two pillows all of feathers three blanketts a rugge a paire of curtaines and vallens a bedsteddle and a matt valued att	5	10	0
Item foure chaires one round table a carpet a fire shovell and a paire of tongs valued att		12	0
Item one trunck a looking glass and a forme valued att		6	0
Item In the Maids Chamber			
One old feather bed a flock bed a flocke boulster two blanketts a rugge a bedstedle and a matt valued att	2	10	0
Item a drawing table a deale box and a table baskett valued att		6	6
Item three paire of sheets two pilow coats three table clothes a dozen and halfe of napkins and halfe a dozen of towells valued att	1	12	0
Item thirteene pounds weight of yarne and tyre valued att		13	0
Item alvether [?leather] sackes		3	0

Item the said deceaseds Library valued att	8	0	0

Item In the Kitchin

One Jack one spitt two dripping pans tinne one tosting iron one gridiron one iron two pett potts on a fender one paire of potthangers a paire of brandirons a paire of doggs a smoothing iron two heaters a fire shovell and a paire of tongs — 1 0 0

Item a brasse candlestick snuffers and snuffe dish and a grater		3	0

Item a warming panne a chafing dish a candle box two extinguishers a saveall and a lanthorne — 7 0

Item a still and a bunting hutch — 1 0 0

Item a table and a forme — 15 0

Item a wheele a pr of yarne winders and a table — 10 0

Item Six pewter dishes a dozen of trencher plates one pye plate one salt seller two sawcers one bason two candlesticks and five spoones valued att — 1 0 0

Item One tinne cullender a flowr box a tinder box a basting ladle a pr of bellowes and a tin meat cover — 2 0

Item Six window curtaines and two curtain rodds valued att — 3 0

Item in the Brewhouse

One furnace a vate a tunne tubb and cooler a wort tub a bucking tubb a three leggd tubb two keelers a powdring tubb five small beere tubbs a meale baskett three bucketts and three wooden bowles — 4 0 0

Item In the Buttery

3 kilderkins — 8 0

Item one frying panne — 3 0

Item one flaskett and three basketts — 2 0

Item two brasse skilletts a tinne sawser panne a funnell and some small earthenware bottles — 5 0

Item one iron pott a pott lidd an iron kettle and an iron slice — 8 0

Item two joyned chaires and two joyned stooles and other things unseen — 5 0

Item in the Barne and stable

Wood and the Hay vallued att — 4 10 0

Item an old Mare — 1 10 0

Item Due and owing to the estate of the sd dced in debts sperate and desperate about the sume of — 70 0 0

The sume totall of this Invry is — 111 9 11

[TNA PRO PROB 4/15943]

Administration 23 Dec 1680
To Charles Alexander clerk, principal creditor, first cousin or nephew (*consobrinus*) John Oglevy having renounced.   [TNA PRO PROB 6/55]

[1] Called MA c. 1679. Curate of Slinfold c. 1675. Vicar of Ifield c. 1679–1680. Died 1680; buried Ifield.

87. Iping 9 April 1663 LEONARD ALEXANDER [1]

Appraisers: Arthur Bonian, John Hamlinson

	£	s	d
In primis his [war]eing Aparrell and mony	5	0	0
Item in the halle			
one cubbard one table and summe other Smale things 4 stolls 3 chares		12	0
Item in the parler			
one table 12 chares 4 stolles one cubard one pare of andiernes tonges and firepan and summe other things	3	0	0
Item in the studdy			
on little table one deske one chare and his bookes and other things	7	10	0
Item in the buttery			
8 barles two renn…	1	0	0
Item in the chichen			
one pare of andierns on rack 4 Spittes twoe driping panes the brasse and puter and summe small things beside	5	0	0
Item one hog of baken	1	0	0
Item the brueing vessell one reone 4 civeres and other old tubes	1	0	0
Item in the chichen loaft			
one truckle bed one bolster and cuerlet		10	0
Item in the hall chamber			
two fether beds one bolster two pellowes one rugge curtines and valiones one side table 4 chares and other small things of litle valew	6	0	0
Item in the parler loaft			
two bedstedles two bedes two bolsters 4 bellowes [?]canisle and cushiones	5	0	0
Item 6 pare of sheates 4 dozen of napkens table cloaths and other small things	4	0	0
Item two chestes two old trunckes		10	0
Item wood and faggets	5	0	0
Item one mare bridle and sadle	3	0	0
	42	2	0

[WSRO Ep I/29/110/08]

Administration 24 April 1663
To Catherine, wife   [WSRO STC III/H/288]

[1] Son of Francis, of Winchester, Hants, LLD. Oxford, New College, matriculated 1627 aged 19, BCL 1634. Ordained priest 1632 (bishop of Salisbury). Vicar of Barton Stacey, Hants, 1630, patron dean and chapter of Winchester. Possibly vicar of Collingbourne Kingston, Wilts, c. 1642–1661; ejected 1647. Rector of Iping with Chithurst 1660–1663; of Kings Worthy, Hants, 1662, patron Thomas, earl of Southampton. Prebendary of Exceit 1662–1663. Died 1663.

88. West Itchenor 4 May 1613 ROGER SMITH, parson [1]
Appraisers: Allen Tomsonne, Henrie Warner, Allyn Diggins, Edward Leigh.

	£	s	d
In the parlour were these			
In primis one standing bedd 2 fetherbeds 1 feather boulster and 2 pillowes 3 Coverletts and 1 blankett wth curtaine rodds	6	13	4
Item one table and 3 stooles carpett wainscott and bench		15	0
Item 1 Cupborde trucle bedd 1 cheste and deske	1	0	0
Item 1 payre Andirons and tongues		2	6
Item his bookes	2	0	0
In the Hall			
Two Tables 2 Formes 4 Cheyres and 1 Cupborde wth cloth and 7 quishens and all other implements there	1	10	0
In the kitchen			
One table and Forme 4 brasse pots and 1 yron pott 6 kettles and morter and pessell 1 chaffer and warming pann 3 brasse candlesticks and five posnets and other brasse	4	0	0
Item Foure duzzen pewter	1	10	0
Item 3 spitts and 3 dripping pannes 4 payre pot hookes 3 pothangers two payre andirons and other implements of yron		12	0
Item an old furnisse		6	8
Item shelves and bunting hutch and troes and other woodde Lumberment		3	4
In the Milkhouse			
Two cheese presses 6 bowles 6 truggs 1 vate Kiler 2 charns and all other wodde vessels drie or wett crockes and shelves and other Lumberments	1	10	0
In the store house			
Wheat maulte and barley	2	0	0
Wheeles and hempe		6	0
In the Chamber over the Parlour			
One Tubb 1 Chest 1 truncke and box		13	4
In the Chamber over the Hall			
A bedsteddle fetherbed 1 rugg 2 blanketts 1 boulster 2 pillowes	3	0	0
Item 2 Chests 2 truncktes and box Wickett Chayer and stayned clothes	1	0	0
Item 16 payre sheetes 6 table clothes 3 payre hollond pillowbeers 2 duzzen table napkins and five twoels and other lynnen	6	13	4
In the Chamber over the buttery			
A bedsteddle 1 fetherbed truckle bedd flockbedd 2 boulsters 2 Coverletts 3 blanketts and paynted clothes	1	0	0
In the Chamber over the Kitchen			
A steddle a bedsteddle a trucle bedd a fetherbedd and coverlett and blankett and other Lumberment	1	0	0
In the buttery			
an old cupborde tubb and trow and shelves		5	0
In plate a silver salt and 5 silver spoones	2	0	0
His apparell and money in his purse	4	0	0

		£	s	d
	Item these abroade			
First 13 acres of wheate		5	0	0
Item barley 9 acre		6	0	0
Item 17 acr oates		11	0	0
Item 7 kyne and 5 calves		17	10	0
Item 10 Ewes and 8 lambes		3	10	0
Item 5 hogs and 6 piggs		1	3	4
Item geese cocke and hennes			3	4
Item cart plowes and harrowes and other implements for husbandrie		2	0	0
Item wood and Tymber and all other Lumber		3	0	0
Things forgotten			5	0
	Sum	103	11	2

[WSRO Ep I/29/112/2]

Administration 21 May 1614
To Catharine, wife   [WSRO STC III/F/32]

[1] Possibly of Lancaster; and Oxford, Brasenose, matriculated 1585 aged 18, BA 1589, MA 1592. Ordained deacon and priest 1599 (bishop of Rochester). Rector of West Itchenor 1599–1613, patron Crown. Died 1613.

89. West Itchenor 3 May 1662 JOHN KNIGHT [1]

Appraisers: William Squire, Thomas Searle

	£	s	d
In primis for bookes	10	0	0
Item for foure sheep and five lambs	1	10	0
Item for A olde hors	1	5	0
Item for A sowe hogge and foure pigs		16	0
Item for five acres of wheate for seed and syliage	5	0	0
Item for six quarters and seaven bushels of barley	10	0	0
Item for foure quarters and a halfe of wheate	14	0	0
Item for twentie bushels of peese	3	0	0
Item for seaventeene bushels of fetches	2	2	6
Item for six fletches of small dried bacon	2	6	0
Item for twelve bushels of oates	1	8	0
Item for a littill tabell and frame and A side Cobert		15	0
Item for six lether'd Chaires		15	0
Item for six plaine Chares		6	0
Item for A paire of angrierns		6	8
Item for twoe paire of bottrells		3	0
Item for twoe paire of tonges a slice and a fire pan		4	0
Item for a loockinge glas		1	0
Item for a tabele and frame and twoe formes		7	0
Item for a paire of angrierons		5	0
Item for Three spits and A jacke		10	0
Item for three Iron potts		1	0
Item for foure bras potts		12	0

Item for three bras kettels		10	0
Item for six bras skillats		12	0
Item for A bras Morter and pistele and other lumber in the Cechen		3	0
Item for a bed pan		3	4
Item for A Charne		2	0
Item for peuter	2	10	0
Item for a littill Coberd		6	0
Item for five tubes and a bole and a Cooler		16	0
Item for twelve beere vessels and other lumber	1	4	0
Item for A winnoinge sheete and Sacks	1	6	6
Item for a halfe bushell		3	4
Item for twoe Carpits and six Cushens		12	0
Item for a bedstedle and a chest and other Lumber		15	0
Item for a Silver bole	2	10	0
Item for twelve trayes		6	0
Item for one fether bed furnished	7	0	0
Item for A fether bed furnished	1	0	0
Item for A flock bed furnished	2	0	0
Item for woollan yarne and other lumber	1	10	0
Item for A fether bed furnished	5	0	0
Item for A fether bed furnished	1	10	0
Item for three truncks and one Chest	1	0	0
Item for eighteene paire of Sheets and other linnan	7	0	0
Item for A littill tabell and other lumber		13	0
Item for the planckes of the barne	1	0	0
Item for bords and hoggtrowes and other lumber	1	0	0
Item owinge to the deaseased	3	0	0
Item for the deaseased's Moneyes in his purs and wareing Apparrell	8	0	0
Tot	110	5	10
Exhibited 15 October 1662	[WSRO Ep I/29/112/020]		

Administration 5 April 1662
To Margaret, wife   [WSRO STC III/H/246, 267]

[1] Son of John, of Sussex. Oxford, Magdalen Hall, matriculated 1621 aged 17, BA 1624. Rector of West Itchenor 1640–1662, patron Crown. Married Margaret Taylor at West Itchenor 1642. Died 1662.

90. West Itchenor 12 Dec 1691 HUMPHREY DAY [1]
Appraisers: Robert Fearne, Thomas Billinghurst, John Woolland

	£	s	d
Money in purse and wearing Close	2	0	0
in the hall			
Item one drawing tabell one ferme and 3 joint stools	1	0	0
Item 7 Chaires		7	0
Item one paire of andorns one paire of doggs 1 fiet pan one pair of tongs 2 slices		8	0
Item one Jack one lanthorn one Looking glase one box Iorn		4	0

in the hall Chamber

Item 2 Beds with steddals and valyons Cortens one Rugg one matt one bolster one pillowe all belonging to them	5	0	0
one Littell teabell one Chest one deske and one truncke one seeing glass		10	0
Item 3 paire of sheats one dussen and halfe of napkins one paire of pelycoats 3 tabell Clothes	1	0	0
Item one paire of andiorns one paire of tongs one small box with som Child bed Lenen		10	0
Item pleate		12	0
Item books of all sorts	2	0	0

in the kitchen Chamber

Item one bed with furnetuer and steddell	2	0	0
Item one Chest with one dussen of peuter dish and 3 flaggins all in the Chest	2	5	0
Item one Chest and 2 boxes and one box with sum houseall Linnen all		15	0
Item one bed and steddell	1	0	0

In the brewhouse

Item one furness one kittell 2 skelletts	1	10	0
Item one [?]veatte and kiver and a tonn and one tubb		15	0

in the kittchen

Item 2 paire of [?]Cotterlins one Iron dripen pan 2 spitts 2 Iorn pan and one pair of gegiorns		7	0
Item 2 puter dishes one small drippen pan and trenchers one teabell one boule		5	0

In the Melkhouse

Item one Cerne and Rening tubb and trays		7	0

In the bottrey

Item 8 drink vessells and a meall tubb and 2 trays	1	0	0
one salting trow with 2 flitches of hogg in him	1	10	0

Goods without dors

Item two small Cows	4	0	0
Item one Fann	1	0	0
Item one hogg hutch and one hoggtrow		6	0
Item a well bucket and Chaine and Corbe and Roope one Chees prese one hogge tubb		7	0
Item wood and other ould Lomber	1	0	0
	32	0	0

[WSRO Ep I/29/112/27]

Administration 12 Dec 1691
To Ann, wife [WSRO Ep I/88/35/6]

[1] Son of Humphrey, of Gedney, Lincs. Alford Grammar School, Lincs. Cambridge, Magdalene, admitted sizar aged 15 and matriculated 1657, BA 1661. Ordained deacon 1666 (bishop of Chichester), priest 1672 (bishop of Ely). Curate of Kirdford c. 1671; of Birdham c. 1675. Rector of West Itchenor 1676–1691, patron Crown. Married Ann Strudwick of Kirdford at Kirdford by licence 1671. Died 1691.

91. Kirdford 14 May 1647 THOMAS HOLLAND, vicar [1]
Appraisers: John Tanner, William Boxall

	£	s	d
In primis His pursse and his apparell	7	0	0
In the Hall			
Item: A round table		16	0
A livery cupboard		8	0
A waincot chaire and 6 joyned stooles		13	0
Six cushins		5	0
A carpet and a cupboord clothe		6	0
A Clock with plummets and lines	2	4	0
An Iron back for a chimney		16	0
A paire of andirons		8	0
A fire shovell a paire of tongs and bellows		3	0
A birding peece a musket and bandaleeres a pistol and a sword	2	0	0
In the Kitchen			
Item: A little table a planck and a frame		3	0
A forme 4: ioned stooles and six chaires		6	0
A Cupboord and A rack		2	6
A dresser benches and Six shelves		4	4
4: spitts an yron dripingpan a fender a tosting iron		10	0
2: latine driping pans 3: little latine pans and an apple roster		2	0
4: yron pots one brass pot	1	5	0
5: kettles a brasse pan and 3: skillets		11	0
2: paire of andirons		14	0
A fire shovell A paire of tongs and bellowes		2	0
A cradle a pillow a curtaine and a curtainerod		2	4
2: wheeles for wollen and for linnen		3	2
In the Closet			
Item: Glasses galliepots Boxes 6: shelves and other hushlement		10	0
In the Buttery			
Item: A round table and A cupboord		10	0
A salting trough and a powdring tub		7	0
five kilderkins and foure firkins and a funnell		14	0
3: stands 2: tankerds potts and other drinking cups		3	0
sixe candlesticks and A sider trough and snuffers		5	0
foure duzne of pewter and A flaggon	3	14	0
In the Bakehouse			
Item: A chest for meale A bin for flower		4	0
A kneading kiver A halfe bushell and a peck		3	0
3: sacks 2: searchers 2: sives and a shaull		7	0
5: shelves and crocks		2	0
In the Brewhouse			
Item: A furnace	1	0	0
A mashfate A stand A tap kiver A cooler		13	0
A tunne A bucking tub and some other tubbs		10	0
A handsaw A hatchet A hammer A spade garden sheeres		2	4
In the passage chamber			
Item: A presse	1	0	0

A Carved bedstead with a cord a mat and curtaine rods	3	3	0
A trundle bedstead with A cord and A mat		3	4
A feather bed and two boulsters	2	2	0
Three white blanquets and A covering		12	0
A tapistry covering 5: curtaines and 2: chests	1	5	0

In the Chamber over the Kitchen

Item: A bedstead wt a cord and a mat A teaster curtaines rods 5: curtaines and valence	2	0	0
A feather bed 2: boulsters and 2: pillowes	3	0	0
Three blankets and A greene rugg	1	0	0
Three window curtaines and two satten cushins		10	0
A trundle bedstead with A cord and a mat		4	0
Two greene cushin chaires and 2: stooles		10	0
A red leather chaire and a wainscot chaire		5	0
A needle worke stoole and a table and a carpet		7	0
A wainscot Chest and A Trunck		12	0
A paire of Andirons and A paire of little dogs		5	0
A fire shovell and a paire of tongs		1	4

In the Chamber over the Hall

Item: A bedstead with a cord A matt a cover curtaine rods and curtaines		14	0
A feather bed Two blankets boulsters and Two pillows	3	0	0
Three blankets and A greene rug	1	2	0
Item: A trundle bedstead with a cord and a matt		4	0
A feather bed A boulster	1	12	0
Three blankets and A covering		12	0
Two window curtains and 2: boxes		5	0
An yronbound trunck and A close stoole with a pan		10	0
A livery cupboord and a cushin stoole		4	0
A paire of Andirons A fireshovell and a paire of tongs		2	2

In the chamber over the buttrey

Item: A bedstead a matt		3	6
Two flock beds and three flock boulsters		18	0
Three blankets and two coverings		15	0
A great chest and A little chest		12	0

Abroad

Item: A mare	7	0	0
A colt A saddle and A bridle	5	4	0
Hay A wheele barrow and Beese	1	10	0
Boords pales with other hushlement		5	0
Item Debts on his books And by bonds	76	4	0
Item: Linnen 21 paire of sheetes	10	0	0
Eight paire of pillow beeres	1	14	0
Six Cupboord clothes		12	0
14 Table cloaths	1	4	0
4 duzne of napkins	1	4	0
And one duzne of Towells		10	0
Item: About 24 yeards of new cloth	3	7	0

In the Studdie

Item: A round table		4	6

A cushen stoole and a red leather chaire		8	0
A nest of drawing boxes and an other boxe		10	0
Item: All the bookes	30	0	0
And a frame of shelves		10	0
Plate:1: bole 3: salts 2: duzne of spoones	12	0	0
Left at Warnham with Mr Morrice			
Item: A carved wainscot bedstead wt cord mat and curtaine rods	3	10	0
Another bedstead with some appurtenances		5	0
A table and A ioyned forme	1	2	0
A brewing vate And the bodie of A cheese presse		7	0
Item: Left with Mr Fist A paire of virginalls	1	10	0
left with Henry Sumersale 2: cheese presses		2	0
Suma totalis	215	8	10

Memorandum that the bookes were valued and priced at £30 May 19th 1647. By us Will. Napper, Maurice Rowlands, John Willshaw. [WSRO Ep I/29/116/76]

Will: made 6 April 1647; proved 1 June 1647
Wife Joan, executrix; two eldest sons: Edward, Henry; eldest daughter: Grace; second daughter: Patience; three younger children: Thomas, Charity, William. All children under 21
Overseers: Richard Deering of Burton, Gregory Hurst
Witnesses: Henry Strudwicke (Crouchland) John Wilshaw [WSRO STC I/21/179]

[1] Of Steyning. Eton College. Cambridge, King's, admitted Eton scholar aged 16 and matriculated 1583, fellow 1586–1590, BA 1588; called MA 1623. Ordained deacon 1623, priest 1624 (bishop of Chichester). Vicar of Madehurst 1625–1626, patron Thomas Page, yeoman; of Warnham 1626, patron dean and chapter of Canterbury; of Kirdford 1638–1647, patron Richard, Viscount Lumley. Prebendary of Selsey 1631–1647. Married Joan Hobbs of Warnham at Houghton by licence 1625. Died 1647; buried Kirdford.

92. Lancing 2 Nov 1622 WALTER GIBBENS, vicar [1]

Appraisers: William Smith of Goring, Richard Horton, William Deans, Henry Grinfielde and John Thomas of Lancing

	£	s	d
In primis in the Hale			
The Table and bench and 6 stooles at		16	0
Item the Cupborde and Cage and litle table and other implements	1	8	0
In the Parlour			
Item 1 Bedsteddle 1 Coverlett and 2 blanketts with a Matt and fetherbed	5	10	0
Item 1 Cupborde 1 table and frame and livery Cupborde 4 Chestes and 2 forms	2	0	0
In the Chamber above			
Item 1 Bedsteddle 2 boulsters 1 fetherbedd 1 blankett and Coverlett and matt	2	10	0
Item 1 flocbedd and blankett 1 Coverlett and boulster	1	0	0
In the Hall lofte			
Item Hemp and Beanes		12	0
Item 6 nayle butter and 6 nayles of hony	1	0	0

Item	£	s	d
Item Cheese 10 nayle		13	0
Item 3 tubs and litle [?]somid peeces 2 Wheeles for Lynnen		8	0
Item Wooll Tyre and Apples		2	0
Item in the Buttery			
16 truggs for milke 16 ferkins 6 shelves and stan for beer		16	0
Item a bunting hutch and Charne and Crocks with Some implements		4	0
Item 4 fletches of bacon	1	0	0
Item Wimmed Corne Wheate and barly		17	0
Item salt 2 flasketts 2 basketts with Breade grate and brushe and 2 …	..	…	..
Item in the Kitchinne			
Item 1 Table 6 benches and forms and stooles with 1 Cup and 8 bowls		12	0
Item 3 buckets 22 halfe bushells a gallon a Corne shovell a spitter axe and hatchett and oven pyle		7	0
Item a Warming pan a Kaldron brasse potts and Kettles and skilletts with smale yetessones [?utensils]	2	5	0
Item 2 spitts 2 yron drippinge Pans 2 potthangers 2 payre pothooks a cleaver gridiron Andiron and tongs at		10	0
Item Woodden platters and dishes and other lumberment		2	0
Item 13 pewter platters	1	11	2
Item 6 smale peeces and 3 sawcers and 3 porringers with Bason and chamber pot		8	0
Item Bason and yowre 4 pewter candlestickes 2 pewter cups and brasse morter with pestle		12	0
Item 17 payre sheetes 6 table clothes 18 napkins 2 payre pillowbers	6	13	4
Item pyke buckanett sworde and Coate		7	0
Item 2 kyne	4	0	0
Item 7 hoggs	2	4	0
Item wheate barley tares and hay	20	0	0
Item Woode	2	0	0
Item rackes and hogg troes		6	0
Item Wheate sowen in grounde	6	0	0
Item some yeares of a lease unexpired	1	0	0
Item drinking glasses a looking glass and [?]style stickes		2	6
Item brake Billowes Laddar prongs forke and some smale implements		5	0
Item Powltrey		10	0
Item his gowne Cloke and other his apparrell	5	0	0
Item in gold £37 which he gave to his sonne Robart Gibbins in his will Nuncupative			
Sum total	112	0	0

[WSRO Ep I/29/118/12]

Will nuncupative: 20 Nov 1622; proved 21 Jan 1623

Wife Ann

All leasehold to son Robert Gibbens, who was 'to beare discharge and paye halfe the charge of the dilapidations of the Vicaridge howse of Lancinge'

Witnesses: Richard Norton of Lancing, gent, Robert Gibbens

[WSRO STC II/S Dean 1622 (7)]

[1] Ordained deacon 1571 (bishop of Chester), priest 1574 (bishop of Chichester). Vicar of Lancing 1571–1622, patron bishop of Lincoln. Married Joan Treadcrafte at Lancing 1577 (died 1592); Agnes [*sic*] Doddinge of Lancing at Lancing by licence 1606. Died 1622; buried Lancing.

93. Lancing 2 June 1639 TIMOTHY HOLNEY, minister [1]
Appraisers: Richard Searle, Steven Standen, Richard Lusher, Edward White

	£	s	d
In primis in the hale			
on table an fworme one benche		3	0
Item 8 giene stooles		5	4
Item one chayar on [?]gray rug one cradele on pet … mantel		3	8
Item 2 brand Irones an Iron slice a payer of tongs and 2 payer of hand arres with other things		4	6
In the Chichen			
Item 4 ketteles 2 posnetes on Iron pot		14	0
Item 4 ferkins for drink		2	8
Item 2 toubes on couller on pouddring toube		3	0
Item a halfe bushall on chorne one payle		2	0
Item on weminge sheat		3	0
Item on olde coubbard 2 brakes		3	0
Item an axe on hachat on beke on spett a payer of hangers		2	6
In the millk house			
Item 7 milke boules with shelfes an other things		5	0
In the buttery			
Item 2 toubes one couller on payell		3	0
Item on driping pan a friing pan a choping knife on cleaver on skimmar		4	0
Item one wollon whele one lenen whel and for deshis and tranchars		2	0
Item on morter 3 candelsteckes		2	0
Item 7 peeces of pautar one Dousson of sponnes 2 salt sellers		8	0
Item …fe an shelvfes an other things		3	4
In the lettell parler			
Item one low … bedsteddell one fether bede 2 fether boulsters blankett coverlet on pelow 2 payre of sheats all this was the womans before she was marred	1	10	0
Item one warming pane one Chayar with other things		2	0
In the chichene loufte			
Item of broke hempe one toube with othere things		3	6
In and othere louft			
Item one Chayar one cheest with othere things		3	0
In the Studie			
Item for his bookes and other things there	[?]	[?]	[?]
In the lodging chambar			
Item of sheate 5 payar	1	0	0
Item 4 table clous 2 towwells		4	6
Item 22 table napkens		11	0
Item 2 pelow Cotes		1	6
Item the Chestes that was hers before 2 and 6 boxe		6	0
Item on bedsteddell one fethear bed and that belongeth to hem	2	1	0

Item 2 Chestes 2 boxes	10	0
Item one truckell bedsteddell one flockbede and that belongeth to hem	10	0
Item one … ter	5	0
Item 3 cheastes	3	0
Item his gound and waring apparrell and mony in his purse	2 0	0

Things in the gats

Item the wood and a wataring trouf and a hogge trouf with other things	1 0	0
Item one acare and …	1 6	0
Item 2 acares of tares	1 0	0

For the cattell

Item one Cow	2 6	8
Item one young barren hogge a yonge sow with 5 young piges	16	0
Item old Iron and other thinges forgotten	1	0
The Somm is	19 9	0

[WSRO Ep I/29/118/28]

Administration 29 June 1639
To Joan, wife   [WSRO STC III/H/116, 124]

[1] Called BA 1618. Ordained deacon 1618, priest 1620 (bishop of Chichester). Curate of East Lavant c. 1620; of Albourne 1621. Licensed curate Lewes archdeaconry 1621. Vicar of Lancing 1626–1639, patron bishop of Lincoln. Married Joan Dunstall at Henfield 1627. Died 1639.

94. Lewes 7 Feb 1712 EDWARD NEWTON [1]
Appraisers: Walter Brett the elder, John Maynard

	£	s	d
In primis the deceaseds wearing			
Apparrell and money in his Purse	13	0	0

In the Kitchen

Item 14 Pewter dishes One pewter Bason a dozen of Plates 6 Pye plates One small pewter Dish 7 pewter Sawcers One Bed pan 2 pewer Candlestickes One pewter Flaggon a parcell of old pewter 6 Turkey worke Chairs 7 Cushions one amrd Chair One small Chair a Table a joind stoole a Chimney Back a pair of Andirons Firepan Tongs and Fender a Jack 3 Spits a Chopping Knide a brass Skimmer a brass Spoon a brass Candlestick an iron Forke a small Cupboard a Pot hanger 2 Curtains and a Curtaine rod and a Bacon Rack	3	13	0

In the Brewhouse

Item One brass Furnace 4 Tubs 3 Keelers 2 small brass pots 4 skillets a brass Kettle a fish plate a frying Pan a Gridiron 2 iron Candlesticks 2 Pails	2	11	6

In the Cellar

Item 5 small beer Vessells a Stallage a dozen and an halfe lass botles		8	0

In the Kitchen Chamber and Closett

Item a Looking Glass a pair of brass Andirons 4 little Stools a Cushion a parcell of earthen Ware and other small things		10	0

In the Brewhouse Chamber

Item 2 feather beds 2 blanketts 2 bolsters One old Rugg one Bedstedle matt Cord Curtains and Vallance 2 old pillows a Chest of drawers a large Trunke a small looking glass	5	10	0

In the Fore Garrett

Item 3 Chests One Trunke and one Table		8	0
Item in the Trunke Four pair of Sheets One single diaper Sheet 2 diaper Table Cloths One other Table Cloth a dozen of fringe Napkins and a fringe Table Cloth 16 pillowbers a dozen o diaper Napkins 2 dozen other Napkins One damaske sheet and Two damaske Table Cloths	8	15	6
Item in the in laid Chest One dozen of Napkins 3 Table Cloths 3 pairs of sheets 6 Pillowbers 5 Towells 19 more Napkins One other Table Cloth 15 Diaper Clouts	2	16	0
Item 2 small Ruggs 2 old blankets a Coverlett 2 old Pillows a peice of Tapestry and an old Turkey Carpett		6	0

In the Back Garrett

Item one halfe headed Bedstedle matt and Cord a Feather bed bolster and pillow 3 blankets a small Press 4 old stools a deal Box and a small wooden Chest	1	6	8
Item a Pewter Still Close Stooll and Pan		8	0

In the Study

Item 55 ounces and 9dn of Plate	13	2	6
Item 2 old Watches an old pair of silver Buttons a small Silver Seale a Gold Ring and ... silver Buckles	1	10	0
Brought from the other side	54	5	2

In the Study

Item a Chair a Stoole a deske a Side board ^a litle Trunke^ and a parcell of old Books		15	0
Item a Clock on the Stairs		10	0

In the Stable

Item Wood Faggots and Charcoale	1	5	0
Item Lumber and things unseen and forgotten		5	0
Suma totlis huius Inventy	57	0	2

[ESRO W/INV 266]

Will: made 6 Dec 1711; proved 12 March 1712
Wife Elizabeth; sons: John, executor (with son-in-law John Holmwood)
Witnesses: William Garland, Samuel Walls, William Brett　　　　[ESRO W/A 48.173]

[1] Born Maidstone, Kent. Cambridge, Emmanuel, admitted 1644; Jesus, admitted 1645, BA 1647. Oxford, Balliol, fellow 1649, MA 1650. Cambridge, incorporated MA 1652. Ordained 1652 (presbytery of Salisbury). Rector of Kingston by Sea 1654. Rector of St Anne's, Lewes, with Southover 1657, nominated by Lord Protector; ejected for nonconformity 1662. Licensed preacher 1672. Denounced by grand jury 1685. Married daughter of Benjamin Pickering, his predecessor at St Anne's and Southover; Margaret Lane of Southover, widow, at Falmer by licence 1689 (buried St Anne's 1689); Elizabeth Downer, widow, at Pagham 1691. Died 1712 aged 84; buried St Anne's.

95. Lyminster 30 March 1688 FRANCIS WRIGHT, vicar [1]
Appraisers: Isaac Duke, Andrew Horrist, John Wilkins

	£	s	d
In primis for his wearing apparill and mony in his parse	1	0	0
Item for 2 fether beeds 3 flock boulsters one fether bolster and 2 bedsteds one rugge and 2 blanketts one payre of Curtens and vallians Cords and matt	2	1	6
Item for five payre of Course sheets 6 Course table Cloaths 6 Course touells	1	1	6
Item one small buck [*sic*] cubbard 2 Chestes one boxe one syd Cubbard		10	6
Item for one furnice one Cittell one warmingpan and one ould brase pott one Iorne pott 2 payre of pothucks 2 payre of poyhangers one payre of small brandirons one fier pan and tonges one payreof grydiorns	1	9	9
Item one Jack one spitt one dripingpan one fender one sryding knife one payre tosting iornes		7	6
Item one Cubbard 2 small tables one greate 2 Chayes 2 Joyne stooles	1	0	0
Item for one seeingglas		1	6
Item 4 drink vessels 6 tubbs 3 trays		12	6
Item one horse	1	10	0
Item three swine		15	0
Item for other Lumber infitt and unseene		5	0
Item for three dishes of pewter		1	3
Item for bookes		15	0
Sume totall	11	11	0

Exhibited by Margaret Wright, widow, 30 May 1688   [WSRO Ep I/29/131/95]

No will or administration found

[1] Born Buckinghamshire, son of Richard, of Everdon, Northants, cleric. Oxford, Merton, matriculated aged 19 and BA 1629, fellow 1630, MA 1634. Vicar of Cocking 1654–1683; of Lyminster 1684–1688. Ordained deacon and priest 1662 (bishop of Chichester). Curate of Littlehampton c. 1684. Died 1688.

96. Madehurst 30 March 1652 ADAM PAGE [1]
Appraisers: James Goble, John Ludgater

	£	s	d
In primis his Wareinge parell and money in his purse	2	0	0
Item Toward Twenty Pewter dishes a Chamber pott and a salte seller	1	10	6
Item a dripinge panne a bell skillet a brasse Morter and a ladle tow brasse kitells a brasse panne a bed panne and a brasse potte	1	15	0
Item tow Iron spitts one pare of gridIrons and a Tosteinge Iron a fender and an Iron plate and an Axe		10	0
Item a Tunn and one ferkine three Tubes tow kealers tow Joine stooles tow Buckets one Chaire and three other stooles and other Lumber		15	0
In the Chamber			
Item one Joined bedsteddle one Feather bed tow boulsters tow pillowes tow coverlets and tow blanckets	2	10	0
Item one peece of Canvis		9	0

Item tow Cheastes and foure pare of Sheetes a dussen of napkines and tow pillow bers	1	10	0
Item one Linen Torne		1	4
In the Lofte			
Item one Truckell Bedstedlle one flocke bed and a flocke boulster		4	0
Item one sowe Hogge and tow weaner Pigges	1	0	0
Item woode in the gate		12	0
Item one pare of skales with an Iron Beame		2	6
Item Boockes in his Study	4	0	0
Sum is	16	18	10

[WSRO Ep I/29/132/14]

Administration 26 Oct 1652

To John Page, next of kin, relict … Page having renounced   [WSRO STC III/K/158]

[1] Of Sussex. Oxford, Balliol, matriculated 1610 aged 18, BA 1612, MA 1615. Ordained deacon and priest 1614 (bishop of Oxford). Vicar of Tortington 1614, patron Crown. Rector of Middleton 1619, patron Crown. Married Margaret Gratwick of Yapton at Middleton 1635. Died 1652.

97. Up Marden and Compton 22 May 1655 ANTHONY GRAY [1]

Appraisers: John Marner, Nicholas Fayremaner, John Valler

	£	s	d
[In] his lodging Chamber			
In primis his w[earing] Apparrell and [mo]ney in his purse	5	0	0
Item… bedstedle with Curtaynes … 1 featherbed and boulster 2 pillowes 2 blankets and a coverlet	5	0	0
Item one other bedstedle with featherbed and a boulster … pillowes 2 blanckets and a coverlet	[?]1	0	0
Item 1 great cheste … truncke and a presse	1	0	0
Item all the lynnen there	1	10	0
Item 1 table paire of Andirons		1	6
In the Parlor Chamber			
Item 1 bedstedle with Curtaines and rods 1 feather bed and boulster 2 pillowes 2 blankets and a rugg	5	0	0
… 2 chayres …		10	0
…		1	0
[In the] Chamber over the kitchen			
Item 1 bedstedle with curtaines and curtain rods featherbed and boulster 2 pillowes 2 blankets and a coverlet	4	0	0
Item 1 other bedstedle 1 featherbed and boulster and 3 blankets	1	10	0
In his Study			
Item his Books there with a table and chayre and shelves	1	10	0
In the Parlor			
Item 1 drawing table with a carpet 6 chaires 6 joyned stooles and a side Cubbord	2	0	0
Item 1 paire of Andirons		6	8
In the hall			
Item 1 long table … Chayres and an …	1	0	0

In the kitchen

Item … peuter and flag … chamber potts	2	10	0
Item 4 brasse ketles 2 brasse potts 1 brasse pann 4 brasse skilletts 1 brasse chaffing dish a warming pann and a brasse skimmer	1	15	0
Item 4 iron dripping pannes 4 spitts a paire of racks a paire of andirons a paire of tongs and fire pan a slice a pire of gridirons 2 iron … ..iron furnaces a paire of … A Jacke with an iron backe … Ch … and an iron morter and pestle …	[?]2	0	0
Item 2 small flitches of bacon		12	0
Item 1 table and a chayre		5	0

In the Ba …

Item … and two buckets	..	..	..

In the …

Item a safe … a few shelves …	1	6	0

In the Celler

Item a Tunn a keeler …tubb a kiver … 5 barells and 3 firkins with the … siltingtrough and an … a boultinghutch and 2 old …	2	10	0
Plate and debts owing Item 1 silver bowell and 2 silver spoones	2	0	0
Item owing by Nicholas Fayremaner	3	5	0
Item owing more uppon a bond	30	0	0

Goods abroad

Item faggotts	2	0	0
Item a … two Coults with a bridle and [sad]le	2	10	0
Item 2 ho …	1	0	0
Item … small wheeles	1	10	0
Sum Totall at	88	10	2

Debts owing by the said deceased at the tyme of his death

In primis owing unto Mr Thomas Gray for rent of certeyne land for sevrall yeares	75	0	0
Item owing unto Mr William Thomas Clerke for officiating for the sayd Deceased	16	0	0
Item owing to divers other persons sevrall small summes of money amounting in all to	1	10	0
Item for the funeral charges of the said deceased	5	0	0

[WSRO Ep I/29/135/18]

No will or administration found

[1] Of Sussex. Oxford, New College, matriculated 1604 aged 22, BA 1609, MA 1612. Ordained deacon and priest 1613 (bishop of Oxford). Licensed preacher Woolbeding and Winchester diocese 1615. Vicar of Alciston 1616–1619, patron bishop of Chichester; of Compton with Up Marden and chapel of West Marden 1619–1655, patron Thomas Gray of Woolbeding, gent. Possibly married Ann Bragg at Up Marden 1651; second wife Hester. Died 1655.

98. Mayfield 2 April 1730 PETER BAKER, vicar [1]
Appraisers: Joseph Beale, Alexander Reade, mercer

	£	s	d
In primis his Wearing Apparell and Money in his Purse	150	0	0
In the Kitchen			
Item One Clock One Jack Two tables and One Bunting Hutch Six Chairs Five Dozen of Pewter Plates Fourteen Pewter Dishes Three Spitts Two pair of Andirons Fire pan and Tongs Two Gridirons Two Copper Te Kettles and Three Sopper Pots Two Case Irons a pair of Stilliards and Some other things	15	8	0
Item One Iron Back		10	0
In the Little Parlour			
Two Tables Six Cane Chairs A Corner Cupboard and Weather Glass	1	5	0
In the Hall			
One Iron Back		5	0
Two tables Six Cane Chairs One Couch One Looking Glass Fire pan Tongs Andirons and a pair of Bellows	3	5	0
Item One Bag Gammon Table		6	0
In the Great Parlour			
One Ovell table One Hand Tea table and Two other Tea tables Seven Cane Chairs Cane Couch and Cushion One Looking Glass Two Sconces Fire pan and Tongs a pair of Bellows And a pair of Andirons and Seven pictures in Frames	6	5	0
Item three Setts of China Cupps Saucers and Basons	3	3	0
In the Lower Kitchen			
Five Iron pottage potts one iron Kettle One Bell Brass Pottage Pott and Fish Kettle Five Bell Brass Skilletts and One Iron Skillett Three Coffee potts two Saucepans Four Dripping panns One Brass Mortar and pestle One Stew pan Two Warming Pans Two Tin Covers a pewter Cistern and Bason and Pewter Flaggon Two Pailes One Iron pipe Box Three Cutting Knives Two Dozen of Trenchers Wooden Platters Some Earthen Ware and other Lumber One iron back Three pair of Pothooks One Slice and An Iron Oven Door	9	1	0
In the Bakehouse			
Two Keelers One Wooden Horse Two Fry Pans Two Churnes and Some Earthen Ware	1	10	0
In the Brewhouse			
Two Copper Furnaces	4	4	0
Item Two Bucking Tubbs One Cheese press Leaden Cistern pipe and Wheels Two Tubbs and two Keelers and Pailes One Mash Tubb one Cooler Two Wort Tubbs	9	0	0
In the Strong beer Cellar			
Six hogsheads and Six Barrells and Four Brass Casks	3	10	0
Six Dozen of Bottles		9	0
In the Small Beer Cellar			
Seven Barrells Three keelers Three Powdering Tubbs One Bacon Trough and Stalders	3	8	0
In the Milk Cellar			
Three Milk Leads Three Milk Bowles Eight Crocks	1	0	0

Upon the Staires			
Six old paper Pictures		5	0
In the Best Chamber			
One Feather Bed with Mohair Curtains and Vallence Coverlett Blancketts and Bolster and All things belonging to it	15	0	0
Item One Easy Chair and Seven other Cane Chairs	2	0	0
Item One Chest of Drawers One Looking Glass and Jappan Table Hangings and Curtains A pair of Tongs Firepan and Andirons a pair of bellows and Iron Back and Fender and Stoole and One Picture	7	0	0
In the Study Chamber			
One feather Bed Coverlett Curtains and Vallence blanketts and Bolster and All things belonging to it One table Window Curtains and Hangings of the Room	5	10	0
In the Hall Chamber			
One feather Bed with Camblett Curtains Vallence Coverlett blanketts and Bolster and All things Belonging to it Two Tables Six Chaires One Close Stool and Looking Glass	7	0	0
In the Chamber over the old Kitchen			
One Feather bed China Curtains and Vallence Coverlett Blanketts and Bolster with all things belonging and One other Truckle Bed One Small Table one Looking Glass and One Chair and Window Curtains	5	0	0
In Mrs Bakers Chamber			
One Feather Bed workd Curtains and Vallence Coverlett Blanketts and Bolster and All things Belonging	12	0	0
Item One Chest of Drawers Looking Glass Close Stool and Table one Clock and Six Pictures and Some other odd things and one Armd Chair	8	0	0
In Mrs Bakers Closett			
In Plate of Severall kinds	50	0	0
Item China Bowles Cups and Plates	2	2	0
Twelve small pictures and other odd things	1	0	0
In the Kitchen Chamber			
One Old Feather Bed Rugg and Blanketts and All things belonging Six Chests Four Trunks One Looking Glass One Pillio [*sic*] Pillion Cloth and Some other old Lumber	3	0	0
In Linnen of All Sorts Fine and Coarse Old and New	60	0	0
Upon The Stairhead			
One Press for Cloaths		18	0
In Mr Bakers Study			
One Old Chest of drawers and Old Cabinett and two Chairs		13	0
The Library of Books	20	0	0
In the Garrett			
Three Brass Kettles one Timbe Jack Two Seives Four Pailes Six Cheese Bailes	4	11	0
Item Seven Bell Cucumber Glasses and Seven Framed Cucumber Glasses one keeler One Tubb Three Bowles Some Beer Glasses Six Earthen Chamber Pots and Other Lumber	1	0	0
In Cattle			
Item Two Coach Horses	25	0	0
Two Cows and Two Calves	10	0	0

	£	s	d
One Saddle Mare	4	4	0
Three Hoggs	2	2	0
Item One Garden Roll and Iron Frame		10	0
Item One Charriot and Glasses and Harness	20	0	0
Two Saddles and bridles	1	1	0
Item One Waggon Two Courts with Wheeles and Two Pair of Court Wheeles	4	0	0
In the Woodhouse			
One Apple Mill and Press	1	5	0
One Stack of Hay	15	0	0
At Mr Leatherborrow's			
Two feather Beds One with Curtains and the other without One kettle One Pottage pott one Fire pan and Tongs One pair of Andirons	5	0	0
Item Some old Goods and Lumber at the Place	10	0	0
Item for Woods Sold to Mr Fuller and Mr Hussey	159	0	0
Item for Principall and Interest upon Severall Securitys	350	0	0
Item Debts due on Book	100	0	0
Item things unseen and forgott	5	0	0
	717	13	0

[ESRO W/INV/SM 2]

Administration 18 March 1731
To wife Martha
Sureties: Joseph Bell of Mayfield, yeoman, and Alexander Read of Mayfield, mercer
[ESRO W/SM/D 6.129]

[1] Third son of John, of Mayfield Place. Cambridge, Emmanuel, admitted 1690, matriculated 1691, BA 1695, MA 1698. Ordained deacon 1695, priest 1696 (bishop of Lincoln). Vicar of Mayfield 1696–1730. Married Marthanna Baker of Mayfield at Mayfield by licence 1716. Died 1730 aged 58; buried Mayfield.

99. Merston 16 Feb 1677 DAVID BLANEY [1]

Appraisers: William Coxe, Henry Hall, James Launder

	£	s	d
In the Kitchin			
In primis Three paire of Potthangers Fyve paire of Potthooks Twoe small spittes and Three lattin panns		13	0
Item One fire pann Twoe paire of tongs one Iren Trist one paire of gridirons one paire of doggs		8	0
Item One paire of gridirons one Iren Forke one Iren Fender Fower smoothing irens and a grate		5	0
Item One Jacke … Twoe shreding knives		6	0
Item Three Brasse Potts Twoe Iren Potts Three brasse Kettles Three brasse skelletts and one warming pann	1	11	0
Item one brasse Furnace one brasse morter	1	11	6
Item Tenne Pewter dishes Twoe pewter plates Twoe pewter candle sticks one Flagon Twoe pewter Chamber potts and other small peeces	1	15	0
Item one Table Three Joyned stooles and Twoe Chaires		10	0

In the Parlour			
One Cubbard Eight Chaires one Forme Sixe Cushions and Twoe olde Carpetts	1	10	0
In the Butterie			
One Saltinge Trow Seaven beere vessells and some other Tubbs	1	10	0
Item Twoe small Flitches of Bacon in salt	1	0	0
In the Milkehouse			
Sixteene Bowles and Trayes One Charne and severall other things	1	10	0
In the Wash house			
One Cheese presse Fyve Tubbs and other lumber	1	10	0
In the Parlor Chamber			
One Bedsted with Curtaines and vallence One Feather Bed one Boulster one Rugg One Coverlett and one Blankett	4	0	0
Item One Table Three Chaires Twoe Trunkes and one Chest	1	0	0
Item Twelve paire of sheets Three dozen of Napkins Nine Pillow Coates Five Table Clothes Three Towells and other olde linnen	6	10	0
In the Hall Chamber			
One Bedsted One Fether Bed with furniture	4	5	0
Item One Trundle Bed Furnished	1	5	0
Item olde Chests and lumber		12	0
Item Bookes in The Studdie	5	0	0
In the Chamber over the Entry			
One little Bed with other materialls	1	10	0
In the Backside			
Item haye and ….in Cocks Wood and Faggotts and an olde Cart and Wheeles	10	0	0
Item Wheate Thrashes and unthrashed	25	0	0
Item Barly Thrashed and unthrashed	5	0	0
Item Oates Thrashed and unthrashed	3	0	0
Item in Pease	2	0	0
Item One Sow and Piggs	1	0	0
Item Seaven Younge Shouts	4	0	0
Item Three Cowes and Three Calves	9	0	0
Item One Nagge and a Mare one Cart … sadle and pillion side Sadle and Pannell	8	0	0
Item Sacks Wimsheet and Fann	2	0	0
Item Three silver spoones	10	0	0
Item Money in The house and abroad and his wearinge Aparrell	184	0	0
Summa Totalis	296	12	6

[WSRO Ep I/29/136/20]

Will nuncupative: made 28 Jan 1677; proved 19 Feb 1677
Wife Hester, executrix
Witnesses: Joan Bignall and others   [WSRO STC I/26/107b]

For probate account see **186**

---

[1] Possibly Oxford, Exeter, MA. Rector of Merston 1655, nominated by Lord Protector; instituted 1660–1677, patron Crown. Died 1677.

100. Midhurst 15 Sept 1614 RICHARD GUY [1]
Appraisers: Robert Ruffin, John Fatchen, John Bishop

	£	s	d
In the hall			
In primis 1 payre of tressells 1 tubb 1 old fourme 2 old chayres 1 Joyned stoole 1 payre of belloes 1 slyce 2 payre of potthangers and 1 little table with a bench	4	0	0
In the lofte over the hall			
Item 1 old standing bedsteadle with an old tester 1 truckle bedsteadle 2 flockbeds 2 flock bolsters 3 pillowes 3 coverletts 3 little chests and a little table	1	13	8
The linnen cloathes			
Item 3 payre of sheets 3 napkins 1 table cloath		16	0
Item his wearing apparell	1	10	0
Item his books	5	0	0
Item 1 little table 1 old chayre with 2 old shelves		1	0
In the kitchen			
Item 2 brassed kettles 1 Iron pott		17	0
Item 2 platters 1 little basen 4 sawcers 1 little pewter pott 3 spones of tyn		3	4
Item 1 still		6	8
Item 2 tubbes 3 firkens 1 bole 1 keever 3 tankerds 1 spitter 1 well buckett and a rope 1 forme 1 huche 1 old axe 1 old hatchet 5 ropes of oynions		10	0
Item certeyne wood with other lumbrye		3	0
The totall sume is	11	4	8

[WSRO Ep I/29/138/8]

Will nuncupative: 16 Aug 1614; proved 17 Sep 1614
Wife Elizabeth; 3 sons (includingOnesiphoras)
Books to be equally divided among two sons
Witnesses: Robert Ruffin, John Fachen, John Bishop [WSRO STC II/M Dean 1614 (37)]

[1] Possibly Oxford, Magdalen, BA 1599. Ordained deacon and priest 1606 (bishop of Rochester). Curate of Easebourne c. 1606. Married Elizabeth Holden at Billingshurst 1602.

101. Midhurst 8 March 1717 RICHARD TOWNSEND [1]
Appraisers: Jeffrey Dawtry, John Mitchell

	£	s	d
In primis his wearing apparell and money in Purse	34	0	0
In the Chamber over the Kitchin			
One Feather Bed and Bolster Three Blanketts one Quilt two Pillows Curtains and Valence rods and steddle	6	0	0
A table Chest of Drawes 6 Chairs Close Stool and Trunke 8 Pictures and Curtains to the windows	4	4	0
In the Parlour Chamber			
Eighteen Pictures and Glass	1	0	0

In the Garrett			
One Feather Bed one Bolster Two Pillows Four Blanketts Coverlet Curtaines and Steddle One Desk Box one Spinning Wheel	3	0	0
In the Passage Chamber			
Twelve Boxes		12	0
Books in his Study	3	0	0
Seven pairs of Sheets	2	16	0
Two dozen of Napkins	1	0	0
Thirty Towells		10	0
Eight table Cloths	1	0	0
Eight Pillobers		12	0
In the Kitchin			
Fire pan and tongs a Jack Two Doggs one Fender one pair of Andirons one pair of Potthooks one Still Two spitts Gridgirons Chopping knife Cleaver and Candle Box heaters and Box Iron iron Slice and rack 6 Chairs 3 Tables	2	15	6
In the Parlour			
Eleven pewter dishes Cake Plate Two pewter rings and Cake hoop Two pair of Andirons Fire pan and Tongs warming pan one Dripping pan one stewpan Eleven Iron Skivers Seven brass Candlesticks Five Iron ditto 2 brass skimers Scales and Copper Lamp Cullender pye and pudding Pan 6 Pye pans Two small Chairs and Two Tables 13 pictures window curtains and rods	7	0	0
In the Brewhouse			
One Furnise 3 potts 1 brass kettle 2 Skilletts one tea kettle and Coper Pott 10 Tubs and kevers 7 Barills 3 stands one salting Trough seven Douzen of Bottles and rack One wooden horse one Chest and other Lumber	8	19	0
One Tankerd one Salver Two salts Two watches Two spoons and 6 tea dishes	16	0	0
Due to the Deceased	150	0	0
	242	8	6

[WSRO Ep I/29/138/186]

Administration 22 March 1717
To Jane, wife   [WSRO STC III/N/9]

[1] Possibly son of Anthony, of Chipping Campden, Glos; Oxford, Trinity, matriculated 1699 aged 17. Ordained priest 1716 (bishop of Chichester). Licensed and appointed perpetual curate of Midhurst 1716. Married Jane Alderton at Terwick 1708. Died 1717.

102. North Mundham 16 Feb 1625 JOHN KEAY [1]

Appraisers: John Wooddier, John Tuckishe, John Ivrynge

	£	s	d
In the parler			
In primis 1 Table and his frame and carpet		5	0
Item 4 Chayres		8	0
Item 1 side boord and 1 lyvery Coubord		10	0

Item 6 Joyned Stooles		8	0
Item 1 Joyned bedstedle 1 feather bedd 2 feather bolsters 2 blanquets			
and one green Rugg and the Courtenes and valiences	5	0	0
Item 6 Cushings	1	0	0
Item 1 payer of Aundyornes		5	0
Item 2 Glasse grates		5	0
Item 6 nyld worked stooles		12	0
Item 1 stayned cloth		2	6
In the halle			
Item 1 Table and a frame and 6 joyned stooles		6	0
Item 1 Couboord		13	4
Item 1 Chest and 1 old chayer		5	0
Item all the Pewter	2	10	0
In the kitchin			
Item 1 Jack		6	8
Item all the Brasse	2	10	0
Item 3 yorne potts		6	8
Item 3 payer of pothangers 1 fier pan 1 payer of tongues 2 aundyornes 1			
yorne for the fier 1 tosting yorne		7	0
Item 4 spitts 3 payer of pothooks 1 driping pan 1 Clever 1 shreding			
knyfe 1 Chopinge knyfe		8	0
Item all the letten plates		5	0
Item 1 musket furnished		15	0
Item 1 dresser and 6 shelves		5	0
Item 3 fliches of Bacon	1	0	0
Item 1 payer of Bellows 1 payer of gredyornes		1	0
Item 1 Still		5	0
Item 5 dozen of trenchers and earthen dishes		2	0
Item 1 foulinge peace		15	0
In the old kitchen			
Item Brewing vessells and ould tubbes	1	0	0
Item Boules and boule dyshes and truggs		10	0
Item 1 formes		13	4
Item 1 wymbesheete and sackes		5	0
Item 1 Lanthorne			10
Item 2 Hen Coulpes		2	0
Item 1 fryeng pan			6
Item 1 lytle table			8
Item 2 serches		1	0
Item 1 half bushell 1 pecke and 1 halfe pecke		2	0
Item 1 old sawe		1	0
Item 1 salting trowe		1	0
In the milke house			
Item 1 querne		10	0
Item 1 safe Coubboord		6	8
Item 6 shelves		1	1
Item 1 bracke		1	0
In the loft over the Parler			
Item 1 feather bed furnished	5	0	0

Item 1 Truckelbed furnished	1	0	0
Item 1 feather bed and a flocke bed 2 blanquets and a coverlet	4	0	0
Item 1 side boord and his cloth		6	0
Item 5 boxes and 2 trunckes		16	0
Item 1 box with a frame		4	0
Item 2 Chayres		3	0
Item 6 Cushings		2	0
Item 1 litle table		1	0
Item 1 bed pan		1	6
Item 1 payer of Aundyornes 1 fier pan on slyce 1 payer of tongues and a fender		5	0
Item 2 trencher baskets		2	0
Item 20 payer of sheets	6	0	0
Item 11 table clothes	1	10	0
Item 12 dozen of table napkins	3	0	0
Item 8 payer of Pillowe beeres	1	0	0
Item 1 Chrystenyng sheet and 1 pall beerer	3	0	0
Item 1 dozen and a halfe of hand towells	1	0	0
Item halfe a dozen of Coubboord clothes		10	0
Item 8 pillowes	1	4	0
Item 2 silver boules and 6 silver spoones	4	0	0
Item 1 wyndowe Curtayne and a curten rood		1	6
In the chamber over the halle			
Item 1 feather bed 1 flocbed 1 payer of blanquets 1 coverlet and curtaynes	4	0	0
Item 1 chest 1 deske		3	4
Item lynnen and … towe	1	10	0
In the studie			
Item 1 square table 6 shelves		4	0
Item bookes in the studie	10	0	0
In the inner chamber			
Item 1 presse 1 truncke		18	0
Item 1 flocke bed 1 payer of blanquets 1 Coverlet 1 bolster and 1 bedstedle	1	0	0
Item tryer 1 shelfe 1 lynen torne 1 roode sadle 1 bag of hopps		15	0
The apparell of the dead	10	0	0
Money in his purse	10	0	0
Money owyng to the testator	65	0	0
Item 1 still and 1 payer of hannpes		6	8
Item 1 Clock	1	0	0
Item in beanes		6	0
In the gates			
Item wood faggats and hoppoules	3	0	0
Item 1 long cart with wheeles			
Item 2 dong carts and 1 payer of wheels	1	10	0
Item 1 mare an a colte	3	0	0
Item 1 cowe	2	8	0
Item 2 plowes and wheeles 2 harrowes	1	0	0
Item 1 sowe and pigges		13	0

Item 1 stalle of bees	3	4
Item 1 vanne	2	0
Item 1 wheele barrowe 1 garden rake and ould yorne and other lumberment	10	0
Item 1 Eawe sheepe	5	0

Sum total 174 12 7

[WSRO Ep I/29/141/24]

Will: made 13 Feb 1624; proved 4 March 1625
Wife Sara; children
Overseers: 'cosen' Thomas Bowyer esq, John Woodyer
Witness: John Woodyer [WSRO STC II/B Dean 1625 (3)]

[1] Cambridge, Christ's, matriculated sizar 1584, BA 1588, MA 1591. Vicar of North Mundham 1612–1624; of Hunston 1616–1624; patrons of both, Thomas and Jane Bowyer of Leythorne. Died 1624; buried North Mundham.

103. North Mundham 30 Nov 1668 GEORGE MOORE [1]

Appraisers: Robert Addams, George Payne

	£	s	d
In primis his wearing apparrell and money in his purse	2	12	0
Item for his books	7	8	0
Sum total	10	0	0

[WSRO Ep I/29/141/65]

Administration 30 Nov 1668
To Richard Kercher, principal creditor [WSRO STC III/I/67]

[1] Oxford, Christ Church, matriculated 1651, BA 1654; Oriel, fellow, MA 1658, BD 1665. Ordained deacon and priest 1660 (bishop of Oxford). Vicar of North Mundham 1668. Died Madrid 1668 while in attendance on English ambassador.

104. North Mundham 12 Oct 1680 THOMAS CARR [1]

Appraisers: Thomas Woodyer, Robert Edmonds gent

	£	s	d
In the dyninge roome			
1 dossen of Turkeywork Chaiers	6	0	0
One Couech two tabells two Carpetts	2	15	0
One pair of Andirons one fire Shovell 1 pr of tongs	1	0	0
One Chimney peece and 2 windoe Curtens	1	0	0
In the beste Chamber			
One pair of Curtens and 2 pair of Valyences one tester one head peece one silk Quilt one bedsted two paire of blanncketts and hangings for the roome one Chimney peece eight Chaiers	50	0	0
One tabell one Lookeinge Glas one pr of Stanns	4	0	0
Two pr of bras Andirons one fender one fire Shovell and 1 pr of tongs and hoocks and Screnes and 1 pr of bellos	1	5	0

In one other Chamber			
Greene hangings 1 Littell tabell and one box	2	0	0
Severall peeces of Silver Plate	20	0	0
In one other Chamber			
One bedd and stedell 2 bolsters 2 pillowes one littell tabell 3 blanncketts	4	0	0
In the Maides Chamber			
3 fether bedds one steddle one pr of Curtaines	4	0	0
Item six boulsters 6 pillowes 6 blanncketts 4 Ruggs	2	10	0
Item one Studdey of books	20	0	0
Item Severall Sorts of Linen	13	0	0
In the kitchen			
Severall Sorts of Pewter and brass 2 Coper potts 1 pair of Iron Greats with other Small things	8	0	0
In the brewhouse			
One Furnis with Iron Greats with other brewing vessells	10	0	0
In the Parlor			
6 Chaers 4 Stools 1 littell tabell	1	10	0
1 littell furnis with Greats …		10	0
In the Milkhouse			
One pott of butter Severall Cheeses and Milk vessell and Charne and Cheespres	2	10	0
Item 10 Wether Sheepe	4	10	0
One horse and 2 Mares	15	0	0
2 hoggs and 6 Shutts	4	0	0
4 Cowes 3 other bease and 1 Caufe	14	10	0
Poultry and 3 geese		8	0
Item his wareinge Aparrell and Mony in his Pockett	20	0	0
Item two Ricks of Hay	6	0	0
Mony due for rents	150	0	0
Mony due upon Security	200	0	0
Sum total	568	8	0

Exhibited by Joan Lane, spinster, for Elizabeth Carr widow   [WSRO Ep I/29/141/76]

Will: made 24 Aug 1680; proved 11 Sep 1680
Wife Elizabeth, executrix (with Thomas Woodier); daughter: Mary (under 18)
Money for redemption of Turkish slaves
Witnesses: Mary Peckham, Thomas Bickley, William Peckham, Francis Goater
                                                              [WSRO STC I/27/177]

[1] Son of Thomas, of Petworth, gent. Oxford, St Edmund Hall, matriculated 1666 aged 15; Merton, BA 1670, MA 1673. Rector of West Thorney 1673–1680. Vicar of North Mundham 1678–1680. Died 1680.

105. North Mundham 26 Aug 1706 EDMUND LANE [1]
Appraisers: Richard Streton, William Goble

	£	s	d
In the Kitchen			
In primis two tables Seven chares one Joyne Stoole and four Cushins one Lanthorn Sixten pewter dishes and thirty Six pewter plats two Salts two pewter candle Sticks two dripingpans one brass Morter and pisle one Stile one Jack and line one Spit one paire of Andirons and one paire of dogs one fender one Chafeing dish one Warming pann one pare of tonges and fier pann one pothanger and gridirons one pair of billows one Smothiniron one dreser and Shevels and two benches one woaden rack and bacon two Iron candlesticks Six patte pans two Window curtens and rods a case of Knives and forks	5	10	6
In the Parlor			
Item twelfe Lether chares two tables two Skrens one clock and case two chares a paire of Andirons a paire of doggs three Window curtens and two roods a paire of tongs	3	11	0
In the Butterry			
Item four dussen of Glass botles one table two poudering tubbs		10	0
In the Parlor chamber			
Item twenty paire of Sheets tenn dussen of Napkins twenty pillo coots Fiften table clothes one dussen and a halfe of towells and two wallets one beed and curtens and vallions and all that belongs to him one press a ches of drawers a paire of Andirons one paire of doggs and tongs four chares one close Stole one Glass three window curtains one hollend Sheett	26	14	0
In the Butterry chamber			
Item one Fether beed With curtins and vallions and belonging one truckle beed and all belonging one chest and one trunck	5	0	6
In the Kitchen Chamber			
Item one Fether beed curtins and vallions and all belonging there unto six Sharge chares one chest of drawers one table to Stands Four Window curtis and Iron roods one Glasse and thirten Silver Spouns one Silver Suerver and six Silver Saltes one Silver tumler one Silver Porringer two Andirons a paire of tonngs and billos	21	6	0
In the Litle roume			
Item five pillos one rugg one chest	1	0	0
In the Studdy			
Item the bookes in his Studdy	3	1	0
Item his Wearing aparrell and mony in his Pockett	5	0	0
In the Clossett			
Item three Spining Wheeles and other things		10	0
In the Wash house			
Item one Furnice and three Iron pots and Bruing vessells and other Smale things and eight drinck vessells and two Stands	3	0	6
Item two hogs and one horse	2	5	0
Item for Wheat in the barn and Six acres of oats	14	0	0
Item for clover hay in the Stable	3	15	0
Item for one Load of Sackes one busshell	1	0	0

Item for Wood and Fagots and old Lumber		2	0	0
Total sum	98	3	6
Item mony due to the deceased upon Bond	300	0	0
Item a desprate debt due to the deceased owing on Bond	50	0	0
	478	3	6

[WSRO Ep I/29/141/92]

Administration 31 Aug 1706
To Elizabeth, wife   [WSRO STC III/M/61]

[1] Of Sussex. Cambridge, Jesus, admitted sizar and matriculated 1676, scholar 1679, BA 1680, MA 1683. Ordained deacon and priest 1680 (bishop of Chichester). Vicar of North Mundham 1680–1706. Curate of Westhampnett c. 1684. Rector of Rumboldswyke 1694–1706. Married Elizabeth Nash of North Mundham at Hunston 1683. Died 1706.

106. Newick 7 Oct 1710 JOSEPH HOYLE [1]
Appraisers: Peter Gard, Mr Langford

	£	s	d
In primis his wearing apparel and money in his purse	10	0	0
In the kitchen			
Item two tables six chairs one stoole one forme one cubbard one Screen one glass cage one Rack the spits two pair of brandirons one pair of Creepers one porridge pott one fire plate one pair of gridirons a fire shovel one clock two pair of tongs an oven door and other small things	5	6	8
In the parlor			
Item one table one couch twelve chairs one pair of brandirons one pair of creepers nine maps three cushens and a chimney back	3	15	0
In the Buttery			
Item one press one dresser one bras kettle one bell bras pott ten dishes of pewter two cheese plates three dozen and a halfe of plates one pewter basin one still one wheel a pair of yarn winders	5	12	4
In the Brewhouse			
Item one Copper one brew fatt one keeler an iron kettle and the leaden pipe and some other things	9	6	3
In the drink roome			
Item four tubs two keelers ten beer vesels a gross of bottles a fry pan and some crocks	2	12	6
In the Bakehouse			
Item two tubs a meal trough some sives baskets and other small things a warming pan pillion and lanthorn	1	8	0
In the parlor Chamber			
Item two beds bedstidles curtains and other furniture thereto belong	7	0	0
Item one great Camlet chair four turkey workt stooles an old chest of drawers a Close Stoole a Chimney back a pair of brandirons bellows fire shovel and tongs	3	8	6
Item a pair of pistols a sword two small tables and some China cups and three maps	1	14	6

Item his library of books	50	0	0
In the little Chamber			
Item one bed and the furniture thereto belonging a turky workt stool			
one Cushen a glass and window curtain	5	4	0
In the maids Chamber			
Item one bed bedstedle and furniture	1	5	0
In the Brewhouse Chamber			
Item four feather beds and three stedles and the furniture thereto			
belonging	6	10	0
In the outer Chamber			
Item two feather beds one old stedle and the furniture thereto			
belonging	3	10	0
Item a press at the top of the stairs		12	0
Item twenty pair of sheets	10	0	0
Item twelve table clothes and six dozen of napkins	4	16	0
Item twelve towels		18	0
Item twelve pair of pillowcotes	1	0	0
Item Six Silver Spoons and a tumbler	3	0	0
Item a Steel mill	1	5	0
Without doors			
Item a bout twelve quarters of oats	7	4	0
Item about a quarter of tares	1	0	0
Item a horse	3	5	0
Item a hogg	1	5	0
Wood and fagots	3	14	0
In the Schoole			
Item three tables three formes wheelbarrow and a chimney back		13	4
Item in moneys due to the testator att interest	1200	0	0
Things unseen and forgotten		16	8
Totall	1356	1	9
[ESRO W/INV 90]			

Will: made 25 Aug 1710; proved 17 Jan 1711
Wife Jane, executor; son: John; daughter: Jane
Witnesses: Thomas Standen, Elizabeth Newnham, John Langford   [ESRO W/A 48.65]

[1] Of Yorkshire. Cambridge, Emmanuel, admitted sizar and matriculated 1680, BA 1684, MA 1687. Ordained deacon 1685 (bishop of London), priest 1687 (bishop of Chichester). Curate of Wivelsfield 1686. Rector of Newick 1690–1710, patron Francis Millington, esq. Married Jane Wright at Keymer 1695. Died 1710.

107. Northchapel 9 March 1629 JOHN FORMAN [1]
Appraisers: William Booker, Richard Ede, Richard Baker
[Original damaged]

	£	s	d
In primis his wearing apparel	5	0	0
Item in ready mony in his purse	1	0	0
Item 2 feather beds 2 feather boulsters 4 feather pillows	7	0	0

Item 5 coverlets	1	10	0
Item 2 flock beds 2 bolsters		13	4
Item 2 bedstidels and 2 Chists	1	0	0
Item for sheats	3	0	0
Item 3 table Clothes 3 pillibers with other smale linen	1	10	0
Item 3 pare of blanckets		13	4
Item 1 bedstidle 3 Chests 2 boxes	1	0	0
Item one pise of new ...	1	1	0
Item all the pewter in the house	1	6	8
Item the brase	2	0	0
Item the yron vessels	1	8	0
Item 3 spits 3 branIrons 2 pare of pothangers and one fyer pane		9	0
Item one Cubbord one table 4 stoles 4 Chares 2 formes and the staine Clothes and 4 Chusens	1	3	4
In the Milk house			
Item one bulting huch and one neding trough and one clyvor and other lumbery in that rome	1	0	0
In the Chichen			
Item one table 2 tubs 2 benches with other lumbery		10	0
Item the iorne and woats in the house	1	14	0
Item one Chise prese and other lumbery		13	4
Item the baken in the house	1	10	0
Item the Cise and other provision		10	0
Item 2 kyne and one mayre	8	0	0
Item 13 Shipe	2	12	0
Item the woode and fagots and soyle about the house	1	0	0
Item a Cart one pare of Whiles 2 yockes and a chaine		6	8
Item 3 piges		15	0
Item the haye		6	8
Item one old Cubbord and 3 plankes		5	0
Item the pultery		5	0
Item the bookes	2	0	0
Item he had owing upon bonds and other wayes and mony in his house	100	15	0
Item one ringer the bils and axes and other Implements wich are unpraysed		6	8
The whole sum is	166	15	0

[WSRO Ep I/29/142/15]

Will: made 12 March 1628; proved 14 May 1629
Wife (second) Catherine; two sons; four daughters
Witness: Richard [...]   [WSRO STC I/17/268]

---

[1] Called BA 1592. Ordained deacon and priest 1592 (bishop of Peterborough). Curate of Northchapel 1597–1629. Died 1629.

108. Northiam ... 1699 RICHARD SEAMER [1]
Appraisers: ..., Richard ...
[Original damaged]

	£	s	d
... the sum of	[?]25	3	4
Item wearing apparell	15	0	0
In the Parlour			
... Chaires	3	12	0
Item ...	1	2	0
Item ... four cushions		10	0
Item ...	4	0	0
In the Kitchin			
Item ...	..	..	..
Item ...	..	..	..
Pewter	3	0	0
Item one table eight chaires two warming panns a paire of bellowes a paire of tonges two spitts a paire of Andirons and other small things	2	1	0
In the Brewhouse			
Item one Copper another small Copper	7	0	0
Item one brew tubb		15	0
Item one buck tubb and seven keelers	1	10	0
Item four iron potts two bell brasse skilletts two other brasse skilletts four payles and other small things	1	12	0
In the milkehouse			
Item six milke trayes a cherne and other small things		18	0
In the bunting roome			
Item the bunter a table a still and some small things	1	10	0
In the Beere Buttery			
Item fourteene barrells and pinns and one frying pann	1	16	0
In another Buttery			
Item one powdring tubb two other tubbs one Meallbagg one [?]douett one Gallon and two sacks	1	1	0
In the best Chamber			
Item the bed and furniture therein	15	0	0
In the Parlour Chamber			
Item the bed and all its furniture	5	0	0
Item the hangings	1	0	0
Item one looking glasse		6	8
Item one Chest of drawers wherein is four diaper table cloths two dozen and a halfe of diaper napkins two diaper voyder Cloaths two diaper side board Cloaths seven large flaxen table cloaths and other plaine Linnen	6	2	6
Item one paire of bellowes a paire of tongs a fire shovell one paire of andirons and a paire of creepers		10	6
In the Kitchen Chamber			
Item the bed and furniture thereof	5	0	0
Item one armed chaire one other chaire two stooles One case of drawers and one looking glasse	1	13	0
Item one chest wherein is fourteene table cloaths six towells six paire of sheetes and other ordinary Linnen	6	1	6

In the Closett			
Item a dozen of silver spoones	5	0	0
Item four salts two small silver tasters	5	0	0
Item one old silver watch and other old silver	2	0	0
Item a little case of drawers and other small things		16	0
In the Study			
Item the deceaseds bookes	15	0	0
In the milkhouse Chamber			
Item a servants bed and furniture	1	5	0
In the Garrett			
Item another servants bed and its furniture one table and other small lumber	1	13	9
Without doores			
Item two horses	17	0	0
Item a Cowe	4	0	0
Item two hoggs	2	0	0
Item the hoppground and the poles which are valluable	10	0	0
Item the horse Court [?]dugg saddle and wheeles	1	5	0
In the Stables			
Item two saddles two bridles one maids pillion one [?]slip curry combe and a brush	1	1	0
Item a spade a shovell two axes one handbill two prongs one trowe one paire of hedge sheeres and old sithe one shovell and one spade		11	6
Item sixteene Cord of new wood	6	0	0
Item five hundred and a halfe of faggotts	1	16	9
Item things not seene and forgotten		2	6
Debts due and oweing to the said deceased upon specialty vizt			
Item a Mortgage from Mr Walter Everenden for five hundred pounds four hundred pounds paid thereof one proper … of Mr Walter … an Ideott … son in Law of whome he had the Custody … of the said Mortgage there is of the Testatory onely the sume of one hundred pounds	100	0	0
Item due for three quarters of a yeare interest of the said sum of one hundred pounds	3	15	0
Item one other Mortgage from Mr John Steer for the sum of	200	0	0
Item due for three quarters of a years interest thereon	7	10	0
Summa totalis	565	15	3
Another specialty due to the deceased which is desperate vizt			
Item a Mortgage from Charles Crouch gent for the sum of	200	0	0
Item tithes due from the Parishoners and … of Lanes in … ford at East Guldford in Sussex …	52	10	6
other desperate debts upon … contracts vizt			
Item from severall poore people the sum of	5	4	7

[TNA PRO PROB 4/6048]

Will: made 1 May 1685; proved 12 June 1699
Wife Mary, sole heir and executrix
Poor of parish. £5
Witnesses: Sam [?]Potten, John Goodwin, John Trim   [TNA PRO PROB 11/451/103]

[1] Born Raisthorpe in Wharram Percy, Yorks, son of John, of Raisthorpe, yeoman. School at ?South Dalton, Yorks. Cambridge, St John's, admitted sizar aged 17 and matriculated 1665, BA 1669, MA 1672. Ordained deacon 1671 (archbishop of York); signed for priest's orders 1674 (bishop of London). Curate of Deptford, Kent. Rector of East Guldeford 1694–1699, patrons William Boys and Thomas Frewen, esqs. Married Mary Frewen, widow, at Beckley 1684. Died 1699; buried Northiam.

109. Nuthurst 6 July 1640 WILLIAM ANDREWES, rector [1]

Appraisers: William Agate, Henry Stone, Thomas Walder

	£	s	d
In primis his wearing apparrell and money in his purse	10	0	0
Item foure Acres of wheat	4	0	0
Item eight Acres of Oates	8	0	0
Item two oxen	13	0	0
Item three horses	15	0	0
Item Hey in the Barne	2	0	0
Item Dung in the gates and other places	2	10	0
Item one wayne and wheeles		3	0
Item two dung Courts		8	0
Item two Ploughs		10	0
Item two Harrowes		10	0
Item two Sowes and eleven pigges	4	0	0
Item Wood and Faggotts	3	0	0
Item in the Parlour chamber			
four pillobers [a] feather bed one rugge one blanket one [pair] of sheetes one bedstedle and Curtaynes two ... es two Livery tables twelve stooles and [ch]eires six Cushens two trunckes one wicker Cheire one paire of Brandirons one paire of tongues one fire pan and two boxes	13	0	0
Item hoopes		13	0
Item silver and gilt plate	31	10	0
Item hangings in the parlour Chamber		10	..
Item a painted Carpet		10	..
Item in the Chamber over the Hall			
two [hi]ghe beds two truckle beds and all belonging to them	11	0	0
Item foureteene paire of sheetes and six paire of pillocotes	26	10	0
Item in the Hall Chamber six Diaper table Clothes seaven sideboard Clothes six dozen of diaper napkins one diaper towel . . . Cupboard Clothes three other towels foure dozen of napkins wth other Course Linnen two rugges three Coverlets three blankets three Chests one truncke three boxes one table and one Chaire	36	5	..
Item in the Kitchen Chamber			
one bed for servants wth all thinges belonging to it. . . .ton tyer and wooll	4	0	0
Item in the Parlour			
one Cupboard one table one Livery Cubberd eight cheires six stooles a form one greene ... two greene stooles one Carpet [on] paire of Brandirons a paier of tongues a fire pan and the hangings in the roome	10	0	0

Item in the Hall
two great tables two little tables two formes one Cupboard one Chaire
two small Cupboards one Chest a still and other things   4   0   0
Item Pewter   12   0   0
        Item in the Kitchen
six brass kettles two brass potts six Iron potts three spitts a Jacke wth
other thinges   10   10   0
        Item in the Milke house and Buttery
the Barrells trugges and other thinges   5   10   0
Item one Cheese presse Mill boardes and other thinges   3   0   0
Item wheat   8   0   0
Item a Musket and thinges thereunto belonging   1   10   0
Item one other parcell of Hey   3   ..   0
Item yokes Cheynes and other ymplementes   2   10   0
        Item the Bookes in his studie   30   0   0
        Item Due from William Davie   ..   0   0
        Item in the Hall Chamber
foure feather beds bedsteds and all other thinges to them belonginge   12   0   0
                      Summa totalis   298   19   4
                     [WSRO Ep I/29/143/27]

Administration 31 July 1640
To Elizabeth, wife   [WSRO STC III/H/153, 166]

[1] Born London c. 1600, son of Nicholas, citizen of London, and nephew of Lancelot, bishop of
Chichester. Cambridge, Jesus, admitted and matriculated fellow-commoner 1619, BA 1621, MA
1625. Ordained deacon 1625 (bishop of Rochester), priest 1626 (bishop of Peterborough). Rector
of Nuthurst 1625–1640, patron bishop of Chichester. Died 1640; buried Nuthurst.

110. Nuthurst 1 Sept 1645 GEORGE EDGLY [1]

Appraisers: Henry Bacon of West Grinstead, John Mann

	£	s	d
In primis one Cubbard and one truncke		10	0
Item one Settle 3 Chayers and 2 stooles		2	0
Item one wollen whele		1	0
Item one pair of hampers			10
Item one oyron plate		6	0
Item one pair of Spit rackes		5	0
Item one paire of brand eyrnes 2 paire of tongues 2 fire shoveles		5	0
Item 6 Spites and 2 fire pronges		3	0
Item 2 paire of gridgeyrones one oven peele one paire of tongues and one fire slice		2	0
Item one eyron quarne and one Chafer		5	0
Item one paire of brandeyrons and one trest		1	6
Item one paire of Scales and one Sconce		2	0
Item som olde eyron		1	6
Item one paire of pothangers		1	0
Item one logchaine		5	0

Item	£	s	d
Item one Rounde table and one deske		3	0
Item 3 firkins and one linnen whele		5	0
Item 2 buckets 2 boules one peck and one gallan with som other wooden vessell		1	0
Item one paire of brazen brandeyrons one still one paire of tongues one fire shovell	1	0	0
Item 2 brazen posnets 2 Candelstickes and one Chafing dish		5	0
Item one stone morter		1	0
Item som lattin stuffe		1	0
Item 2 sawes and one grindstone winch		3	0
Item 4 pronges 3 mathookes one shovell one Donge rake one olde ax one bill		2	0
Item 6 crockes 6 pannes with other earthen vessell		1	6
Item 5 white earthen dishes one tankard and one earthen poot		1	6
Item som glasson weare		1	6
Item one Beed and one boulster	2	0	0
Item one Beedsted with Curtaines and valiantes therunto belonging	1	0	0
Item another Bedsted with curtaines and hanginges therunto belonging	1	1	0
Item one Carpit one Cubard cloth 6 cushines with one paire of window curtaines		10	0
Item 2 Carpites 3 Cubard clothes 4 cushines and dornis curtaine		10	0
Item 6 fether pillowes 3 flocke boulsters		10	0
Item one rug and 3 blankets		10	0
Item 11 paire of sheetes	4	0	0
Item 3 dossen of napkines 6 pilabeures 4 Cubard cloathes one dossen of towells	1	10	0
Item 10 table Cloathes	1	10	0
Item 2 trunkes and 2 Chestes		16	0
Item 7 Chaires	1	0	0
Item one warming pan and one Chafeing dish		10	0
Item one wodden Cestern one Chamberpot one darklanthorne and one tinen candlestick		2	6
Item one Sack seller and one hot water seller		5	0
Item one candle basket one screene 2 mustardpots 2 skiming dishes and one Cup		2	0
Item 2 Cubardes and one little deske		10	0
Item 12 little boxes and one straw basket		4	0
Item one bed and one boulster	1	2	0
Item one little bedsted for a Child one Cradle one standing stole and one flasket		5	0
Item one hogshead one barrell 2 halfe tubes and 2 Chickincipes		5	0
Item 2 olde tubes and 2 dust basketes		2	0
Item one bed and one boulster	1	2	0
Item in silver plate 76 ounces	18	1	0
Item one writing deske and standish		2	0
Item 2 loade of healing stoone		14	0
Item one plow		5	0
Item 3 yoakes		1	0
Item one eyron plate and one eyron barr		10	0

	£	s	d
Item in ready mony in the house	9	0	0
Item Received uppon a bonde	8	0	0
Item in Bukes	23	5	0
Item in Pewter	4	0	0
Item for a weane and wheles	2	2	0
Item for 3 wattls and 3 sakes		8	0
Item for one flockbed		12	0
Item for one Coverlet and one Rugg	1	0	0
Item for one brasse kittel and one eyron kittell		11	0
Item for two draft Chaines		3	2
Item for one black ragg and a bucking tob		4	0
Item for 10 milktroages		5	0
Item for darnix hangings	1	16	0
Item for a Coutch		10	0
Item for 2 tinn dripping pans		2	6
Item one table basket		1	6
Item for a fagg to wim Corne		7	0
Item for a [?]Panscip		4	0
Item for 5 dossen of trenchers		1	6
Item for timber	3	5	0
Suma totalis	99	0	0

[WSRO Ep I/29/143/34]

Administration 16 Sep 1645
To Elizabeth, wife   [WSRO STC III/K/23]

[1] Cambridge, Trinity, matriculated sizar 1620, BA 1624, MA 1627. Oxford, DD 1644. Ordained priest 1626 (bishop of Llandaff). Prebendary of Heathfield 1630–1644. Vicar of Donnington 1630–1641, patron bishop of Chichester; of Lyminster 1634, patron Eton College. Rector of Nuthurst 1642. Died 1644; buried Didcot, Berks.

111. Nuthurst 10 March 1682 JOHN TAYLOR [1]

Appraisers: Thomas Tingler, Richard Seale, John Wood

	£	s	d
In primis his weareinge apparrell and money in his purse	18	18	0

In the kitchen

	£	s	d
Item twenty four peeces of pewter two candle sticks one bason three kettles five scillets one warming pan two brasse potts one brasse frying pan two Iron kettles one driping pan four spits one Jack four andirons two pothangers three Gridgirons one round table one gun three Iron potts one Iron Morter one Cupboard of drawers four Chaires togeather with other lumber	9	0	0

In the out Roomes

	£	s	d
Item one brasse fornace six tubs three coollers three poudering tubs two milk leads ten barrels and ferkens two Cheespresses with other Lumber	7	0	0

In the Hall

Item one table two foarmes one Sideboard one pewter still one paire of virginals one Cloth two Andirons one Sideboard two tinne sconces four

Chaires two Joyned Stooles one greene Carpet one Case of knifes … dossen of glasse and stone bottles with other Lumber	5	10	0

In the Parlor

Item one oval table Six greene Chaires one litle table three Carpets two Andirons fire pan and tongs one Iron plate one Cowch one Cupboard one leather Chaire and hangings	2	19	6

In the parlor Chamber

Item two bedstedles one truckle bedstedle two feather beds one flock bed four bolsters four pillows with all other things thereunto belonging one paire of andirons one litle table three Chaires four stooles one Chest and other Lumber	12	10	0

In the Hall Chamber

Item two bedstedles two feather beds and all thereunto belonging three. . . one chest two Chaires one table	1	10	0
Item in the back Chamber Lumber	1	10	0

In the litle Chamber

Item one feather bead and Stedle	2	0	0

In the litle Iner Chamber

Item twelve diaper napkins one towel seaven paire of Sheets two dossen of ordinary napkins Six towells Six pillow cloaths nyne table Cloaths two diaper table cloaths and new cloth	5	17	0

In the Closet

Item Six ounces of Silver lace		16	0
Item three Silver buttons		1	6
Item two paire of Silver buckles		4	6
Item one Silver Isene Clasp		2	0
Item one Silver Cup	3	8	0
Item one Silver dish	3	1	3
Item ten Silver Spoones	3	18	3
Item one Silver porringer	1	17	6
Item two Silver Salts		10	8
Item one Silver watch	1	15	0
Item one Silver tobacco box		11	0
Item two gold rings		15	0
Item wood fagets and Coles	3	5	0
Item lime and bricks		5	0
Item his wearing Apparell goods forgotten and not seene two flitches of baccon and a crock of butter	9	0	0
Item att John watertons in Horsham eleaven Sheetes two side board Cloths twenty Six napkins seaven table cloths four towells	5	0	0
Item his Librarie of books	10	0	0
Item debts owing him	15	3	0
Item att John watertons one Chest of drawers and one other Chest	1	5	0
Item one silver porringer four ounces a quarter	1	1	3
In desperat debts	..	16	0
Suma totalis	141	0	3

[EpI/29/143/58]

Will nuncupative: made 22 Feb 1682; no probate date
Four children under 21
Executors: Richard Bridger of Coomb, or John Roberts gent and John Stone yeoman of Nuthurst
Witnesses: Thomas Tingler, Mary Pierce, Margaret Waterton   [WSRO STC I/27/342]

For probate account see **187**

[1] Cambridge, Trinity, admitted sizar and matriculated 1658, scholar 1661, BA 1662. Ordained priest 1664 (bishop of Lincoln). Possibly curate of Cuckfield c. 1665; of Lindfield c. 1673. Licensed preacher Nuthurst 1674; rector 1674–1682. Died 1682.

112. Oving 10 July 1682 JOHN DRAKE [1]

Appraisers: Henry Peckham, Richard Crisgnas, Thomas Copar

	£	s	d
In the Kechen			
In primis 15 pewter dishes	2	10	0
Item 12 plates		6	0
Item 4 sassars			8
Item 3 puter candell stickes		5	0
Item 2 puter saltselears		2	0
Item a fyre plate		1	6
Item a puter bason		1	0
Item 4 pothengars		1	6
Bell mettel 2 potts		15	0
A brass kettell		2	6
3 brass skelets		2	0
A brass candell sticke			6
A warming pan		2	6
A brass ladell			4
A brass frying pan		2	6
A grid Iern		2	0
A small grid Iern			8
A shredding knife and a clever		1	6
9 Irn sceaeres a bessfork and a chopping knife		2	0
A par of ...ear Ironns with Racks and a par of Doggs		10	0
2 slyces a pare of tonges and a fendor 2 pare of Cottrells and ... a Jacke		5	0
2 speters		3	0
3 smothing Iearnes		1	10
A laten pasti pan and an appell Roster and fissh plat			8
A pan of snoffars and bred grat			6
a Tabbell a furme and benches and 3 shelves and a dresserbord		8	0
3 bullRush chayers		1	6
A new dell press cubberd		8	0
In the Back Rome			
7 woden Trayes		2	0
4 Tubes and half bushell		4	0
A marbell morter and pessell		5	0
2 wodden plates and 8 dishes		1	4

2 dressers and 2 shelves	3	0
2 cherches	1	4
12 plat trenchers	2	6
In the Bruhouse and seller		
A furnness	14	0
A vate and 9 Tubes and wash boule and 2 stands	12	0
8 beare vessells and 2 stands	13	0
12 glass potts and bottels	4	6
2 dozen of quats	5	0
A duch pot for bear and 2 other small potts to drinke in	1	0
In the hall		
A tabell 2 benches a forme and a wenscot by the dor and a shelfe	9	0
A Stell	10	0
A picke and a gon	5	0
In the parlor		
3 Tabells	12	0

6 Turky chayers	1	10	0
4 bullRush chayers		4	0
A pare of doggs with brass heds and fier pan and tonges		5	0
Grene hangings and curten and the Iorn Rods		8	0
2 carpets		2	6
In the parlor chamber			
A bedsted with sacking curten rodes curtenes and valence and counterpane and tester of paragin 6 chayers of the same with a tabell cloth a goss fether bed with brasell ticke 3 blankets a bolster 2 pelowes	10	0	0
A side Tabell a pare of Doggs with brass heds		4	6
4 tenchar salts a cadell cup with a cover 2 small copes 3 spones all selver	4	0	0
8 picktuers	1	0	0
In the sellar chamber			
3 half hedded bedsteds with canapeyes mats and cords and 2 fether beds 2 bolssters a Red Rugg 5 blankets a side tabell	7	0	0
In the ferst kechen chamber			
A half hedded bedsted mat and cord a fether bed and bolster 2 chests 2 blankets	2	0	0
In the ener kechen chamber			
2 half hed bedsteds canapes mat and cord 2 fether beds 2 bolstars 2 coverlets 2 blankets	5	0	0
In the hall chamber			
A bedsted a mat and Cord and Curtens tester of lensey wolsey a fether bed and bolstar 2 pelowes 2 blankets 4 bulRush chayers a par of doggs and tonges	4	5	0
A chest of draws		8	0
A looking glass		2	0
14 pare of shetes 4 pare of pillocotes Diaper and damaske tabell clothes 4 and Napkins 3 dozen and a half 12 Towells	10	0	0
In the Studdy			
For his Bookes	40	0	0
His aparrell	5	0	0

In mony	4	0	0
A bedsted bed bolster 2 blankets which John Drake have at ….. Within the feld	1	0	0
A Riding horss saddell and bridell	3	0	0
A Cowe	2	0	0
2 hoges and 2 piggs	1	2	0
Item owing to the deceased what is owing to Mr Drake	50	0	0
Sum total	174	15	0

[WSRO Ep I/29/145/55]

Will: made 23 June 1675; proved 17 July 1682
Proved by wife Jane for son; son: John (minor), executor (all books); daughters: Mary, Jane
Burial to be without 'vain riotous intemperate and gluttenous pompes and ceremonies too often used'; long statement (six pages) of personal belief and pious declamation
Witnesses: William Cobden, Ann Tayler   [WSRO STCI/27/313]

[1] Probably of Suffolk; and Cambridge, Emmanuel, admitted sizar 1655. Called BA 1667. Ordained deacon 1663 (bishop of Salisbury), priest 1665 (bishop of Chichester). Vicar of Oving 1667–1682. Curate of Westhampnett c. 1675. Married Jane Stanesby of Elvetham, Hants, at Oving 1668. Died 1682; buried Oving.

113. Oving 1721 JOHN WOODYER [1]
Appraisers: John Groome, George Libbard

	£	s	d
In primis Ready money in Pocket and house	37	9	3
Item the deceaseds wearing Apparel	70	0	0
Item Fourteen Gold Rings valued at	4	18	0
Item money on Mortgage bonds and Notes	817	14	10
Item Also a Bond on Mr Hutchinson being a desperate debt besides the Interest being tis fearfull lost	80	0	0
Item due upon book besides 2=12=4 desperate Debt	143	14	2
Item Plate being a Tankard one Caudle Cup three Casters four Salt Sellers Thirteen spoons one silver one pair of Silver Buckels	19	10	0
In the Study			
Item Bookes Desk and Shelves	20	0	0
Item for Linnen being Ten pair of Household sheets Nine pair of fine sheets Six pair of Pillowcoats Two dozen of Towels five suites of fine Table Linnen and other Household Linnen	15	12	0
In the Hall Chamber			
Item one bed and boulster Two blankets one Quilt Stedle Curtains and valance and hangings one Chest of Draws one Table and Glase and a set of Dressing Boxes five Chairs one Press one Close Stool one pair of Window Curtains and … Trunk	11	10	0
In the Parlour Chamber			
Item one Bed and bolster 2 Blankets one Quilt one Stedle Curtains and vallance Eight Caine Chairs six squabs one Table one glase Two pair of Brass Doggs fire pan and Tongs Hangings and window curtains	13	0	0

In the Buttery Chamber

Item one bed and stedle and bolster Two blankets one Quilt Curtains and vallance one Chest of Draws one Table three Chairs and one looking Glass	4	0	0

In the Kitchen Chamber

Item one bedstedle and bolster two blankets one Rug Curtains and valance and one Table	2	10	0

In the Boys Chamber

Item one bedstedle bed and bolster Two blankets one Rug one press Two Trunks Two Chests and a Pocket of Hops	3	0	0
Item for Eight Pillows	1	0	0
Item one Still and a bed pan		12	0

In the Parlour

Item Thirteen Cane Chaires Four Tables one Corner Cupboard Two sqabs one pair of Iron dogs one pair of bellows one pair of Window Curtains and Hangings	5	0	0

In the Hall

Item … Twelve Chairs Two Tables one Clock and a looking Glass	5	0	0

In the Kitchen

Item one dozen of Pewter Dishes Five dozen of Pewter Plates Two spitts Two driping pans one Jack three bell brass Skelets one stone Morter Two pair of brass Candlesticks severall small brass things one dozen of Knives and forks Four Iron Candlesticks one pair of Iron brandirons one pair of Iron doggs and severall small things three Tables one foldingboard one press and Cupboard one Dresser one bacon Rack six Chairs Four shelves one Skreen one pair of Stilliards	8	19	0

In the drinking Room

Item Two stands one new vessel six dozen of Bottels and one old barrel	2	0	0

In the Brewhouse

Item one Copper furnese one brewvate one Tun Tub six Kealers one bucking Tub Two brass pots one Iron pott one brass Kettle one frying pan one pewter bason Two stands one brass Cullender three Wooden Trays 2 handishes and one copperpott	4	0	0

In the Buttery

Item Two powdering Tubs one Sive five drinking vessels Two flower tubs Two stands	1	0	0

In the stable

Item one Little horse one Mare Two saddles Two Bridles one Pillion one pair of Gambadoes and a sidesaddle	15	5	0

In the Barn

Item Wood and faggotts	2	10	0
Item Things forgott		5	0
Total	1228	9	3

[WSRO Ep I/29/145/72]

Will: made 28 Oct 1718; proved 13 April 1721
Wife Constance, executrix; son: John, under 20, (books); brother: Thos Woodyer, Lindfield, gent; daughters: Jane, Constance, Anne (under 18)
Trustees: Wife, brother-in-law John Mathews, vicar, Steyning, William Woodyer, Chichester, John Whitehead, rector, Tangmere
Witnesses: William Peckham, Thomas Austin, John Worlidge   [WSRO STC I/33/18]

[1] Of Sussex. Cambridge, Jesus, admitted 1676, matriculated 1676 (in his absence, due to prevalence of smallpox), BA 1680, MA 1683. Ordained deacon and priest 1682 (bishop of Chichester). Vicar of Oving 1682–1721; of Bersted 1704–1721. Curate of Sidlesham c. 1695. Chaplain to Frances, Dowager Lady Howard of Escrick. Died 1721; buried Oving.

114. Parham 21 April 1666 RICHARD LEWES [1]
Appraisers: John Willet, John Harwood

	£	s	d

Item for his wareing Apparell and money in his purse
Item for 1 bed and bedstedell and Chestes and ….. and other things in his Loging Chamber
    Item in the next Chamber
for sheets and nap[kins] and other Linan
Item in the same Chamber 2 beds and bedstedes with chestes and other things
Item for Corn and other things in the corn Loate
    Item in the little Loate atope of the stares
1 still and other things
    Item in the Paller
1 Table and stouels and Arndians with other things
    Item in the hall
1 Table 1 form with brase d … and pewter and other things
    Item in the kitchen
barrells and bruing … with other things
Item for 6 working Cattell
Item for 3 chows and other young bea[se]
Item for 14 Ackers of corn
Item for hogs and 4 sheepe
Item for A dunkpot and A plow and harrow and Chains and other takiling
Item for husbandry towls and other Lomber

                              Sum total   [88   15   0]
                                         [WSRO Ep I/29/147/8]

Will: made 21 March 1666; proved 27 April 1666
Wife: Mary, executrix (with step-daughter); step-daughter: Anne Archer (6 silver spoons); George Gouldsmith, Sir Cecil Bishop's warrener (a gun)
Witnesses: Edward Warner, William Andrew   [WSRO STC I/23/307]

[1] Son of Richard, rector of Parham. Oxford, Magdalen, matriculated 1640 aged 18. Rector of Parham c. 1660–1666. Died 1666.

115. Parham 2 Dec 1708 WILLIAM BROWN [1]

Appraisers: George Streeter, Richard Lockyer

	£	s	d
In primis his money in Purse and wearing Apparrell	4	0	0
In the Kitchen			
Item One Table One sideboard with Drawers and one Jack with other small things	1	10	0
In the Brewhouse			
Item One Furnase One Brewing Vate Two Tubbs Two Kivers with some other small things	1	15	6
In the Backroome			
Item One Old Cubbord Two Kettles Three Potts with other small things	1	0	0
In the Seller			
Item Six Barrells and Two Stands		12	0
In the little roome			
Item 7 Dishes of Pewter and 3 Dozen of Plates with some other small things	1	5	6
In the Parlor			
Item Two Tables One Clock One Dozen of Chaires with other small things	2	10	0
In the Study			
Item Books One Table One Trunk and one Box with some other small things	8	10	6
In the Parlour Chamber			
Item One Bed with all things thereunto belonging One Dozen of Chaires One Sideboard Table One pair of broad Irons with some other small things	3	10	0
In the Kitchen Chamber			
Item Two Beds with all things thereunto belonging One Box of Drawers and Trunk with some other small things	6	5	10
In another Chamber			
Item One Bed with all things thereunto belonging and Five Chaires and some other things of small value	4	9	6
In another Chamber			
Item Two Boxes of Linnen	40	0	0
Sum total	38	8	10

[WSRO Ep I/29/147/14]

Administration 3 Dec 1708
To wife, Sarah   [WSRO STC III/M/83]

[1] Called MA 1698. Ordained priest 1691 (bishop of Chichester). Rector of Parham 1691–1708, patron Sir Cecil Bishop, bt; of Wiggonholt 1698–1708, patrons William and Maria Mill. Died 1708.

116. Peasmarsh 27 Aug 1722 STEVENS PARR [1]

Appraisers: Samuel Furner gent, Thomas Martin

	£	s	d
In primis			
Purse and Apparell	34	11	2½
Plate and Rings	6	12	0
Bonds and Mortgages	250	0	0
In the Cellar			
Barrells Tubbs Bottles etc	1	19	3
In the Wash house			
A Furnace Mash Fatt Tubbs etc	3	8	6
In the Kitchin			
Pewter Brasse Jack Irons etc	4	13	7
In the Pantry			
One Bacon Trough porridge Potts Frying pan Crocks Knives and forkes etc	1	5	11
In the Parlour			
One Clock Table Chairs Pictures etc	4	16	6
In the Best Roome			
One Blew bed and bedstead feather bed Bolster Pillows Table Looking glasse etc	8	6	6
In the Maids Room			
One Bedstead vallens Curtains etc	1	1	6
In the Mans Roome			
One Bed Bedstead Bolster pillows etc	1	10	0
In the Garrott			
One grate one old Jack pulleys etc		12	0
In Mr Parrs own Chamber			
One Bedstead Curtains vallens feather Bed Bolster pillows etc	5	0	0
Books and case	25	0	0
Twelve pair of sheets and other Linnen	6	18	6
Without Dores			
Hay wood Coales etc	3	13	10
Debts in Tythes and Rents etc	35	0	0
Things unseen and forgott		3	4
Sum Totll	395	8	7½

[ESRO W/INV 1510]

Administration 27 Aug 1722
To brother, Richard Parr, of Northampton, gent   [ESRO W/B 16.121r]

---

[1] Baptized All Saints, Northampton, 1683, fourth son of John, of Northampton, mercer. Houghton Conquest Grammar School, Beds. Cambridge, Sidney Sussex, admitted aged 16 and matriculated 1698, BA 1702, MA 1705. Ordained deacon 1705 (bishop of Peterborough), priest 1709 (bishop of Chichester). Curate of Spratton, Northants; of Udimore 1715. Vicar of Peasmarsh 1709–1722, patron Sidney Sussex College. Died 1722 aged 39.

117. Petworth 7 May 1633 WILLIAM BEEDING [1]

Appraisers: Henry Fullerton gent, John Milles yeoman, Richard Keyse husbandman, John Putocke tanner, Richard Wakeford blacksmith

	£	s	d
In primis redie monie in his purse and [ap]p[a]rell	6	13	4
In the parlor			
Item his bookes	4	0	0
Item one bedd furneshed	4	0	0
Item one side cuberd		4	0
Item one truncke and one cheaste with linane in them	4	0	0
Item one table two chares and sixe Joyned stooles		10	0
The Chamber over the hale			
Item two featherbedds beeing old and the bedstedles with all theireunto belongeing	3	10	0
Item one folding table one chaire one chiste and other lumber	1	3	4
Item the pewter thiere with the bedpanne	1	0	0
The Butterie			
Item fowre Wooden vesseles and other lumber		6	8
The hale			
Item one table with the carpite and frame one livrie cuboard and fowre chaires	1	0	0
Item three small hoggs of baken	2	0	0
Item one Jake two pr of brandirons one burding peece one Ierone pote two pr of pote hangers one chafing dishe one pr of tos[t]ying ierons one pr of gurdierons one speete with other such like smale things	2	0	0
The kitchen			
Item one brace furnese one pr of andiarons two litle kitles one pote three smale tubes two posenets with other lumber	2	2	0
The Milkhowse			
Item 14 trougs and other lumber		10	0
The chamber over the kitchin			
Item one ould flocke bed with certaine Ierone		10	0
Then Without the doores			
Item Fowre oxen one Waggon with yowkes and chaines theireunto belonging	17	13	4
Item Fowre horse beasts at	7	0	0
Item three kine with Caves by thiere sids at	6	0	0
Item two hiffers and Fowre smale beace	6	6	8
Item five younge shotts	1	13	4
Item two ould dounge courts one ould plowe and two ould harrowes		13	4
Item three akcers of ots	1	10	0
Item Fowre akcers of pease and tares	2	10	0
Item one litle plote of beanes and flaxe		6	0
Item two cords of wood		10	0
Item one wimsheete with ould sakkes one welbocket and well roope		8	0
Item one turkie cock and henne		5	0
Item two geese and one gander		2	0
Sum total	78	7	0

[WSRO Ep I/29/149/50]

Administration 22 May 1633
To Catherine, wife   [WSRO STC III/G/231, 235]

¹ Oxford, subscribed 1613; Magdalen Hall, BA 1616, MA 1619. Rector of Burton with Coates 1623–1633, patron Crown. Died 1633.

118. Plumpton 24 May 1682 [*sic*] JAMES BENNETT ¹
Appraiser: Anthony Nethercott

	£	s	d
In primis Cloths and wearing Apparell	4	0	0
Item Money in the House with allowance for [?]Guineys	62	0	0
Item Corne in the Barne and Strawe	18	11	10
Item Goods in the Yard and Fields	47	3	0
Item Goods and Householdstuffe sold	45	16	0
Item pewter sold and unsold	2	13	4
Item Lynnen sold and unsold	9	7	8
Item Bedding and other Goods unsold	11	15	8
~~Item Goods and Householdstuffe sold~~	~~45~~	~~16~~	~~0~~
Item Due to the Deceased upon Bond with Interest from Mr Springett	207	10	0
Item from Mr Middleton on Bond with Interest	46	0	0
Item from John Beard with Interest	36	4	6
Item from John Browne upon Note	1	0	0
Item from Captain Challoner	2	15	0
Item from John Banks upon a Note	3	14	9
Item received for Tithes due at the time of the said Deceaseds ~~death as may appear by particular~~	72	15	0
Item Tithes hopefull but not paid	7	10	4
Item Rent at Milton in Kent due at the testators death and since received	42	15	6
Item Money Lent to Mr Lintott without a Note	30	0	0
Item due from Thomas Verrall at the testators death and since received	7	0	0
Item due from Goodman Burlinger	2	0	0
Item from Mr Steatton for his Board	3	0	0
Item for Butter sold	11	6	0
Item from mr Middleton	2	0	0
Sum	657	13	1
Item Tythes that are Desperate and lost	6	17	6

[TNA PRO PROB 5/2248]

Will: made 7 May 1680; codicil 26 Oct 1680; proved 22 Nov 1680
Wife Jane, executrix (with son-in-law, Anthony Nethercott); 'sons': Anthony Nethercott, clerk (books); Thomas Lintott; John Swinoke; daughters: Jane (Burnsall), Mary (Lintott), Elizabeth (Nethercott), Katherine (Swinoke)
Witnesses: John Teeling, Thomas Veruell, William Burges, servant

[TNA PRO PROB 11/364]

For probate account see **188**

¹ Possibly Cambridge. Rector of Plumpton 1656–1680. Died 1680; buried Plumpton.

119. Plumpton 15 Feb 1711 THOMAS TRAVERS [1]
Appraisers: John Pennall, [?]Michell Coppead

	£	s	d
In primis A bed Bedsteadle two Blanketts one Pillow and a Bolster	2	10	0
Item Two arm Chairs		4	0
Eight small Chairs		8	0
One leafe Table		4	0
A Table with a drawer		3	0
A large table Leafe		7	0
A Clock and Clock Case	1	5	0
A Firepann Tongs and pair of Andirons		3	0
Two Iron Scewers and Fork		1	0
A pothook			6
A Salt box and pair of bellowes		1	0
A box Iron 2 heats and ...		1	8
In the Buttery			
Two dozen of Plates		12	0
Six dishes and a pye plate		7	0
Two porringers two saucers and a Sale		2	0
Two Candlesticks and one more		1	0
Six small tinn pye plates			6
Two powdering Tubbs		6	0
A sauce pann		1	0
An Iron pott		2	6
A brass Kettle		2	6
A bell brass Skillett		2	6
A bowl a Trugg a platter and Tunnell		2	6
A Frying pann		1	0
A Lanthorn			8
Two Sieves		1	0
A brass Chafing dish and snuffers		1	0
A Nutmegg Grater and brass Skimmer			6
Tenn Wooden Trenchards			6
Four Earthen Muggs		1	0
An Apple roaster			6
In the Cellar			
Two Coolers		5	0
Eight barrells	1	0	0
In the Chamber over the Kitchin			
A Table Cloth and a dozen of Napkins		10	0
A doz of Napkins and table Cloth		10	0
A dozen more and table Cloth		10	0
Two pair of Sheets and 4 pillowcoats	1	0	0
Two pair of Strong flaxen Sheets	2	0	0
Four towells		2	0
Three pair of Tow Sheets		18	0
One pair of Hemp Sheeys		5	0
One pair more of tow Sheets		5	0
Five shirts		12	6

A Course table Cloth	7	0
Three Table Clothes	3	0
Seven course Towells	3	6
Three more course Towells	1	0
Nine Napkins	2	0
A bed one Blankett 2 bolsters and Coverlid	1 0	0
A Cloth prop	4	0
In the Washhouse		
A Bucking tubb and long tubb	2	6
A Brewing tubb	8	0
A Furnace	1 15	0
A Wicker Chair	4	0
In the Woodhouse		
One Cord and Quarter of wood	15	0
Halfe an hundred of Faggotts	5	0
Besides		
Six Silver Spoons	1 10	0
One Silver Tobacco box	10	0
One Silver Watch	10	0
In Mony	4 17	6
Five Gold rings	1 0	0
Five doz of Bottles	10	0
Mony due to tythes	8 8	0
Mony Due on Note	50 0	0
	68 6	5
More in mony	10 3	6
Books value att	3 0	0
	101 5	9

[ESRO W/INV 124]

Will: made 26 Sep 1710; proved 1 March 1711
Executor: Anthony Springett, gent
Witnesses: John and Edward Verrall, John Page   [ESRO W/A 48.94]

[1] Biographical details not found.

120. Poling 5 Dec 1722 THOMAS SCRIVENS [1]
Appraisers: John Booker, Ralph Grevatt
[Original damaged]

	£	s	d
In primis in the Hall the g ... valued at			
Item in the Kitchen	1	10	0
Item in the Parlour	..	...	..
Item in the Wash hou[se] ...	..	...	..
Item in the Dr[ink room] ...	..	...	..
Item in the best ...	..	...	..
Item in the Hall [Chamber] ...	..	...	..
Item in the Kitchen Chamber	2	0	0

Item in the Maids Chamber	1	0	0
Item for Linnen and Plate	4	10	0
Item Money on Bond	5	0	0
Item wearing Apparell and money in Purse	5	0	0
Item wheat in the Straw	12	0	0
Item barley in the Straw	5	0	0
Item Pease and Tares unthrashed	5	0	0
Item Four Horses	8	0	0
Item Three Cows	..	...	..
Item Eleven P …	..	...	..
Item Hay …	..	...	..
Item a Wagg[on …	..	...	..
Item one Plo[w]…	..	...	..
Item Four Horse Harness	1	0	0
Item Bacon and Porck and Cheese	2	0	0
Item Books in the Studdey	5	0	0
Item things unseen and Forgotten		5	0
	96	0	0

[WSRO Ep I/29/150/47]

Will: made 1 July 1722; proved 5 Dec 1722
Wife: Mary, executrix
Witnesses: Henry Hare, Susan Barnard, John Booker   [WSRO STC I/33/108]

[1] Called MA 1706. Vicar of Poling 1706–1722, patron Eton College. Curate of Patching c. 1722.
Married Mary Harding at Burpham 1715. Died 1722.

121. Pulborough …. 1668 RICHARD RAWLINSON [1]
[Original damaged and illegible]   [TNA PRO PROB 4/2688]

Will: made 20 July 1668; proved 29 July 1668
Proved by one of executors, Walter Nicholson
Wife Bridgett (10 pieces of gold for mourning, silver chafeing dish, linen etc, £500);
sister: Anne; brother and sister Nicholson; in-laws Sir Robert and Lady Croke and family
Sill family
Poor of parish £3; Queen's College, Oxford £5
Witnesses: Robert Beale, Richard Hichcock, Anne Andrewes
[TNA PRO PROB 11/327/96]

[1] Son of Richard, of Milnthorpe, Westm. Oxford, Queen's, matriculated 1636 aged 18, BA 1641,
MA 1643, BD 1657, DD 1661. Ordained deacon 1644, priest 1646 (bishop of Oxford). Chaplain
to William, duke of Newcastle. Rector of Pulborough 1665–1668. Married Bridget Crooke at
St Katherine Cree, London, by licence 1666. Died 1668; buried Pulborough.

122. Rottingdean 21 June 1732 THOMAS PELLING [1]

Appraisers: John Gold, John Friend

	£	s	d
In primis his Wearing Apparrell and money in purse	20	0	0
Item in Cash	300	0	0
Item Principall money due upon a Mortgage	250	0	0
Item Principall money due upon a Bond	170	0	0
Item Intrest money and Sundry Debts due upon Book Account or otherwise some good and Some Dubious	150	0	0
In the Kitchen			
Item a pair of fire grates fire pan Tongs Poker Slice Brandirons 1 Jack 1 spitt with other small Iron things and pair of Bellows	2	10	0
One Morter and pestle 2 Candlesticks 2 Coffee potts 1 floor 1 pepper box 1 Coffee pot 1 Coffee Mill with some other things of Brass or Copper	1	5	0
One Table 2 Firmes 6 Chairs 1 Loaking Glass 1 Bacon rack with about 4 flitches of Bacon 1 Screen 1 Cupboard or nest of Drawers	4	10	0
In the Hall			
Item 2 Tables 5 Chairs 4 Pictures 2 Birdcages	3	0	0
In the Parlour			
Item One Table 10 Chairs 1 Clock 1 Couch 1 weather glass 1 Screen 2 pictures with Severall drinking Glasses and some Earthen ware	6	0	0
In the Bakehouse			
Item 3 Copper or Brass potts 2 Stew pans 1 Clever a pair of old Brandirons with Sundry earthen potts wooden dishes and other small things and Lumber	3	0	0
In the Pantry			
Item 10 Pewter Dishes 3 Dozen of Plates 1 fish Kettle 2 Skilletts 2 Saucepans 1 frying pan some earthen potts and pans with other small things and Lumber	5	0	0
In the Brewhouse			
Item 2 Furnaces 1 Brew Tub Tun Tubb and Cooller with other Brewing and Washing Tubbs and Water Pailes	10	0	0
In the other Pantery			
Item One table 1 Tubb and 2 Crocks		5	0
In the passage up Stairs			
Item One old Cupboard 1 Sta ... d 1 warming pan and an Wooden Horse for drying Clothes with other small things		10	0
In the mild beer Cellar			
Item 3 Cask of mild beer four empty Cask and 2 Stands	2	3	0
In the Small Beer Cellar			
Item 7 Beer Cask 1 Stand or Stollage	1	0	0
In the Little Cellar			
Item Two powdring Tubbs with some Pork and 2 Beer Cask	7	0	0

In the Wine Cellar

	£	s	d
Item 3 Empty Cask 2 Cheeses a bout 4 Dozen bottles of Wine and about 2 Dozen of other Liquour	6	5	0

In the Parlour Chamber

	£	s	d
Item One Feather bed with the Steddle and appurtenances Chairs 1 Table 1 Looking Glass 1 Stove with the fender fire pan and Tongs 1 Close stool and Window Curtains	8	8	0

In the maides Chamber

	£	s	d
Item One Feather bed and Steddle with the appurtenances 2 Chairs and 1 Chest	3	0	0

In the Bakehouse Chamber

	£	s	d
Item One feather Bed with the Steddle and appurtenances 1 press 1 Chest and 2 Chairs	5	0	0
Fourteen pair of Sheets and other Linnen	15	0	0

In the Kitchen Chamber

	£	s	d
Item One Feather Bed and Steddle with the appurtenances 1 Screetore 1 Table a pair of Brand Irons firepan Tongs and Bellows	7	10	0
One Silver Tankard 1 porrenger 11 Spoones 6 Tea Spoons 1 Watch and 4 Gold Rings	17	0	0

In the Studdy

	£	s	d
Item About 800 Books a pair of Globes 1 table 2 Ring Dyalls 1 Tellescope 1 Speaking Trumpett 2 Chairs and other things	100	0	0

In the Garrett

	£	s	d
Item 2 feather Bedds with appurtenances a parcell of malt and a Steel mill	17	0	0

In the Court and Gardens about the House

	£	s	d
Item about 2 Gross of Empty Bottles with the Bottle Racks 1 Stone Roller 13 Hives of bees about 2 Chaldron of Sea coal 1 welbuckett and Rope	7	17	6

In the little Stables

	£	s	d
Item Some fire wood and faggotts 3 Saddls and Bridles	3	0	0

In the Parsonage Barne

	£	s	d
Item Three Tubbs with a Small quantity of Pease and Barley	2	15	0

Live Stock

	£	s	d
Item 55 Sheep and 35 Lambs	28	0	0
3 Sows 7 Shoots or young hoggs 6 Sucking piggs and Two Cows	16	10	0
Six Cart Horses 2 Riding Horses 2 Colts with the cart Harness and Plough Harness	60	0	0

In the Coach House Great Stable Closes and Elsewhere

	£	s	d
Item One Chariott 1 Chaise and Harness for 4 Horses	15	15	0
3 Waggons 3 Dung courts 2 ploughes 3 Harrows 1 Roller 1 watering Trough 1 Winnower 3 Sacks 4 Sives 2 Corn Shovells 1 Bushell measure 1 Shall 1 Winnowing Sheet	28	3	6
One Stack of Wheat and the Frame	33	0	0
about 2 Load of Hay	3	0	0

In the Grainary

	£	s	d
Item Four quarters of Oates	2	12	0
2 Tubbs and a [?]Gord Two bushells of tares		7	0
55 fleeces of Wooll and Some Lambs wooll	3	12	0

Corn upon the Ground

	£	s	d
Item Wheat	10	0	0
Barley	31	0	0
Pease	7	0	0
Tares		15	0
Item Things unseen and forgotten	2	0	0
	1364	13	0

But on the Contrary he being indebted to Severall persons upon bond
(before other Debts) principall money being deducted   300   0   0

Remaines   1064   13   0

[ESRO W/INV 2426]

Will: made 26 May 1732; proved 8 July 1732
Executrix: Mary Jeffrey, housekeeper
Sister: Martha Betsworth (books)
Witnesses: Thomas Stonestreet, John Snashall junior, John Grover   [ESRO W/A 54.37]

[1] Son of Edward, of Boxworth, Cambs, cleric. Westminster School, king's scholar 1686. Oxford,
Christ Church, matriculated 1689 aged 18, BA 1693, MA 1696. Ordained deacon 1697 (bishop of
Oxford), priest 1698 (bishop of Rochester). Vicar of Rottingdean 1698–1732, patron Charles, earl
of Dorset and Middlesex. Curate of Kingston by Sea c. 1725. Died 1732.

123. Rudgwick 4 Oct 1670 THOMAS MEADE [1]

Appraisers: Richard Napper of Hies, Michael Harmes

	£	s	d
In primis His wearing apparrell and money in purse	5	0	0
Item at his Land called Lemmons three cowes	6	10	0
Item three horse beasts	10	10	0
Item Dung		6	0
A Cart		4	0
Two Harrows		9	0
One Ladder		1	0
Two Quarters of Wheate	3	0	0
Seven quarters of oates	3	10	0
Hay	1	1	1
One Fagge		5	0
… A prong coller and cart harnes		1	0
One …			6
Yrne		2	6
Item at his Land called Pipers			
Three hundred and a halfe of spray fagotts		7	0
Wood		4	0
Hay and one prong one rake one bedstedle		14	6
In the barne at the vicaridge House			
Two breakes and one cord and halfe of wood		9	0
Item boards a sider presse with other Lumber		8	0
In the Hall			
On cupboard and stone table and frame	1	3	0

On long cupboard		7	6
On table forme and bench		7	6
On Jack five spitts and a drawing candlesticke		13	0
On Muskett a paire of brandirons		11	0
Pott hangers one fender and iron plate		13	0
A paire of Tongues and fire shovell		2	0
… and glass cage and one glasse		8	4
4 chaires 6 stooles a settle bench		3	6
A Tosting iron and greater		1	6
3 wedges A cradle		3	0
A pestell mortar and Gridirons		1	6
A paire of ... sh knives		1	0
8 dripping pans 2 formes one bench and shelves		6	0
Roopes and irons		1	6
2 vatt a kever Gimbletts and Mall		1	0
Blades and weights four brasse kettles one skimer 3 A cleaver 2 chopping knives and flesh hooke		1	2
… pieces of Latten		2	0
24 pewter dishes one flagon a chamber pott 3 candlesticks one pott 4 poringers a bason with all other small pewter	2	10	6
Earthen Ware and 3 drinking potts		5	0
In the parlour			
… Silver spoones one silver cup and two salts	3	5	0
A table and frame six chaires 3 carpetts	2	0	0
One cupboard one round table 3 cushions two brandirons and a backe		15	0
Item In the Buttery			
5 Kinderkins 5 firkins and a safe	1	10	0
3 Beer stands and one poudering trough		5	6
A table and six cheese shelves 4 tubs and a kiver		11	0
2 spinning Wheeles one riste and a shaule		2	0
25 cheeses Bees wax and Honey and a pott	1	8	0
Bottles and potts and all other Lumber		3	0
One naile of Butter and Bacon		6	6
One brasse warming pan and Latten Lanthorne		3	4
In the Milkhouse within the House			
3 dozen of Trenchers 2 iron potts with Hookes one iron boate and iron frying pan		9	6
Crocks and all other Lumber in that Roome		6	0
Item 7 sacks a sadle and bridle		12	0
Without doores			
4 Hoggs one stack of fagotts	2	14	0
A Hog Hutch and trough and 14 geese		15	0
24 poultry		10	0
In the Milkhouse without doores			
Ten Truggs 8 earthen pans one irone pott and a cheese presse and table and frame with all other Lumber in that Roome		18	0
Item a wash tub and Hop poles		3	0
In the Brewhouse			
5 tubs 2 kivers a cheese presse 4 bucketts 2 strainers a brasse furnace			

one iron kettle an iron barr with other tooles and all other lumber in that Roome	4	9	0
In the chamber over the Buttery			
One high bed and stedle with the appurtenances and one truckle bed with the appurtenances	4	14	0
In the best chamber			
The best bed and stedle with the appurtenances and one twigg chaire 3 chests one chaire and stoole and eight paire of Tire sheetes	13	0	0
Item 3 Tire table clothes 11 paire of Tow sheetes and 4 Tow table clothes	3	14	0
13 diaper napkins and towell and table cloth and cupboard cloth all Diaper	1	2	0
10 tire napkins and 21 course napkins seven holland pillowcoates 2 ells of tire cloth one paire of Tire pillowcoates one cupboard cloth and Kearcher 3 paire of course pillowcoates 2 twigg basketts	2	8	0
In the entry to the best chamber			
8 towells and other small Linnen and 2 chests		12	6
In the chamber over the Hall			
One bed and stedle with the appurtenances and one litle table and chest	3	16	6
In the Long chamber			
One presse Wooll one truckel bed with the appurtenances an old Trucke with flax and Hemp with all other lumber in that Roome	1	12	0
Item in the West chamber			
One high bed and stedle with the appurtenances	3	0	0
In the Garrett			
Apples peares Hopps and boards and all the other Lumber in that Roome	1	10	0
In His study			
His Bookes	5	0	0
In the Garden and about the house			
One cole basket a halfe bushell a sundiall and all other goods belonging to the deceased not before prized		3	6
Good debts owing to the deceased	9	0	0
Desperate debts owing	5	0	0
	[117	3	11]

Exhibited by Edward Johnson [?nephew]   [WSRO Ep I/29/160/69]

Will: made 14 Sep 1670; proved 18 Nov 1670
Wife: Sarah, executrix (with son and daughter Anna); son: Thomas, London, grocer (new coat); daughters: Anna (feather bed, silver spoon and cup, little brass kettle, skillet, 2 pewter dishes), Sarah (minor); son-in-law: Thomas Oram, vicar, Billingshurst (best gown); brother: James, D.D.
Overseers: Thomas Constable, Ockley brewer, Thomas Oram
Witnesses: John Butcher, Mary Willetts, Thomas Oram   [WSRO STC I/24/101]

[1] Son of Thomas, of Wheatley, Oxon. Oxford, Magdalen, matriculated 1635 aged 17, BA 1638. Called curate 1641. Vicar of Rudgwick 1646–1670, patron bishop of Chichester. Married Sarah Willett at Wisborough Green 1641. Died 1670.

124. Rudgwick 20 June 1681 JOHN SMYTH [1]
Appraisers: Richard Weste, Michael Harmes

	£	s	d
In primis his wearing Aparell and mony in his purse	19	17	3
Item one horse	5	6	8
Item three small Ringes		18	6
Item one watch	2	10	0
Item one Cheeste and som small Things Therein	1	17	8
Item his Bookes		9	6
Item one bond of good debte	20	0	0
Item one other bond of debte	25	0	0
Item Two small peeces of linen Cloth A Riding whipe and whatsoever			
els of and belonging to the Aforesaid deceased not before prised		12	6
The some tottall is	76	12	1

[WSRO Ep I/29/160/84]

Will: made 14 June 1681; proved 15 July 1681
Friend and countryman George Reith, vicar of Rudgwick, executor
Brothers (in Scotland): Robert, William; five sisters
Reference to disposal of Scottish property
John Nisbet, Horsham schoolmaster
Witnesses: Robert Wood, John Butcher, Richard Wood   [WSRO STC I/27/284]

[1] Biographical details not found.

125. Rusper 24 Oct 1633 JOSEPH BROWNE [1]
Appraisers: Richard Evershed and Robert Chattfeilde of Newdigate, Thomas Steere

	£	s	d
Item 2 Mares	5	0	0
Item 3 hoggs and 3 piggs	4	6	8
Item one sheepe		6	8
Item the wheate in the barne	8	0	0
Item wheate in the house	2	0	0
Item …	10	0	0
Item two acres on wheate on the grounde	4	0	0
Item haye	9	0	0
Item one olde wayne wheeles courte a plough yokes chaynes and			
harrowe and other ymplements of husbandry	1	3	4
Item …			
Item boardes and pales		10	0
Item maulte		13	4
Item one Flitch of bacon	1	0	0
Item butter and cheese	2	0	0
Item sope and grease		3	8
Item oate meale		4	0
Item apples and peares		6	0
Item in the haull			
one table forme a falling table chayres and stooles with other things		10	0
Item more there one plate 2 brandirons 4 spitts pott hangers and other			

fire ymplements	1	14	0
Item in the parlour			
one table and frame one livery table and one litle table 8 joyned stooles six cushions 2 litle brandirons and waynescot	3	8	0
Item at the parsonage			
one bedsteddle one table and frame and one joyned chayre	1	0	0
Item there one frame uppon a slyde for swine		6	8
Item in the chamber over the parlour			
one bedstedle and fetherbedd boulster rugg blanket ...	6	0	0
Item one coverlett five carpets	1	6	8
Item in the chamber over the haulle			
one fetherbedd and flockbedd three blankets 2 coverletts 4 pillowes	5	10	0
Item one cupboard 4 chests one close stoole one warming pan and bellowes with other things	2	5	0
Item one truckle bedstedle		4	0
Item all the pewter	4	0	0
Item all the linnen	15	0	0
Item plate	5	0	0
Item 2 flockbedds and bolsters with the appurtenances one olde trunke and one olde cheste	2	2	0
Item 2 flockbedds and stedles in the garrets with olde coverletts and blanketts	1	3	4
Item his bookes and other things in the studye	10	0	0
Item a musket and other armour	1	0	0
Item certayne things in the chamber over the milkhouse	1	1	0
Item one cheesepresse hoopes and followers		5	0
Item milke vessell		10	0
Item vinegar		10	0
... boulting hutch poudring trough with other things there		10	0
Item brasse and iron vessell	4	3	0
Item dripping panns and a morter		4	6
Item 2 aumbries and a glasse cupboard		12	0
Item drinke vessell tubbs and kimmells	1	10	0
Item crocks potts and glasses		10	0
Item Flaskets and baskets		2	0
Item flax and yarne		10	0
Item sives shaulls sacks and baggs a lanthorne and measures		13	4
Item wooll and cloth	1	16	0
Item a grinding stone well bucket with other things apperteyning		6	8
Item a treste and ringer with all workeing tooles and other things not named	1	0	0
Item beeswax and hony		5	0
Item poultry aboute the house		14	0
Item spinning wheeles		3	0
Item a boulster ticke		4	0
Item his apparell girdle purse and mony in his purse	6	2	0
Item debtes oweing to him ... some desperate	25	0	0
Sum total	172	11	2

[WSRO Ep I/29/163/7]

Will: made 18 June 1633; proved 1 Nov 1633

Sons: William, executor, John; daughters: Susan (Leachforde) Sarah (Fenner) Phebe (Simons); son-in-law: Arthur Fenner (chest in study)

Maid: Mary Fowler ('hye chamber in south end of howse where Robert Mathew dwelt during her life'; liberty to make fire in hall 'against stacke where oven is'; bed in chamber over millhouse 'where menservants used to lye'); executor to 'dressse up the Chamber granted to Mary Fowler healing and walling it well'

Witnesses not recorded [WSRO STC I/18/278b]

[1] Of Surrey. Cambridge, Queens', matriculated 1579, BA 1583. Ordained deacon and priest 1588 (bishop of Winchester). Rector of Rusper 1590–1633, patron Cecilia Lewknor of Rusper. Possibly married Elizabeth Stone, widow, at Rusper 1607. Died 1633.

126. Rusper 20 March 1677 WILLIAM PRIAUX [1]

Appraisers: William Greenfield of Capel, William Hill

(Goods left unadministered by Joan Priaux widow deceased)

	£	s	d
In primis the remaynder of his wearing Cloathes	-	-	-
Item In the Parlour			
one Table and Carpett of Turkeyworke one sydeboard wth a Cloth fowre Chayres and two stooles Andirons fireshovell Tongs and Bellowes five Cushions and a lookeing glass	7	2	0
Item In the passage			
One Bason and Ewre and two leather Chayres		6	8
Item in the kitchin			
two tables one forme one Cuppboard three Chayres three joyned stooles one Musquett fowre pistolls dishes pottingers and other vessells of white Earth one Jack six spitts one Cast Iron back and Andirons potthangers fireshovell Tongs and Bellowes smoothing Irons with some other small things	5	18	4
Item In the Hall			
two Tables one Carpett one napkinpress one still one little Cuppboard one Glasscase and Glasses and Tenn China Dishes six small Trenchers salte one brass clock twelve Chayres Eight Cushions wth some other small things	7	10	0
Item In the Pantry			
a Joynd stoole and two old Cuppboards thirteene beere vessells three dozen of Bottles a stand and other small things	2	10	0
Item In the Wash house			
Three Iron potts two Iron kettles two Cleavers two Gridirons two Iron dripping pans fowre brass kettles and fowre brass potts two warming panns of brass two brass skilletts two brazen Chafing dishes one brass Candlestick one brass morter and pestle one old Cupp board wth some Lumber and also a brass scimmer	5	9	0
Item In the Bakehouse			
one powdring trough seaven old tubbs two mealesacks three searchers three stands for barrells wth other lumber	1	5	0

Item In the Brewhouse

	£	s	d
one Copper furnace three brass kettles and a Brass pann an Iron back for Roasting one Brewing fatt and Tunn fowre keelers one bucking tubb two Iron Oven lidds a pyre of Andirons two peeles and a forke two pothangers an halfe bushell one Chorne and five payles with other lumber	6	16	6

Item In the Parlor chamber

	£	s	d
one large Cypress Chest a pyre of blanketts one Ash colour'd Rugg Curtaynes and vallons sideboardcloth and Tablecloth of Redd two Window Cushions of satten and alsoe one greene Carpett	6	5	0
In the same place two featherbedds two feather boulsters two feather pillowes three blanketts	8	0	0
Beddstedd Cutaynes and vallons alsoe six Chayres brass Andirons and brass fireshovell and Tongs	2	10	0

Item In the Chamber over the Entry

	£	s	d
one featherbedd Two boulsters one pillow three blanketts two Ruggs one Quilt Beddstedd Curtaynes and vallons one Chest one Stoole and one Cushion and a small looking glass	8	2	0

Item In the kitchin chamber

	£	s	d
one featherbedd and one Quilt one boulster two pillowes two blanketts one Rugg beddstedd Curtaynes and vallons	4	0	0
In the same place one featherbedd beddstedd and an old Rugg	4	10	0
In the same Chamber three Chayres two Chests and a looking glass		18	0

Item In the Chamber over the Wash house

	£	s	d
one flock bedd two blanketts a Coverlett and boulster a beddstedd and two old Chests and a Joyndstoole	1	0	0

Item In the Garrett over the Parlour Chamber

	£	s	d
one Cauldron and a pyre of large brass Andirons	1	10	0
In the same place three old Chests two trunkes a beddstedd a pillow a large window Cushion	2	0	0

In the Entry Garrett

	£	s	d
one saddle and an old chests		12	0

Item In the Garrett over the kitchin chamber

	£	s	d
some Old Lumber		4	4

Item In the Milkehouse

	£	s	d
fowreteene Wooden trayes For milke and a brass Milke pann and Powderingtubb and other Lumber		18	0

Item In the Cheeshouse

	£	s	d
one Cheespress two Chees Tubbs scales Weights and spinning wheele	1	0	0

Item In the manns Chamber

	£	s	d
one beddstedd and a Flockbedd and boulster an old Coverlett and two Course blanketts		15	0
Item one horse in the stable	3	0	0

Item abroade

	£	s	d
One Wayne Dungpotte and two pyre of Wheeles	5	0	0
Item Yoakes Chaynes harness other husbandry Tooles and Implaments	1	15	0

Item In the Garrett over the Parlour Chamber

two and twenty pewter Dishes a Bason and Ewer of Pewter a Pasty
plate and five Pye Plates a Dozen small Trencher plates of pewter six

	£	s	d
small pewter Dishes six saltsellers a Dozen of Alchymy spoones	4	17	0
Item elswhere about the house seaventeene pewter platters one Bason three Candlesticks of pewter three pewter Chamberpotts six sawcers and three Pottingers	3	14	0

In the study

	£	s	d
In primis the bookes	40	0	0
Item twelve Cesars	5	0	0
Item Two tables a sideboard three deskes a beddsteddle and three Joyndstooles	2	10	0
Item his weareing Rings	10	0	0
Item an account of Tythes unreceived	3	7	6
Item Money uppon Bond	81	4	8
Suma total	244	0	0

Exhibited 8 October 1677 by John Rooke [TNA PRO PROB 4/11933]

Administration 6 Mar 1674
To his widow Joan Priaux; TNA PRO PROB 6/49]

Administration 11 Jun 1677
New grant to his son Peter Priaux, the widow Joan being now also deceased
[TNA PRO PROB 6/52]
[NB: the inventory seems to go with the later grant]

[1] Son of Peter, of Southampton, merchant, previously from Guernsey. Cambridge, Trinity, matriculated 1625, scholar 1627, BA 1629, MA 1632. Oxford, incorporated 1634. Ordained deacon 1633 (bishop of Ely), priest 1634 (bishop of Winchester). Rector of Rusper 1633–1673, patron Sir John Mill, bt. Licensed preacher Chichester diocese 1635. Married Joan Stone, widow, c. 1635. Died 1673 aged 62; buried Rusper; memorial to 'Ye late painfull and faithfull pastor of this church'.

127. Rusper 10 Oct 1712 JOHN PRIAUX [1]
Appraisers: Richard Curtis, James Chapman

	£	s	d
In primis His Wearing apparell and money in pockett	5	0	0

In the Kitchen

Item One Table Two stoolls Eight Chairs One Clock one bunting hutch one warming pan Two Cupboards Fourteen pewter dishes Four porringers six dozen of plates one Copper Coffee pott Three of Tin Two pair of brass Candlesticks one pair of pewter one pair of brass snuffers and Case Two Salvers one pint pott Two Tin Tunnells Two rings one Cheese plate Three spitts Four Iron Candlestickes Two Tin graters one Tin Toster one brass ladle one Skimer one Fish plate one Tin Cover Two Tinn pans Two Tin Dripping pans Two sheets of Tin Two box Irons and heats one Tin Candlebox one pair of Andirons one pair of Doggs Firepan and Tongs one Iron Fender Two paier of potthangers one pair of gridirons one pair of bellowes Two Curtins and rods one pair of small tongs one good huswife one Iron Ovenlid one Iron plate one plate pott one pair of Iron wafer plates one Rack and one small brass Chaffing dish

	£	s	d
	10	0	1

In the parlour next the Court

Item Eight Chairs one Table one pair of doggs one pair of bellowes
Firepan and tongs one seeing glass the hangings of the room one brush
Curtins and rodds pictures 8 cusheens and Almanacks   2   2   6

        In the Closett

Item One pair of playing tables one spinning wheell Five glasses and
shelves   4   6

        In the Inner parlour

Item One table seven chairs one Tea Table one pair of Andirons
Firepan and tongs Four Curtins vallance and rods and Four pictures   1 13   6

        In the Inner Closett

Item Two Earthen basons one Earthen plate one hand Tea table one
decanter several syllybob glasses one mugg one China bason and
shelves   5   8

        In the Buttery

Item Two Keelers one old cupboard one Meal tubb three Iron potts one
brass kittle one leather sack one Iron Chafing dish one brass ffrying pan
a pair of wooden blades and weights a pair of Yarn winders severall
potts and Crocks Formes shelves and dressers and an Iron Trest and
some Odd things   1   9   0

        Item In the Milkhouse

Five kilderkins seven small runletts one brew Tubb one wooden
Tunnell one powdring tubb one safe one old cupboard one old chair one
sieve about Ten dozen of glass bottles one old baskett dressers shelves
and some other odd things   2   7   6

        Item In the Entry

one lanthorne Four pewter dishes and a few odd things   6   6

        Item In the brewhouse

one brass Furnace one brewing vate one bucking tubb one brewing tubb
one Three legged tubb Three bucketts Four kivers one Stann one brass
stew pan one Tin Cullender one pair of potthangers one Fire Forke one
brass skillett one bell brass skillett Three sause pans one small brass
kittle one sack and some other odd things   2   8   6

        Item In the Outer Sellar

Two kilderkins one Firkin Three Stanns Two brass Cocks Eleven
bottles and one pan   16   0

        Item In the Inner Sellar

About Ten dozen of bottles with liquor in them   15   0

        Item In the Parlour Chamber

one Feather bed One Feather bolster Two Feather pillows bedstedle
sacking bottome Curtins vallance and Curtin rods one quilt Three
blanketts one easy chair Six other chairs one table Two Stans one glass
and dressing boxes one pair of Andirons Firepan and tongs window
Curtins vallance and curtin rods and the Hangings of the room and for
odd things about the chimney   9 18   6

        Item In the Parlour Chamber

Closett one bell brass skillett and a few odd things   5   6

        Item In the Study

One Desk Four old chairs one pair of Doggs an old pair of bellowes and

old Trunck and Shelves Curtin and Curtin rod and severall books valued at	30	0	0

Item In the passage at the Topp of the Stairs

Three old pictures		1	0

Item In the Chamber over the kitchin

One Feather bed Two Feather bolsters Two Feather pillowes bedstedle Matt and Cord Curtins vallance and Curtin rods and Three blanketts One press bedstedle one Feather bed one Feather bolster one rugg one old Carpett Two blanketts and a sacking bottome one Table one looking glass one dressing box one picture a few odd Cups upon the Mantle window Curtins and Curtin rods Two old Truncks some boxes and a few odd things	6	14	6
Item One silver Tankard Four Silver Salts Twelve silver spoons and one silver sugar Castar	12	0	0
Item Six paier of Fine Tire sheets Two Damask Tablecloths Sixteen Damask Napkins Seven Diaper Tablecloths Thirteen Diaper Napkins Nine Flaxen Tablecloths one huckabeck Towell Eleven huckabeck Napkins one huckabeck Tablecloth Nine Napkins and a Towell of the same sort Three old Diaper Towells Eleven Flaxen Towells Four pair of holland pillow coat Two ells and a halfe of New Cloth one Napkin and a dressing tablecloth Two other tablecloths and some old peices of linnen	12	0	0

Item In the Closett belonging to the kitchen Chamber

one silver tobacco box one old watch one small [s]crutore and dressing box one table and tablecloth about sixteen bottles a small Window Curtin and rodd some old boxes shelves an old Trunck book and a few odd Things	2	9	6

Item In the Chamber over the buttery

Two Chests of drawers one Stan Three chairs Four window Curtins vallance and Curtin rods a green tablecloth and hangings of the roome	2	12	0

Item In the Milkhouse Chamber

One Feather bed one Feather bolster one Feather pillow bedstedle Matt and Cord and Curtins rods one old table and Two Chairs	2	15	0

Item In the Entry Chamber

one halfe bedstedle Matt and Cord one Feather bed one Feather bolster one rugg Two blanketts one press one chest one Trunck one old bed pan and a few odd things	3	4	0
Item Three pair of Old Towen Sheets three pair of Tire Sheets one other old pair of sheets Two tablecloths Four pair of pillowcoats Five dozen and Four Napkins Twenty Towells and Six tablecloths	6	7	0
Item Three pair of Flaxen sheets and one pair of Towen sheets in the beds up one pair of Stairs	1	10	0

Item In the Inner garrett

Two Truckle bedstedles Two Feather beds Two Feather bolsters Four Ruggs Two blanketts Matts and Cords one pair of Towen sheets and one pair of flaxen sheets	3	10	0

Item In the Outer garrett one

Close stooll and pan one Trunck portmantle one watering pott one still six kilderkins Two Feather pillows one pillow coate one pair of Tire

	£	s	d
Sheets one Flaskett eight yards of New Ticking Three sadles and some Old lumber	4	0	0
Item In the Old Study			
one Napkin one old Tablecloth one Truncke one Chest one old press and one Limbeck		12	0
Item In the Barne			
A parcell of hay Two Ladders one Wheellbarrow Two Sawes one hay cutter one Sythe one Matthoock one sledge Two wedges one handbill one pannell one Wanty one halter one halfe bushell one Old Chest one prong one Old Shovell one Dung spud one Ladder one horse one spitter one shovell more Three Hoes one Old Tubb and Three Rack reells	10	7	6
Item Tenn Stack of Wood	4	0	0
Item Owing to the Deceased for Tythe	96	0	10
Item Things forgotten unseen and not apprized		10	0
	100	10	10
Sum Tot	236	6	1

[WSRO Ep I/29/163/022]

Administration 29 Nov 1712
To Elizabeth, wife   [WSRO STC III/M/118]

[1] Son of John, of Fovant, Wilts, later archdeacon of Salisbury, and nephew of William, rector of Rusper (**126**). Oxford, University College, matriculated 1674 aged 16, BA 1678, MA 1681. Ordained deacon and priest 1681 (bishop of Chichester). Rector of Rusper 1681–1712. Died 1712.

128. Selham 5 Oct 1614 JOHN LEIGH [1]

Appraisers: Nicholas Alderton, John Randall, Henry Sandom

	£	s	d
In primis Eight Oxen	32	0	0
Item Seaven Steers	14	10	0
Item eight kine	20	0	0
Item foure heyfers	7	0	0
Item Six weniers	4	0	0
Item two Naggs	3	0	0
Item a Mare	3	0	0
Item another Mare and colt	2	0	0
Item two great Colts	10	0	0
Item Sheep 184	28	0	0
Item one Boare eight hoggs two Sowes and 11 Shoots	8	0	0
Item Geese Hennes and Ducks and other poultrie		10	0
Item Corne at Selham	36	0	0
Item Corne at Waltham	34	0	0
Item Corne at Northwood	35	0	0
Item Corne at Shortlande	13	0	0
Item Hay and Straw at the forenamed places	18	0	0
Item Mault in the house	1	0	0
Item Butter Cheese Honie Wax melted Tallow and grease	7	0	0
Item Plough geare Cart geare Harrowes and all necessarie implements belonging therewith	3	10	0

Item a grindstoane Axes hatchets Billes prongs Awgers all other tooles of husbandrie and old yron	1	0	0
Item a Musket furnished a Callyver and three pistols	1	10	0
Item an Haire cloth winnowing sheets sacks and baggs	2	0	0
Item household stuffe in the Haule			
two tables a Lyverie Cubboard Chaires and stooles	2	10	0
Item in the Parlor			
two tables a lyverie Cubbord Chaires and stooles	1	10	0
Item in the kitchen			
an henne Coope boards and shelves the brewing vessels tubbes buckets measures and all other woodden vessels in and about the house	5	0	0
Item in the Buttrie			
Cubboard and shelves Chists and boxes boards standes and other woodden stuffe	1	0	0
Item a litle furnace and all the Brasse	5	0	0
Item Pewter	4	0	0
Item yron racks spitts dreeping pannes an yron pott an yron kettle fyre tonges fyre pannes an yron backe and yrons and the yron tooles in the kitchen	2	10	0
Item fyve peece of silver plate and silver spoones	12	0	0
Item in the new Chamber			
a presse Cubbord a rownd table two bedstedds a wyned Chist Chaires and stooles	2	0	0
Item foure featherbeds bolsters pillowes Rugg blankets and Coverlets Curtaines and all the bedding in the new Chamber	20	0	0
Item in the Chamber over the haule			
two bedsteeds foure Chists a Trunke and a Boxe	2	0	0
Item two fetherbeds two flocke beds bolsters pillowes Coverlets blankets Curtaines and all the bedding in the Chamber over the haule	10	0	0
Item in the litle inner Chamber			
two featherbeds two flockbeds bolsters pillowes blankets Coverlets and all other bedding there	5	0	0
Item in the utter Chamber			
a bedsteed bedding feathers and wooll	9	0	0
Item Carpets and Cushions	2	0	0
Item Linnen sheets pillow beeres Cubboard clothes table clothes napkins towels and other lynnen	40	0	0
Item the Menservants bedsteed and bedding	2	0	0
Item in his stoodie			
a table three chistes a deske and shilves		13	4
Item Bookes and Pictures	20	0	0
Item his wearing Apparell Ryding furniture and money in his purse	20	0	0
Item debts owing him	3	17	0
Item the lease of Snape land	40	0	0
Item Timber boards and wood	5	0	0
Item Hemp flax Ropes and other smale things	1	10	0
Sum total	501	4	0

[WSRO Ep I/29/165/2]

Will nuncupative: made 29 Sep 1614; proved 20 Oct 1614
Wife Jennet,[2] three daughters
Books distributed: 'such books as shall be fit' to Free school of Farnworth in Lancaster;
Parens in epistolas Pauli, 2 vols, to Dr Bound; St Ambrose works to Lawrence Alcock;
Stella in Lucam to Richard Blundell; divinity notebooks and other divinity notes in his
study together with the books 'Mr Sephton hath of him' to Thomas Sephton; Downham's
Warfare to John Randall
Witnesses include: Thomas Sephton of Bignor, Richard Blundell, rector of Dogmersfield

[WSRO STC II/M Dean 1614 (1)]

[1]   Called MA 1590. Ordained deacon 1590, priest 1592 (bishop of Chichester). Curate of
Fittleworth 1591. Rector of Upwaltham 1592–1614, patrons Henry and Dorothy Dawtrey; of
Selham 1595–1614, patron Thomas Bennett of Arundel. Died 1614.
[2]   Patron of Selham after her husband's death: see **16**.

129. Selham 3 Feb 1641 JOHN PRICHARD [1]

Appraisers: William Ayling, Edward Blackman

	£	s	d
Item his Wearinge apparell and money in his purse	2	0	0
In the hall			
One table 4 Joyne stooles	1	0	0
Two Joyne Chayres		4	0
One hanging Cobord		3	4
Old Chayres and stooles		2	0
Two paire of pothangers one paire of brandirons one paire of tonges			
one paire of bellowes		5	0
In the parler			
One table and Forme		5	0
In the buttery			
Two barrelles five ferkines one tun two stands	1	0	0
Three Candle stickes and dishes		1	6
In the bedd chamber			
One standing beddstedle with a bedd bolstres and blanketts	2	0	0
One littell table and to Joyne stooles		6	0
Eight paire of sheetes	1	16	0
In the chamber over the hall			
One bedstedle one flocke bed bolstres and blankets	1	0	0
One dozen and a halfe of napkines and two short table clothes		12	0
A litle wooll and a baskett		5	0
In the littell Chamber			
One bedd stedel a truckel bedstedel and two flockbeds with bolsters and			
blankets	1	0	0
In the brewhowse			
In brewing vesales		16	0
In the kitchen			
One Iron Furnes	1	10	0
Brasse and putter	1	0	0
Iron potes and spits		10	0

In the milkhowse			
Fowre Truges		2	0
In lumbrey		10	0
In the barne			
Planckes for the flower		13	4
In the mawlt howse			
One vate		13	4
One wellbucket with a chaine and Roope		2	6
Other lumbrey		2	6
Fower fleches of bacon	1	0	0
Sum is	18	9	6

The debtes owinge by the said John Prichard deceased

Item to the Widdow Leggat due upon bond	5	4	0
Item to Mrs Dobell	1	0	0
Item to Henry Banfield upon bond	5	4	0
Item to John Scut	3	0	0
Sum is	14	8	0

[WSRO Ep I/29/165/5]

Administration 19 Feb 1641
To wife, Elizabeth   [WSRO STC III/H/164]

[1] Called literatus 1632. Rector of Selham 1632–1641, patron John Randall of Upwaltham, yeoman. Died 1641; buried Selham.

130. Selham 23 Sept 1681 THOMAS LOWE [1]

Appraisers: Isaac Woodruffe clerk, Edward Morrise, Henry Clare

	£	s	d
In primis his wearing Apparell and money in his purse	4	0	0
In the Chamber over the Parlour			
Item one silver Tankerd	4	0	0
Item one Feather Bed one bolster two pillowes one Rugge with a Bed Tester and all other furniture belonging to him	3	0	0
Item one chest one Livery Cubberd with foure Chaires		10	0
Item one Looking glass and two Black Jacks		7	0
In his Studdy			
Item his Bookes with other furniture therein	4	0	0
In the Hall Chamber			
Item Seaven Paire of Sheetes with other Course Linnen	3	0	0
Item two Trendle Bed steds two flock Bedds with Coverings and furniture belonging to them	1	0	0
In the Parlour			
Item two tables Six Chaires with other small necessaryes	1	0	0
Item one Clock	2	0	0
In the Hall			
Item one Table six joyned stooles one great Cuppboard	1	10	0
Item one screene one iron Jack two paire of Pothangers two spitts two paire of Brandirons one fire panne one paire of tongs	2	5	0

	£	s	d
Item Eleaven Pewter dishes one paire of Pewter Candlsticks with other small things	1	15	0
Item one Brass Furnace two Brass Kettles and three Brass skilletts	1	0	0
Item one iron pott		2	6
In the Brewhouse			
Item one Brewing Vate one Tunn with other Brewing Vessells	1	4	0
Item one flitch of Bacon with the Butter and Cheese in the house			
Item all the old Lumber		10	0
In the Barne			
Item the Wheat and Rye and Barly and other Corne with the two Reekes	40	0	0
Item two hoggs and three piggs	3	0	0
Item fower Cowes and one Heyfer	11	0	0
Item one Mare and one horse	8	0	0
Item Moneys oweing to him for Tyth	4	0	0
Sum total	98	12	6

[WSRO Ep I/29/165/10]

Will: made 5 Sep 1681; proved 2 Nov 1681
Wife Elizabeth, executrix; brother: Peter, London vintner
Witnesses: William Woods, Eliza Marshall, Thomas Burges   [WSRO STC I/27/237]

[1] Son of Edward, of Middlewich, Ches. Oxford, Brasenose, matriculated 1661 aged 18, BA 1662, MA 1665. Ordained deacon 1666 (bishop of Oxford), priest 1667 (bishop of Chichester). Rector of Selham 1667–1681. Curate of Lodsworth 1675. Married Elizabeth Burges of Graffham at Graffham by licence 1668. Died 1681.

131. Selmeston 12 Aug 1710 WILLIAM GREEN, vicar [1]

Appraisers: John Hawes, Thomas Newington

	£	s	d
In primis for his Wearing Apparrell and money in his Purse	6	13	4
Item in the Kitchin			
Three Tubbs and seven Chaires	1	0	0
Item one Clock one looking-Glass and three Guns	5	0	0
Item two Brass-Kettles two Brass-Pots and one jack	2	0	0
Item one Iron Pott two pair of Pott-hangers four Spitts three pair of Andirons a pair of Stylliers two Slices one fire-pan one pair of Gridirons one Clever one pair of Tongues one Fender An Iron forke a Chopping-Knife a Pott-Iron a Tosting iron one Iron Candlestick one Iron Scraper two Case Irons with five heaters two flattirons and two pair of Tongues more	2	11	2
Item seventeen Dishes of Pewter and three Pye-Plates	2	3	0
Item five Dozen of Plates	2	10	0
Item two Peutar Candlesticks five Brass Candle -sticks with two pair of Snuffers		12	6
Item In the Parlour			
One Table six Turkey wrought Chaires six Leather Chaires and five other Chaires	1	1	6

Item in the Pantery			
One Warming-pan one frying-pan and one Still three Brass-Skellets and three Skellets of Bell-Brass and a Table	1	7	0
Item fourteen Bear-Vessels two Powdering-Tubbs and seven Milk-Trayes	1	10	0
Item in the Brewhouse			
One Furnace four Tubbs eight Kivers and a Steel-Mill	5	10	0
Item in the best Chamber			
One Feather Bed and Boulster two Pillows two Blanketts and a Quilt with the Bed-Steadle and Curtaines	6	0	0
Item One Cheest of Drawers two Tables six Cane Chaires one Looking Glass and a Picture	2	17	0
Item one Armd Chaire and an old Couch		2	0
Item in the Chamber over the Kitchin			
One feather Bed with a Boulster and Coverings a Bed-steadle and Curtaines	3	10	0
Item one pair of Andirons a pair of Tongues fire-pan and Bellows a Table a looking-glass A Press and two Chaires	1	1	6
Item a Trunk with three Cheests with Linen	15	5	0
Item In two other Chambers			
Two Beds with theire Coverings and one of them with Curtaines one Looking glass a Table two Chaires and two small Cup-Boards	5	0	0
Item In the Study and the Press Bookes	40	0	0
Item In the Barne Gate and Feilds			
Two horses one Cow one hogge and to Piggs	11	15	0
Item a parcell of New hay and a parcell of old Hay	1	0	0
Item Wod and Faggotts	5	0	0
Item Plate valued att	8	0	0
Item Lumbar things unseen unthought of and things forgotten	1	6	8
Item Debts due and oweing	13	19	0
	146	14	8

[ESRO W/INV 75]

Will: made 27 Sep 1706; proved 3 Oct 1710
Wife: Elizabeth, executrix; daughter: Catherine
Witnesses: Thomas Newington, Catherine and Ann Richester   [ESRO W/A 48.50]

[1] Son of R Green of Uffington, Berks, minister. Oxford, Balliol, matriculated 1670 aged 16, BA 1673, MA 1676. Ordained deacon 1673 (bishop of Oxford), priest 1675 (bishop of Bath and Wells). Vicar of Selmeston 1681–1710, patron Joseph Sefton. Licensed preacher. Married Elizabeth Read of All Saints, Lewes, at All Saints by licence 1685. Died 1710; buried Selmeston.

132. Selsey 15 May 1639 HUGH FRENCH [1]

Appraisers: Clemens Kirby, William Halle, William Warner

	£	s	d
In the halle			
Item a table one Cupboard and three Chayres		13	0
In the Chamber			
Item on bed furnished and one Chest	1	10	0

	£	s	d
Item the third part of a booate		13	8
Item a bed in the loote		6	8
Item nine pecesse of pewter and a quart pot and a pint pot of pewter		8	0
Item a owld brewing kittel and twoe other small kittels and tow pans		15	0
Item a little box and a little duske one Ceffer and one tubbe and two firkins five wooden disshes and six tien spoones and eight trenchers with other lumberment		6	8
Sume is	4	14	4

[WSRO Ep I/29/166/56]

Administration 17 May 1639
To wife, Alice   [WSRO STC III/H/110]

[1] Of Cheshire. Oxford, Brasenose, matriculated 1603 aged 19, BA 1606, MA 1610. Ordained deacon and priest 1608 (bishop of Oxford). Vicar of Selsey 1627–1638, patron bishop of Chichester.

133. Shipley 25 April 1617 ROBERT WATERS [1]

Appraisers: John Coates senior, Richard Hurst senior, James Hurst, John French

	£	s	d
Item his Apparrill And mony in his Purse	5	0	0
Item hir warringe apparill 3 gownes 3 petticoates 2 hatts on sylke Apron and other Lynem worth	6	13	4
Item 10 payre and an od sheete whereof 5 payre of the best att 10s the payre and the 5 pare and the od sheete att 6s 8d the payre	4	6	8
Item other lynen as napkines toweles pillow cots with other peeces of linen worthe	1	17	8
Item one Joynd bedstedle with one flockbed 2 flock bolsters one fetherbed on feather bolster 4 fether pillowes 1 coverlid 3 blanckets an old black Rugg 4 curtynes to the same att	5	0	0
Item on old blancket 2 old cradle clapes and a peece of cotten		2	0
Item on livery table on Joynd chayre on old Rodd chayre 2 low stooles a flasket 2 joynd chystes A desk and 2 Joynd boxes	1	3	0
Item on new Joynd press on chyst and one Iron fyre herth	1	0	0
Item of pewter 7 platters 2 dishes 1 basson 2 chamber potts 6 porringers 6 bras spoones 8 pewter spoones 5 saultes one pewter candlestyck and one of brasse and old bottles	2	3	6
Item 2 baskits one panyer and 3 old tanckalds		2	0
Item in the buttry			
1 chyst 3 sault boxes and 2 fyrkines		5	0
Item of brass 1 cauldron 3 kitles 2 cast posnets 2 skillets one skymer on ladle and one chafynge dysh	1	15	0
Item in the bakehouse lofte			
6 augores 3 wimbles 1 post ax A mattock 2 wedges on old ax 3 bylles 3 sickles 3 stanes A beame and 2 bordes for skayles 2 fannes on styll and on old topp of a styll 1 halfe bushell 1 old sadle and A panell 1 payr of old bootes 1lb of hopes 1 lb of fethers 1 bow and old arrowes	1	17	4
Item 2 Iron potts on cast trevit 1 old caste morter and pestell A			

	£	s	d
fryingpan A fleshhook A grate A shorte pothook 1 downe grate A smootheinge Iron and 2 sellinge stickes		6	0
Item 2 spites 1 Iron drippingpan and 2 of tynn A tynn potlid 2 gridIrons 2 payre of tonges 2 fyreshovels on payre of cast brandIrones and on of wrought Iron 2 cast plates on curey come 1 payer of pothooks and 1 payer of pothangales 1 payre of bellows 2 spitters 2 shredding knives and 2 small cleavers	1	4	0
Item on lether bagg dishes trencher crockes and other wodden vessell		2	0

Item in the haule

	£	s	d
on frame table and 7 Joynd stooles		16	0
Item on Joynd cubbard 3 matt chayres 3 buckets 2 urynols a [?]lonth		12	0
Item on fyre wheele at Mr Sands howse on [?]sheckstone on [?]cugg glas and divers voyales and watterglasses		3	4

Item in the litle parlor

	£	s	d
1 bedstedell on shorte table 1 stoole 2 hangings and 2 picktures of papers		5	0

Item in the milkhowse

	£	s	d
on bryne tubb 2 butter tubbs 5 tubbs and keelers 2 churnes 1 herne sive 3 other sives 8 truggs 1 peck and halfe peck 2 woodden platters and certain erthen potts on great bucket som flax 2 skaynes of yarne and one old posnyt	1	0	0
Item divers bookes of divinity and physick and surgery besydes bookes that Mr Cooper and others doe clame A tytle unto worth		14	0
Item other lumberment as planckes shelves tressles and else [?]hat wheras som is lent forth som theras is seene and som unseene estimated to be worth		3	4
	36	11	2

In primis ther was An Invytory taken and prayed the 8th day of Apryll past of the goods of the sayd within named Roberte Waters deceased that were withoute the doores of the within named selfe same party which then entred not within doores by Reason they fered som infeccon which God be thanked proveth otherwyse

	£	s	d
Item 5 keene 4 of them havinge calves valued worth	17	0	0
Item on 12 monthinge bullock praysed at	1	0	0
Item on old mare £3 3 yearling Coulte £6 and one 12 monthinge mare coulte 20s all praysed att	10	0	0
Item 2 younge hoggs or shutes		14	0
Item on turke cock and on henn		3	4
Item 3 hennes and on cock		2	6
Item 4 watles		2	0
Item 5 bushels of oates		4	4
Sum total is	65	17	4

[WSRO Ep I/29/168/5]

No will or administration found

[1] Ordained deacon 1577, priest 1578 (bishop of Chichester). Curate of West Grinstead c. 1606.

134. Shipley 2 Feb 1622 [*sic*] RALPH ANTROBUS [1]
Appraisers: [?]William Crockenden, Michael [?]Woodyer, Henry White
[Original damaged]

	£	s	d
[In primis] his wearing aparell [and] mony in his purse	1	0	0
... nine working oxen and ... ... horses	8	0	0
... [?]keene	4	0	0
... Yonge bullocks	2	0	0
... x ... sheepe	5	0	0
... hogs 5 piggs	1	10	0
... of wheate	6	0	0
... haye in the barne	4	0	0
...	3	0	0
...		3	0
...		5	0
...		5	0
...		4	0
...	2	0	0
... crocks with other	1	10	0
... toobs		8	0
... and a frying pan ... vessals		10	0
... a hichell and a brasse ...		2	0
... with dyshes spoones ...		2	0
... with olde stuffe		5	0
...		3	0
...			
Whole sum is	60	14	10

[WSRO Ep I/29/168/17]

Will: undated; proved 7 July 1621
Sarah, wife executrix; son: Joseph executor; daughters: Sara, Mary, Hannah
Overseers: William Crockenden, Michael Woodyer
Witnesses: Henry Whitt, Michael Woodyer   [WSRO STCII/S Dean 1621 (2)]

[1] Cambridge, Corpus Christi, matriculated sizar 1566, BA. Ordained deacon 1576, priest 1577 (bishop of Chester). Vicar of Trimdon, Durh, 1578–1579. Possibly curate of Shipley 1599. Subscribed Chichester diocese 1609.

135. Shipley ... 1679 JOHN BUCKLEY [1]
[Original damaged and illegible]   [TNA PRO PROB 4/20409]

Will: made 17 May 1679; proved 13 June 1679
To be buried in West Grinstead
Sons: Samuel, executor; John (old bible, all law and school books); Thomas (books in study put forth by Mr Reynour of Lincoln); Nicholas (Book of Martyrs, books put forth by Mr Love); daughters: Sarah Gregory; Mary (books put out by Mr Burrows, linen in trunk and litle trunk)
All books not bequeathed to be sold

Overseers: Matthew Woodman, John Beaton, John Holland, Thomas Tingler
Witnesses: Thomas Cole, Charles Weston, William Cooper   [TNA PRO PROB 11/360]

[1]   Son of a cleric. Oxford, Magdalen Hall, matriculated 1632 aged 19, BA 1633. Vicar of Ditchling 1645. Curate of Shipley 1647; perpetual curate 1658; ejected 1662, after which an itinerant. Licensed preacher Shipley 1672. Died 1679; buried Shipley.

136. Sidlesham 20 Jan 1625 WILLIAM WHALLEY [1]

Appraisers: Richard Stronge, John Woodyer, Robert Carden, John Beare

	£	s	d
In the parlar			
In primis a table and a frame		10	0
Item 3 ioyne stooles		3	0
Item 4 smale ioyne stooles		6	0
Item 7 chayers	1	0	0
Item 10 quooshions		10	0
Item a grate		2	0
Item glasses		2	0
Item a litle cheast a stained clothe		2	4
Item one silver salt		16	0
In the hall			
Item a table and a frame		13	4
Item a cubberd a cubberd cloth		6	8
Item a forme a backe and a chayre		18	0
Item a Jacke		6	8
Item a payre of andirons 2 payre of pothangers a fire shovell a payre of tonges		3	4
Item 4 spitts a drippinge pan a fire slice		6	0
Item a pot and a payre of pothookes		2	6
In the Kitchen			
Item 2 kittells a brase pan a chafing dish a brazen ladle and a skimmer 4 skillets	1	6	8
Item a payre of gridiorns			8
Item a saltinge trough		2	6
Item a lanterne			8
Item 2 Candlestickes with dishes trenchers shelves and other implements		2	0
In the Buttery			
Item 8 firkins		7	0
Item a stone pot		1	4
Item 7 boards		2	0
In the outhouse			
Item 4 bowles a tub and 4 shelves		3	0
Item 2 stills		13	4
In the Brewhouse			
In primis a furnace		13	4
Item a welbucket a chayne and a winch		2	6
Item 6 tubbs		6	0

Item hempe in the shales with boards and other Lumberment		6	0
In the inner loafte			
In primis a bedstedle and a fetherbed furnished	5	0	0
Item 4 cheasts a box and a deske		13	4
Item a basket chayre and another chayre		4	0
Item 2 tables with other boards over the loaft		5	0
In the midle loaft			
In primis a bedstedle with fetherbed a feather boulster a feather pillowe a coverlet 3 blankets with a mat and coard curtines and curtine rods	3	10	0
Item an other Bedstedle a fether bed a feather boulster a coverlet and 3 blankets	2	0	0
In the outer loafte			
In primis 3 cheasts		10	0
Item a vate		6	8
Item a triar 2 warbills		3	4
Item a payre of seales a wayte of led of 16lbs		3	4
Item a ladder with other things		1	0
Item a tub with hoops		1	4
Item threescore and foure pound of peuter	2	8	0
Linnen			
Item 10 payre of sheets	1	10	0
Item 3 pillowbers of holland and a damaske cloth		4	0
Item 4 home made pillowbers		2	6
Item 2 duzen of napkins		12	0
Item 3 table cloathes and 3 towells with 4 course napkins		10	0
Item 2 hogges of bacon	2	0	0
Item 3 live hogges	1	0	0
Wood in the gates			
Item 4 coard of woode and a hundred of faggots	1	5	0
Corne in the barne			
In primis wheate unthrasht by estimation 7 quarters	6	0	0
Item barly unthrasht by estimation 7 quarters	5	12	0
Item pease by estimation 3 quarters	3	0	0
Item vatches by estimation 2 quarters	3	0	0
Item one stall of bees		2	6
Item one auger with hog trough and other thinges		4	0
Item a halfe bushell and three sackes and a wimminge sheet		6	0
Item money due upon bonds	2	3	0
Item 2 silver bowles and 2 silver spoones	5	0	0
Item his bookes	5	0	0
Item his apparell with money in his purse	10	0	0
Sum total	113	16	6

[WSRO Ep I/29/173/39]

Will: made 2 Nov 1624; proved 22 Jan 1625
Wife: Agnes executrix; son William executor; two married daughters
Witnesses: Richard Strong, Robert Carden, John Thomas

[WSRO STC II/B Dean 1625 (24)]

[1] Cambridge, St John's, matriculated 1581; St Catharine's, BA 1584; called MA 1590. Ordained deacon and priest 1590 (bishop of Rochester). Vicar of Sidlesham; instituted 1597, patron William Fussarde; collated 1603–1625, patron bishop of Chichester. Married Agnes or Ann Milles, widow, at Sidlesham by licence 1613. Died 1625.

137. Sidlesham 3 Oct 1639 JOHN TAYLOR [1]

Appraisers: Richard Stronge, Randolph Cutte, Richard Ward

	£	s	d
In the Hall			
In primis a Table a forme a bench a back bord 3 formes a dresser with winscot fower shelves a napkin presse 2 deskes a Cubbard and a salfe a Joyned stoole a Racke and other Lumber	1	0	0
Item a fowling peece a Jack 2 spitts two dripping panes two Iron potts a payre of Andirons a paire of tonges and fire shovel two payer of pot hangers twoo payr of pot hooks with other small Iron things	1	10	0
In the Parlor			
Item the bedstedle a fether bed boulsters pyllowes and the furniture to it belonginge	6	0	0
Item a table and frame fower Chaires eight Joyned stooles a winscot back and bench a side Cubbard 2 Carpets a Racke to burne Coales in and an Irone backe with other things	2	0	0
In the Closet			
Item a limbeck a Could Still with other things	1	0	0
In the Kitchen			
Item a siltinge trow shelves dressers kivers with other Lumber		10	0
In the Buttery			
Item the Drinke vessels and other Lumber		10	0
In the bake house			
Item the furnice with other brasse and pewter with tubbs and other Lumber	5	0	0
In the Chamber over the Parlor			
Item a Joyned bestedle a fether bed with all things therunto belonging	5	0	0
Item a Round table 3 Chaires five stooles a truncke a payre of Andirons with fire shovell and tongs and other small things	1	10	0
In the Chamber over the Hall			
Item two fether beds furnished two Chests 3 truncks with other things	5	0	0
In the loft over the kitchen			
Item a Cubberd hempe and other Lumber		13	4
In the Studie			
Item two presses a trunce two Chaires a Joined stoole with the shelves other small things with all the books	7	0	0
In the Garret			
Item a few apples and hopps and other small things		5	0
Item 14 payre of sheets napkins table Clothes and other Linen	6	13	4
The barnes and out houses			
Item the wheat pease and beanes and haye and haslers and other things	20	0	0
Item a Cowe and a Calfe a mare a sowe and 4 shutts	6	0	0
Item the wood and the Coales a Coope and other Lumber	3	0	0

	£	s	d
Item his Wearinge apparell money and plate	7	0	0
Item things over seene and forgotten		10	0
Sum is	80	1	8

[WSRO Ep I/29/173/58]

Administration 3 Oct 1639
To wife, Elizabeth   [WSRO STC III/H/123]

[1]   Son of Richard, rector of Maresfield and prebendary of Sidlesham. Oxford, Queen's, matriculated 1624 aged 17, BA 1628; Hart Hall, MA 1631. Ordained deacon and priest 1631 (bishop of St David's). Licensed curate Lewes archdeaconry and of Willingdon 1634. Vicar of Sidlesham 1635–1639, patron his father. Married Elizabeth Edwards of Willingdon at Willingdon by licence (sponsors his father and William Carpenter of Lewes, hostler) 1636. Died 1639.

138. Slinfold … 1617 PHILIP MUSTIAN, parson [1]
Appraiser: William Maslyn

	£	s	d
In primis twoe old gownes as they weare sould	2	4	0
[Ite]m twoe old Cloaks as they weare sould	1	8	0
Item soulde twoe old payre of breeches with drawers for		8	0
Item two old doublettes as they weare soulde		4	0
Item twoe old Coates as they weare sould		6	0
Item receaved in money due to the sayd Philipp Mustian.......for tithes		9	6
Sum	4	19	6

[WSRO Ep I/29/176/3]

Administration of goods left unadministered 12 Sep 1617
To Roger Mustyan, nominated by William Martin, supervisor of will, during minority of daughters Catherine, Joan and Alice, on death of Catherine, relict

[WSRO STC III/F/100]

[1]   Ordained deacon 1572, priest 1573 (bishop of Chichester). Rector of Slinfold 1573–1616, patron bishop of Chichester. Married Catherine daughter of John Staplehurst of Slinfold at Nuthurst by licence 1597. Died 1616; buried Slinfold.

139. Sompting 2 Sept 1706 ISAAC BOARDMAN, vicar [1]
Appraisers: Hugh Penfold, Robert [?]Lowfeild

	£	s	d
In primis His Wareing Apparrell and Moneys in his Purs	5	0	0
Item In his Lodging Roome	5	2	6
Item In the Chamber over the Parlor	3	10	0
Item In the Chamber over the Buttery	3	15	0
Item In the Chamber over the Kitchin	7	0	0
Item In his Studdy in Books	5	0	0
Item in the Parlor	4	5	0
Item In the Kitchin	4	17	0
Item In the Brewhouse	5	17	0

	£	s	d
Item In the Butterys	2	17	6
Item In Linnens	9	15	0
Item In the Stables		15	0
Item In Hay	1	10	0
Item In Corn	5	0	0
Item A yong black Horse and an Old black Mare	4	0	0
Item One Hogg	1	0	0
Item in ready moneys in his owne keeping	40	0	0
Item in Bonds and Securities	236	0	0
Item what is due to him on Account	40	0	0
Item in Food Faggotts Lombar and other things forgott	3	0	0
Sum is	388	4	0

[WSRO Ep I/29/177/71]

Will: made 5 Aug 1706; proved 9 Sep 1706
Brother: Jeremy, executor
Witnesses: Thomas Holladay, Mary Brasier, Hugh Penfold   [WSRO STC I/30/875]

[1]   Born Bury, Lancs, son of Ralph, of Bury. Bury Grammar School. Cambridge, St John's, admitted sizar 1671 aged 17, BA 1675, MA 1687. Curate of March, Cambs, 1683. Rector of Coombes, patron John Shelley, bt, and vicar of Sompting 1690–1706. Died 1706.

140. Stedham 28 March 1623 JOSEPH CHITTY [1]
[Appraisers not given]

	£	s	d
In primis a devines gowne	3	0	0
Item a Chest of books	3	0	0
Item a bachelers gowne	1	0	0
Item two clokes	2	10	0
Item his wearing apparell	5	0	0
Item monie in his purse	4	18	0
Item two truncks		13	4
Item desperat debts	6	10	0
Sum total	27	0	4

[WSRO Ep I/29/182/78]

Administration 2 April 1623
To Richard Chitty, brother   [WSRO STC III/F/203]

[1]   Possibly Oxford, Magdalen, BA 1615, MA 1619. Died 1623.

141. Steyning 17 March 1643 LEONARD STALMAN, vicar [1]
Appraisers: John Parson, Samuel Lucke

	£	s	d
In the Parlor Chamber			
In primis one joyned bedstedle wth Curtaynes and vallens two featherbedes one boulster and two pillowes one rugge two blanketts	10	0	0

Item one featherbedd and Coverlet	2	10	0
two Chayres three stooles a side Cubbord a great Truncke and two boxes	3	0	0
fourteene payre of sheetes six payre of pillowbers five tableclothes besides one diaper tablecloth and twelve napkins and three dozen and three of an other sort prised at	8	16	6
One Cubbardcloth and seeing glasse	1	0	0
one silver tankard and other plate	17	0	0
27 pewter dishes one flagon foure payre of pewter Candlestickes three Chamberpots three brass Candlestickes 23 small pewter dishes a pewter salte and two pottes and a warming pann praysed at	5	10	0
In the Greene Chamber			
one bedstedle vallens and curtaynes and one joynd Chest and sideboard	2	10	0
one featherbedd two boulsters one pillow foure blanckettes and a greene rugge and a bedsteddle prised at	4	0	0
In the Gallery and Study			
In Bookes	10	0	0
Three Chayres a great Chest and a litle table a litle Chest prised at	1	6	0
In the Closet in pottes and glasses	1	0	0
In the Parlor			
one long Table six stooles one round table foure Chayres two payre of Andirons two payre of tonges six Cushens one fire slice and a payre of seacoale irons	3	9	0
one Cubbard and Cubbard cloth		15	0
In the hall			
one long table six joyned stooles three joyned formes one high Cubbard two Chayres and two Cushens	2	10	0
one Cubbard and Cubbord cloth		6	8
In the kitchin			
one round table one litle table one hanging Cubbord foure Chayres and three dripping pannes in brasse and pewter and two spittes a payre of gridirons a Chaffing dishe	3	5	0
one iron ketle two payre of potthangers three Iron pottes one litle iron ketle prised at	1	15	0
In the Brewhouse			
one furnace and brewing vessells	2	0	0
In the seller			
in Barrells and hogsheades and shelves and Crocks and Chest and [*sic*]	1	10	0
In an out Chamber			
one trucklebedd one still a road saddle and bridle	1	0	0
In the woodhowse			
Five Coard of woodd	2	10	0
one Coup and one Cheespresse		10	0
In the wheat Lofte			
five Bushells of wheat	1	0	0
his wearing Apparell and money in his purse	10	0	0
debts owing by William [?]Rinvell of Ringmer	17	0	0
John Butcher	1	0	0
John Vincent		6	6

Francis Burden	13	0
In lumber forgott	5	6
More uppon bondes	[blank]	

suma totalis 116 8 2

[WSRO Ep I/29/183/60]

Will: made 20 June 1641; proved 1 April 1643
Wife: Joan, executrix; son: Henry; daughters: Joan, Elizabeth (Streater); grandsons Daniel Stalman: ('nest' of three silver cups), William Stalman: (silver tankard); granddaughter Bridget Stalman: (silver bowl)
Overseers: sons Henry and William, kinsmen William Clagett of Barcombe and Richard Burdett of Lewes
Witnesses: Richard Russell, George Stonestreet   [WSRO STC II/S Dean 1643 (2)]

[1] Born Craven, Yorks. Cambridge, Christ's, matriculated sizar 1604, BA 1608, MA 1611. Ordained deacon 1610 (bishop of London) aged 25, priest 1610 (bishop of Chichester). Licensed preacher Chichester diocese 1610. Licensed sequestrator of St Michael's, Lewes, 1622. Rector of Southover 1624–1630, patron Crown. Vicar of Steyning 1630–1639, patron George, Lord Goring. Married Joan Ampleford of Portslade at Portslade 1611. Died 1643; buried Steyning.

142. North Stoke 5 April 1620 THOMAS HEARE, curate [1]

Appraisers: Thomas Harwood, Thomas Harmen, Henry Spencer

	£	s	d
In primis his wearing apparell and money in his purse	1	10	4
Two paires and one ode sheete		7	6
Five pillows a blanket a coverlet and a boarded bedstead		16	0
Five empty chests		8	0
Certen oulde lumber in the chamber		2	0
Two empty chests in the hall		3	0
A flock bed a bedstead and a blanket		5	0
A pan of brasse an iron pott and three dishes		12	0
A tub a bucket a spitt and other lumber in the kitchen		3	0
A parsell of fyerwood		2	0
A parsell of old bookes		2	0
A pigge		2	0
Total	4	18	0

[WSRO Ep I/29/184/5]

Will: made 8 Feb 1620; proved 17 June 1620
Wife: Joan, executrix
Estate to wife
Witnesses: Henry Spencer, Samuel Searle   [WSRO STC I/16/140]

[1] Licensed reader North Stoke from 1574. Married Joan, maiden name unknown, (possibly at North Stoke 1619). Died 1620.

143. North Stoke ... 1690 JOSEPH LISLE [1]
Appraisers: Thomas Griffin, William Dobson

	£	s	d
In primis For ... earing Clothes and Aparrel and money in his Pocket	8	5	0
Item for Books	7	0	0
Item Seven small Tables	1	15	0
Item Seven Chaires one Stooll and one old Couch	1	3	0
Item Two paire of Andirons two paire of Tongs and two fire Shovels		10	4
Item One Spit and one Dripen pan		2	2
Item One small Brass Kettle		5	4
Item One Bed and Bedstead one Boulster and two pillowes two Blanketts and one Quilt with Curtaines and Vaillings	6	15	0
Item Three Beds Three Boulsters and three Pillows	6	0	0
Item Thirteen paire of Sheets	9	15	0
Item Nine Pillowe bares	1	2	6
Item One Dusson and halfe of Towells	1	5	6
Item Ten Table clothes	2	0	0
Item Five Dusson of Napkins	2	16	0
Item Ten Peuter Dishes	1	8	0
Item Two Dusson of Peuter Plates		16	6
Item Two Candlesticks one Porringer and Three Saucers and one Chamber Pott		7	6
Item Foure Small Chaires one Large Chair		8	6
Item Foure Trunks one Chest three Boxes		19	6
Item One small plaine Chest of Drawers		6	0
Item One Ollive Box and Looking glass and two small Powder boxes		14	6
Item Two plaine Stands		2	6
Item In Ready money	30	0	0
Item for things unseen and forgotten		6	8
	84	4	6

[WSRO Ep I/29/184/26]

Will: made 20 Jan 1690; proved 19 Nov 1690
Wife: Margaret, executrix
Witnesses: William Dobson, Mary Dobson   [WSRO STC I/29/80b]

[1] Charterhouse. Cambridge, Trinity, admitted sizar (as John) and matriculated 1662, exhibitioner, BA 1666; called MA 1679. Vicar of Tortington 1676–1690, patron Sir William Morley. Curate of South Stoke 1679; of North Stoke c. 1684. Married Margaret (possibly Margaret Bocock of North Stoke at North Stoke 1684). Died 1690.

144. West Stoke 31 May 1652 GEORGE WELBORNE [1]
Appraisers: William Cooper gent of Ratham, Adam Dallington, Thomas Combes of Funtington

	£	s	d

       In the parlor
In primis one drawe table six stooles three letherne chares one paire of
angerons one paire of tongs one fire shovell one litle table a small side

	£	s	d
cubbord one paire of playing tables	3	2	0
Item one clocke two old carpetts a paire of virgineholes fower vialls six cushions three maps 2 coats of armes	6	13	1
Item small glasses		6	8
In his studdie			
Item his bookes and other lumber	6	0	0
In the chamber over the hall			
Item his wearing apparrell and monie in his purse	10	0	0
Item one stanninge bedstedle with beddinge and curtaines belonging to it	4	0	0
Item one liverie bedstedle a fether bedd a flocke bedd with bolsters to it a coverlett	2	10	0
Item one old table a peece of wainscote two old truncks		10	0
In the chamber over the kitchen			
Item three bushells of wheate two bushells of barle and some festhers with lumber	2	10	0
In the chamber over the parlor			
Item a stanning bedstedle one featherbedd with curtaines and other things belonging to him	7	0	0
Item one small silver tankerd and six silver spoones	6	0	0
Item thre paier of holland sheetes and seaven paire of howshold sheets	6	0	0
Item seaven table clothes thre dossen of napkins six towells five cubbord clothes	4	0	0
Item one little table two small chests thre old chaires two old truncks five small boxes one seeing glasse a [?]chamed dishe and small paier of angerons fire shovell a paire of billowes a table baskett	1	0	0
In the maids chamber			
Item one truckle beddstedle with a flockebedd	1	0	0
In the kitchen			
Item fower score and tenn pound of pewter	4	10	0
Item one greatt brasse kettell	1	10	0
~~Item six and thirtie pound of brasse~~			
Item one brasse kettell fower little brasse skilletts two bell skilletts two small brasse kettells one bedd panne three brasse potts one iron pott	2	6	..
Item one still		10	0
Item two iron dripping panns five spitts one [?]tinning panne one paire of grigdirons and other small things	1	0	0
Item one paire of angerons one paire of doggs one fender two paire of potthangers fier shovell and tongs one iake	1	0	0
Item one small table one ioyn stoole two chaires a little cubbord and other lomber		10	0
Item fower small fletches of bacon	1	10	0
In the milk howse			
Item some selves some crocks with other things		10	0
In the hall			
Item eleven cheeses five bushells of malte one torne a side sadell a pillion three sakes one bedstedle one tabel a forme and other lomber	2	0	0
In the washowse			
Item one cheese presse brewing vessels one irone pill one butter charne			

with other lomber		1	10	0
In the millehowse				
Item one salting trow a milke tubb a small table two bills one hatchett			10	0
In the gate				
Item one stalle of bees two cord of wood tenn hundred of faggotts		4	0	0
In the stable				
Item one racke and manger one rope			5	0
Item three cowes one mare		13	0	0
Item three hoggs		1	10	0
Item two ackers of pese		3	0	0
Item two ackers and a halfe of barly		1	10	0
Item a plott of beanes			10	0
Item a desperatt dett		2	4	0
	Sum	104	17	2

[WSRO Ep I/29/186/7]

Administration 1 June 1652
To wife, Deborah   [WSRO STC III/K/151]

[1] Possibly (as Wilborne) Cambridge, Jesus, matriculated sizar 1617; called literatus 1623; ordained deacon and priest 1623 (bishop of Peterborough); vicar of Great Shelford, Cambs, c. 1625.

145. West Stoke 23 Oct 1696 THOMAS BRAGUE [1]
Appraisers: John [?]Tondene, William Chalcroft

	£	s	d
In primis his wearing apparrell and money in his purse	31	5	0
Item three small presses with books	50	0	0
Item three feather beds and his bolsters	10	0	0
Item Ruggs blanketts pillows bedsteads Curtains and vallence a flock bed and bolster	5	2	0
Item nine pair of Sheets twelve pair of pillow beers and three damaske table cloaths	4	1	6
Item three dozen of diaper and damaske Napkins and fourteen dozen of other course old napkins	2	2	0
Item fourteen diaper table cloaths and eight plain Course table cloaths and other old linnen of a Small value	1	11	6
Item five old Chairs a joined Stoole and five Cushions	11	6	0
Item three old small tables three old trunks and other old boxes	1	2	6
Item a pair of doggs fire pan and tongues		4	0
Item a warming pan and two Chamber potts two basons and two Candlesticks		6	0
Item a Silver Tumbler three Spoons two porringers three rings	4	15	0
Item a Chariot and Harness	15	0	0
Item Debts due to the deceased at the time of his death	250	0	0
Item three dozen of bottles and other Lumber of a Small value		11	6
Summa totalis	376	0	0

[TNA PRO PROB 4/17380]

Will: made 19 Dec 1695; codicil 4 Jan 1696; proved 30 Oct 1696
Wife: Catherine Le Gay, executrix
Sworn as genuine by Samuel Le Gay
No witnesses recorded   [TNA PRO PROB 11/434]

[1] Rector of Ardingly 1645. Lecturer Maidstone, Kent, 1651. Assistant to Hampshire Commission 1658. Assistant minister Portsmouth, Hants, 1660. Living at Southwick 1662. First wife died 1654; second, Hannah Locke, died 1687. Died 1696.

146. Stopham 21 Aug 1661 JOHN CHALONER, rector [1]

Appraisers: Edward Fogden, Nicholas Duke

	£	s	d
In primis all his wearing apparrell and the money in his purse	10	0	0
In the parlour			
[Item] one drawinge [ta]ble and other old ... with frames 2 ... es Carpets	2	0	0
In the Studdy			
Item all his books	5	0	0
In the Kitchin			
Item one payre of andirons 2 payre of tonges one old ax one bill and other iron thinges		6	0
Item one flagon 1 Candlesticke 1 salt 2 porringers		3	4
Item 2 gold ringes 2 small silver salts and one silver spoone	2	0	0
In the parlor Chamber			
Item one fether bed 1 fether boulster 1 coverlet 1 blanket 1 payre of sheetes with the Curtaines	2	10	0
Item 2 bedstedles 1 truncke 1 desk 1 box and one side Cubbard	2	0	0
In the Milke house			
Item 1 cheespresse 2 drinke vessels with other wooden things		6	0
Item in redy money and debts oweing to the Testator uppon specialtie	94	0	0
Item in desperate debts oweing to the testator	25	0	0
Item one bridle and saddle		6	8
Item 3 horse beastes and one colt	11	0	0
Item 5 smale ~~kine~~ Cowes	12	12	6
Item 2 heifer bullocks 1 little bull and 2 wenyers	7	0	0
Item 8 sheepe and 5 lambes	2	2	6
Item 3 smale hogs and six shuts and 1 smale sowe and ... sucklinge piggs	4	6	0
... e barley bucbeans oats and haye and some pease	5	10	0
... [ca]rt and wheeles and [hor]se harnesse	1	0	0
... forgot unseene and so unprized		6	8
Sum total	187	9	8

[WSRO Ep I/29/187/17]

Will: made 25 Sep 1658; proved 13 Sep 1661
Brothers: Richard (executor), James, Thomas; sisters: Mary (Brandon) Elizabeth (Duke)
'My Tutor Peele'
Witnesses: William Goddard, William Goodman   [WSRO STC I/22/84]

[1] Cambridge, Clare, admitted 1635, BA 1640. Rector of Stopham ?1644–1661. Died 1661.

147. Stopham 1667 ROBERT DENNIS, rector [1]

[original fragmentary]   [WSRO Ep I/29/187/20]

Will: made 11 Feb 1667; proved 31 May 1667
Wife: Jane, residual legatee and executor; sons: John (all books except those in a chest),
Robert (one trunk 'marked with my name' and Bible); daughters: Elizabeth, Dorothy,
Mary (under 21)
Witnesses: Edward Fogden, Anthony Dalton   [WSRO STC I/23/390]

[1] Son of John, of Broughton, Hants. Oxford, Merton, matriculated 1630 aged 20, BA 1631.
Ordained deacon 1632 (bishop of St David's), priest 1634 (bishop of Winchester). Sequestered
curate of Capel, Surr. Vicar of Warnham 1656. Rector of Stopham 1661–1667, patron Walter
Bartelot. Died 1667.

148. Stopham 25 June 1705 JOHN DENNIS [1]

Appraisers: Robert Dennis, John Woods

	£	s	d
In primis His money and wearing Apparrell	5	0	0
Item his Study of Books	5	0	0
In the Parlour			
A Clock two tables and nine chairs One pair of Andirons fire shovell and tongs	2	0	0
In the Hall			
Two tables five stools one pair of small Andirons and One Iron Back		10	0
In the Parlour Chamber			
One feather bed and Bedstead Curtains and vallens a Quilt and two Blankets one Bolster and two Pillowes [fou]r chairs and four stools One small table a looking glass three window Curtains One p[air of A]ndirons and a pair of tongs	5	0	0
In the Hall Ch[amber]			
One Feather bed and B[edstead] Curtains and Vallens one rug and … Blankets two Bolsters a Chest of drawers … [c]hairs two window Curtains One pair of An[dir]ons	3	0	0
In the Entry Cha[mber]			
One Feather bed and Counterp[ain] Curtains and vallens	1	10	0
In the Kitchen Chamber			
One feather Bed and Bedstead Curtains and Vallens two blankets one Counterpain one Bolster and two Pillows a press and Box eight pair of sheets five pair of pillow Coats four table cloaths one dozen and half of napkins eleven towells	4	0	0
In the Kitchen			

One Furnace 5 Chairs 3 pair of Pot hangers 3 spits 2 pair of Gridirons 7
Candlesticks 2 box Irons one warming pan one Iron Mortar and pestle 3
Brass Skillets one Brass Skimmer and two Brass Ladles one flesh fork
and a Brass Chafing dish a Cleaver and a Shredding Knife One Stone

Mortar 3 Iron Pots One Iron Kettle One Brass Kettle one Iron Skillet 18
pewter dishes three dozen of Plates a py plate One Bason One Gun 2
frying pans a dozen of Iron scewers two dripping pans two grates One
Cover and Candle box Flower Box and Candle Snuffer 1 Iron Fender
and Back One table and Stool a case of Knives a pot plate and One pair

of Andirons	3	10	0

In the Brewhouse Chamber

One Flock Bed and two Bedsteads		5	0

In the Brew House

One Meal Bin 9 tubs 4 Coolers a Cheese Press a Cyder trough One Old

table and Cupboard One Iron Bar Bill and Ax Saw Spitter and Shovell	1	0	0

In the Cellar

16 Beer vessells One Tun dish one Keever and 7 dozen of Bottles	1	5	0

In the Milk house

10 Milk treys 2 Curns 3 Buckets a Cheese plate 4 hoopp and vallors 15

Cheeses 8 pound of butter and 4 flitches of Bacon	1	10	0
One Waggon One Dung pot and thills two harrows and one plow	2	10	0
Three foddering racks and 12 Elm boards		7	6

One Fan One Corn Binn one half Bushell 4 sacks one Grindstone 1 well

Bucket rope and Chain	1	15	0

One Pair of Oxen 3 Milch Cows One Small Steer Bullock 3 Yearling

Calves	14	0	0
Two old horses and 1 pair of harness	3	0	0
One Ladder		1	0
5 Hoggs	2	10	0
3 Acres of Rie	2	10	0
3 Acres of Oats	1	5	0
A still and two spinning wheels		3	6
An Iron Pot hook Bar		1	0
A pannell and two Leathern sacks		4	6
Lumber		1	0
Sum total	61	8	6

[WSRO Ep I/29/187/26]

Administration 19 Oct 1705
To Elizabeth, wife   [WSRO STC III/M/55]

[1] Son of a cleric. Oxford, St Mary Hall, matriculated 1657; Magdalen, demy 1659–1664, BA
1661. Ordained priest 1663 (bishop of Chichester). Rector of Parham 1666–1691; of Stopham
1667–1705; of Barlavington 1691–1705, patron Sir William Goring, bt. Possibly curate of
Coldwaltham c. 1684. Died 1705.

149. Storrington 25 Oct 1692 EDMUND COLES, rector [1]

Appraisers: Weeley Cale, Thomas Purser

	£	s	d
In primis Wearing apparrell and money in Purse	5	0	0
Item 1 Feather bed and appurtenances	4	10	0
Item 15 pair of coarse sheetes	3	10	0

	£	s	d
Item 8 dozen of coarse Napkins	2	0	0
Item 3 dozen ½ of coarse Table clothes	2	4	0
Item 1 dozen and 3 pillow coates coarse		15	0
Item 1 dozen and 4 Coarse Towells		8	0
Item 14 pair of fine sheetes	7	0	0
Item 2 Dozen of fine Table cloths	3	0	0
Item 9 dozen ½ of fine Napkins	4	0	0
Item 20 fine Pillow coates	1	10	0
Item 15 fine Towells		15	0
Item 11 Silver Spoones	2	10	0
Item 1 Silver Tankard 2 Silver porringers 1 Silver cup and Sugar box	7	10	0
Item 3 dozen of pewter plates	2	4	0
Item 6 chamber pots and 5 Basins		10	0
Item 2 dozen ½ pewter Dishes	1	10	0
Item 1 dozen of fruit dishes		5	0
Item 3 pair of Candlesticks and other small things		15	0
Sum total	48	16	0

[WSRO Ep I/29/188/85]

Will: made 10 Oct 1692; proved 8 Nov 1692
Wife: Elizabeth, executor (with son Mathew); sons: John, …, and Mathew (books to be equally divided); daughters: Elizabeth (Forfar), Ruth (Cale)
Witnesses: Thomas Purser, Hen[?] float, Elizabeth Lassiter   [WSRO STC I/29/139]

[1] Of Winchester, Hants, son of a cleric. Oxford, New College, matriculated 1635 aged 19, BA 1638, MA 1642. Ordained priest 1646 (bishop of Oxford). Rector of Storrington 1647–1692, patron Richard Kidder jun. Vicar of Preston with Hove 1663–1692. Prebendary of Bursalis 1671–1692. Died 1692; buried Storrington.

150. Stoughton 29 Oct 1657 MATTHEW MAIOR [1]

Appraisers: George White gent, Thomas Bayly yeoman

	£	s	d
In the room where he dyed			
First one Bedsteddle one Feather bed one feather bolster two pillowes and other furniture belong	2	10	0
Item his wearing apparell and money in his purse	2	0	0
Item one greate ioyned Chest one little table and Frame and 2 Joyned stooles		15	0
Item one Trunck one Chest and one old chest one Box and some woll	5	0	0
In one little Roome called his studdy			
The Boocks one Patch and a deske	5	0	0
In the Hall			
Item one Table and Frame and six Joyned stooles		10	0
Item Five Chairs one little Table and one side table		10	0
Item one payre of Cast Andirons and one still		3	0
In the Kitchen			
Item one little Table 3 Joyned stooles 2 Chaires with trenchers and dishes		3	0

Item 18 pewter dishes 2 Chamberpotts and one pewter salt	1	0	0
Item 3 Brass kettles 2 brass Potts one Skillett and one Yron pott	1	0	0
Item one Bedd pann one frying pan one jack 2 spitts one morter and pestle		15	0
Item one paire of Andirons a paire of doggs one yron back one paire of Tongs one fire slice and one yron dripping pan one letten dripping pann and one paire of potthangers	2	16	0
Item 3 gunns and one muskett	1	0	0
Item 5 drinke Vessells one Tonn one Kiver and 4 Tubbs		10	0
Item one brass furnace and six spoones		7	0
Item Corne in the Barne and hay	5	0	0
Item 3 hoggs	1	16	0
Item wood and all other lumber in and about the house	3	0	0
Sum total	31	14	0

[WSRO Ep I/29/189/30]

No will or administration found

[1] Oxford, called scholar of New College 1606, scholar of Christ Church 1607, BA 1609. Ordained deacon 1606, priest 1607 (bishop of Oxford). Vicar of Stoughton 1609–1657, patron bishop of Chichester.

151. Stoughton 9 March 1691 JOHN HARRISON [1]

Appraisers: William Pannell, John Penfold junior

	£	s	d
In his Lodging Chamber where he used to Lay			
In primis His wearing Apparrel and mony in his purse	10	0	0
Item one featherbed one boulster two pillows two blankets one Rugg bedsted Curtains and Valliance	4	0	0
Item one Chest one trunck side Cubbord two Chairs		7	6
Item one silver Colledge pott one silver salt six small silver salts one silver tumbler seven silver spoons one gold Ring	15	0	0
Item seventeen sheets two dozen and halfe of napkins four pair of pillow Coats five table Cloaths two towells	5	0	0
In the Chamber over the Parlour			
One feather bed and boulster two pillows one Quilt one Rugg two blankets bedsted Curtains and valliance	8	0	0
Item one small table seven Chairs two small boxes brasse andirons fire pan and tongs and other small things	1	10	0
In the Clossett one Chest one trunck one Cabbinett one small box and other small things		12	6
In a little Room one feather bed and boulster and pillow bedsted and Covering	1	15	0
In another little room and in the Garrett a kiver 1 trey one meal tub a stone morter and other small things		6	8
In his Study			
books and Chest and old side Cubbord	50	0	0

In the Parlour
Two tables one Couch twelve Leather Chairs two Carpetts one Clock
two pair of Andirons firepan and tongs and bellows Iron back   7   0   0
     In the kitchen
One table five stools four Chairs one forme one presse one grate bakon
rack one screen   1   0   0
Item one Jack two spitts one brass ladle two Skimers a pair of andirons
and dogs one firepan two pair of tongs two pair of Cottrels two box
Irons and other small things and Iron back Iron fender   1   10   0
     In the buttery
Two brasse kettles three skillets three brasse pots a stone pan Iron
dripping pan warming pan one Cleaver a lanthorn and other small
things and frying pan   1   10   0
     In the brewhouse
One furnace one brewing vate one tun five beere vessels four smal tubs
three kevers three stands one powdring tubb a pott of butter and other
small things   3   10   0
Item ten pewter platters two Candlesticks two Flagons thirteen plates
Eight small dishes two Chamber potts and other small pewter   2   5   0
Item a well buckett and Chain Iron barr wood and faggots and other
Lumber   1   5   0
A horse and bridle and sadle   2   0   0
                                                           106   11   8
[WSRO Ep I/29/189/56]

Will: made 11 Feb 1691; proved 10 March 1691
Wife Ann, executor; daughters: Elizabeth (Wheeler) Abigail (Benson)
Witnesses: William Bayley, John Battine, Thomas Sone, John Penfold junior
                                     [WSRO STC I/29/91b]

[1] Possibly rector of Warblington, Hants, until 1662 and licensed preacher Havant, Hants, 1672.
Called 'of Ashling, near Chichester, noe certaine knowledg of his state' 1690. Second wife Ann
daughter of Anthony Prowse, rector of Alverstoke, Hants.

152. Sutton 14 Jan 1663 AQUILA CRUSO, minister [1]
Appraisers: Thomas Garrett, curate of Duncton, John Wallwyn curate of Petersfield

	£	s	d
In primis The Books	20	16	0
Item An old table in his Study		2	6
Item An old trunke		2	0
Item 2 Firkins		2	0
Item An old stoole and chaire		1	6
Item a standish			4
Item A urinall			4
Item the Barrell of a muskett and Bandileers		3	6
	21	8	2
Hereunto is to be appended			
Arrears of Rent in his Tenants house for Sutton Rectory	3	0	0

Money returned which he had given to the reliefe of the Protestants in
Piemont etc   5   0
From Westwittering Prebend Ten bushels of Wheat for Micklemas
Quarter 1660 at 3s 6d a bushell deducting £2 5s 1d for Sole money and
Taxes rests   9   11

Total   35   3   1

[WSRO Ep I/29/191/19]

Administration 11 Jan 1663
To Thomas Thornton, clerk, principal administrator[2]   [WSRO STC III/H/276, 340]

[1]   Third son of John, of Norwich, esq., a Fleming. Norwich Grammar School. Cambridge, Gonville and Caius, admitted 1610 aged 15, matriculated 1611, scholar 1611–1616, BA 1614, fellow 1616–1634, MA 1618, BD 1626; university preacher 1623. Ordained deacon and priest 1620 (bishop of Peterborough). Rector of Sutton 1633–1660, patron Algernon, earl of Northumberland. Prebendary of Wightring 1637–1660. Died 1660; buried Sutton.
[2]   Presumably his successor as rector: see **153**.

153. Sutton Feb 1682 THOMAS THORNTON, rector [1]

Appraisers: Henry German clerk, Joseph Sefton, William Langley, Richard Croucher, Maurice Ford

	£	s	d
In the House			
In primis His Whearing apparell and money in his purse	10	..	..
Item in Plate	8	..	..
In the lodging Chamber			
Item Three Beds with the coverings and appurtenances	..	..	..
In Linen vallued at	..	..	..
Item Hangins a Chest of Drawers and other things	..	..	..
In the second Chamber			
Item Two old Beds with the appurtenances	2	..	..
Item a side board Chest etc	..	..	..
In the Parlor Chamber			
Item One Bed with the appurtenances 3 Chaires … two stools of the same	20	4	..
Item the Hangings and other things	1	14	..
In the Study Chamber			
Item one feather Bed with the appurtenances	..	..	..
Item a Presse for Clothes and other things vallued at	..	..	..
In the Study			
Item English Books vallued at	5	..	..
Item Latin and other bookes	45	..	..
Item shelves and other things	1	..	..
In the Mans Chamber			
Item one old Bed with appurtenances	..	..	..
In the Parlor			
Item Tables Chaires and other things	..	..	..

In the hall			
Item One Cider presse one Clocke and other things	..	..	..
In the Buttery			
Item Bacon and Cyder	11	0	6
Item Butter Cheese and Lard	1	..	..
Item Vessells shelves and other things	..	..	..
In the Kitchen			
Item Pewter	..	..	..
Item Brasse	..	..	..
Item a Furnace steele Mill and a presse	2	0	..
Item Iron pots a Jack spits driping pans slices weights and other things	1	..	..
Item Tubs and other wooden utensils	1	7	..
In the [?]Ortch Yard			
Item Hay 14 Tun	14	..	..
Item Wood	1	..	..
Item Hoghutch well bucket and rope	..	..	..
In the Barnes			
Item Corns vallued at	72	12	..
Item Hay	2	10	..
Item Corne on the ground	2	0	..
In the Gates and Stales			
Item Horses and Colts	..	..	..
Item Oxen Cows and young Beasts	..	..	..
Item Hoggs	..	..	..
Item Waggons Carte Plows and Harrows	..	..	..
Item Boards Timber lathes etc	..	..	..
Item Dung Carts Yoakes and Chaines	..	..	..
Item Iron Barrs a Musket Gunne and sword	..	..	..
Item Dung	..	..	..
In Other Places			
In primis Sackes winnowing sheet Poakes and Haire Cloth	2	10	0
Item Poultry and Beese	1	10	0
Item Things unseen things unthought off and things forgotten	1	0	0
Sum total	357	7	4
[Mon]ey due upon Bond	200	0	0
[D]ets (as neare as we can judge and reckon) to the vallue of	88	2	4
.... to the value of about		15	0
Sperate debts to the value of about	10	6	0
[De]bts to the vallue of about	35	19	1
Another debt owing at Chichester for a Pension Procurations etc about	..	..	..
Received in Credits about	5	10	0
Received in Goods about	6	10	0

[WSRO Ep I/29/191/32]

Will: made 2 July 1681; proved 8 March 1682
Wife Elizabeth, executrix (English books); sons: George (Ridders dictionary) Josuah (books) Thomas; daughter: Eliza
Witnesses: Joseph Sefton, Thomas Quennell, Thomas Leggatt   [WSRO STC I/27/252]

[1] Son of George, of Yorkshire, gent. Oxford, Queen's, matriculated 1647 aged 18; Corpus Christi, scholar 1648, BA 1651; University College, fellow 1653–1655, MA 1653, elected master by fellows but election overturned by visitors. Rector of Sutton 1660–1682; of Barlavington 1672–1682. Married Elizabeth daughter of Thomas Quennell of Sutton. Died 1682; buried Sutton.

154. Tangmere 9 Nov 1674 PAUL LAWRENCE [1]
Appraisers: Richard Syres of Chichester, gent, Henry Masters of Chichester, brasier

	£	s	d
In primis his wearing apparell and money in the house	60	0	0
Item due upon bond	20	0	0
Item due for Rent from Wm and A ... Baldie	120	0	0
Item owing from severall persons for Tythes being desprate	30	0	0
Item hogges and pigges	5	0	0
Item 40 sackes and a wimsheete	3	0	0
Item an old Cart dung pot and wheeles with other husbandry tackling	2	0	0
Item a gelding	10	0	0
In the Parlor			
In primis twelve rushen Chayres	3	12	0
Item 4 sidebord Tables and three Carpetts	2	0	0
Item a Clock a payre of brasse Andirons firepan and Tounges a payre of Iren dogges and a payre of bellowes	3	0	0
Item two pictures a curten and an Iron rod		6	8
In the kitchen			
In primis Brasse and pewter of all sorts a furnace Iron potts five spitts a Jack an Iron back two payre of Andirons a payre of racks	16	0	0
Item six leather Chayres two Cubbords one Table three bulrush Chayres a Childes Chayre and three Joyne stooles	2	0	0
In the wash howse and buttery			
In primis 25[?] Drink vessells one mershvate fower kivers a bucking Tub and other woodden things	2	0	0
Item fower dozen of bottles an old Table three stands with Other lumber	1	0	0
In the Chamber over the wash howse			
In primis one feather bed and boulster a payre of blanketts a greene rug one halfe headed bedsted mat and Cord with Curtens and Iron rodds	3	0	0
Item two Cheasts a bulrush Chayre with other lumber		5	0
In the Chamber over the kitchen			
In primis a feather bed a feather boulster two feather pillowes a payre of blanketts a rugg a payre of Curtens a bedstedle with other appurtenances thereunto	3	10	0
Item two presses fower Truncks an old Cheast a Cubbord with other lumber there	2	0	0
Item sixteene silver spoones one silver Tankard six small silver salts with other silver plate	10	0	0
Item lynnen of all sorts	15	0	0

In the maides Chamber			
One feather bed a boulster three blanketts a halfe headed Bedsted mat and Cord	2	10	0
In the roome over the entry			
One Trunk one Cheast one box one Chayre	1	0	0
In the Chamber over the Butterie			
In primis one feather bed three pillowes a rugg one payre of blanketts a bedstedle Curtens and Vallence with other appurtenances therento belonging with six Chayres and stooles	12	0	0
Item a Cheast a Table a side Cubbord a Cabbenet a payre of Andirons and tounges a fire pan with all other things in the sayd Chamber	3	0	0
In the Chamber over the Parlour			
In primis one feather bed one boulster two pillowes a greene rugg a payre of blanketts a bedstedle Vallence Curtens and Curten rodds with all belonging thereto	14	0	0
Item eight stooles seaven Chayres a payre of Andirons two Tables with other things in the sayd Chamber	2	0	0
Item a feather bed boulster and pillow a greene rugg three blanketts Curtens and Vallence with a bedstedle disposd off	5	0	0
Item a flockbed with other appurtenances thereto belonging in the maides Chamber	1	0	0
In the studdie			
Bookes of all sortes	60	0	0
Item lumber and all other things forgotten and unseene	1	0	0
	(416	3	8)

[TNA PRO PROB 4/12565]

Will: made 5 March 1672; proved 24 Nov 1674
Wife Jane, executrix; sons: Edward, Thomas (under 21); brothers-in-law: Thomas and William Palmer
Witnesses: George Payne, John Stuart   [TNA PRO PROB 11/346]

[1] Of Sussex. Cambridge, Jesus, admitted and matriculated 1625, scholar 1626, BA 1629, MA 1632. Ordained deacon 1639 (bishop of Winchester), priest 1640 (bishop of Chichester). Curate of Pulborough 1640. Vicar of Burpham 1640–1660, patron dean and chapter of Chichester; of Poling 1661–1674, patron Eton College. Rector of Tangmere 1660–1674. Possibly married Elizabeth Chatfield of Cuckfield (?died 1651) at West Grinstead 1638 when he was living at Pulborough. (?Second) wife Jane. Died 1674.

155. Thakeham 26 March 1668 WILLIAM CORDEROY [1]

Appraisers: Thomas Mellersh, yeoman, Richard Greene husbandman

	£	s	d
In primis his wearing apparell and mony in his purse	2	10	0
Item in the Kitchen			
Fourteen peeces of Pewter and six porringers	1	15	10
Item one quart pot and 1 pint pot		1	6
Item Candlesticks and chamberpots with other small things		5	0

Item 2 kettles 2 skillets 1 warming pan 1 chafendish 1 morter 2 brasse ladles		14	0
Item 2 Iron pots and Pothooks		3	0
Item 4 Chairs and 4 Stools		7	0
Item 3 spits 2 p of brandirons 1 p of tongs 2 p of pothangers 1 fender		10	0
Item Porke and Bacon		5	0
Item one Cupboard with other things		6	0
Item one Jack		5	0
In the hall			
Item 1 side board 2 tables 2 chairs 4 joynstools 6 Clothstools	1	8	0
Item his books	5	0	0
Item a Carpet and Cupboard 1 Cloth		8	0
In the Chamber over the hall			
Item 2 mantles and childbed lynnen		13	4
Item 3 beds steads		18	0
Item 2 featherbeds	3	0	0
Item 9 pillows and 2 bolsters	1	4	4
Item 4 flockbeds and 5 bolsters	1	18	0
Item 3 rugs 2 Coverlets 5 blankets	2	8	0
Item 3 p of Curtains and valence	1	10	0
Item 5 p of fine sheets	3	6	0
Item 2 dozen of fine Napkins		18	0
Item 6 p of ordinary sheets	2	2	0
Item 2 dozen of ordinary Napkins		7	6
Item 2 Cupboard Cloaths		8	0
Item 8 fine Pillowcoats and 2 other		12	0
Item 8 Table Cloths		13	0
Item 12 Towells		4	0
Item 7 course Pillowcoates		5	0
Item 2 Chests and 2 boxes with other things		10	0
Item 2 p of Curtains	1	0	0
Item one Coverlet		10	0
In the Cellar			
Item 1 barrell and 1 Tub with other lumber		2	0
In the Beakhouse			
Item 2 trugs 2 bowls 3 shelves with other things		4	0
In the Entry			
Item 1 Tub 1 bowl 1 halfe bushell and 1 Gallon		5	0
In the Washhouse			
Item 1 Bedstead		6	8
Item 2 keelers		3	0
Item 2 Tubs with other Lumber		5	0
In the Milkhouse			
Item 4 bedsteads with other Lumber	1	6	6
At Storrington			
Item a flockbed bolster and coverlett		5	0
At Petworth			
Item 5 old chayers one tub and other lumber		5	0
Item good debts on bond to the use of his children	40	0	0

	£	s	d
Item one bond more	10	0	0
Item a desperat debt due from Ed. Cooke	6	18	0
Item due from his brother Keyn		10	6
Item due from Wid. Lee	1	0	0
Item things unseen and forgotten		10	0
Sum total	87	3	2

[WSRO Ep I/29/195/43]

Administration 10 July 1668
To Margaret, wife   [WSRO STC III/I/60]

[1] Son of William, of Finchampstead, Berks. Oxford, Trinity, matriculated 1639 aged 17. Curate of Duncton c. 1653; minister *pro tempore* 1660; ejected. Kept boarding school at Steyning but forced to leave it after Five Mile Act 1665. Retired to Thakeham. Married Margaret Moris at Petworth 1656. Died 1668; buried Thakeham.

156. Thakeham 23 Oct 1680 HENRY BANCKES, rector [1]
Appraisers: [Not given]

	£	s	d
In primis The deceaseds wearing aparell Linnen And woollen and money in his purse; plate and Rings	130	0	0
In the Parlour			
Item Two tables and carpets six Rushia leather chaires one paire of brasse andirons fire panne and tongs and cushions and Curtaines to the windowes	3	13	4
In the Long Roome			
Item Two tables and carpets three chaires one stoole One fourme two old maps and one Pike	1	5	0
In the hall			
Item One table one carpet six chaires one stoole two Curtaines One side board and carpet two paire of andirons one paire of tongs a paire of tables and a chess board	1	6	8
In the Kitchen			
Item One Table one stoole one fourme one chaire one cupboard two Jackes five spits one paire of andirons iron racke one fender one fire panne and tongs and bellowes one fire slice and fire forke and a musquet Pothooks and Pothangers one iron candlesticke and two iron dripping pannes	2	7	6
Item Two warmeing pannes foure brasse kettles two brasse potts three brasse candlestickes three brasse Skimmers two brasse skilletts two mortars and pestles three brasse sconces one brasse chafeing dish two iron potts and one iron Kettle	3	13	0
Item Two hundred and fourty pound weight of pewter	8	0	0
Item Tinne and a paire of pistolls and other Lumber		10	0
In the Brewhouse			
Item One furnace one brewing fatt one Tunne three keelers foure Tubbs one Three Leggs five buckets and other Lumber	3	0	0
In the Sellar			

Item One cheese presse one Quarne fourteen Kilderkins six small
vessells two powdering Tubbs and other Lumber   2   10   0
     In the Buttery
Item One safe Two stills thirty cheeses Tenne payle of butter Crockes
and bottles and other Lumber   4   5   0
     In the Milke house
Item Three Leaden pannes Crockes pannes fourmes churne and
shelves   2   11   8
     In the Bakehouse
Item One meale Trough two meale Tubbs three searches Leather sacke
and other Lumber   13   4
     In the closet within the Parlour chamber
Item Twenty six dozen of napkins old and new Twenty two table
clothes nine Towells Two Cotton Counterpaines   12   8   0
Item One brasse sconce   6   8
     In the Parlour chamber
Item Two feather beds Two boulsters and Two pillowes six blancketts
one rugge one Coverled mat and cords one Table and carpett firepanne
and Tongs and looking glasse   7   10   0
     In the Dining Roome
Item Seaventeene paire of sheets five dozen of napkins sixteen table
clothes eight pieces of flaxen cloth eleaven Towells eight Cupboard
clothes and Tenne paire of pillowe Beers   14   1   8
Item Foure Turkey worked carpetts two sideboard cloathes one
damaske carpet two paire of vallans five ~~paire of~~ cushions one piece of
wrought stuffe one piece of old Cotton Carpet two green Carpets   6   5   0
Item Seaven course Table cloathes one peice of Course cloath for
napkins   18   0
Item One downe bedd one boulster two pillowes one silke Quilt
Curtaines and vallans with mat and cord one paire of andirons fire
panne and tongs foure chaires and one chest of drawers two Trunckes
and one chest and the hangings   8   7   6
Item Two old pictures   5   0
     In the entry chamber
Item eighteen paire of sheets and three table cloathes   6   0   0
Item One feather bed and boulster bedstead two Blanckets rugge and
counterpaine and the hangings   3   3   4
     In the Hall chamber
Item One downe bed one feather bed and bedstead two ruggs four
blanckets one paire of curtaines and vallans matts and cords one table
two chaires fire panne Tongs and andirons Sideboard and glasse case
and the hangings   11   10   0
Item One old clocke   10   0
Item One little deske wth the things in it   1   5   0
Item Two old leather boxes   5   0
Item One Chinah dish with other earthen ware   10   0
     In the Study
Item The deceaseds Bookes   40   0   0
Item Three deskes with a watch and all things in them and one chaire   2   0   0

In the wash house chamber

Item One feather bed and ~~blanckets~~ bedstead two blanckets and one coverled mat and cord and the hangings	3	0	0
Item foure paire of sheets nine dozen of napkins eight table cloath nineteen Towells and three pillowe beers	6	13	4
Item One satten mantle and two petticoats	3	0	0
Item foure old Trunckes and a Little Table	1	0	0
Item Two mantles Two sideboard cloathes and some other small things in a Truncke	3	0	0

In the Kitchen chamber

Item Two feather beds and bedsteads boulsters and pillowes two blanckets one rugge mat and cord and chaire and the hangings	3	0	0

In the mens chamber

Item One featherbed and boulster bedstead two blanckets one coverled mat and cord	1	10	0
Item One old presse		10	0
Item six downe pillowes and two old wrought cushions Thirty three paire of sheets and fifteen table cloathes and two old chests	22	5	0
Item Three dozen of course napkins Two dozen of Towells eight pillowe beers and eight table cloaths	2	9	0
Item Corne in the West Land Barne a ricke of pease and a ricke of hay there	20	0	0
Item Barly in the three Barnes	30	0	0
Item wheate in the barne	16	0	0
Item Oates	1	0	0
Item Hay	3	0	0
Item six Oxen	28	0	0
Item Two mares and two colts	8	0	0
Item foure cowes	12	0	0
Item two steers and a bull	7	5	0
Item One mare and one horse	5	0	0
Item Twenty one sheep	8	0	0
Item One waggon and wheeles dung potts chaines harrowes with other husbandry Tackling	7	10	0
Item seaven hogs and eleaven Piggs	6	13	4
Item Cord=wood and faggots	8	0	0
Item the welbucket ropes and leaden cisterne and pipe	3	13	4
Item tenne sackes and one fagg	1	0	0
Item wooll flaxseed and a piece of blacke cloath	1	0	0
Item Things unseen forgot and soe not appraised		10	0

Debts due to the deceased followe vizt

Item A bond dated the 15th of July One thousand six Hundred and eighty wherein Robert Belward of Ditchingham in the County of Norfolk yeoman and Ralph Pell of great yarmouth in the County aforesaid gent stand bound to Alane Cliffe of the Citty of London Esq in the sume of Two hundred pounds for payment of One hundred pounds upon the first of January next following the date of the said bond the said monies belonging to the Testator Henry Banckes and the name of the said Alane Cliffe being ... sed in Trust onely for him	100	0	0

Item A Bill obligatory dated the fourteenth of November 1679 wherein
Alane Cliffe Esq aforsd binds himselfe his heires Executors and
administrators in the penall sum of twelve hundred pounds for
payment of six hundred and thirty pounds together with interest
for the same at the rate of five pound p Cent p annum upon demand to
the said Doc. Henry Banckes his heires Executors or Assignes   630   0   0
Item another bill obligatory dated the sixth of October 1680 wherein
the said Alane Cliffe binds himselfe his heires executors and
administrators for the payment of ninety eight pounds upon demand
with interest at the rate of five pounds p Cent p annum to the said
Doc. Henry Banckes his Executors and Assignes   98   0   0
Item a debt of eighteen pound or thereabouts due to the Testator from
Mr Thomas Jordan upon account of rent by him reced for the Testator
in his life time   18   0   0

Sum total   1337   19   8

[TNA PRO PROB 5/4331]

Will: made 24 Nov 1678; proved 9 Dec 1680
Brother ?Clis… ; nephew … Bankes (lands and tenements); sister Bennet (£10); niece
Rebecca Bankes (£250); brother Humphrey; sister An; cousin Mary … ; cousins
Elizabeth Wickens, An Jenden, Rebecca Bankes (mourning rings)
Poor of parish. 4s
Executor, Richard Bankes, cousin
Witnesses: Edmund Coles, John Fortrie, William Wheeler [TNA PRO PROB 11/363/89]

[1] Of York. Cambridge, Magdalene, matriculated 1637; Jesus, admitted 1638, BA 1642, probably
DD 1671. Rector of Thakeham 1640–1680. Died 1680 aged 70.

157. Thakeham Dec 1682 ROBERT PUTT, vicar [1]
Appraisers: William Jenden, rector West Chiltington, Richard Harraden, John Ratley

	£	s	d
In primis the deceaseds wearing apparel & money in his purse	10	0	0
Item his books valued at five pounds	5	0	0
Item six Russian leather chaires	1	4	0
Item foure Bullrush chaires		3	0
Item a rugg valued at ten shillings		10	0
Item two paire of andirons		4	0
Item three C... nckes [?]glass at 3s 6d		3	6
Item … Barrelles and two Kilderkins	..	..	0
Item a tun tubb and a Vate		10	0
Item two Powdring tubbs		6	0
Item a Jacke [?]bowle with Ladle and foure small wooden dishes		1	4
Item two Sieves		1	0
Item two little tables		4	4
Item three bedstead and valued at 10s		20	0
Item tenn dozen of glass bottles tenne single bottles	1	0	0
Item Thirteene pounds of hopps		6	6
Item a Bell		2	6

		£	s	d
Item a saddle and bridle			5	0
Item wheate in the barne valued at the sume of foure pounds		4	0	0
Item the Mow of Barly pease and hey		6	0	0
Item neare thirteene cord of wood at the rate of five shillings p Cord		3	5	0
Item Timber valued at		2	10	0
Item lumber about the house and Things forgott			5	0
Item dung valued at			5	0
	Suma totali	38	5	2

[TNA PRO PROB 4/20685]

Will: made 5 March 1681; proved 12 Dec 1682; testator described in will as of Lubenham, Leics
Mother, Mary Putt, executrix (house in Lubenham where she lives and other property for life; then to Arabella and Mary Clarke junior of Gilmorton, Leics daughters of sister Mary wife of William)
2nd house
Poor of Thakeham 40s
Overseers: two uncles (Perkins of Herrington and Bull of Sutton)
Witnesses: William Waters, James Middleton, Robert Drake

[TNA PRO PROB 11 371/149]

[1] Cambridge, Clare, admitted 1670, matriculated 1671, BA 1674. Ordained deacon 1674, priest 1677 (bishop of Peterborough). Rector of Thakeham c. 1680–1682.

158. West Thorney Feb 1638 GODFREY BLAXTON [1]

Appraisers: George Edgley, clerk, Thomas Hooker, clerk, William Alridge, clerk

	£	s	d
In the great chamber in the house of Chichester			
In primis on drawing table a Cubord and a little syde table		15	0
Item an old chayre an old wicker chayre two lowe old chayres and two little old stooles		3	4
Item a Waynescott chest and three trunks		10	0
Item a presse Cupbord		12	0
Item on truckle bedstedle with matt and cord		2	0
Item two feather beds and two bolsters and two pillowes	3	0	0
Item on Rugge and three blanketts	..	..	..
Item a payre of tongs … payre of Andirons on payre of …		10	0
Item ~~six quish~~ two window quishons and six other quishons		10	0
Item an old greene Coverlett and an old greene Carpett cupbord cloth and a little Turkey carpett and a greene Coverlett	1	6	0
Item three pictures		5	0
Item on loakinge glasse and 2 hower glasses		1	0
Item the pewter	1	10	0
In the chamber over the kitchen			
Item an old bedstedle with dornix curtaynes curtayne rods with matt and cord and an old peece of dornix		12	0
Item one feather bed one two feather bolsters a flocke boulster one Coverlett two blanqetts one pillowe and a peece of an old rugge and			

	£	s	d
~~Item~~ one old truckle bedsted with one old little low table	2	0	0
Item a payre of toungs a payre of andirons and a payre of billowes a little olde low chayer and … stoole		3	4
Item a little cupboard for glasses and three little boxes		2	0
Item an olde bedstedle and a chest and a little table and three old boxes	..	..	..
Item a little pott tipt with sylver and two silver spoones		10	0

In the Chamber over the kitchen

	£	s	d
Item … bedstedle a bolster and two one pillow and an old chest a little table and fower boxes a Coverlett and a blankett		10	0

In the Hall

	£	s	d
Item an old drawinge table fower ioyned stooles a presse Cupbord a syd Cupbord and five chayres	1	10	0
Item an old little mape and five little old pictures		2	0
Item a brasse sconce			6
Item a little … of cast iron and irons and a payre of doggs		2	0
Item two old little boxes		1	0
Item two quishions and a bench			6
Item three dozen of trenchers		1	0

In the Buttery

	£	s	d
Item five fowre firkins a little tubb and a little pudringe tubb twoe pastry peeles a shelfe and a little olde cupbord and fower beere bottles		5	0
Item two payre of saffes			6

In the kitchen

	£	s	d
Item two brasse potts three kittles a skillett a chafinge dishe an other little kittle two brasse Candlesticks a brase skimer a warming [pan and a] little brasse hand candlesticke	1	11	8
Item a fryinge pan a drippinge pan three spitts fender a payre of scales fowre irons two payre of Cotterils a payre of toungs		6	6
Item an old iacke		3	4
Item a thinge of latte[n] to [?]briople meate			6
Item a little table a Cupbord and an olde forme		5	0
Item two bulrushe chayres and a childs wooden chayre		2	0
Item a salt box a bread greate and little shelves		1	0
Item three iron potts two bell skilletts a little brasse pott two bell two bell skelletts an olde kittle and a skillett and a warming pan		12	0

In the wash house

	£	s	d
Item fower old tubbs with other old lumber		3	4

The Linnen

	£	s	d
Item fower six payre of sheets five table clothes fower dozen and fower napkins two Cupbord clothes five payre of course pillowbers a longe towell three smale towells	2	1	0
Item on table cloth and a dozen of diaper napkins with other linnen at Mr Aldridges	3	0	0
Item a carpett and a cupbord cloth at Mr Aldridges		13	4
Item a pare of an olde coslett at Mr Aldridges		1	0

Item More at Mr Aldridges the bakehowse

	£	s	d
Item a bedstedle matt and cord	..	..	..
Item a deske with boxes		1	6
Item other lumber		1	6

	£	s	d
Item a bedstedle with old Curtaynes and matt and cord		11	8
Item three trunks a chest a payre of little doggs and a little deske	..	..	..
Item the deceaseds books	6	0	0
Item his wearing apparell	3	0	0

Att the barn in the Clopsle Street which was brought from Thorney

	£	s	d
Item an old bedstedle a halfe bushell a pecke a gallon an old fryinge pan a powdringe tubb a settle with other lumber		6	8

Att the backhowse

	£	s	d
Item an old trunke a cupborde with other lumber		10	0
Item the wood and old lumber in the seller		10	0
Sum total	36	10	2

[WSRO Ep I/29/196/6]

Administration 7 March 1638
To wife, Thomazine   [WSRO STC III/H/63, 93]

[1] Born Higham Ferrers, Northants, c. 1570, son of Henry, prebendary of Wightring 1572–1606. Chorister Chichester cathedral 1580. Cambridge, Trinity, matriculated 1586, BA 1590; Clare, MA 1593. Rector of St Peter the Less, Chichester, 1593–1596; of Rumboldswyke 1596–c. 1608; of Eastergate 1596–1631; patron of all three dean and chapter of Chichester. Rector of West Thorney 1607–1638, patron Crown, but for another institution on same day patron Joan Blaxton, widow. Vicar choral of Chichester cathedral 1594–1634. Possibly vicar of East Marden 1595. Sub-treasurer of Chichester cathedral 1606. Married Thomasine daughter of Thomas Brigham, alderman of Chichester, at Tillington by licence 1595. Died 1638.

159. Treyford 3 Feb 1686 WALTER TOMLINSON [1]

Appraisers: John Sadler, Richard Newman

	£	s	d
in his Logen Chamber			
wollen and Linen and Money	20	0	0
For a bed bolster and toe piller pare of blankets and Coverled	7	0	0
For toe beds steeds and A tronke and Chest and table	1	6	0
For his Study of Book in all	15	0	0
in the Chamber over the hall			
For A bed bollster and blankets and Ruge and bedsteed	2	10	0
For toe presses and boxses and one Chest and A ne ...	2	0	0
in the roome over the back kitchen			
For A bedstead and bed and blankets and bollsteres and Coverled	2	10	0
in the back Chitchen			
For toe kitells and three scillets and a Letell bras pot and An iren one	1	10	0
For three [?]chefors		4	0
For Laten pans Aboute the hows and A [?]Bruen fates and [?]lefores	10	2	0
For A fornes Grates and spites 4 of them	1	15	0
For An iren sliss and pisell and Morter and A pare of forks and [?]comer		15	0
For puter in all	1	5	0
For A bucket Chaine and well Rope		10	0

For barell 14 of them and boatell A boute th howes all	2	2	0
in the parler			
For A bed bolster and toe pilloes and A pare of blankets all	5	0	0
For A table and forme and Chare		7	0
For toe fletches of bakon	2	0	0
in the pantrey			
Item plats and trencheres and table and safe		15	0
Item toe tables 4 joynte stolls and A forme		13	0
For A backen Rack Cobarte and Grate		9	0
in the Hall			
A Clock and Jack	2	10	0
For hay and fackotes and billet	2	10	0
Item for a hors Bridell and other thing	5	0	0
Item three pare of dogs and andirens and fierpaines and tongs		9	0
Item for A backsword kepor and pistell and pick		11	0
For A wormenpan and Chefendish		6	0
For A Liad pig		17	0
For 5 spuns and a Letell Sellver dish	2	10	0
For A [?]haywich and [?]querren	1	5	0
Item Lomber in all About the howes	1	5	0
Suma totalis	85	16	0

[WSRO Ep I 29/199/8]

Fee for lost will 17 March 1686   [WSRO Ep I/43/6]

[1] Son of Robert, rector of Trotton (**160**). Oxford, Magdalen, matriculated 1635 aged 18. Rector of Trotton (after his father's sequestration) 1646–?1662; of Treyford c. 1661–1686. Called rector of Tuxlith (now Milland) c. 1662. Married Elizabeth Drew at Treyford 1662. Died 1686; buried Treyford.

160. Trotton 3 May 1663 ROBERT TOMLINSON [1]

Appraisers: Thomas Bradshawe, Richard Smith, Anthony White, Richard Bridger

	£	s	d
In primis his weareinge			
appell and money in his purse	5	0	0
Item in the greene chamber			
one Bedd and Bedsteddle two Bowlsters and one Rugge	3	0	0
Item in the same chamber one			
side Cupboard one litle table fower joyned stooles one payre of			
Brandirons	1	0	0
Item in the chamber over the hall			
one Flocke bedd two Bedsteddles o(ne) Bowlster one Chest one side			
Cupboard one side table one Deske one Truncke one payre of			
Brandirons	2	1	6
Item in the same chamber two			
Coverletts one Coveringe for (a) Bedd one windowe Cushion	2	1	0
Item for his bookes	2	0	6

Item in the same chamber			
one close stoole		1	6
Item in the Parlor			
one joyned Table two litle Tables one side Cupboard two greate chaires eight covered stooles one Jacke two payre of Andirons two payre of Tonges one firepan one payre of pothangers the wainscoate and the Benche in the same roome	3	13	4
Item in the hall			
one Table one side Cupboard two Formes one Chayre one greate Cup board one payre of Rackes one Brandiron one pothanger one iron Jacke	1	6	8
Item in the chamber			
one Bedd and Bedsteddle and ... nett bowlster and one Rugge one swoard and Bandaleers wooll & hopps one Truncke		1	0
Item in the chamber over the milke house			
one old Cheste and Barley	3	0	0
Item in the seller			
three Barrells two Firkins		5	0
Item one silver salte one silver spoone	1	0	0
In the litle roome next			
the seller one pewter Still two Flaggons one Bason ten peises of pewter two brasse Candlestickes and one warminge pan one posnett two skilletts one Chamberpott three latten Candlestickes one latten pan one Morter and pestle one salte one brasse skimmer one ladle		1	6
Item in the kitchen			
one iron pott one iron kettle two brasse kettles one Vate one greate kiver one spitter Bill and Ax one Clever one hollowe shovell pecke and gallon two payre of pothookes one payre of gridirons one Furnesse two Bucketts one payre of Tonges one Tubbe & kivers one fryinge pan and other lumber and two spitts	2	15	0
Item three Flitches of Bacon	2	0	0
Item one payre of holland sheetes two payre of Canvesse sheetes two Dyaper Table clothes one Dyaper Cupboard cloth nine Napkins wth other small linen	1	15	0
Item two horses and a Colte	6	0	0
Item six hogges	4	16	0
Item the waggon and all thereunto belonginge	1	12	6
Item one Van and fower pronges	1	0	6
Item for Corne in the Barne	10	5	0
Item fower Sackes		4	0
Item for Beanes upon the ground		15	0
Item for two Saddles and two Bridles		6	8
Item for the Corne upon the land	12	0	0
Item for two payre of blancketts three Cushions three pillowes		8	8
Item for a lookinge glasse			6
Item fower hennes and a Cocke		2	6
Item one Teinnt sauwre one hamer and broad Ax		2	6
Suma totalis huius Intry	73	13	10

[WSRO Ep I/29/200/24]

Will: made 22 Nov 1661; no probate
Sons: Walter, Robert (deceased), Anthony (administrator of will); daughter: Ann (Gale)
Trustees: Walter Bockland, Arthur Bold
Overseers and witnesses: Mr Nicholas Love of Terwick, Henry Aylinge

[WSRO STC I/26/170]

[1] Son of William, of London. School at London. Cambridge, Gonville and Caius, admitted sizar 1590 aged 15, scholar 1591–1597, BA 1594, MA 1597. Oxford, incorporated 1607. Possibly rector of Sessay, Yorks, 1606. Ordained deacon 1607, priest 1608 (bishop of London). Schoolmaster in household of Sir Francis Leigh of Westminster, Midd, 1608. Licensed preacher Chichester diocese 1609. Rector of Trotton 1609, patron Crown, but for another institution on same day patrons John Mill, esq., and Constance Glemham, widow; dispensation for non-residence 1631; sequestered 1645.

161. Upwaltham 27 July 1718 HENRY WRIGHT, rector [1]
Appraisers: William Moore, Robert Russell

	£	s	d
In primis In the Cellar			
Ten Dozen of Bottles	1	0	0
Item Four Vessells of Beer and The Vessells	4	15	0
Three Stands		5	0
Two brass Cocks		2	0
A Powdering tubb		2	6
Small bear		4	0
Two Searchers		3	6
In the Woodhouse			
Wood and Faggots	2	0	0
A Leathern bag Lanthorn and Couple tub		6	0
In the Kitchin			
Bacon		3	0
Six knives and six forks		3	6
Eight Chairs		8	0
Table and Lock		4	0
A Dresser and Shelves		15	0
Two Smoothing Irons		4	0
A Dozen of Wooden plates		2	0
A Rack		2	0
Glasses Muggs		2	0
S ... res and Tobacco tongs		1	6
A Chaffing Dish		2	6
White Ware		1	0
Coffee Pots and 2 Candlesticks		4	0
A puding pan drudger and Tunnell		2	0
In the Parlour			
Pipes			6
Hair Line		1	6
Table		10	0

In the Chamber

Two tables		8	0
Bed and what belongs to it	2	0	0
Wareing Cloaths	10	0	0
A Press		14	0
A Hair Broom			6
A Bedsteddle and Cord		6	0
Shooes and Boots		12	0
Wigg and Hats	2	0	0
A Gun		15	0
A Trunk and Drawer		3	0
Item pair of Sheets	2	0	0
Table Linnen	1	4	0
A Parcell of Books	1	15	0
Two Basketts and Iron Cloth		1	6
Moneys	4	7	6
	38	15	0

[WSRO Ep I/29/201/4]

Administration 29 July 1718

To Richard Goodyer, creditor, mother, Elizabeth Wright, widow, having renounced

[WSRO STC III/N/13]

[1] Son of Samuel, of Oxford, cleric. Oxford, New College, matriculated 1698 aged 15; University College, BA 1702. Cambridge, incorporated 1711; Corpus Christi, MA 1711. Ordained deacon 1705, priest 1706 (bishop of Chichester). Schoolmaster at Petworth 1705. Rector of Upwaltham 1706–1718, patron Thomas Dawtrey; of Burton with Coates 1713–1718, patron Crown. Died 1718.

162. Walberton 29 Sept 1650 THOMAS JAMES [1]

Appraisers not given

	£	s	d
In primis 1 high bedstedle and matt and cord [curt]aines and vallens	1	4	0
Item 1 greene bulrush chaire		1	8
Item an iron backe		6	0
Item 18 peeces of pewter weighing 28lbs	1	8	0
Item an ewer and a salt seller		2	6
Item 1 fetherbed of 71lbs	3	5	1
Item another featherbed of 40lbs	1	13	4
Item 3 boulsters of 6lbs	1	13	..
Item 2 feather pillowes of 8lbs		7	..
Item 3 blankets		15	..
Item 1 greene rug		18	0
Item 3 sheetes		13	4
Item 1 dozen of napkins		7	0
Item 2 tableclothes		6	0
Item a paire of pillocoates		1	6
Item 2 chamber potts		2	0

Item		£	s	d
Item 1 brasse pott			4	9
Item a brasse ladle			1	0
Item 2 velvet cushens			2	0
Item 1 drawing table		1	0	0
Item 1 still			9	..
Item 2 wainscott chaires and a livery cubbard			13	..
Item 4 leather back't chaires			13	0
Item 7 high stooles covered with leather and 2 low leather stooles			9	4
Item 6 joyned stooles			9	0
Item 1 round falling table			3	4
Item 2 cloth cushens		..	..	..
Item …		..	..	..
Item 1 boxe and 2 …		..	..	..
Item 2 formes …			2	0
Item 2 tables		1	0	0
Item 6 joyned stooles more			9	0
Item 1 chaire covered with dornix and 1 stoole			4	0
Item earthen potts and pannes			2	0
Item a picke and a spitter and a shovell			1	4
Item a sadle and 2 bridles			12	0
Item his waring apparrell		1	0	0
Item money in the house		5	5	0
Item all his bookes		5	0	0
Item shelves and bords about the house			10	0
Item a welbuckett rope and chaine			2	0
Item one mare		7	0	0
Item one henn				4
Item owing to him for tithes		8	0	0
Item owing more by John …		2	0	0
Item owing by Richard …		2	10	0
Item received for pasture since his death		1	0	0
	Sum total	58	15	0

[WSRO Ep I/29/202/31]

Will nuncupative: 12 May 1650; proved 27 July 1650
Brother Richard (of Asten in Sussex in ?Friston or Alfriston) executor
Witnesses: Augustine Payne, minister of Eastergate, Eleanor James

[WSRO STC I/21/419]

[1] Called MA 1627. Ordained deacon and priest 1627 (bishop of Llandaff). Licensed preacher Chichester diocese 1635. Vicar of Walberton 1635–1650, patron bishop of Chichester. Died 1650.

163. Warbleton 14 Aug 1644 EDWARD TREDCROFT, rector [1]
Appraisers: Richard Dicker, John Ellis, Abraham Cruttenden

	£	s	d
In the Parlor			
In primis one Table	1	0	0
Item one Livery Coberd		10	0

	£	s	d
Item one Table and Coberd carpet		16	0
Item 6 letheren Chaires and one of a biger sort	9	0	0
Item 12 Cushens	2	0	0
Item 10 eight ioyne stooles and 6 lowe ones		14	0
In the Hall			
Item one Cupboard	1	10	0
Item 1 Table	1	0	0
Item 3 Chairs		3	0
Item one jacke		10	0
Item one payre of Brandirons		5	0
Item the skels to waigh hopps		12	0
Item 16 hundred and [?]oad of hops	10	0	0
In the Kitchen			
Item one iron furnace	2	5	0
Item 2 bruing tubs	1	5	0
Item one Bucking tub		2	0
Item one Iron Kettel and 2 iron pots		9	0
Item one brasse kettel		17	5
Item 2 fire panes and one payre of Brandirons		..	6
Item one rake and one payre of tonges		4	6
Item one Fender 3 payre of pot hangers and a litle hooke		..	..
Item 2 payre of pothooks		1	0
Item one iron barr wch the pothookes hang upon			3
Item one old Dresser		2	0
Item 4 spitts		6	0
Item 7 keelers		14	0
Item 8 Tubes and one long legd keeler	1	0	0
Item 2 payre of Bellowes		1	6
Item 4 Buckets		5	0
Item one Clever and one Choping knife		1	0
Item one Shreddinge knife one Chafeing dish		1	6
Item one Morter and pessell		1	4
Item 9 Traies		13	0
Item one forme and one Table in the milke house			3
Item 2 Chaires		2	0
Item one Warming pan and one frying pann		3	0
Item one Tosting iron			4
Item one Bread grate			6
Item 2 Latin driping pans		1	0
Item one Charne		2	0
Item one Cheese presse		8	1
Item one Skimmer			6
In the Parler Chamber			
Item one feather bed one Bolster and two pillers a blew rugge 2 Blankets Bedsteed Canopie curtains vallens	12	0	0
Item one Table one chest one Truncke one ioyne chaire		1	8
In the hall Chamber			
Item one Bedsteedell cutaines and valens one bed 2 Bolsters 2 pillars one Coverlet 2 blankets	10	0	0

Item one littel tabell		6	8
Item one great ioyne chest	1	0	0
Item 3 chests one wicker Chaire		8	0
In the other littell Chambers			
Item one Bedsteed Curtaines featherbed one bolster 2 pillers one coverlet and one blanket	9	0	0
Item one chest 2 boxes and one duske		12	0
Item one cradle		3	0
Item one halfe heded bedstedell and one Trukelbed			
Item 2 Fetherbeds 2 bolsters 3 pillers 2 coverlets 2 blankets	8	0	0
Item 2 chests		6	0
Item one halfeheaded Bedstedell one chafebed one bolster one blanket	1	7	0
Item on Truckell bedstedell one chafebed one bolster one blanket	1	0	0
Item one halfheded bedstedell one flockebed one chafe bolster one blanket	..	..	..
Item one halfheaded bedstedell one flockbed one flockebolster one blanket	..	..	..
Item one new Coper furnace	1	16	0
Item 3 payre of old flexen sheets and one payre of new flexen sheets	2	0	0
Item 2 payre of new hemppen sheets and seven payre of new towen sheets and 2 payre of old towen sheets	4	0	..
Item 2 payre of fine Hollen Pillicoats		8	0
Item 4 payre of other Pillicoats		16	0
Item one Diaper Tablecloth one Diaper towell 6 diaper napkins		16	0
Item 2 other fine Table cloths 2 other fine towells 12 other fine napkins		10	0
Item 2 dozen of fine Towen napkins and 2 dosen and a halfe of other towen napkins	1	0	0
Item 2 fine towen Towels and 9 corse towen Towels		10	0
Item 7 corse Tabel cloths		12	0
Item Yarne fine and corse	8	0	0
Item Flexen and Hempen Tyere	1	5	0
Item Hempe from the Brake	1	0	0
Item wool	..	..	..
Item one Dosen of great pewter	..	..	..
Item one Dosen of the lesser sort	..	..	..
Item Poringer and Sasers one Dosen	..	..	..
Item 5 chamber pots	..	..	..
Item 5 Candelsticks	..	..	..
Item 5 Saltsellers	..	..	..
Item one peuter pot and one candle cup		14	0
Item Hopp poles	12	0	0
Item the Hoggs	8	0	0
Item the Hay	8	0	0
Item 5 Keene	15	0	0
Item 5 young Beese	7	10	0
Item 2 mares and the Colt	10	0	0
Item 4 sheep	1	4	0
Item wheat in the Barne	7	10	0
Item Oates	5	0	0

	£	s	d
Item pease	1	0	0
Item Barley		10	0
In the hall			
a payre of scales and swings		2	0
the musket sord hedpease bandaleers	1	5	0
Item 10 barrels and 2 firkins	1	15	0
his purse and girdle	2	0	0
his Wearing apparrell	5	0	0
Item a bedstedle flockbed and a fether bolster and a blanket mat and cords	2	0	0
Item 2 of Shears		16	0
Item the wool	2	0	0
Item 10 naile of hempe	1	0	0
Suma totalis	194	19	8

Exhibited 22 August 1648 by John Tredcroft gent, son and administrator

[WSRO Ep I/29/202/24]

Administration 17 Aug 1648
To John Tredcrofte, gent, son;
Wife: Elizabeth　　　　　　　　[WSRO STC III/K/90]

[1] Of Sussex. Oxford, Brasenose, matriculated 1616 aged 18, BA 1619; called MA 1621. Ordained deacon 1620, priest 1621 (bishop of Chichester). Licensed preacher 1621. Curate of Shipley 1621. Rector of Warbleton 1640–1644, patron Richard Middleton, gent. Married Bridget Parvys at Wisborough Green 1622; second wife Elizabeth. Died 1644.

164. Warnham 13 Jan 1685 WILLIAM AVERY [1]

Appraisers: Edmond Michell, William Porter

	£	s	d
In primis his wareing Apparell	10	0	0
Item Ready mony by him	5	9	0
In Parler chamber			
Item Two bedsteed 1 feather bed and Bolster two Desks 2 chests 1 cubord 1 pr of Iron brandyrons 1 pr tongs & 1 wicker chaire	4	0	0
Item Eleaven paire of sheets wth pillow coates Napkins handtowells and other linnen	8	10	0
In the buttry chamber			
Item one Bed wth all furniture therunto foure chests 1 chaire and two stooles	4	0	0
In the hall chamber			
Item Two Beeds wth coverlet and blanketts 2 trunkes 1 old chest wth A close stoole and other Lumber	2	0	0
Item The library of Bookes	10	0	0
In the Parloar			
Item one clock two Tables two settles 1 pr of brandirons one chaire and two stooles	5	0	0
In the hall			
Item Two cupbords 1 Table 6 joyned stooles 4 chaires 1 pr brandyrons			

fire pan and tongs 1 small Jack & A glass cage wth other lumber	3	0	0
In the brew house			
Item Two keelers 3 skilleets 3 potts A warming pann A copper wth all ye other matterialls of brewing vessells & other lumber therto belonging	6	0	0
Item fifty pounds of Pewter two spitts and A driping pann	2	0	0
Suma totall	60	4	0

[WSRO Ep I/29/203/066]

Will: made 11 Aug 1681; proved 10 March 1685
Sons: William, executor, Thomas, Robert (silver spoon, feather bed, blue curtains and valance); daughter: Mary
Witnesses: Robert ..., William Booker, J[n?] ...   [WSRO STC I/27/443]

[1] Son of Edward, of Kingston upon Thames, Surr. Oxford, New Inn Hall, matriculated 1638 aged 18, BA 1642. Vicar of Warnham 1648, by letters patent of Commissioners of Great Seal; probably deprived; instituted 1660–1684. Parish register of Warnham 1653; resigned by 1656. Ordained deacon and priest 1660 (?bishop of Chichester). Wife Mary (died 1670). Died 1684; buried Warnham.

165. Warningcamp 12 Jan 1635 GEORGE PAGE [1]
Appraisers: Mr Richard Page, Richard St ... William Voakes

	£	s	d
Item in the Halle			
In primis a Coubbard and a falling Table three Chayers one Joyned forme and three Joyne stoolles	2	8	0
Item for the pewter Conteyning 50lb	2	10	0
Item a brasse morter and pessel a brasse kandstick a brasse pott 3 brasse ketteles a brasse possnet 3 small scilletes a scimer and a warminge pane and a brase Chaffinge dish	1	8	0
Item 3 Cushenes an yorne potte a wicker Chayer a small powderinge toube a small boule with other Lomber a Clever and a choppinge knife		10	0
Item the Jacke a fyershovele a payer of tonges and a payer of Ayndyornes and a payer of gridyarnes and 2 payer of potthangers and 2 spitts a smothinge yorne one yorne fender	2	0	0
Item in the Lodginge Chamber			
Item a table and a forme and Six Joyne stoolles		15	0
Item a bedstedell matt and Coard		14	0
Item a trouclbed matt and Coard		2	0
Item a fether bed one fether boulster 2 blancketts and a rouge	5	0	0
Item 4 fether pillowes and 2 small fether pillowes		13	0
Item one payer of Courtines and vallents		6	0
Item a myll flocke bedd 2 boulsters a Coverlet and a blancket	1	6	0
Item a payer of Courtines and a ...	..	..	..
Item 2 nedell work Chayers ...	..	..	..
Item 3 frame stooles and a frame Chayer ... worke and a smale chayer	..	..	..
Item a Livery Coubard a Couberd ...	..	..	..
Item a brase pott and a Limbacke at Chichester	..	..	..

	£	s	d
Item 4 Trounckes	1	..	..
Item one Cheste Locke and kea a Joyne box Lock and kea and tow			
Littele boxes	..	..	..
Item a wicker Chayer	..	..	..
Item a payer of Ayndyornes and a payer of tonges and fyershovell and a			
payer of bellows	..	..	..
Item a silver boule and five silver spoones	..	..	..
Item Seven payer of sheetes	..	..	..
Item 3 doussen of Table napkins	..	..	..
Item five payer of pillowbers	..	..	..
Item tow Coubbard Clothes	..	..	..
Item fower Table Cloth and a … Cloth		9	0
Item seven Towelles		2	6
Item for his wearing Apparrele	7	10	0
Item mony in his pours	1	14	0
Item for the horse for my account	2	0	0
Item in mony in my Mothers handes not yet receved	80	0	0
Item in Bookes	10	2	2
	135	11	4

[WSRO Ep I/29/204/9]

Will: made 27 Dec 1634; proved 16 Jan 1635
Wife: Mary, executrix; daughters: Mary, Anne
Witnesses: Andrew Niell [rest illegible]   [WSRO STC I/18/352]

[1] Ordained deacon 1628, priest 1630 (bishop of Chichester). Licensed schoolmaster at Arundel 1631. Curate of Warningcamp. Married Mary Nashe at St Peter the Less, Chichester, by licence 1629. Died 1635.

166. Wartling 7 Oct 1712 DAVID FORSYTH, curate [1]
Appraisers: Mr. William Jarratt, John Holland

	£	s	d
It: For Mony in his pockett and wearing Apparrell	3	14	6
It: Books in his study	2	0	0
It: for Moneys due upon Book to the deceased	13	19	0
	19	13	6

[ESRO W/INV 361]

Administration 7 Oct 1712
To Mary Iton, widow, principal creditor   [ESRO W/B 15.94r]

[1] Edinburgh, MA. Licensed curate of Wartling 1710. Died 1712.

167. Washington 27 July 1671 NICHOLAS GARBRAND, BD, vicar [1]
Appraisers: George Hutchinson, John Berdmore, Robert Parkhurst, John Jutley

	£	s	d
In primis wearing apparrell and money in his purse	30	0	0

	£	s	d
Item for his study of Bookes	50	0	0
Item for one mare	2	10	0
Item for one Bull	2	0	0
Item in the Granary			
6 bushels of wheat 2 bushels of Barley 11 sacks with other lumber	2	0	0
Item in the Barne			
One quarter of wheat	1	4	0
Item for wood	5	10	0
Item for slabs hoggetroughs whattle and other lumber in the yard		5	0
Item for one Bore		8	0
Item for stocks of Bees		10	0
Item for a rope chaine and buckett pegs and wire in the orchard		5	0
Item in the milkhouse			
a table truggs salting trough and other lumber	1	10	0
Item in the cheesehouse			
a cheese presse wimsheet prongs [?]saies rakes and other lumber	1	10	0
Item in the Brewhouse			
a furnace Fatte tubbs bucketts charne	2	0	0
Item in the cellar and roome adjoyning			
table barrells and other lumber	2	10	0
Item in the Kitchin			
brasse pewter iron bacon and Jacke spitts gunns and other utensils	11	10	0
Item in the Hall			
Table chests clock steel wheels brandirons	5	0	0
Item in the parlour			
tables Chares couch hangings carpets cupboard brandirons glasse	9	0	0
Item in the Pantrey			
a cubberd with other Lumber		5	0
Item servants chamber			
1 bed bedstead rugg and cupboard	4	0	0
In the parlour chamber			
2 beds 2 bolsters 2 pillows rugg Table cupboard brandirons	8	0	0
Item in the Hall chamber			
for one bed 2 bolsters 2 pillows blankets rugge brandirons tonges trunkes glasse table	9	0	0
Item in the study			
for one table chaire and a box		10	0
Item for one trunk of Linnen	9	0	0
Item for course linnen abowt the House	7	0	0
Item for silver plate	8	0	0
Item for childbed linnen	3	0	0
Item for a drawer of linnen	5	0	0
Item in the Kitchen chamber			
One bed and all belonging to it	5	0	0
Item for hangings table andirons etc	1	10	0
Item in the Brewhouse chamber			
3 beds 3 coverlets blankets presse	8	0	0
Item for blankets flasket trunke		10	0
Item the rent for this yeares tithes	80	0	0

Item for debts	12	0	0
Item desperate debts	3	0	0
Suma totalis	289	6	0
[WSRO Ep I/29/205/045]			

Administration 31 Aug 1671
To daughter Frances Garbrand, spinster   [WSRO STC III/L/80]

[1] Of Oxfordshire; member of a Dutch Protestant family. Called Nicholas Harkes alias Garbrand 1638. Oxford, Magdalen, matriculated 1618 aged 18, demy 1618–1619, BA 1618, fellow 1619–1639, MA 1621, BD 1631. Ordained deacon 1622 (bishop of Oxford). Licensed preacher 1635. Vicar of Washington 1638–1671, patron Magdalen College. Rector of Patching 1660–1671, patron archbishop of Canterbury. Prebendary of Somerley 1660–1671. Married Mary Byssh of Burstow, Surr, widow, at Burstow 1652; Judith Allen, of St Bride's, London, widow, at Washington 1656 (after publication of banns in St Bride's market). Died 1671.

168. Westbourne 31 March 1614 THOMAS WILSHA [1]
Appraisers: John Tilley, William Eayles, William Guilford

	£	s	d
In primis his wearing apparell purse and girdle prized at	20	0	0
Item one Bedstedel and Curtens and curtayne rodds in the little chamber	3	10	0
Item one featherbed 2 boulsters 3 downe pillowes five blanketts and one Irish Rugge	6	0	0
Item 2 chests and one green chaire		13	4
Item 2 curtaynes for windowes 2 curtaine rodds and the staine clothes about the chamber and the curtaine for the dore	1	0	0
Item one bedstedel and one paire of Blankets	2	0	0
Item one Bedstedel curtaines and curtaine Rodds one featherbed 2 boulsters one pillow 2 blankets and one coverlet	6	10	0
Item one presse and table of beach		15	0
Item 4 chests and an old trunck	1	0	0
Item all the pewter and pewter candlestikes and salts Bason and ure and chamber potts	4	0	0
Item 24 paire of sheets 6 paire of pillow coats	20	0	0
Item table clothes and table napkins liverie cubbard clothes	10	0	0
Item 3 silver Boales 3 silver salts and one dozen of silver spoones	20	0	0
Item one saffe one beach table in the buttrie and one candle chest		6	8
Item 3 carpetts and 6 Cushons	1	6	8
Item 3 tables in the hall and one forme and side [?]plange and bench	1	0	0
Item 2 chaires in the hall one [?]rage and one shelfe		10	0
Item one wainscott furnished	1	6	8
Item one caliver sword and dagger flask and torchbox		10	0
Item one Coslett furnished	1	0	0
Item 2 stained clothes in the hall		3	4
Item one bedstedel curtaines and curtain rodds	3	10	0
Item one featherbed 2 bolsters one flockbed 2 feather boulsters and 2 downe pillowes three blankets and one arras Cover	10	10	0
Item one truckle bedstedle and featherbed	1	6	8

Item on tubb in the Chamber one liverie Cubbard and 12 stooles and one Cushion for a Cubbard	4	0	0
Item the painted clothes in the Chamber and Curtain and Curtaine rodd		10	0
Item one Bedsteddle one featherbed one boulster and one blankett	3	10	0
Item one bedstedle one featherbed one boulster one pillow 2 blanketts one Coverlett	2	0	0
Item one truckle bed one livery Cubbard and one little table		15	0
Item in the parlour one table 2 formes one livery Cubbard one chaire one planke and tressels at		12	0
Item in the milkhowse			
Item 22 cheeses	1	10	0
Item 16 trugges		15	0
Item one charne and renning tubb and two powdring tubbes		5	0
Item the cheese woots and cheese presse		5	0
Item one fatt 2 tunnes 9 kevers one bucking tubb and one other tubb and one wash tubbe	2	0	0
Item the Coopes		5	0
Item 5 barrels 3 ... and 2 firkins		10	0
Item the bucketts and dishes and trenchers		3	4
Item 4 pair of potthangers 3 barres 2 paire of Andirons one paire of Racks five spitts 2 paire of pott hooks and three Iron dripping pannes and the gridirons the [?]shuggs for [?]Larrells	2	10	0
Item all the Brasse and Brasse Candlesticks ... Mortars skimmer and basting Laddle cleaver chopping knife and chaffing dish and grate and 2 warming pannes	6	13	4
Item one kever one turne one bolting hutch and one meale chest		5	0
Item 10 charks 2 leather sacks one ... one bushell half bushell and peck buckett and shelves	1	6	8
Item hoopes and feathers	2	0	0
Item wedges prongers weights axes and other lumber		5	0
Item the Bacon at	4	0	0
Item 15 quarter of wheat and 5 of Barley	60	0	0
Item all the hogges in the gatts	9	0	0
Item 2 Carts 2 dung potts and wheles plowes and harrowes	6	13	0
Item 2 yoake of Bullocks	13	0	0
Item 6 other bullocks	10	0	0
Item 3 heifers	5	0	0
Item 2 geldings and sadles and briddles	10	0	0
Item four ... horses carte horses and plow ... yoakes and plow chaines	8	0	0
Item 8 kine and Calves and other Cowes and one Bull	30	0	0
Item ... load of Logs and the Rackes Ladder ... and planges and the hogge troughs	1	10	0
Item the pales and posts	2	0	0
Item all the poultrey in the gates		10	0
Item the billet in the gates and one grindstone	1	0	0
Item the sheep at	7	10	0
Item in the sume of ...	30	0	0
	345	1	0

[WSRO Ep I/29/206/9]

Will: made 1 May 1610; no probate found [1614]
Wife Bridget; three sons; one daughter (wife of William Mattocke); cousin John
Mattocke, archdeacon of Lewes
Two gold angels; property and land
Witnesses: John Croulle, William Upton, William Poate

[WSRO STC II/B Dean 1614 (35)]

[1] Of Derbyshire. Cambridge, Jesus, matriculated 1569, BA 1573, fellow 1573–1585, MA 1576,
BD 1586.   Ordained deacon 1585 aged 31 (bishop of London), priest 1585 (bishop of
Peterborough).   Rector of West Blatchington and of Hangleton 1585, patron of both Edward
Bellingham; of Westbourne 1592–1614, patron Richard Bellingham. Licensed preacher throughout
England and Wales 1586. Prebendary of Seaford 1587–1614. Vicar of Cuckfield 1607–1609,
patron bishop of Chichester. Married Bridget Jutton of Greatham at Greatham by licence 1590.
Died 1614; buried Westbourne.

169.Westbourne 16 March 1678 WARBERTON OWEN [1]
Appraisers: Richard Bouncer, George Sherlocke

	£	s	d
In primis his money In his Purse and all his wearing Aparrell	5	0	0
Item the Beding and Bedstedles And all In this Room where he dyed	5	0	0
Item five pair of Sheets and five Pair of pillabers 1 dozen and A halfe of napkins and four Table Cloathes	3	0	0
Item one dozen and a halfe of Spoons one Silver Bowl one dram Cup	5	10	0
Item Bookes and notes In his Study	6	0	0
Item One Bed one Bedstedle and Valians and Curtins to itt	4	10	0
Item four Chaires two gine Stooles one Little table one pair of Angerns one pair of tongs one fire panne	1	10	0
Item one Lookeing glasse one Carpett		5	0
Item one Bed and Bolsster and Bedstedle	1	10	0
Item four brasse pots Eight Brasse Kittles two warming pans four Brasse Skilletts	4	0	0
Item three dozen of putter dishes and one dozen of puter Plates four pair of puter Cansticks one dozen of puter Porringers and half a dozen of Sacers and two puter tankards one puter Chamber pott	3	0	0
Item two tables one dozen of Lethern Chaires two Carpetts Six gine Stools one pair of angerns and one pair of tongs	2	10	0
Item four Spits two driping Panns one table one pair of Angerns two Cotterels one Cubord		15	0
Item Barrels tubs and kivers and al other Lumber within doors whatsoever	1	0	0
Item one Bay mare Bridle and sadle	1	10	0
Item one Chest		2	0
Sum total	45	2	0

[WSRO Ep I/29/206/161]

Will: made 4 Feb 1678; proved 5 April 1678; testator clerk of Racton and curate to John
Clark of Westbourne
Wife (unnamed); son: William, executor; daughters: Ann, Mary (both under 23)

Overseers: Mr Pitfield vicar of Warblington, Hants, Richard Bounser, bricklayer
Witnesses: John Clark, Francis Hunt, Edward Wood, John Hurst, John Wheeler

[WSRO STC I/27/8]

[1] Baptized Abbotts Ann, Hants, 1612; son of Morgan, cleric. Oxford, New College, matriculated 1628 aged 18, BA 1633. Rector of Racton 1660–1678, patron Crown. Died 1678.

170. Westbourne 28 May 1678 GEORGE SIDGWICK [1]

Appraisers: John Bexhill, ...

	£	s	d
In primis his waring aparell and money in his purse	20	0	0
In the parler			
Item one table and sid table and 1 Couch and 8 Chaires	1	0	0
In the Parlor Chamber			
Item one Bed and beadstedell and bolster 2 pillowes two blankets one Rug one quilt and one Counterpane one table and sid Cubbard 2 Chairs 3 stooles at	3	0	0
In the little Chamber			
Item one bed and boulster one pillow 2 Coverlets one p of Curtins and vallins one bed stedell one little table 2 trunks one Chair one loking glas one window Curten	2	10	0
In the Chichen Chamber			
Item one bed and bed stedell one bolster 3 pillows 2 p of Curtins one Rug 2 Chests one sid cubard 1 p of Angians and tongs one basket Chaire at	2	0	0
In the iner Chamber			
Item one other bed and bed stedell one old coverlet and blanket and other lumber at		10	0
In the Studdey			
Item one table and Chaire and his books at	6	0	0
In the Kichen			
Item one table one Dreser one p of Angrens and tongs and fier chuffell 5 Chairs 3 joint stooles one furner and fier shuffell 2 p Cotrells one Jack one Iren Pot on Warming pan on kittle one skillet one glas Cubbard 2 spits one bras pot	2	10	0
Item in puter	2	0	0
In the buttry and Brewhous			
Item brewing vessells and other Lumber	2	0	0
Item Linen	5	0	0
Item in plate	5	0	0
Item in Money and Debts	200	0	0
Sum total	239	10	0

[WSRO Ep I/29/206/163]

Will: made 10 Nov 1676; 14 June 1677; proved 30 May 1678
Wife: Cicelye; son: John, executor, daughter: Anne (Blake)
Witness: Henry Ball   [WSRO STC I/27/25]

[1] Cambridge, St John's, matriculated 1619, BA 1623, MA 1626. Ordained deacon and priest 1626 (bishop of Llandaff). Vicar of Westbourne 1630–1678, patron Christopher Swale, rector. First wife Audrey (died 1639); married Cicely Standen, widow, at Westbourne 1644 (died day before he did). Died 1678; buried Westbourne.

171. Westbourne 29 Jan 1679 THOMAS PRYNNE, rector [1]
Appraisers: Richard Crockford, Peter Hirring

	£	s	d
In primis his weareing Apparell and money in his purse to the vallu of	15	0	0
Item three Gold rings and one Silver Spoone to the vallu of	2	0	0
Item All the Libery books to the vallu of	20	0	0
Item In old putter to the vallu of		10	0
Item foure dusks to the vallu of	1	5	0
Item one Great Cheast and one other Cheast to the vallu of	1	0	0
Item one Press one Cheast of drawes to the vallu of	1	0	0
Item Five boxes to the vallu of		5	0
Item Foure Leatheren Cheares and two other Cheares to the vallu of		18	0
Item two Little tables to the vallu of		10	0
Item one fether bed and all that belongs unto him to the vallu of	5	0	0
Item one paire of Angeraines one pare of tongs one fire pan to the vallu of		3	0
Item one hower Glase and other small things to the vallu of		5	0
Item Debts owing to the vallu of	37	10	0
Sum is	85	6	0

[WSRO Ep I/29/206/165]

Will: made 28 Oct 1678; proved 26 Feb 1679
Nephew: George son of John Clark, both executors
Witnesses: Thomas Cooper, Henry Stevens, Richard Crockford, Richard Silverlock

[WSRO STC I/27/17]

[1] Of Somerset. Oxford, Oriel, matriculated 1618 aged 13, BA (as William) 1623. Ordained deacon 1627 (bishop of Salisbury), priest 1628 (bishop of Bristol). Possibly curate of Woolley, Som, c. 1639. Rector of Westbourne 1646–1679. Licensed preacher Chichester diocese 1662. Died 1679; buried Westbourne.

172. Westbourne 29 Oct 1705 CHRISTOPHER SPENCER [1]
Appraisers: Henry Clement, Francis Hunt

	£	s	d
In the Bedchamber			
Item one Feather bed and bolster and Two Pillows One Blankett and one Callicoe Quilt and a Rugg One Bedsted matt and cord and a Suite of druggett Curtains and Curtaine rodds	8	0	0
Item One Wallnutt Tree Table and a Chest of Draws Three large Stools and Three stools sixteen small P[?ictures]	1	10	0
One close stoole and Two stands and some Earthen Ware		5	0
One pair of billows and a p of Iron doggs		5	6

In the Inner Chamber			
Three old Chests		9	0
His wearing Cloaths	4	0	0
One Screen and a deal Chest and some small Pictures		5	0
Item Twelve pounds of Tobacco		12	0
In the Maids Chamber			
Item One Feather bed and bolster and Two Pillows and a green Rugg and a bedsted matt and Cord	3	0	0
One looking Glass and One Chaire and Stoole		4	0
In his Studdy			
A parcell of Books and an old Table and one Chaire	10	0	0
In the Little Parlour			
Two Ovill Tables Six Cane Chairs Five Leather Chairs One Needlework Chaire One Lookeing Glass Sixteen small Pictures One pr of Tongs and a pr of doggs	2	15	0
In the Kitchen			
Two pair of iron dogs two fire shovells and tongs and fenders one Jack three spitts one dresser and shelves Ten Rush bottom shairs two square tables one box iron and three flatirons one pair of Gridirons and a saltbox one Coper furness four brass Candlesticks four pewter two iron Two and Twenty pewter plates one and Thirty wood plates one pewter Chamber pott one pewter bason Ten pewter dishes two pair of Cotrells one pewter Tankard one pewter bed pann and Twelve spoons one brass warming pan one pewter Ring one Tinn puding and three Coffey pots two pair of brass snuffers and snuff dish some eartheware one pair of Bellows	8	0	0
In the Sellar			
Twelve bruing vesells one botle Rack one powdring tubb three kivers and one tunn one wass tubb two bucking tubbs two brass kitles one brass pott and a parcell of Botles two buckets and a lantorne and some small things	3	10	0
In the Stable			
A parcell of Hay	5	0	0
A parcell of wood	1	0	0
A parcell of Linning	5	0	0
	53	11	6

[WSRO Ep I/29/206/207]

Will: made 4 Oct 1705; proved 5 Nov 1705
Wife Ann, executrix, with brother Nathaniel Spencer of London
Friends: Charles Leaver, rector, Racton, John Shore, physician (both living in Chichester)
Witnesses: Richard Bridgewaters, Richard and John Silverlock   [WSRO STC I/30/804]

[1] Born London, son of John, of London. School at Tinwell, Rut. Cambridge, St John's, admitted sizar 1665 aged 17, matriculated 1667, BA 1669. Oxford, incorporated 1669. Ordained deacon 1671 (bishop of Ely). Vicar of Sidlesham 1671–1680. Prebendary of Selsey 1675–1705. Died 1705; buried Westbourne.

173. Westfield 3 Jan 1688 ROWLAND PRIGG [1]
Appraisers: Ralph Edwards, John Jorden, tailor

	£	s	d
In primis In ready money	18	0	0
Item his wearing apparell	2	0	0
Item for two Little Silver Cupps and two Silver Spoones	2	0	0
In the Kitchin			
Item one Table one Old Carpett Eight Old Chayres two Joyne Stooles One Old press one Clock and Case	1	5	0
Item Two glass Cages Four Andirons two Old fire Shovels One paire of Tongs One Old Bunter		10	0
Item three Spitts an Old Jack an Old case iron and one Old warming pann		8	0
Item Eight pewter dishes and other small Pewter three Chamber potts an Old bedd pann and three porringers		15	0
In the Parlour			
Item Two feather bedds two bolsters two ruggs two Old blanketts one Old paire of Curtaines and vallence	4	0	0
Item Six leather Chayres one litle table one Cabbinett and one joynt stoole		15	0
In the Drink Buttery			
Item one Old Powdering tubb one Old Cubbord foure Drink Vessells a litle porke and an Old Tunnel		12	0
In the Wash house			
Item One Kettle one Cauldron one litle Kettle one Old Dripping pann two Old Settles seaven Olde tubbs and one Old Keeler	1	0	0
In the Parlor Chamber			
Item Ten paire of Sheets flaxen and towen	2	0	0
Item two Chests and two boxes		6	0
Item one Old flock bedd and two Old bolsters one Old bed stedle and Curtaines		6	0
In the Hall Chamber			
Item one bedstedle and bedd one Blankett one Coverlett curtaines and vallence	2	0	0
Item two Dozen of Napkins and pillowcoats	1	0	0
Item one press and books	2	0	0
Item one case of drawers one Joyne Chest and one box	1	0	0
Item Six Cushions		6	0
Item Two litle paire of AndIrons an Old fire Shovel and a paire of tongs		4	0
Due to the Testator upon specialty Item upon Bond	1	0	0
Debts without specialty			
Item due from the farmer of the Rectory of Westfield	18	0	0
Item due at Mich'as last for a yeares Pension	5	6	0
Item due for arreares of Tithes	10	0	0
Item for things unseen and forgott	5	0	0
Sum totall	170	15	0

[TNA PRO PROB 4/7800]

Will: made 4 April 1685; proved 11 Feb 1688
Wife Emme, executrix (library and manuscripts); sons: Nicholas, Thomas
Witnesses: John Thorpe, John Dan, Susannah Tolhurst   [TNA PRO PROB 11/390]

[1] Son of John, of Bristol. Oxford, Oriel, matriculated 1635 aged 16; Merton, BA 1638.
Commended by sergeant of House of Commons c. 1640. Vicar of Westfield 1655, nominated by
Lord Protector; after Restoration conformed and was collated by bishop of Chichester. Buried
Westfield 2 Jan. 1688.

174. Whatlington 7/22 June 1685 JOHN ELDRED of Battle, rector [1]

Appraisers: Thomas Smith, Thomas Watts; John Back, George Bishop

	£	s	d
In primis his wearing apparrell of all sorts	4	16	4
Item in ready money	6	14	11
Item his Watch	2	0	0
Item one small feather bed a boulster 2 blanketts and a Coverlid	1	10	0
Item a Chest of Drawers one small trunk anf five Boxes		17	6
Item four peier of sheetes and four pillowbeers eight napkins three Course towells and three table Clothes very mean	2	8	6
Item one Gun and Pistoll	1	5	0
Item one horse with Bridle and sadle	2	17	6
Item his bookes	12	16	0
Item a sword and belt		6	8
Item mony due upon a mortgage	60	0	0
Item in debts sperate	50	0	0
Sum totalis	145	12	5

[TNA PRO PROB 4/12352]

Administration 30 Apr 1685
To brother Samuel   [TNA PRO PROB 6/61]

[1] Of Huntingdonshire. Cambridge, St Catharine's, admitted sizar 1659, matriculated 1661, BA
1663. Ordained priest 1663 (bishop of Chichester). Rector of Whatlington 1663–1685, patron
Thomas Sackville. Died 1685; buried Whatlington.

175. Whatlington 23 July 1734 JOHN DODDERIDGE [1]

Appraisers: Nicholas Cheesman, Thomas Lynn

	£	s	d
Money in pocket	14	11	0
Wearing Apparrell	2	0	0
In the Kitchen			
one Clock one Jack two Spitts one fire Shovell	1	5	0
one pair of tongs three andirons one pair of Stillards one Case iron one warming pan one Gridiron one trevet		10	6
seven iron Skivells one tin driping pan one tin haylor one pewter Bason one Clever three iron Candle Sticks two small old Tables two stooles Nine Chairs		13	6

	£	s	d
one old Bunter one Cubbard twenty one pewter plates ten pewter dishes one pewter poringer one Brass pestle and Mortor	1	6	6
one Silver sale one pair of pot hangers ten pewter Spoons one Brass Grater Six trenchers		3	3
In the Parlor			
four Chairs and one Round Table		12	0
In the Little Buttery			
three powdering tubs one Cubboard one old Bunting huch ten Earthen Crocks one frying pan sum Glass bottells one stone pot two wooden trays two wooden platters one Gun	1	3	6
Sum pork and frying	1	17	6
In the Great Buttery			
one old Chair two iron porridg pots two Brass Skellets two Shruf Brass Skellets one stone morter		12	0
one wooden Gallon one ax two handbills one pair of Garden Sheers one iron Skellet and one Tovel		5	0
In the first Seller			
three old Barrells two Stolders one Chees press one Brass Cheafing dish		9	0
In Small Beer Seller			
four old Barrells one Stolder one Safe one wooden Tunnell		6	6
In the Brewhouse			
one Copper one Brew tub one Bucking Tub one form one apple trofe three old pailes	1	1	6
one hand dish two small Tubs four Small Keellers one small iron Kettell one old Table one old Lanthron one old Saw		9	0
In the Seller Chamber			
one feather Bed and Steddle and all thereunto belonging and one old deal Box	1	15	0
In the Kitching Chamber			
one feather Bed and furniture one pair of Creepers one pair of Tongs one fire pan	2	15	0
two Chairs one table one large box one pair of Bellows one old Close stool		9	0
In the Studdy			
a parcell of old Books one old portmantue one male pillion one old watch	3	3	0
In the Great Garrat			
one old parchment Scry two Sives a few old hops Eleven old Sacks one old Small Brass Kettle two old Yoaks one ox chain one horse harness two Blindfold Bridles a pair of old Quoilers som old hame woods	1	0	0
In the Little garret			
one Small old Bed one pair of Brandirons		15	0
In the Parlor Chamber			
one feather Bed and thereunto belonging	2	0	0
one Chest four boxes two Trunks		13	0
three huckleback Napkins two Damust Table Cloaths one dussen of Dammust Napkins	2	12	6
two pair of fine sheets one pair of pillow Coats five Course Table Cloaths Nine tow Towells twelve pieces of old Linen	1	4	0

Eleven flaxen Towells Eighteen Course Sheets	1	16	0
two old Stands and a pillion		5	0
In the Stable			
two old Sadles two Bridles one halter		5	0
In the yard			
one old hay syack and two pigs	7	0	0
a parcell of Cordwood and fagots	2	0	0
one old wagion four old prongs two Reaks one pair of old swifts one hog huch two Troufs	1	0	0
two old Ladders one old hay Cutter		2	0
Things unseen and forgot		1	6
Tot	55	12	9

[ESRO W/INV 2572A]

Will: made 2 Aug 1730; codicil 14 June 1732; proved 2 Aug 1734
Executors: William Hammond, Mr William Dodderidge of Sandford
Witnesses: Thomas Lynn, Edward Hussey, Richard Edwards, John Young, John Godwin
Trustees: Revd John Sorsby, Mr Giles Watts, Mr William Hammond

[ESRO W/A 54.252]

[1] Son of Robert, of Sandford, Devon. Oxford, Exeter, matriculated 1671 aged 16; New Inn Hall, BA 1674; called MA 1675. Ordained deacon 1674, priest 1675 (bishop of Exeter). Rector of West Worlington, Devon, 1676; of Whatlington 1685–1734, patron Charles, earl of Dorset. Died 1734.

176. Wiggonholt 11 May 1630 RICHARD BOLEY, minister [1]
Appraisers: Thomas Butterwicke gent of Bury, Richard Hale senior of Coldwaltham, William Chambers

	£	s	d
In primis his wareinge apparrell money in his purse and his bookes	8	0	0
Item in bonds and other specialties	77	0	0
Item one Mare and a colte	3	10	0
In the hale in the parsonage house			
Item one tabell and the tressells 2 ioyned stooles one cubbert twoe Chaires A wainescote back and three shelves	1	0	0
Lynnen			
Item twoe paire of sheetes and a table cloth	1	0	0
In the Kitchen			
Item some pewter plattors twoe litle brasse kettls and one olde iron dripping pann	..	..	..
Item one olde brasse furnace		16	0
Item one paire of Andirons		2	0
Item one olde Coverlett and blankett		5	0
Item in desperate debts	4	0	0
Item wood and other Lumbermt	1	10	0
Item all other thinges unpraized and forgott		2	0
Soma total	98	15	0

Exhibited 26 May 1630 by Edward Boley, son

[WSRO Ep I/29/209/5]

Will: made 23 April 1630; proved 26 May 1630
Daughter: Ann (wife of John Butcher); two sons: William ('a colt and 'all my wearing apparrell whatsoever both lynnen and woolen, one furnace as yet now standeth in the parsonage house, one payre of my best sheetes') [WSRO STC I/18/8]

[1] Ordained deacon 1585, priest 1586 (bishop of Gloucester). Rector of Wiggonholt 1596–1630, patron Crown. Possibly married Mary Butcher at Storrington 1612. Died 1630.

177. Winchelsea 1 May 1723 JOHN PROSSER [1]

Appraisers: Abraham Kennet of Rye, John Richardson of Udimore

	£	s	d
In primis: His silver plate redy money and apparel and four gold rings	37	0	0
His books and shelves	20	0	0
In the Kitchen			
A jack 2 spits a round table and an old musket	1	15	0
2 doz of pewter plates and 13 pewter dishes	1	14	0
Brass and Copper ware and a warming pan	1	17	6
Iron ware and Tin 10 knives and forks		17	6
A dresser and shelves and 8 ordinary chairs		13	6
In the little parlour			
Six black chairs a small table tea table and card table a corner cuppord and a dozen of tin patty panns		19	6
In the best parlour			
Cheyney and glasses in the bouffet	1	1	0
a weather glas 4 black chairs fire pan and tongs	9	0	0
In the Buttery			
3 brass pots a sopper drinking pot 2 sause pans a stew pan fish kettle calendar 3 tin pans 2 tin plates a fry pan a lamp a keiler a linen wheel 2 sives meal tub a basting ladle 11 earthen dishes 2 pewter potingers 2 spoons a safe and other small things	3	5	0
In the Brew house			
one copper 2 brew Tubbs wort tub and two keiler 4 pails and an hand dish	2	7	6
An iron kettle a pewter bason 2 sives		10	6
6 trenchers 4 sacks and a leatherne bagg		4	0
a pair of bellows working tools and a stallage		5	0
In the Cellar			
2 stands 4 Stallages 6 barrels and a charn		17	6
2 Tubbs a yest keiler 4 glas bottles four milk pans 2 brine tubs a crok and 2 stools	1	2	6
In the best chamber and stairs			
A clok wth the case and a watch	6	0	0
A pair of drawers and dressing glass	2	2	0
8 walnut tree chairs inlaid	3	4	0
fire pan tongs poker and fender		3	0
In the outer Chamber			
3 pair of flaxen sheets 3 pair of towen	3	11	0
4 table cloths 12 towels 6 workt napkins	1	12	0

	£	s	d
24 napkins 6 pillow coats and 10 towels	1	0	8
one large table cloath 10 small ones		16	0
2 towels 6 napkins 2 pair of pillow coats	5	0	0
a case of bottles and 40 dutch tiles		5	0
Flax and thread spun		18	0
A small bed and healing	1	10	0
In the little Chamber			
A bed furniture window curtains a table a glass and 2 chairs	2	17	0
In the Kitchen Chamber			
A bed and furniture	6	10	0
A small table a glass a brush 3 chairs fire pan and tongs bellows window curtains and a pewter chamber pot	1	0	0
In the little parlour Chamber			
A bed furniture and window curtains	4	0	0
an old glass and 2 old baskets and pictures		4	0
A pair of callocoe window curtains	1	10	0
In the Iner Garret			
A pair of Iron grates fender and close stool	1	1	0
A pillion and 2 pillion cloths		10	0
a pair of lethern baggs and an hand saw		4	0
3 small [?]chairs		3	0
provision of pork and the tub	1	3	0
for sack of oates another of buck wheat		10	0
Without Doors			
Two Horses and a colt and 2 saddles	12	0	0
Some hay in the barn	1	15	0
oweing to him			
In tiths at Winchelsea	20	0	0
In tiths at oare	25	0	0
In good debts as supposed	45	0	0
In desperate debts	2	0	0
Things unseen not apprised and forgot		6	8
Sume totall	231	2	4

[ESRO W/INV 1573]

Will: made 27 Jan 1723; proved 11 May 1723
Executor: Edward Wilson, vicar, Rye
Witnesses: Samuel Chittenden, Judith Hills, Isabella Smith, Ann Coburne

[ESRO W/A 51.186]

[1] Possibly Oxford. Called BA 1708. Curate of Winchelsea c. 1705; rector 1708–1723, patron Thomas Muchell, gent. Rector of Ore 1718–1723.

178. Wiston 13 May 1718 SAMUEL PADIE [1]

Appraisers : Mr Thomas Elliott and Mr Hugh Haine
[Poor original]

	£	s	d

In the Parlour
Two square Tables Six turkey work chairs one stoole one pair of

andirons one mapp of the world one other mapp and five small pictures
two pair of window curtains four drinking glasses one salt and one large
picture   ..   ..   ..
        In the Parlour Chamber
One feather bed and Bolster bedstead matt and Cords Six blanketts and
Quilt with Hangings and all belonging to it   4   ..   ..
one Table and Sideboard three chairs one pair of Tongs one pair of
bellows five window curtains one Desk and other odd things   1   5   ..
        In the Hall
fourteen quart bottles one table and carpet and one settle   16   6   ..
Two Basketts two chairs one table and forme one stand and one
hanging shelf one keeler one old sword and one small desk   14   6   ..
        In the Hall Chamber
one feather bed matt and cords curtains valiants & healing and all
belonging to it   5   ..   ..
one Chest of Draws two other chests two curtains and one stoole and
one paire of window curtains Nine pair of sheets and one odd sheet   4   ..   ..
Twelve hand towles five and twenty fine Napkins five other old napkins
Ten table Cloths and four pair of Pillow coats and one small looking
glass   3   ..   ..
        In the Library
The books and shelves   10   ..   ..
        In the Kitchen Chamber
one bedstead Matt and cord and hanging one boulster two Blanketts one
Rugg   15   ..   ..
Six older Chairs one Table and cloth three Window curtains one Silver
Tankert and two silver spoones   10   ..   ..
        In the Brewhouse
One Furnace and Tub and two keelers   15   ..   ..
one Bucking Tubb one iron kettle one stand a half bushell and one half
Tubb one Flaskett two bucketts a gallon and a half gallon two Iron potts
a block two skilletts some trenchers and other odd things   1   ..   ..
        In the Barn
A Cyder Mill and press and frame to hold apples and a small ladder   2   10   ..
two Hundred of Fagges and a half a Cord of wood a well buckett and
Rope and a Coup for chickens   1   15   ..
                                                                        157   14   6
                                    [WSRO Ep I/29/211/49]

Will: made 2 Nov 1709; proved 31 May 1718
Wife: Anne, executrix
Daughters: Hannah (decd.) Mary Burrell (decd.) Anne
Witnesses: Thomas Lancaster, Abraham Coom, junior, Richard Jackson
                                    [WSRO STC I/32/152]

[1]   Born Shrewsbury, Salop, son of James, of Shrewsbury, clothier. Shrewsbury School.
Cambridge, St John's, admitted sizar aged 19 and matriculated 1654, BA 1658; called MA 1660.
Ordained deacon and priest 1660 (bishop of Chichester). Rector of Wiston 1670–1718; of

Southease 1673–1718, patron John Amherst, esq. Licensed preacher Chichester diocese 1675. Died 1718.

179. West Wittering 1663 JOHN HARRISON [1]

[Original damaged and illegible]   [WSRO Ep I/29/213/49]

Will: made 23 Sep 1661; proved 23 Dec 1663
Sons Nicholas, executor and residuary legatee, John, of 'Rumney', Kent; daughter: Frances Vallor; brother-in-law Richard Sherryer
Witnesses: John Voake, Phillip Lock   [WSRO STC I/23/174]

[1] Attested West Wittering parish register 1661; still there 1662.

180. Woolavington 25 Feb 1647 DANIEL GERMAN [1]
Appraisers: John Ede and Anthony Todman of Waltham, Francis Sandeham and Robert Carver

	£	s	d
In the Barne at Waltham parsonage			
In primis Barley Oates peaze and Tares in the straw	30	0	0
In the gate at Waltham parsonage			
Item Five steeres	16	0	0
Item Five Watles		10	0
In the parsonage barne at Woollavington			
Item six quarters of Wheate	12	0	0
Item Fower Bushells of Peaze		10	0
Item a load of hay	1	0	0
In the parsonage gate at Woollavington			
Item three Mares and a litle stone Coult	10	0	0
Item Six Cordes of Wood	2	0	0
Item Five yonge shootes	2	10	0
In the Coppyholde barne at Woollavington			
Item Five quarters of Barley	5	0	0
Item a Load of hay	1	0	0
In the Coppieholde gate			
Item Fower cowes and a Calfe	14	0	0
Item Fortie one sheepe and six lambs	16	0	0
In a Barne at Duncton nere Wollavinton			
Item Thirteen quarters of Wheate	26	0	0
In another barne at Duncton			
Item seaven quarters of Barley	6	13	4
Item halfe a Load of hay		10	0
Item Wheate uppon the ground	7	0	0
Item One Waggon one cart Three Harrowes and other ymplements of husbandry	6	0	0
Within the parsonage house			
In the parlor			
Item One Joyned table and frame and six Joyned stooles	1	4	0

	£	s	d
Item three Joyned Chaires		12	0
Item one Court Cupbord		10	0
Item seaven Wrought Chaires and a little stoole	2	0	0
Item three Carpetts		12	0
Item Fower Cushions		4	0
Item one paire of Cast Iron Andirons With …		10	0

In the Hall

	£	s	d
Item one Joyned table and frame and six Joyned stooles	1	..	..
Item One Joyned cubbord and a chaire		13	4

In the Kitchen

	£	s	d
Item one litle table and a Chaire		2	0
Item one Iron Jack		5	0
Item twentite and two pewter dishes	2	4	0
Item One pewter Voider and a Bason and Eure of pewter two other pewter Basans and two pie plates	1	1	0
Item Eight pewter porringers and six pewter sawcers		5	0
Item two Chamber pott		3	0
Item one double pewter salt		1	4
Item One pewter pinte pot		1	0
Item One pewter flagon and one Wyne quart pott		6	0
Item two pewter Candlesticks		2	6
Item three Brasse potts and three bell skilletts	3	0	0
Item three Brasse ketles and one brasse pan	1	10	0
Item two Brasse Warminge pans		10	0
Item One Brasse Chaffinge dishe one Brasse skymmer one Brasse ladle one Brasse pessell and Morter and two Brase Candlesticks		13	0
Item two Iron potts and an Iron ketle		12	0
Item One Brasse Furnace	1	4	0
Item Five spitts three drippinge pans and an Iron Ladle	1	0	0
Item a paire of Andirons a paire of Iron Racks two paire of potthangers a fender a paire of Tongs and a fyer shovell	1	10	0
Item Dishes and spoones shelves and other Lumbery		5	0
Item one grediron and Chaffinge dishe and a leaden Weight		5	0

In the Buttery

	£	s	d
Item Eight Barrells	1	0	0
Item three kevers a Tunne a litle Vate and a Renynge tubb		10	0
Item a Bakinge trough and a Boultinge hutch		5	0
Item three standes		5	0
Item two serses a leather Botle a Baskett and a garden Rake		3	0
Item an hoo and two spitters		3	0

In the Chamber over the hall

	£	s	d
Item One Downe Bedd a Boulster and a paire of pillowes	6	0	0
Item a paire of Blanketts and a Counterpane	2	10	0
Item Five Curtins and Curtin Rodd		5	0
Item one Joyned Bedstedle Matt and Cord		13	0
Item one olde Chest and two tronkes		8	0

In another Chamber over the hall

	£	s	d
Item one Fether Bedd boulster and two pillowes	3	0	0
Item a paire of Blanketts and a Rugge	1	10	0

Item Five Curtins and Vallance and Curtin Rodd	1	0	0
Item one Bedstedle Cord and Matt With Buckrum		10	0
Item One Flockbed and Boulster one Litle Coverlett and Blanketts and one truckle bedstedle		14	0
Item One Court Cupbord With an olde Cloth thereuppon		7	0
Item and earthen painted Basan and Eure a Wooden Cupp and a paire of gould Waites		7	0
Item a paire of Andirons fier shovell and tonges a litle furr Box and a truckle Bedstedle		5	0
In the Chamber over the parlor			
Item one Fether bedd one Boulster and a paire of pillowes	2	10	0
Item One Rugge and Blankett	1	0	0
Item one Joyned Bedstedle Matt and Cord		12	0
Item One other Fether Bedd and boulster a paire of Blanketts a Coverlett a paire of sheetes a Bedstedle Matt and Cord	2	0	0
Item one Closestoole and a Chest		5	0
In another Chamber over the parlor			
Item one Flockbedd and boulster a Coverlett a Blankett a Bedstedle Matt and Cord		13	0
Item one other Flockbedd and Boulster a Coverlett and Blankett and two Borded Bedstedles and another olde flockbedd and boulster		10	0
Item Thirteene paire of sheetes and fower paire of pillowbers	5	0	0
Item Fower tableclothes a Cupbordcloth and three towells	1	0	0
Item a dozen and a halfe of table napkins		12	0
Item three Course tableclothes		3	0
Item Fowerteene silver spoones	5	0	0
Item one double guilt salt and one silver sewger Box With a litle silver spoone in it	3	0	0
Item his Wearinge apparell and Money in his purse	14	0	0
Item in good debts	10	0	0
Item Eight flitches of Bacon	5	0	0
Item Fortie pound of Butter and Eight pounde of Cheese	1	0	0
Item Poultrey		6	0
Item Tenne Sacks	1	0	0
In the Coppieholde house Within the Milkehouse			
Item Twelve truggs		6	0
Item Tenne pounde of lard		3	4
Item a Butter cherne a stand a powdring tubb a dresser table a pair of Butter skales and Fower shelves		5	0
In the Study			
Item the Library of Bookes	30	0	0
Item a deske and a table		6	0
Item Olde Iron and an Iron Beame		10	0
In the Maulthouse			
Item Five hundred of Board	2	0	0
Item two dry Vates		15	0
Item an olde Tubb and other Lumbery		2	0
Item Fower Busshells of Rye	1	0	0
Item a Mault Mill		5	0

In the Chamber over the Maulthouse

	£	s	d
Item Eight quarters of Oates	5	6	8
Item a quarter of Barley	1	0	0
Item Tenne Busshells of Tares	1	0	0
Item two Busshells of Beanes		7	0
Item Twentie and three pound of Wooll	1	3	0
Item two hundred and a halfe of lath		2	6
Item Wenscott and other Lumbery		10	0
Item Twelve pound of hopps		4	0
Item a lease of a parcell of land at Northwood Worth	100	0	0
Sum total	396	18	0
Item in Desparate debts	6	0	0
The total of all	402	18	0

23 April, Jane German, widow

[WSRO Ep I/29/215/21]

Will: made 13 Feb 1647; proved 13 April 1647
Wife: Jane, executrix; sons: Thomas (feather bed in own chamber, green rug), Robert, Peter, Henry (books now in my study in copyhold house, best gown, cloak, cassock); daughters: Jane Penicod, Grace Browning, Dorothy
Overseers: Francis Sandham, Robert Carver
Witnesses: Henry Barnard, Dorothy Gaston, Constance Bateman

[WSRO STC I/21/140b]

[1] Cambridge, King's, matriculated 1603, BA 1606, MA 1613. Oxford, incorporated as MA 1615. Ordained deacon 1608 (bishop of Rochester), priest 1609 (bishop of Lincoln). Rector of Woolavington 1609–1647, patron Crown; of Upwaltham 1614, patron Daniel Dun. Died 1647.

181. Yapton 18 March 1671 ROBERT DALGARNO [1]

Appraisers not given
Goods left unadministered by Margery Sturt, widow deceased, administratrix

	£	s	d
In primis a silver Tankard	10	0	0
Item a silver watch	5	0	0
Sum total	15	0	0

[WSRO Ep I/29/225/46]

Administration 24 Sep 1661
To Margery Sturt, mother, on behalf of Ann Dalgarno, relict, minor

[WSRO STC III/H/226]

Administration 18 March 1671 of goods of Robert Dalgarno left unadministered by Margaret Sturt, widow, deceased
To Thomas Edmonds, gent, husband of Anne Edmonds als Dalgarno, formerly wife of Robert Dalgarno   [WSRO STC III/I/134]

[1] Curate of Middleton and vicar of Yapton 1661. Died 1661; buried Yapton.

APPENDIX 1
TWO INVENTORIES WITH MAJOR COLLECTIONS OF TITLED BOOKS, 1451 AND 1791

182. Oxford 9 May 1451 HENRY CALDEY [1]

Inventory taken by John Moore, bookseller and John Mathugh, tailor[2]

	£	s	d
Unus liber 'De potentia Dei et malo' secundum Thomam, secundo folio 'poma'		13	4
Commentator super libros propheticorum, secundo folio '-cæ igitur'		3	4
Liber vocatus 'Petrus paludis' super primum sententiarum, secundo folio '-gra quo'		2	0
Psalterium glossatum, secundo folio 'titulus aliorum'		6	8
Liber Homiliarum Gregorii Papæ, secundo folio 'dum transit'		6	8
Liber vocatus 'Digestus Fortiati', secundo folio 'et quarta'		6	0
Liber vocatus 'Digestus Vetus', secundo folio 'in nomine Domini'		4	0
Liber vocatus 'Sextus' cum glossa cardinali, secundo folio 'spem gratiæ'		5	0
Liber vocatus 'Digestus Fortiati', secundo folio 'animam'		5	0
Liber vocatus 'Codex', secundo folio 'generalium'		4	0
Liber 'De diversis contentis', secundo folio 'dein fanu-'		1	8
Liber vocatus 'Casus Bernadi', secundo folio 'sum nisi'		5	0
Liber Prisciani 'in majore', secundo folio 'de corporativis'		4	0
Liber Anselmi vocatus 'Cur Deus homo', secundo folio '- lo nec'		2	4
Liber de communi glossa secundum Mattheum, secundo folio '-col lacol'		1	0
Liber 'doctrinalis', secundo folio '-er vel -ur'		1	0
Liber 'De diversis contentis', secundo folio 'propria nomina locorum'		5	0
Liber de Epistolis Senecae ad Lucilium, secundo folio 'est tecto'		2	0
Unum portiforium,[3] secundo folio 'dicentur'		6	8
Hugo de Victore de … et …,secundo folio 'fecisse et mali'		1	4
Liber vocatus Martialis, secundo folio 'nam soliditatem'		1	0
Plato in Timæo, secundo folio 'Platonis'			6
Liber 'Clementinus', secundo folio 'ipsum Dei verbum'		3	4
Vetus liber Decretalium, secundo folio 'seu natura'		1	4
Liber 'De diversis contentis', secundo folio '-tare clerici'		5	0
Pro omnibus aliis quaternis [4]		3	4
Summa [for books]	5	0	6
one old feather bolster			8
one blanket			8
one canvas ['carentinillum']		1	4
one other canvas			8
one old mattress		1	4
one blanket			8
another blanket			6
a pair of linen sheets		2	0

three linen sheets torn and repaired ['cum commissuris']			10
a coverlet		2	8
one coverlet three curtains and one red say tester			8
one russet doublet		1	0
one white tabard coat		1	8
one short green gown with hood		4	8
one other short blue gown		2	8
one hood of mixed blue colour			10
one mustard yellow ['musterde-velys']hood		1	0
one old mustard yellow ['musterde-velys'] gown		2	0
one gown of mixed red colour and hood		5	0
one other gown of mixed colour with hood		5	0
one habit and hood lined with silk			8
one russet cloak		1	8
one old mantle		1	0
one old curtain			4
one chest without a lock		1	2
a full length green gown and hood lined with silk		10	0
one canopy ['seldre'] over bed			8
various laces ['cordulis']			4
one pair of tongs			2
two pairs of bellows			3
one chair		1	0
one table with two trestles			6
one small chest without a lock			3
in money	5	0	6
Sum	8	18	6
Summa totalis	13	19	0

Goods bequeathed			
To nephew, Nicholas, one short marbled colour gown; 20 marks	13	0	0
To Master Paris: one blue habit with fur-lined hood			
To Dominus Begge: one full-length gown and green hooded habit			
To the church of St Martin		10	0
To the church of St Peter in the East		2	0
To Merton College		13	4
To St Mary Magdalen's Hall	6	12	4

Will: made 4 April 1451; proved 6 May 1451
Body to be buried in St Martin's (Carfax)
Executor Symon Godmeston, clerk
To nephew Nicholas: lands etc. in Ireland
To my fellows at the Hall lately called Maudelen Hall 10 marks for celebration of masses
13s 4d to Bell Tower of Merton College; 6s 8d to St Martin's for burial and 3s 4d for
high altar; 16d to St Mary's; 2s to St Peter in the East
Witnesses; Peter Paris MA, Thomas Smyth MA, W Heeward. MA, Richard Beernys,
chaplain, John Wellys

[Inventory and will published in *Munimenta Academica, or Documents illustrative of academical life and studies at Oxford*, ed. H Anstey (London, 1868), vol. II, p. 608.]

[1] Of Ferns diocese, Ireland. Oxford, MA; Magdalen Hall, ?fellow; St Thomas Hall, principal 1436. Ordained deacon 1437 (bishop of Bath and Wells), priest 1438 (bishop of Salisbury). Granted letters of commendation from Oxford University to archbishop of Dublin and bishop of Ferns 1438. Licensed preacher Berkshire archdeaconry 1440. Vicar of Cuckfield to 1451. Died 1451; buried Oxford.
[2] The first part of the inventory, relating to books, has been kept in Latin; the rest has been translated.
[3] Portable breviary.
[4] Gatherings or small books.

183 Rusper 28 and29 April 1791 JOHN WOOD [1]
Appraisers: Thomas Plumer, John Plumer

	£	s	d
Notes and Money in Purse			
in Bank Notes	145	0	0
In Cash	117	1	6
4 Pieces of Gold £3-12-0 Each	14	8	0
Silver	18	8	6
1 Portugall Piece	1	7	0
Light Guineas 29	30	9	0
	326	14	0

      No 1 In the Glebe Land
6 Hundred of Faggots 5 ¾ Load of Wood
      No 2 In the Hovell and Without Doors
1 Wheelbarrow 1 beer Stand 2 firms 1 bittle 1 Wood Horse a parcell
Slabs About 2 Load of Wood a parcell bricks and Tiles about 3 Load of
Broke Wood a few Chips and a parcell of Wood and poles about 3
Hand of Faggots 12 Tops of Timber and a small parcell of Dung About
2000 of Bricks and some Stone
      No 3 In the Barn and Stable
a Small parcell of Wood and Faggots 1 Garden Seat 1 Hanbarrow 1
Long Step Ladder 4 other Ladders 3 rakes 3 Scythes 5 prongs 1 Rat trap
1 Slab 2 planks 1 Hen Rip 3 Col Baskets 2 parcells of Hay 1 parcell of
Brakes 1 Seive 1 Chaff Binn 1 parcell of Boards, Laths and broomes 1
Holter 1 Horse with Bridle and Saddle 1 Dung Spud 1 Shovell 1 Horse
plogh 1 Oat Chest 2 Chains
      No 4 In the Garden
1 Stone Rowler 2 Water pots
      No 5 In the Kitchen
2 pr pothooks 3 pr tongs 2 fire Shovells 1 pr Dogs 1 pr Roasting Dogs 1
pr Gridirons 2 Trests 1 Slice 1 fender 1 pr Stilliards 1 Salt box
1.Choping knife 1 Doz of Iron Scuers and hook 1 Long Scuer 1 pr
bellows 4 spits 1 Hold fast 1 pot plate 1 Shoe Iron 1 brass Do 1 bird
Spit 7 brass Candlesticks 2 Iron Do 1 Copper Coffee pott 1 Do Tin 2
brass Extinguishers 1 brass Dog Collar 1 Copper Chafingdish 1 flash

fork 1 pr Hand Stilliards 1 pr Snuffers 1 plate Warmer 1 Toasting fork 2
tin flour boxs 1 brass peper box 1 Curtain and Rod 1 Roasting Jack with
Chain Line pulleys and Iron Weight 1 Copper Tea Kettle 1 box Iron 3
Heats 1 Hussey 2 Small Ovall Tables 1 Eight Day Clock in a Wainscott
case 2 Tin Tunnells 1 bottle Crane 2 pewter porringers 1 Eg Spoon 6
Tin pattys 26 pewter plates 12 Dishes 1 Small ps pewter 1 Coffee Mill
11 knives 14 forks 2 boxes 2 Clasp knives 1 Carvingknife 3 Drink
Glasses 1 Glass Salt 1 Vinegar Cruett 2 Viels 1 Stone Dish 2 butter
boats 3 Basens 6 brown Drink pots 3 pewter Spoons 2 pr Window
Curtains and rods 1 Small Seeing Glass 1 Slat 1 Square Deal Table 1
Ironingboard 1 Wainscott pillow and Claw Table 1 Large Oval
Wainscott Table 5 Beach Chairs Leather Seats 2 Armd and 2 Small Ash
Chairs 1 Brass Warmingpan 1 Large Copper boiler 2 flitches of Bacon
1 Silver Watch

      No 6 In the Brewhouse
1 brass furnace 1 Brewhouse 1 Brew Vatt Stand Slirer and Sieve 1
Chafingdish 1 Iron Kettle 1 Tun Tub 1 Small Tea Kettle 3 pails 2
Handishes 1 Tin Cullender 1 Tin Dish Cover 2 tin Sawcepans 1 Bell
Metall Skillet 1 Copper pint pott 1 Old Tub 1 Large brown pan 14
Peices of Earthenware 1 Jug 1 pr Small Dogs 1 firm

      No 7 In the front Parlour
1 fire Shovell tongs Dogs bellows and brush 2 pr Tobacco tongs 3 Maps
2 prints 1 Bell Metall Mortar and pestle 1 Beauroe 3 Tin Cannisters 1
Small baskett 1 bottle Stand 2 Armd Chairs 2 Leather Cushions 6
Beach Chairs Leather Seats 1 Ovall Mahogany Dineing Table and
Green Cloth 1 Wainscott pillow and Claw Table 1 Joint Stool 1 Japand
2 Quart Jug 1 Back Gammon Table and Men 1 brass Ink Stand 1
Jerman Flute Dice and boxes 1 peir Glass in a painted frame and brass
Sconces 1 painted Corner Cubboard 1 Quart Decanter and 1 pr pint Do
2 Glass Quart Mugs 5 Tumblers 17 Wine and beer Glasses 1 Cruett 1
Cream pott 2 Salts 6 Delf blue and White plates 1 Mahogany Waiter 2
China Cups and Saucers 1 bason 1 Stone Cup and Saucer 1 Tea pott 1
Stair Line 1 Iron Mortar and pestle 3 Table Matts 1 small basket 1
Cannister 12 knives 12 forks and box 2 brass Cocks

      No 8 In the Back Parlour
2 fire Shovells 2 pr tongs 2 brushes 1 pr Doggs and bellows 1 Armd
Walnuttree Chair Matted Seat and Leather Cushion 6 Small Chairs
Leather Seats 1 Cloaths Horse 1 Small Sa Table 1 Mahogany Pillow
and Claw Table 1 Walnuttree Beauroe 1 Wainscott Bofett 3 Mahogany
Tea board 1 Do Waiter 2 Maps 7 prints 1 peir Glass in a Gilt frame with
2 brass Sconces 1 Mahogany Tea Chest 1 Stand Call Bell 4 Psm Books
1 pitch pipe 1 China Bowl 5 China basons 2 Delf bowls 1 Ladle 10
plates 1 Dish 11 blue and White China Cups and 12 Saucers 12 China
Coffee Cups 6 Red and White Coffee Cups 1 Large and 2 Small Tea
pots 1 brown Quart pott 1 pint Stone pot and Stand 6 Handle Cups 3
Glass Casters and Stand

      No 9 In the Studdy
Etchards History of England in folio 1 Vol
Stackhouses Body of Divinity in folio 1 Vol

Chambers Dictionary in folio 2 Vol
Burkits Exposition in folio
Stackhouses History of the Bible in folio 2 Vols
Taylors Life of Christ in folio 1 Vol
Patricks Paraphraise in folio 1 Vol
Lowths on the Prophets 1 Vol in folio
Crudens Concordance 1 Vol in Quarto
Dr Peirceson on the Creed 1 Vol in folio
Gays Fables 2 Vols in Octavo
Paradice Lost 1 Vol in Octavo
Practice of Piety 1 Vol in Octavo
The Present State of Great Britain 1 Vol in Octavo
The Geographicall Grammer 1 Vol in Octavo
The Military History of Europe 1 Vol in Octavo
The Life of Mahomet 1 Vol in Octavo
The Life of King David 2 Vol in Octavo
The Director or Young Womans best Companion 2 books
Nomens Claturam 1 Vol
2 Bibles
A Tour through Great Britain and Ireland 4 Vol
Browns Miscellereus 4 Vol
Dean Swifts Works 14 Vol in Twelves
Baileys Dictionary 2 Books
Dr Wilkins on Naturall Religion 1 Vol in Octavo
Reeves Apology 2 Vol in Octavo
Puffendors Duty of Man 1 Vol in Octavo
Kennetts Antiquity 1 Vol in Octavo
Etchards Ecclesiasticall History 2 Vol in Octavo
2 Psm Books
Jevenall 1 Vol in Octavo
Farrringtons Sermons 2 Vol in Octavo
Dr Hicks on the Priesthood 2 Vol in Octavo
Greys Ecclesiasticall Law 1 Vol in Octavo
Joseph Andrews 2 Vol in Twelves
Preeches Odes of Horris 1 Vol in Twelves
Jno Johnson on Bloody Sacrifice 1 Vol in Octavo
1 Prayer Book
Jno Johnsons Naturall Law 1 Vol in Octavo
Colyers Sermons 1 Vol
1 Lattin Common Prayer Book
Grotius 2 Vol in Twelves
Parish Officer 1 Vol
The 39 Articles 2 Vol in Octavo
The Clergymans Companion in Visiting the Sick 1 Vol
Stanhope on the Epistles and Gospells 4 Vol in Octavo
Matthew Hole practical Discourses 5 Vol in Octavo
Spectator 9 Vol in Twelves
Homers Iliad 6 Vol in Twelves
An Explanation of Clarks Church Catichism 1 Vol

Articles of Religion 1 Vol
A Pantheon 1 Vol in Twelves
Officium Hominis 1 Vol in Twelves
An Answer to Dissenters 1 Vol in Octavo
Tatler 4 Vol in Twelves
Venners Exposition on the 39 Articles 2 Vol in Octavo
Guardians 2 Vol in Twelves
Pyles Paraphraise 2 Vol in Octavo
17 Yearly Registers
Hornicks Great Law of Consideration 1 Vol in Octavo
Beveridge thesaurus 4 Vol in Octavo
Etchards Roman History 5 Vol in Octavo
Rodgers Sermons 4 Vol in Octavo
The Religious Philosopher 3 Vol in Octavo
The Common Prayer Book
Gibsons Cicero 1 Vol in Octavo
Sherlocks Sermons 1 Vol in Octavo
2 Small Common Prayer books
Sherlock on Judgement 1 Vol in Octavo
Inness Sermons 1 Vol in Octavo
Sherlock on Death 1 Vol in Octavo
Naturall Philosophy 1 Vol in Octavo
Gentlemans Calling 1 Vol in Octavo
Bise on the Common Prayer 1 Vol
The Vanity of Arts and Sciences 1 Vol in Octavo
Beveridges Private thoughts 1 Vol in Octavo
Littletons Dictionary 1 Vol in Quarto
a Greek Lexicon 1 Vol in Octavo
Russells Works 2 Vol in Octavo
Virgill 1 Vol in Octavo
Horace 1 Vol in Octavo
Homers Eluid 2 Vol in Octavo
Wheatlys Elustration of the Common Prayer 2 books
Nelsons Feast and fasts 2 Books
Clarks Paraphraise 2 Vol in Octavo
A Defence of Infant Baptism 1 Vol
Walls History of Infant Baptism 1 Vol
Cornelius Nephus 1 Vol in Octavo
Sallust 1 Vol in Octavo
Pilgrims Progress 1 Vol in Twelves
The Clergymans Vademecum 2 Vol
Phedruss Fables 1 Vol
T Terence 1 Vol in Octavo
Eutropius 1 Vol in Octavo
Homilies 1 Vol
Midwifery Improvd 1 Vol
A Greek Testament 1 Vol
English Particulars
An Examination of the Bishop of Londons Discourses

14 Od Books

The Modern Gazzeteer 1 Vol

1 pr Doggs bellows a brush 1 pewter Ink Stand 2 Tables 1 Armd and 3 Small Chairs 1 Chest 4 boxes 1 brush 4 Horse Whips 1 Gun Rod 2 Mud Scuppets 1 pr bellows 1 Small Seeing Glass 7 prints 18lbs of Candles 1 pr of Garden Sheers 1 fender 1 Bell 1 Dog Chain Sundry Nails and pins 2 pr Seizzars 1 Rule 36 Marbles 1 Girdle 1 poatch bag and shot 2 Window Curtains 2 Rods About 2lbs Soap 1lb of Thread Some paper and brush Hammer 1 pr pinchers 1 pr Hinges 2 Gimblets g with 2s and 6d in Silver and 4s and 11d in halfpence

No 10 In the Passage

Dogs 1 Jack Candlestick 1 Powdering tub 1 Dust Shovell 1 Lanthorn 2 baskets 1 Bridle

No 11 In the Wood Room

Parcell of Wood 7 Barrells 1 Bucking tub 2 Deal Ceelers 2 Ovall Ceelers 1 Stand 5 Round Ceelers 1 Tan Tub 1 Bushell Basket 4 flag do 2 Hand baskets 3 Wood bottles 2 Axes 1 Hanbill 1 Spitter 1 pr Garden Sheers 2 Saws 1 Mattock 2 Hoes 2 Garden Rakes 1 Hammer 1 Bag with feathers

No 12 In the Pantery

3 Trays 1 Wood platter 1 Chopingblock 1 small Ceeler 2 brass Skillets 2 Bell Metall Skillets 3 Sawcepans 1 pr Steps 1 Rush boat 1 Marble Mortar 1 Large Safe 1 Large brass pan 1 frypan 1 Drippan and Tin 1 Cleaver 1 Block 1 old Tub 1 pye board 1 brass Boiler 1 Iron pott 1 Spining wheell and reel 2 Large Beams and 2 pr Scales 4 Iron Half Hundred Weights 1:4 Hund 1:14lbs wth 2:7lbs 1:4lbs 1:2lbs and 1:1lbs 1 Meat Screen 12 Trenchers and Rack 2 baskets 2 Mouse Traps 2 Crocks 1 Jug 7 pans 2 Ovall Stone Dishes 17 plates 5 Doz Quart bottles 1 Doz pints

No 13 In the Cellars

8 Barrells 5 Stands 2 brass Cocks 1 Large Stone bottle About 6 Doz Glass bottles

No 14 In the Apple Room

6 Oak Chests 1 box 1 Trunk 8 Pewter Dishes 26 Plates 1 Jack Candlestick 1 Wig block 1 Bell 1 Deal Chest

No 15 In the Maids Room

1 Bedstead and Sacking with Cheyney furniture and Rods 1 Feather Bed 1 boulster 2 pillows 3 Blankets 1 Quilt 1 Armd Cane Chair 1 ash Chair 1 Small Table 1 Small Seeing Glass

No 16 In the Kitchen Chamber

1:4 Post Bedstead and Sacking with Yellow furniture and rods 1 Feather Bed 1 boulster 2 pillows 3 Blankets 1 Quilt 1 Truckell Bedstead and Sacking with Blue Lincey Curtains and rod 1 small feather Bed 2 Boulsters 2 Blankets 1 Quilt 1 Night Stool and Earthen pan 1 Deal Cloathes press 1 Brass Blunderbuss 1 Walnuttree Dressing Table with 4 Drawers 1 Chest Draws 1 Swing Glass in a Walnuttre frame 1 fire Shovell tongs Dogs bellows and brush 1 Night Chair and Earthenpan 6 Walnuttree Chairs Matted Seats 1 Staind Chair 2 prints 1 Cloaths Horse 1 Bed Waggon 2 Deal boxes 1 Oak box 1 Chest 2 Chamber pots 1 Trutt

2 pr Window Curtains 2 Rods 2 Matts 1 portmantua 3 Small Jars 2
Drink pots 1 Hedge Bill

> No 17 In the Housekeepers Room

1 Bedstead and Sacking with Yellow Cheyney furniture and rods 1
Goose Feather Bed 1 boulster 2 pillows 3 Blankets 1 Quilt 1 Dressing
Table with 3 Draws 1 Swing Glass 1 Chest Draws 1 Curtain Rod 5
Beach Chairs Matted Seats 1 Od Chair 2 Maps 6 prints

> No 18 In the Best Chamber and Closett

1:4 Post Bedstead and Sacking with Green Stuff Damask furniture and
Rods 1 Goose feather Bed 1 boulster 2 pillows 3 Blankets 1 Quilt 1
Dressing table 1 pr Checkd Window Curtains and rod 2 old Chest
Draws 1 Swing Glass in a Walnuttree frame with 3 Draws 1 Small
Glass 1 Walnuttree Armd Chair and Cushion and 6 Small Chairs with
Stuff Damask Seats 2 Staind Chairs 2 Stools 1 pr Small Dogs 1 fire
Shovell and tongs 1 pr Dogs with brass fronts 1 brass fire Shovell and
tongs 1 bellows and brush 3 Matts 11yds 2 Guns 1 Stair broom 1
Scrubbing brush 1 Lanthorn 1 Doz bottles 1 pistoll

> No 19 In the Garretts

1 Stump Bedstead and Sacking with old blue Hangings and rods 1
feather Bed and boulster 3 Blankets 1 Coverlet 1 armd Cane Chair 1
Ash Do 1 Oak Chest 4 ½ Quarters of Oats 13 Sacks 1 Iron fire Rack 2
Ratraps 2 flaskets 2 Hampers 1 Wantey A parcell old iron About 7 Doz
bottles 4 old Chairs 1 Small Chest 1 Small Ladder 2 Trussells and
Wings 1 Smoak Jack 1 firm 1 brush and some Lumber 1½ bottles

> No 20 Plate brought from Mr Woods House that was then
> there

4 Table Spoons 2 pr Tea tongs 17 Tea Spoons 2 Ps Spoons 1 Small 2
Handle Cup 2 pr Spurs

Plate at Geo Plumers

1 Tankard 1 Coffee Pott and Stand 1 porringer 13 Table Spoons 1
Cream Strainer 3 Casters 1 ½ pint pott 1 punch Ladle 2 Salts 2 pr Shoe
Buckells 2 Stock Buckels 2 Seals 7 Mourning Rings at the House 1
Large Gold Do 1 pr Sleeve buttens 2 Bath Rings 1 pr Glass buttons 1
Silver Watch

> No 21 Linen

51 pr Sheets 33 pillow Cases 45 Table Cloths 83 Towells 75 Napkins
77 yds New Cloth 5 Ash Cloths 8 Small Cloths 1 White Quilt 4 Yds
Wroch Cloth

> No 22 Wearing Apparell and Sundrys

1 frock and Waistcoat 2 blue Great Coats 1 Grey Great Coat 8 pr
breeches 1 pr flannell Lineings 3 Coats 3 Waistcoats 4 black Gowns 1
Morning Gown 2 Round frocks 49 Shirts 22 Night Caps 15 Colourd
Hancercheifs 7 White Do 1 White Workd Waiscoat 1 pr Sturrup
Leathers and Irons 4 pr Shoes 3 pr boots 1 pr boot Legs 15 pr Stockings
1 Telliscope 4 Psm books 1 pr Money Seales 1 Silk Hancerchief 2
favours 2 yds Ribben

	£	s	d
Houshold Goods, plate, Linen and Wearing Apparell, Horse, Wood, etc.			
	262	8	8
Notes and Cash	326	14	0
All the Within Mentioned Articles Valud and Appraisd at the sum of			
five Hundred Eighty Nine pounds two Shillings and 8d	589	2	8
By Us: Thos Plumer Jno Plumer			

The under Mentioned found since			
14 Coat and 15 brest Silver Buttons			
1 Ps of Portugall Gold	6	15	0
1 Ps of Do	3	12	0
1 Ps of Do	1	16	0
1 Ps of Do	1	7	0

[Horsham Museum MS 358.2]

Will: made 20th July 1790; proved 4 May, 1791
Executors: John Burry of Horsham, apothecary, William Garrett of Ifield
Bequests:
To James Wood of Hickstead Place: Ockley Farm in Keymer
To Henry Wood of Henfield: All other real estate and advowson of Rusper; silver plate 'in memory of the family'
To housekeeper, Mary Stone: £500 (in hands of Thomas Wenham of Newdigate on mortgage); 6 silver teaspoons, pair of silver tea tongs (marked EW); 2 large silver table spoons; choice of bed and all belonging; two pairs of sheets; three blankets; and all goods and furniture sufficient for a single person, unless she 'has anything to do with James Chapman of Rusper', in which case all must be returned to Henry Wood, as 'I esteem JC to be a man of a very bad principal'
To 'my girl' Hannah Boorer: Interest and dividends for life on £1000 bank stock
To John Henry Lintot of Cowfold: Interest and dividends for life on £6000 bank stock
£200 for access road for glebe land
Remainder of moneys between tenants: George Bennett, John Lee and lessor (unnamed)
Witnesses: William Plumer, draper, John Lepard, farrier, James Illman, wheeler

[TNA PRO PROB 11/1205]

[1] Son of James, of Keymer. Oxford, Brasenose, matriculated 1738 aged 19, BA 1742. Cambridge, Peterhouse, MA 1751. Ordained deacon 1742, priest 1743 (bishop of Chichester). Licensed curate of Rusper 1742; rector 1743–1791, patron James Wood of Keymer, probably his father. Died 1791; buried Rusper; monument in church says he was 'very easy in his demands of tythes'.

184. Bosham 28 Sept 1679 SAMUEL TANGLEY [1]

Ingrossetur The Accompt of William Hale principall Creditor and Administrator of all and singuler the goodes Chattells and Credites of Samuel Tangley late of the parish of Bosham in the Countie of Sussex wthin the Diocesse and Archdeaconry of Chichester Clerke deceased made as well of and uppon all such goodes Cattells Chattells and credites of the sayd deceased wch since his death have come to the handes of this Accomptant As also of all such paymentes and disbursementes wch this Accomptant hath paid and appended in and about the Administracon of the same goodes Exhibited this Eight and Twentith day of September Anno Dni 1679

	£	s	d
The Charge			
In primis this Accomptant chargeth herselfe [*sic*] wth all and singuler the goodes Chattells and Credites of the sayd deceased menconed and comprized in an Inventory thereof made and exhibited into the Registry of this Court amounting to the summe of	52	15	0
Summa patet			
The Discharge			
In primis this Accomptant craveth allowance for the funerall expenses of the deceased	8	12	10
Item payd for taking the letters of Administracon wth a day for an Inventory the Kings duty for the Inventory the Proctors Fees and all other charges and expenses for myself and suretyes in and about the same	1	8	8
Item paid for horsehire and other charges and expenses at the time of apprizing the goodes of the deceased		8	0
Item paid to Robert Whicher owing by the Deceased	5	0	0
Item paid to Nicholas Mills	3	0	0
Item paid to John Bucknell	5	12	0
Item paid to George Mills	5	0	0
Item paid to John Peachey Esq	4	9	0
Item paid to James Hartley		9	0
Item paid to the servant maid due for wages	1	6	0
Item this Accomptant craveth allowance for monies due to him from the deceased	23	11	0
Item for ingrossing and exhibiting of the Inventory		5	0
Summa	59	1	6
Ordinary Charges			
In primis for drawing this Accompt and Counsell about the same		5	4
Item for examining this Accompt		3	4

Item for admission thereof			8
Item for the Apparitors Fees		1	0
Item for double ingrossing this Accompt in parchmt		6	8
Item for the Quietus est under the seale		17	0
Summa	1	14	0
Summa totalis expositor et exponendorum	59	6	10

Sic restat in manibus huius Computan[?] nil sed est in surplusagio ultra
vires Inventorii

summa	6	11	10

[WSRO Ep I/33/1674]

¹ His inventory is **21**.

185. Fittleworth 15 March 1670 WILLIAM HINDE [1]

Ingrossatur The Accompt of William Hinde, gent, the son and Administrator of all and
singuler the goodes Chattells and Credites of Mr William Hinde Clerk late Vicar of
Fittleworth wth[in] the Archdenary and dioces of Chichester deceased, made as well of
and uppon all such goodes and Chattells of the sayd deceased as have Come to the handes
of this Accomptant as of all such debtes Charges and paymentes as hee hath payd and
discharged since the death of the sayd deceased and exhibited the 15th day of March Anno
dni 1669

	£	s	d
The Charge			
This accomptant chargeth himself wth all and singular the goodes Chattells and Credites of the sayd deceased comprized in an Inventory thereof made and exhibited into the Registry of this Court extending to the summe of	416	14	2
Summa patet			
The discharge			
Peticons of allowances			
In primis for the letters of Administracon and other charges thereabout	1	3	4
Item for the severall Charges of the sayd deceased	15	0	0
Item for severall small debtes owing by the sayd deceased and the charges of his sicknes since payd by this Accomptant	6	0	0
Item this Accomptant craveth allowance for monies payd by him for The deceasedes bord at Petworth in six yeares the summe of	90	0	0
Item due more to this Accomptant for boarding the said deceased and others at his request	20	0	0
Item payd by this Accomptant unto Mercy Willet als Hinde widow Daughter of the sayd deceased for her part of the remaynder of his goodes the summe of £109 6s. 8d. besides eight hundred poundes wch the sayd deceased gave her for her marryage porcon at and since the tyme of her marryage So he craveth allowance of the summe of	109	6	8
Summa	241	10	0

Ordinary charges of this Accompt

In primis for drawing this Accompt and for Counsell thereabout	5	4
Item for examyning of this Accompt	3	4
Item for admission thereof		8
Item for double ingrossing this Accompt in parchment	6	8
Item for calling this Accompt to pass his Accompt	1	0
Item for the Quietus est under seale	17	0
Item for exhibiting and ingrossing the Inventory of the goodes of the sayd deceased	3	4

Summa	1	17	4
Summa totalis expositorum	243	7	4

Sic remanet in manibus huis Computantis summa	172	17	0

[WSRO Ep I/33/1669]

¹ His inventory is **58**.

186. Merston 19 Feb 1677 DAVID BLANEY ¹

The Accompt of Hester Blayney widdow the Relict and Admistratrix of all and singuler the goodes Cattells Chattells and Credites of David Blayney late of the parish of Merston in the County of Sussex wthin the diocesse and Archdeconery of Chichester Clerke deceased wth his Nuncupative will annexed Made as well of and uppon all such goodes Cattells Chattells and Credittes of the said deceased wch since his death have come to the handes of this Accomptant As also of all such paymentes and disbursemtes wch this Accomptant hath payd and expended in and about the Admistracon of the same goodes Exhibited this Nineteenth day of February Anno Dni juxta etc[?] 1676

	£	s	d
The Charge			
In primis this Accomptant chargeth herself wth all and singuler the goodes Cattells Chattells and Credites of the said deceased menconed and expressed in an Inventory thereof made and Exhibited into the Registry of this Court amounting to the Summe of	296	12	6
Summa patet			

The Discharge			
In primis this Accomptant craveth allowance for the funerall expenses of the decd and a sermon	5	0	0
Item payd for drawing the will the Fees of the letters of Admistracon ingrossing and registering the will ingrossing and exhibiting of the Inventory his Maties duty for the same, the produccon of the witnesses the Proctors Fee and all other charges and expenses in and about the same	1	15	0
Summa	6	15	0

Ordinary Charges

In primis for drawing this Accompt and Counsell about the same		5	4
Item for admission thereof			8
Item for examining this Accompt		3	4
Item for the Apparitors Fee		1	0
Item for double ingrossing this Accompt in parchment		6	8
Item for the Quietus est under the seale		17	0
Summa	1	14	0
Summa totalis expositor et exponendorum	8	9	0

Sworn before me …	288	3	6

[WSRO Ep I/33/1676]

[1] His inventory is **99.**

187. Nuthurst [?]17 May 1684 JOHN TAYLOR [1]

[The tops of each of the three pages of this account are torn]

Franc[?is] … , Elizabeth Tayler and Mary Tayler
 exhibited this [?]seventeenth day of May Anno dni 1684

	£	s	d
The Charge			
In primis these Accomptantes Charge themselves wth all and singuler the goods Cattells Chattells and credites of the sayd deceased menconed and comprized in an Inventory thereof made and exhibited into the Registry of this Court amounting to the summe of	141	0	3
Summa patet			
The discharge			
In primis these Accomptantes crave allowance for the funerall expences of the decd		6	0
Item these Accomptantes likewise crave allowance for the fees of proving the will taking of letts of Admstracon letts of guardianship Proctors fees and other Charges and expences in and about the same	3	7	4
Item payd to Major Bridger in full on a bond of £80 due from the decd	10	11	0
Item payd to Thomas Tingler moneys due to him from the decd as appears by his bill		11	10
Item payd to the widow Lingfeild butcher for meate due from the decd		8	4
Item payd to William Vinall of Cowfold for three Cheeses due from the decd		6	6
Item payd to William Stamper for bottles due from the decd		4	0
Item payd to John Pike for mending the decds Clothes		3	6
Item payd to Mary Waterton for wages due from the decd	1	0	0
Item payd to Will daniel for six bushells of mault due from the decd	1	0	0

Item payd to Thomas Parsons for three nailes of butter due from the decd	8	0
Item payd to Thomas Parsons more for fetching two loads of brickes for the decd	3	0
Item payd to him more for fetching one Loade of goods from Cuckfeild for the decd two loads of sands from the forrest	9	0
Item due to this Accomptant John Roberts for a book debt due from the decd	1 1	4
Item payd to Thomas Parsons for a Loade of lime due from the decd	12	0
… for Oranges and lemons …	..	..
… Paid John Robertes for Phy[si]ck in time of his sickness	1 13	4
Payd to Thomas Sheppard for laying stone over the decds grave	1	4
Item more payd to him for beere at the sale of the decds goodes	4	8
Item payd to Mr Thomas Burrell for Clothes he bought for Elizabeth Taylor when shee lived wth him	16	2
Item payd to Mr George Bridger for materialls to make Up a suite of Clothes for Thomas Taylor	8	6
Item payd to John Pike for making the sayd Thomas Taylor a new suite and mending his old	5	6
Item payd to Richard Simes of Slaugham for bording and schooling Mary Taylor for a yeare	7 10	0
Item payd to him for two paire of shoes and mending the old	4	0
Item payd to Mr Stall for a new suite for Thomas Taylor	1 6	6
Item payd to John Pike for making the suite and mending the old	5	0
Item payd to John Pike senr for making two new coates for Mary and Elizabeth Taylor	6	6
Item payd to John Jenden for … paire of shoes and mending the old	5	10
Item payd to the widow Seale for thred for Elizabeth Taylor		6
Item payd for a paire of shoes the knitting a paire of stockings Incke and a horne booke	1	11
Item payd to Thomas Harman for severall shelves and setting them up at Mr Gobles shop for the placeing Mr Taylors bookes wch shelves Mr Goble afterwardes had for the rent of his shop	6	6
Item payd to John Jenden for a paire of new shoes	2	2
Item payd to Richard Hunt for writing three Catalogues of Mr Taylors books	2	6
Item payd to John Waterton for a Journey for him and his wife to [?dr] Hamtons for the taking the youngest child being her Goddaughter and for hire of two horses	4	6
Item pr to Mr Hall for a new Coate for Mary Taylor	10	0
Item payd to John Pike senr for making two new coates for Mary and Elizabeth Taylor	6	6
~~Item due to this Accomptant John Robertes for Physsike for the decd in his last sicknes 33s 4d~~		4
Item for one paire of gloves for Elizabeth Taylor		3

Item for a knife and a paire of Gloves for Thomas Taylor			8
Item payd to Mr Hart for tuneing the Virginalls		10	0
Item for two paire of Welsh stockings for Thomas Taylor		1	2
Item payd to Mathew Weston for the dying and dressing one old Carpett to make the Children Clothes		3	0
… Botten for … house aft[er the] sale …	..	..	..
Item cleaning three Carp[ets]	..	..	..
[?Mr or Mrs] Tredcrof[t]e	..	..	..
Item payd for the Counting be[ads?]	..	..	..
Item payd for paper at several times	..	..	..
Item payd to Edward Wildfire for Crying at the sale		5	0
Item payd to John Walder for writing at the sale		3	7
Item payd for Carrying the decds bookes to towne		5	0
Item to Will Jenden for a paire of shoes for Thomas Taylor		2	2
Item payd to John Pike for making one new suite and mending two old suites for Thomas Taylor		5	6
Item pd for a paire of gloves for Thomas Taylor			6
Item payd to John Jenden for a paire of shoes for Thomas Taylor		3	0
Item payd to him for soleing two paire of shoes	1	0	0
Item payd to Richard Sims for halfe a yeare's bord and moneys hee disburst for Mary Taylor	4	2	4
Item payd to Mr Hall for Clothes for Mary and Elizabeth Taylor		14	0
Item payd to John Waterton for the bord of Elizabeth Taylor and moneys hee disbursed	3	1	10
Item payd to John Jenden for two paire of shoes for Thomas Taylor		5	6
Item for the Charges of these Accomptants in Coming to Chichester to passe this Accompt	1	10	0
Summa	49	10	0

Ordinary Charges

In primis for drawing this Accompt and Counsell about the same		5	4
Item for examining this Accompt		3	4
Item for the admission thereof			8
Item the Apparitors fee		1	0
Item for double ingrossing this accompt in parchmt		6	8
Item for the Quietus est under seale		17	0
Summa	1	13	0

Summa totalis exposit et exponendor	100	14	1
…	90	5	5

[WSRO Ep I/33/1684]

[1] His inventory is **111**.

188. Plumpton [1682] JAMES BENNETT [1]

The Accompt of Anthony Nethercott Clerk one of the Executors named in the last Will and Testament of James Bennett late of Plumpton in the County of Sussex Clerk Deceased as well of all such Goods Chattells and Debts which have come to his hands possession or knowledge since the said Deceaseds death as alsoe of all such necessary disbursements as hee hath laid out since his death as followeth (videlicet)

	£	s	d
The Charge			
In primis this Accomptant doth Charge himselfe with the summe of Six hundred fifty seaven pounds Thirteene shillings and one penny being the summe totall of the sd Deceaseds personall estate which is come to his hands possion or knowledge since his death particularily mentioned in the Inventary hereunto annexed	657	13	1
Item this Accomptant doth declare that if hee doth hereafter receive ~~any~~ the sume Of six pounds seaventeene shillings and six pence or any part thereof being a Desperate Debt due to the said Deceased alsoe mentioned after the Summe totall of the Inventory hereunto annexed he will charge himselfe therewith			
The Discharge			
This Accomptant craveth allowance for the severall summs hereafter Mentioned by him paid and laid out as followeth (videlicet)			
In primis paid for Funerall Charges	12	11	0
Item ~~paid to Mr Nethercote~~ this Accomptant craveth allowance for the sum of £10 for a Debt due to him by the said Deceased upon a Note	10	0	0
Item paid to Mr Lintott a Debt due to him by the sd Deced on his Booke	6	14	3
Item paid to one Thomas Lee a Debt due to him by the Deceased the summe of	4	8	6
Item paid some other small Debts due by the Deceased	7	16	4
Item paid more some other small Debts	2	1	6
Item this Accomptant craveth allowance for the summe of two hundred Eighty twoe pounds by him paid for the severall Legacyes given by the said Deceaseds last Will	282	0	0
Item Cloths given by Will	4	0	0
Item Expences in Housekeeping after the said Deceaseds death	2	17	11
~~Item for Expences in Housekeeping after the Deceaseds Death~~	~~2~~	~~9~~	~~5~~
Item for Expences in Travelling November the fifth 1681 About the said Deceaseds Estate the Summe of	6	0	0
Item for Expences in going to receive Rent at Milton in Kent And Taxes	6	15	1
Item for Expences for carriage of Goods and repairs for provinge the Deceaseds Will double Ingrossinge the Inventarye Exhibiting the same and for advice concerninge the said Deceaseds Estate the summe of	10	5	9
Item ~~Expences~~ paid by this Accomptant for a journey and for Messengers the summe of	3	0	0
Item paid by this Accomptant to the Thresher	1	1	10
Item spent for Wood	3	10	6
Item spent for Hay	1	0	0

	£	s	d
Item paid for Chimney Money and to the Glaziour and laid out about the Sheepe Walke	16	0	0
Item paid for a journey to Plumpton the first of May 1682 with Letters	7	5	0
Item this Accomptant craveth allownce of the summe of three pounds Eight shillings for his Expences in coming twice ~~severall~~ to London in May 1682 to give this his Accompt	3	8	11
Item hee alsoe craveth allowance for the summe of fourty Shillings by him paid for advice about passing this Inventary and Accompts for draweinge Copyeing and Ingrossing the same Proctors fees Acts of Court and other Charges thereunto Incident	2	0	0
Sum	362	4	0
Soe that there is remaining in this Accomptants hands (all things deducted and allowed) the summe of	295	9	1

[TNA PRO PROB 11/364]

[1] His inventory is **118**.

189. Thakeham 13 Dec 1670 WILLIAM CORDEROY [1]

Ingrossatur The Accompt of Margaret Corderoy the Relict and Admistratrix of all and singuler the goodes, Chattells and credites of Will Corderoy late of the parish of Thakeham in the County of Sussex wthin the diocesse and Archdeconry of Chichester Clerk deceased made as well of and uppon all such goodes Cattells Chattells and credites of the said deceased as since his death have come to this Accomptantes handes As also of all such paymentes and disbursementes as this Accomptant hath paid and expended in and about the Administracon Exhibited the Thirteenth day of december Anno Dni 1670

	£	s	d
The Charge			
In primis this Accomptant chargeth herselfe wth all and singuler the goodes chattells and credites of the said deceased menconed and comprized in an Inventory thereof made and exhibited to the Registry of this Court amounting to the summe of	87	3	2
Summa patet			
The Discharge			
Item paid for the fees of a Comission, the letters of Admistracon and other charges about the same	1	10	0
Item paid John Lee owing by the deceased		9	0
Item paid Henry Coles for Mault owing by the deceased		4	6
Item paid Mr Mellish for wheat owing by the deceased	1	2	0
Item paid … Barnes for meate owing by the deceased		6	6
Item paid Mr Gellibrand owing by the deceased	1	15	0
Item paid ... Parsons a Taylor owing by the deceased		3	0

Item paid to a Tender in the time of the deceasedes sicknes		3	0
Summa	6	13	0

Ordinary Charges			
In primis for drawing of this Accompt and counsell about the same		5	4
Item for examining of this Accompt		3	4
Item for admission thereof			8
Item for warning this Accomptant to passe her Accompt		1	0
Item for double ingrossing this Accompt in parchment		6	8
Item for the Quietus est under the seale		17	0
Summa	1	13	0

79	16	2

[WSRO Ep I/33/1670]

[1] His inventory is **155.**

GLOSSARY
Some of the unusual or obscure words used in the inventories

Andirons	Firedogs for supporting burning wood on hearth
Arras	Superior tapestry hangings
Ashcloth	Placed over the washtub with marshmallow leaves; water was poured through to soften it before washing clothes
Augur	Boring tool to make holes
Aumbry	Large cupboard with doors, originally for food, but later for books, linen etc
Back	Fire back, usually of iron
Bayle	Loop handle of bucket
Beam	Transverse bar for scales
Bed	Filled mattress
Bedstedle	Wooden framework of a bed
Beke	Anvil with two sharpened ends
Bell metal	Alloy of copper and tin
Bill, byll	Pruning tool
Brake	Hook or sickle for uprooting or teasing out; often used in relation to flax or hemp
Brandiron	Gridiron, sometimes an andiron; iron tripod from which to hang cooking vessels over fire
Broche	Alternative term for spit
Bucking tub	Washing tub
Bunting, bolting hutch	Trough for sifting flour
Bushell	Measure for 8 gallons of dry goods
Calliver	Light musket
Canvas	Fabric used in medieval times as material for bedding in mattresses, coverlets and sheets
Cage	Open fronted cupboard for glassware etc
Carpet	Usually a cloth for cupboards, tables & benches
Chaffing dish, chaffer	Small portable iron dish filled with charcoal to keep food placed above warm
Chamber	Usually a first floor room, unless otherwise indicated
Chapes	Hooks to link harness to plough
Clock	Timepiece; mechanism for operating a spit jack
Cooler	All-purpose wooden tub
Cord	128 cubic feet of cut wood (8ft x 4ft x 4ft); see also 'matt and'
Costrel	Flask with pieced projections for a carrying cord or strap
Cradle clapes	?Clasps on which to hang a cradle
Creepers	?Coal tongs
Cruse	Drinking cup
Delfe	Quarry or pit
Desperate debts	Those unlikely to be honoured
Diaper	Twilled, unbleached linen
Drawing table	With pull-out leaves
Dung pot	Tub attached like pannier to carry manure to the fields

Ell	The English ell was 45 inches, to be superseded by the 36-inch yard
Falling table	With hinged flaps
Fan, fann	Winnowing basket or shovel for separating chaff
Fat, vat	Large vessel for liquids
Fetches, vetches	Leguminous plants for cattle fodder
Fire pan	To collect hot ashes; a portable brazier
Firkin	Barrel for 56 lbs or 9 gallons
Flaskett	Clothes basket or tub
Flesh hook	Long bar with two or three hooks for extracting meat from pot or cauldron
Flock bed	Made from wool refuse or torn-up cloth
Follow, vallow	Flat circular piece of wood used in pressing cheese, in conjunction with hoops
Frame	See table
Frying pan	With a long handle, or rings for attachment to pothooks
Furnis, furnace	Boiler
Galleypot	Small earthenware pot used especially for ointment
Glass cage	Shelf or open cupboard for glasses
Graffing saw	For grafting woodwork or trees
Gridiron	Metal grid with short feet and long handle for grilling food
Healing stone	Split sandstone for roofing
Heare	Coarse open fabric of horse hair
Heffer, heyffer	Young cow that has not calved
Hitchell	Tool for dressing flax and hemp
Hogg	Year-old pig
Hogshead	Barrel with 54 gallons of beer or 46 of claret
Holland	Fine linen, named after the Dutch province from which it originated
Hoops	Used in conjunction with follows/vallows in cheese making
Hull bed	Mattress filled with wheat hulls or husks
Hutch	Chest with a curved lid
Irish rug	White embroidery on white ground
Jack	Machine for turning roasting spit
Joyned, joynt	Furniture jointed and pegged by a joiner, rather than of boards nailed by a carpenter
Keeler, cooler	Wooden tub used in brewing
Keen, kine	Cattle
Kettle, kittle	Round iron pot to hang from a chain over the fire
Kilderkin	Barrel measuring 18 gallons
Ladder	Framework to fix to front and back of a wain to take a load of hay or corn
Latten, letten	Alloy of copper, zinc, lead and tin as used for monumental brasses; thin metal plates
Lead	Leaden milk pan
Limbeck	Still (alembic) for making liquor
Livery cupboard	With perforated doors for keeping food
Load	Could be specifically 36 trusses of hay each weighing 56 lbs

Loaft, loate	Loft
Matt and cord	Net-like base formed in bed frame to support woven rush mat on which was placed the filled mattress or 'bed'
Mattock	Pick
Nail, nayle	Weight measurement of 8lbs; length measurement of 2.5 inches
Neding trough	For bread making
Occumy, alcany	Mixed metal harder than pewter
Oast hair	Mesh on which hops were laid while drying
Pair of tables	Usually folding, for games such as backgammon
Panche, panchion	Large earthenware bowl
Panel	Saddle or saddle blanket
Panyer, panier	Basket for carriage by a horse
Peck	Quarter of a bushell
Peel, peel, pyle	Flat, long-handled shovel for placing dough in a hot oven, and drawing out the baked loaves
Petuana	Type of material
Pin	Small cask or keg holding 4.5 gallons
Poke, poak	Sack for hops weighing about 168 lbs
Powdering tub	In which to salt meat
Posnet	Small basin or pot with three feet
Pillow cot, ber	Pillow case
Press cupboard	With doors and shelves for clothes, linen, books
Quarter	Measure of grain equal to 8 bushells; weight measurement of 28 pounds
Quishen	Cushion
Rack	Iron bar or bars to hold a spit; fixed or moveable frame to hold fodder for livestock
Renning tub	For cheese making
Ringer	Crowbar or hammer for driving wedges
Rodd chair	With turned components
Rundlet	Small cask
Rug	Counterpaine
Safe	Food cupboard, usually with woven panels for ventilation
Say	Fine serge material
Scrutore	Escritoire or desk
Searcher	Fine sieve or strainer
Seed lip, lep	Basket for sowing seed
Setting stick	Implement for making pleats or sets of ruffs
Shaul	Wooden shovel without a handle for putting corn into a winnowing machine
Shoot, shut	Young pig
Side board	Long table without a cupboard set against a wall, often used for display of plate
Silting trough	For salting meat
Skillett	Cooking pan with handle and three feet
Skimmer	Shallow perforated implement for skimming liquids
Sledge	Sledge hammer
Slice	Fire shovel shaped like a spade

Specialty	Contracted agreement for payment
Spitter	Spade
Stallage	Barrel stand
Stan, stand	Stand for casks etc
Standish	Inkstand
Stayned clothes	Cheap substitute for tapestry hangings
Steer	Young castrated ox
Steelyard, stillion, stilliard	Counterpoise moved along a graduated beam on scales
Styll, still	Apparatus for distilling
Table with frame	Joined table with top fixed to frame of legs, stretchers and rails
Tacks	Clasps or metal bands
Tares	Variety of vetch; animal fodder
Tester	'Ceiling' for a four-poster bedstead, of wood or fabric
Thills	Waggon shafts
Todd	Weight of wool (28 lbs)
Trencher	Wooden plate, sometimes with depression for salt
Trevet, trivet	Iron stand to support pan over fire
Triar, tryar	Kind of sieve
Troe, trow	Trough
Truckle bed	Low bedstead on castors to run under higher bed
Tun	Tub or barrel
Tundish	Wooden dish with tube at the base which fitted into bung-hole of a cask forming a funnel
Tunnell	Funnel
Turkey work	Woven wool material with a pile
Turn	Spinning wheel; winding gear for grindstone or well bucket
Ure	Ewer
Urinal	Glass bottle used for medical diagnosis
Vallance	Short curtain around top of a four-poster bed, or above window curtains
Voider	Basket or tray for removing crumbs etc after meals
Wainscott	Panelling, or pannelled furniture
Wallet	Bag with two pouches for holding goods or provisions on a journey
Waney	Probably boarded
Warbill	Cutting tool with long blade, possibly for pruning
Wedge	For splitting timber
Weiner, wenyer	Weaned calf
Wimble	Gimlet, augur or brace
Wimsheet	For winnowing
Wool card	Instrument with teeth to card wool

INDEX OF PERSONS AND PLACES

Arabic numbers refer to entries, small roman numbers to pages. Except for London, all English places are in Sussex unless otherwise stated. The others are assigned to their historic, not modern, counties.

Oram, Ann, 17, Ann *or* Anna, (*another*) 17,
    123; John, 17; Mary, 17; Sarah, 17;
    Thomas, xxvi, xxvii, 17, (?*same*) 123,
    (*another*) 17
Ore (Oare), 177
Osborne (Osborn), George, 53; Nathaniel,
    45
Oving, xxvi, 112, 113
Owen, Ann, 169; Mary, 169; Morgan, 169;
    Warburton, xxiv, xxv, 21, 169; William,
    169
Oxford, Oxon, xi, 161, 182; St Martin's
    (Carfax), 182; St Mary's, 182; St Peter
    in the East, 182
Oxford, bishop of, 12, 34, 51, 53, 60, 63, 96,
    97, 103, 121, 122, 130–132, 149, 150,
    167
Oxford University, 58, 110, 117, 126, 160,
    172, 177, 180, 182; colleges and halls:
    All Souls, 15, 41; Balliol, 51, 63, 67, 94,
    96, 131; Brasenose, 16, 34, 64, 88, 130,
    132, 163, 183; Christ Church, 30, 36, 43,
    48, 103, 122, 150; Corpus Christi, 153;
    Exeter, xiv, 12, 53, 99, 175; Hart Hall,
    137; Jesus, 39; Lincoln, 70; Magdalen,
    xiv, 12, 23, 42, 55, 61, 100, 114, 123,
    140, 148, 159, 167; Magdalen Hall
    (Maudelen Hall, St Mary Magdalen's
    Hall), 8, 33, 39, 78, 83, 89, 117, 135,
    182; Merton, 4, 81, 95, 104, 147, 173,
    182; New College, 2, 67, 87, 97, 149,
    150, 161, 169; New Inn Hall, 164, 175;
    Oriel, 24, 49, 103, 171, 173; Pembroke,
    36; Queen's, xiv, 4, 10, 60, 72, 121, 137,
    153; St Alban Hall, 69, 81; St Edmund
    Hall, 104; St John's, 40, 49, 59; St Mary
    Hall, 148; St Thomas Hall, 182; Trinity,
    62, 82, 101, 155; University, 42, 127,
    153, 161; Wadham, 31, 40, 61, 82
Oxfordshire, 167; *see also* Horspath;
    Oxford; Wheatley

Packham, Edmund, 81
Padie, Anne, 178, (*another*) 178; Hannah,
    178; James, 178; Mary, 178; Samuel,
    xxvi, xxvii, 178
Page, Mr ..., 63; Adam, xxii, xxiii, 96;
    Anne, 165; Edward, 80; George, xxii,
    xxiii, 165; John, 19, 96, (*another*) 119;
    Margaret, 96; Mary, 165, (*another*) 165;
    Randall, 41; Richard, 4, 165; Thomas,
    91
Pagham, 94
Pagham and Tarring peculiar, xx

Palmer, Thomas, 154; William, 154
Pancris, Robert, 81
Pannell, William, 151
Pannett, John, 54; Robert, 3
Parham, xxiv, xxvi, ?16, 68, 114, 115, 148
Paris, Peter, 182
Parker, Robert, 48
Parkhurst, Edward, 77; Robert, 167
Parr, John, 116; Richard, 116; Stevens,
    xxviii, xxix, 116
Parson, John, 20, (*another*) 141
Parsons, ..., 189; Thomas, 187
Parvys, Bridget, 163
Patching, 120, 167
?Patte, John, 60
Payne, Augustine, 162; George, 103, 154;
    Henry, 79
Peachey (Peache), John, 65, (?*another*) 184;
    Thomas, 36, (?*same*) 44
Peart, Elizabeth, 80; Mary, 80; Richard, 80;
    Stephen, xxiv, xxv, 80; Thomas, 80,
    (*another*) 80
Peasmarsh, xxviii, 76, 116
Peckham (Peckam), Elizabeth, 44; Henry,
    112; Mary, 104; Richard, 44; Thomas,
    36, (?*same*) 83; William, 1, (*another*)
    104, (?*another*) 113
Peele, ..., 146
Peirce *see* Pierce
Pelham, Thomas, bt, 27
Pell, Ralph, 156
Pellett (Pellatt), Nathaniel, 78; William, 6,
    (?*same*) 16
Pelling, Edward, 122; Thomas, xviii, xix,
    xxviii, xxix, 122
Penfold, Hugh, 63, 139; John, 151
Penicod, Jane, 180
Pennall, John, 119
Percy, Algernon, earl of Northumberland,
    152
Perkins, ..., 157; Mr ..., 18
Peterborough, bishop of, 58, 79, 107, 109,
    116, 144, 152, 157, 168
Petersfield, Hants, 152
Petow, ..., 64
Pett, 75
Petworth, xxii, 59, 77, 104, 117, 155, 161,
    185
Pevensey, xx
Pickering, Benjamin, 94
Piedmont (Piemont), 152
Pierce (Peirce), Mary, 111; William, 70
Pike (Pyke), John, 187, (*another*) 187;
    Thomas, 70